I0816840

EUROPEAN VIEWS OF THE UNITED STATES

Edited on Behalf
of the European Association
for American Studies
by HANS-JÜRGEN GRABBE

Volume 7

ANDREW S. GROSS

The Pound Reaction

Liberalism and Lyricism in Midcentury American Literature

Universitätsverlag
WINTER
Heidelberg

Bibliografische Information der Deutschen Nationalbibliothek

Die Deutsche Nationalbibliothek verzeichnet diese Publikation in der Deutschen Nationalbibliografie; detaillierte bibliografische Daten sind im Internet über *http://dnb.d-nb.de* abrufbar.

COVER ILLUSTRATION

St. Elizabeths Hospital, Washington, DC
© Photo by Tim Lundin | TDLphoto.com

European Association for American Studies
c/o Stiftung Leucorea
Collegienstraße 62
06886 Lutherstadt Wittenberg
Germany
www.eaas.eu

ISBN 978-3-8253-6470-0

Imprimé en Allemagne · Printed in Germany
Druck: Memminger MedienCentrum, 87700 Memmingen

Gedruckt auf umweltfreundlichem, chlorfrei gebleichtem und alterungsbeständigem Papier

Den Verlag erreichen Sie im Internet unter:
www.winter-verlag.de

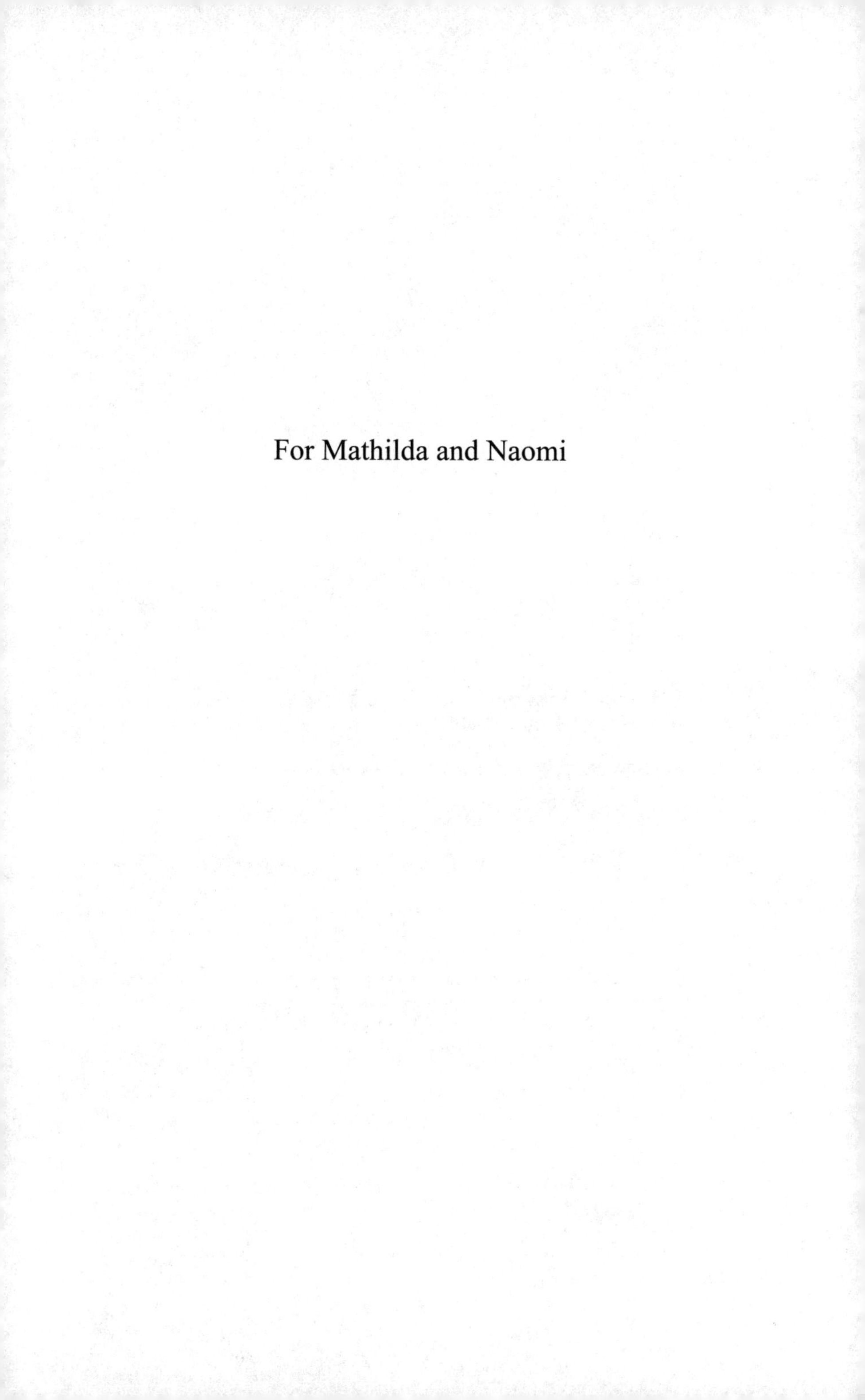

For Mathilda and Naomi

Table of Contents

Preface

The Pound Reaction: Liberalism and Lyricism in Midcentury American Literature won the 2013 Rob Kroes Publication Award. Written by an American, it is a remarkably European book of American studies. In a day and age when many lament the standardization of the world under the influence of imperial academic and disciplinary monolingualism, Andrew Gross's learned and stimulating study takes the reader out of the academic rut.

The book has the qualities of a well-made object produced by an artisan who has refined and polished his gesture so that the erudition has lost much of its heaviness without losing the energy of a writing that is part of a thinking in progress. Thus, *The Pound Reaction* frees Ezra Pound from the closed circles of exegetes to astutely reposition him in the context of American studies. It does not propose an umpteenth "revaluation" or a would-be Pound revolution: Pound's "reaction" and the reaction to Pound are attentively contextualized, which enables the reader to break out of dichotomous debate that has divided the readership between scholars with an aesthetic reading from those with a moral and political reading. The book does not dodge difficult ethical or political questions, but refuses to be bound by them. This is not a study on Pound's poetry *per se*, nor is it another study of the Poundian influence on successive generations of poets. The book thus avoids the trap of presenting Pound as an origin and the followers as deflections of expressions of mourning for the lost voice. On the other hand, Pound scholars and aficionados will we rewarded by this book that takes on board the classic Pound scholarship and expands on it to extoll Pound's lyrical voice. As a result, we never lose sight of Pound's poetic persona, and, quite remarkably in a study in American studies, we never lose sight of the form of Pound's poetry. Andrew Gross never turns the poetry into a pre-text for more trendy considerations and Pound's sophisticated writing always remains the basis of his argument.

Where so many studies home in on one aspect of texts to push one agenda, this book of American studies echoes with the influences of its European multilingual and multicultural background and influences. It reminds us that poetry always speaks more than one language. The company poetry keeps with cultural politics, philosophy and history truly enables the reader to better read Pound. At the same time, the close reading of Pound's poetry is in itself a meta-critical statement and possibly a commentary or a reaction to the disappearance of the literary text from American studies. Gross reinstates the powerful *poein* of the poetry; he shows how the performance of the poetry has triggered chain reactions that have contributed to producing the cultural world in which we live. We are reminded also that poetry is never merely *divertente* ("amusing") as Mussolini had it when he read Pound. Dictators would like poetry to remain a child's game, but Gross shows us how that poetry contributed to shaping the literary, academic, and political climate of the Cold War era. His fine reading, in particular, of Pound's receiving the 1949 Bollingen Prize enables us to see poetry in its cultural performance, and not simply as a symptom of the time when it was written.

The Pound Reaction book elegantly combines disciplinary discourses. It deploys the history of the writing and the reception of Pound's poetry, unravels the complexity of its style, extols its visionary qualities, problematizes its dark facets, and embeds it all in the cultural politics that extends from the Second World War to our contemporary world. A far more comprehensive reading of Pound and of his poetic and political aura thus appears. We get to better grasp the often tortured relations that poets such as Katherine Garrison Chapin, Karl Shapiro, T. S. Eliot, Conrad Aiken, W. H. Auden, Louise Bogan, Robert Lowell, Katherine Anne Porter, Allen Tate, Robert Penn Warren, Léonie Adams, Robert Frost and others entertained with Pound and with his œuvre. We finally get to better read the tensions between those who defended Pound on strictly aesthetic grounds by defending poetry as a form of free speech, New Critics who sought to read it according to objective values, and those who wished to stress its political—and therefore objectionable—nature. By reading Pound with the un-disciplined discipline of American studies Andrew Gross manages to combine these discourses, thus emulating the multifarious style of the poet whose work he enlightens. Few poets are as contradictory in their style and expression as Ezra Pound; reading the reaction generated by his poetry requires a response that is as economic in expression, precise in language and inspirational in style.

Unlike studies that seek to either charge or exonerate Pound, this book shows that the chain reaction started by the *Pisan Cantos* has not come to an end yet. The necessary historical reconstruction furthers our understanding, but most importantly the book projects us into the future of Pound's poetry, which is our present. We see poets of the successive generations, such as Elizabeth Bishop or Allen Ginsberg, come into the contested Pound heritage, but we also see how reading Pound's poetry has profoundly influenced the development of critical and academic discourses that extend beyond them. *The Pound Reaction* thus contributes to enriching the Pound scholarship even as it contributes to defining the field of American studies. It bridges many gaps between ways of reading Pound and takes us a few steps further on Ezra Pound's tortuous path of an American poet in Europe.

Boris Vejdovsky
Chair of the Jury
Lausanne, May 2015

A List of Publications under the Auspices of the European Association for American Studies

EAAS Publications in the Series *European Views of the United States,* Hans-Jürgen Grabbe, General Editor, Heidelberg: Universitätsverlag Winter, 2008–

Gross, Andrew S. *The Pound Reaction: Liberalism and Lyricism in Midcentury American Literature*, vol 7, 2015 (Rob Kroes Publication Award 2013).

The Health of the Nation, eds. Meldan Tanrısal and Tanfer Emin Tunç, vol 6, 2014 (Izmir Conference 2012).

Mehring, Frank. *The Democratic Gap: Transcultural Confrontations of German Immigrants and the Promiseof American Democracy,* vol. 5, 2014 (Rob Kroes Publication Award 2011).

Forever Young? The Changing Images of the United State, eds. Philip Coleman and Stephen Matterson, vol. 4, 2012 (Dublin Conference 2010).

E Pluribus Unum or E Pluribus Plura? Unity and Diversity in American Culture, eds. Hans-Jürgen Grabbe, David Mauk, and Ole Moen, vol. 3, 2011 (Oslo Conference 2008).

Franke, Astrid. *Pursue the Illusion: Ceremonies and Spectacles: Problems of Public Poetry in America*, vol. 2, 2010 (Rob Kroes Publication Award 2009).

Conformism, Non-Conformism, and Anti-Conformism in the Culture of the United States, eds. Antonis Balasopoulos, Gesa Mackenthun, and TheodoraTsimpouki, vol. 1, 2008 (Nicosia Conference 2006).

EAAS Publications in the Series *European Contributions to American Studies,* Rob Kroes, General Editor, Amsterdam: Amerika Instituut, Universiteit van Amsterdam, 1980–1988; VU University Press, 1990–2006.

America in the Course of Human Events, eds. Josef Jařab, Marcel Arbeit, and Jenel Virden, vol. 63, 2006 (Prague Conference 2004).

The Cultural Shuttle: The United States of/in Europe, eds. Véronique Béghain and Marc Chénetier, vol. 57, 2004 (Bordeaux Conference 2002).

"Nature's Nation" Revisited: American Concepts of Nature from Wonder to Ecological Crisis, eds. Hans Bak and Walter W. Hölbling, vol. 49, 2003 (Graz Conference 2000).

Ceremonies and Spectacles: Performing American Culture, eds. Teresa Alves, Teresa Cid, and Heinz Ickstadt, vol. 44, 2000 (Lisbon Conference 1998).

Living with America, 1946–1996, eds. Cristina Giorcelli and Rob Kroes, vol. 38, 1997 (Warsaw Conference 1996).

The Insular Dream: Obsession and Resistance, ed. Kristiaan Versluys, vol. 35, 1995 (Luxembourg Conference 1994).

The American Columbiad: "Discovering" America, Inventing the United States, eds. Mario Materassi and Maria Irene Ramalho de Sousa Santos, vol. 34, 1996 (Seville Conference 1992).

Victorianism in the United States: Its Era and Its Legacy, eds. Steve Ickringill and Stephen Mills, vol. 24, 1992 (London Conference 1990).

In the European Grain: American Studies from Central and Eastern Europe, ed. Orm Overland, vol. 19, 1990 (EAAS Translation Project).[1]

Looking Inward, Looking Outward: From the 1930s through the 1940s, ed. Steve Ickringill, vol. 18, 1990 (Berlin Conference 1988).

The Early Republic: The Making of a Nation—The Making of a Culture, eds. Steve Ickringill, Zoltan Abadi-Nagy, and Aladár Sarbu, vol. 14, 1988 (Budapest Conference 1986).

Social Change and New Modes of Expression: The United States, 1910–1930, eds. Rob Kroes and Alessandro Portelli, vol. 10, 1986 (Rome Conference 1984).

Cultural Change in the U.S. since World War II, eds. Maurice Gonnaud, Sergio Perosa, and Chris Bigsby, vol. 9, 1986 (EAAS Translation Project).*

Impressions of a Gilded Age: The American Fin de Siecle, eds. Marc Chénetier and Rob Kroes, vol. 6, 1983 (Paris Conference 1982).

The American Identity: Fusion and Fragmentation, ed. Rob Kroes, vol. 3, 1980 (Amsterdam Conference 1980).

---

1 Books resulting from an EAAS Board decision to sponsor and finance volumes containing essays produced by European scholars in languages other than English. The selected contributions were translated and published to give the authors a wider audience.

Individual Conference Volumes Published before 1980

Vistas of a Continent: Concepts of Nature in America, ed. on behalf of the European Association for American Studies by Teut Andreas Riese, Anglistische Forschungen 136, Heidelberg: Winter, 1979 (Heidelberg Conference 1976).

Contagious Conflict: The Impact of American Dissent on European Life, ed. A. N. J. den Hollander, Leiden: Brill, 1973 (Geneva Conference 1972).

Diverging Parallels: A Comparison of American and European Thought and Action, ed. A. N. J. den Hollander, Leiden: Brill, 1971 (Rome Conference 1967 and Brussels Conference 1970).

The Role of Universities in the Modern World: A Transatlantic Dialogue, Bonn: Cultural Affairs and Educational Exchange Unit, United States Information Service, 1965 (Aarhus Conference 1965).

"Special Issue European Association for American Studies," *The American Review: A Quarterly of American Affairs*, publ. under the auspices of the European Center of American Studies of the Johns Hopkins Bologna Center, vol. 2, no. 4, March 1963 (Cambridge Conference 1962).

Annual Conference of the European Association for American Studies, Berlin, 27–30 September 1961 [Berlin: EAAS, 1961]. Eighteen typescripts of papers presented at the conference.

Proceedings of the Second Conference of the European Association for American Studies Held at the Fondation des États-Unis, Paris September 3–6, 1957, Paris: European Association for American Studies, 1957 (Paris Conference 1957).

Acknowledgments

Many people and institutions have helped make the writing of this book possible. I want to first express my gratitude towards the Fulbright Program, which sent me to the place that became my intellectual home for over a decade, the John F. Kennedy Institute of the Freie Universität Berlin. Heinz Ickstadt and Susanne Rohr helped bring me to Berlin and keep me there. Heinz has been my mentor and Susanne my collaborator in many projects over the years; the friendships have grown, but I still think of them as the most gracious and welcoming of hosts. While in Berlin I profited from innumerable discussions with my friends and colleagues Catrin Gersdorf, MaryAnn Snyder-Körber, and Ulla Haselstein, who was for many years my department chair and is still my role model. Ulla, Heinz, and Sabine Sielke—who also took me under her wing when I came to Germany—were the first readers to evaluate this manuscript when I submitted it as my habilitation at the Freie Universität Berlin. Their thoughtful evaluations guided me in the revisions necessary to transform the manuscript into a book. The other primary reader was Michael Hoffman, my dissertation advisor at UC Davis and mentor and friend. Thank you, Michael, for standing by me all these years; when I write, you are the reader I have in mind.

Scholars who visited the Kennedy Institute also read chapters and provided intellectual support. Charles Altieri, Joel Pfister, Nathalia King, Christopher Zinn, Donald Pease, and Robert Brinkmeyer offered crucial advice, as did Joshua Weiner, whom I met in Erlangen. Colleagues gave me opportunities to present my work at the Humboldt Universität and the annual convention of the German Association of American Studies. Agnes Mueller and Nicholas Vazsonyi invited me to present a chapter the University of South Carolina and introduced me to Greg Forter, whose insightful comments on an early draft helped me re-think my approach. Antje Kley, who offered me a safe harbor at the Universität Erlangen-Nürnberg, has read many drafts and offered her friendship, guidance, and support. Karin Höpker, my friend and office mate in Erlangen, has patiently listened to me talk about this project more times than I can count. My students in Berlin and Erlangen have also endured my ramblings and contributed their own insights to this story.

I want to thank my colleagues at the European Association of American Studies who honored my efforts with the Rob Kroes Publication Award. This gave me the opportunity to shape the manuscript under the competent editing of Hans-Jürgen Grabbe, who also discovered the photograph adorning the front cover. I wish to thank Wiebke Kartheus for the wonderful work she has done as a formatter. Most of all I want to acknowledge the support, over the years, of my loving parents Joe and Carol Gross, and the encouragement of my own dear family, which has had to share me with the computer while I should have been doing other things.

Finally, I wish to acknowledge the publishers who have printed portions of this manuscript and generously given their permission to reprint the material in book form. Part of the introduction appeared in a special issue of *Telos* 170 (Spring 2015), edited by Johannes Voelz, another friend and colleague from Berlin. Part of chapter one is scheduled to appear in a book entitled *The Art of Walking*, edited by Klaus Benesch and François Specq. A version of chapter two appeared in the *Journal of Modern Literature* 34.3 (Spring 2011). A version of chapter three appeared in *Transnational American Studies* (Heidelberg: Universitätsverlag Winter, 2012), edited by Udo Hebel. The final chapter appeared in *The Journal of Transnational American Studies* 1.1 (Jan. 2009) and in *The Pathos of Authenticity* (Heidelberg: Universitätsverlag Winter, 2010), edited by Ulla Haselstein, MaryAnn Snyder-Körber, and myself.

Introduction: Ezra Pound and the Liberal Aesthetic

Ezra Pound won the first Bollingen Award in 1949 for *The Pisan Cantos*, the book of poems he wrote while imprisoned in a U.S. military disciplinary training center in Italy. He had been arrested for making pro-Mussolini broadcasts for Rome radio during the war—the official charge was treason—and confined in the kind of outdoor cage more recently used at Guantanamo Bay. By all accounts the harsh conditions unbalanced the nearly 60-year-old poet. When Pound was flown back to the United States to stand trial, his attorney pleaded insanity on his behalf. The plea allowed Pound to avoid conviction at a time when other propagandists who broadcast for the enemy were receiving harsh sentences. Pound could not, however, avoid incarceration. The poet was remanded to a federal mental hospital, St. Elizabeths, where he was in the second year of what would prove to be a 13-year internment when the Library of Congress announced him the Bollingen winner.

The announcement caused a scandal. How could Pound be honored by one branch of government while facing indictment by another? Pound's supporters argued that the award proved artistic freedom was alive and well in the United States; only totalitarian regimes forced artists to tow the party line. This free speech defense of poetry made lyricism the proof positive of liberalism. The argument proved influential, but it had the ironic effect of making a fascist poet the symbol of democratic culture, a prisoner the spokesman for free speech.

This book, *The Pound Reaction*, explores how a number of writers struggled with the uncomfortable paradoxes stemming from the liberal defense of lyricism. Those discussed include Karl Shapiro, one of two dissenting members of the Bollingen committee who believed that his vote against Pound ruined his career; W. H. Auden, who supported the prize but suggested Pound's work should be suppressed; Peter Viereck, the poet and conservative thinker who was scandalized by Pound's accolades, in part because Viereck's own father served time in prison for disseminating Nazi propaganda; John Berryman, who struggled with Pound's anti-Semitism in an introduction intended for—but never published with—Pound's *Selected Poems*; and Katherine Anne Porter, the only prose writer on the Bollingen committee, whose *Ship of Fools*, resembling *The Cantos* in its sprawling form, attempts to come to terms with the kind of unreason she saw embodied in Pound. Other writers discussed in relation to the Pound controversy include Robert Lowell, Elizabeth Bishop, Sylvia Plath, Allen Ginsberg, Leslie Fiedler, and several midcentury philosophers and political thinkers. *The Pound Reaction* aims to highlight the changing relation of poetry to politics during the Cold War, and to explore the special significance of the lyric for liberals committed to free speech.

Ezra Pound settled in Rapallo, Italy in 1924.[2] It was partly for the swimming, his publisher and friend James Laughlin would later recall, and partly because the picturesque seashore community was on the main rail-line between Rome and Paris, making it an easy stopover for friends (Laughlin 9). However whimsical Pound's initial reasons for choosing Italy, they rapidly assumed shape and purpose.[3] By 1925 Pound was defending Mussolini in letters, which "were now invariably dated Fascist style, from the 'March on Rome' in late October 1922," as one of his biographers puts it; "His letterhead bore a cubist pen-and-ink drawing of him by Gaudier-Brzeska and a motto by Mussolini: 'Liberty is a duty not a right'" (Heymann 57).[4]

The letterhead's pairing of image and motto suggests one of Pound's motivations for turning to fascism. The sculptor Henri Gaudier had been Pound's friend and collaborator in London. He was killed in World War I, a conflict that shocked and sickened Pound: "There died a myriad, / And of the best, among them, / For an old bitch gone in the teeth, / For a botched civilization" (Pound, *New Selected* 113). Pound was convinced that unsound economic policies led to war. By the 1930s he was dedicating much of his energy to making this argument in verse and prose. Canto 38, written in 1933, paraphrases a key economic concept Pound took over from C. H. Douglas, the advocate of social credit: "The power to purchase can never / (under the present system) catch up with / prices at large" (38/190; Kenner, *Pound Era* 307). The next few lines go on to demonstrate how armament

---

[2] All references to *The Cantos* are to the New Directions 1996 edition and provide first the canto number followed by page number(s).

[3] "The Rapallesi loved him […]. They harbored no resentment about his pro-fascist leanings" because they were all fascists, as Laughlin quotes a local newspaper editor as saying (Laughlin 9–10).

[4] From Pound's letter to Harriet Monroe, dated Rapallo, 30 November, 1926: "I personally think extremely well of Mussolini. If one compares him to American presidents (the last three) or British premiers, etc., in fact one can NOT without insulting him. If the intelligentsia don't think well of him, it is because they know nothing about 'the state,' and government, and have no particularly large sense of values" (Pound, *Selected Letters* 205).

companies like Krupp and Schneider—Pound describes them as "Twin arse with one belly"—circumvented the cash-strapped public sector by selling weapons directly to governments, indeed to governments on opposing sides of conflicts in order to stimulate demand (38/187–92; 191). Pound argued governments should lend money for useful projects—the basic principle of social credit—rather than wasting it on war. However, lending was in the hands of private financiers or "usurers" as Pound insisted on calling them; he defined usury as "a charge for the use of purchasing power, levied without regard to production" and criticized the practice for generating profits "CONTRA NATURAM" (45/230). Driven by his grief over the First World War, and perhaps by his growing fear that another war could not be avoided, Pound became obsessed with the "unnatural" consequences of usury (see Sieburth, "In Pound We Trust" 159). Canto 45, which contains an oblique reference to Gaudier—"Stonecutter is kept from his stone"—revels in abject descriptions of the perversion, poverty, barrenness, and destruction allegedly resulting from usury (45/229–30; see also "Addendum" to Canto 100/818).

Pound thought that fascism could solve the linked problems of usury and war. He believed that Mussolini had the power to implement a system of social credit, or state lending, that would do away with unsound financial practices and encourage traditional craftsmanship, agriculture, and art (Canto 41). Pound met Mussolini in 1933 and presented him with a vellum edition of *A Draft of XXX Cantos* along with a plan for political and economic reform. Mussolini apparently did not have much use for the plan, but "insisting that he found what he had seen of Pound's poetry 'divertente' (entertaining), 'the Boss,' as the poet called him in Canto 41, made an instant and lifelong believer out of Pound," as David Heymann put it (Heymann 58). Canto 41, which begins with the "divertente" remark, goes on to show Mussolini draining swamps and unfair profit margins. The penultimate lines quote Jefferson on money (41/206). This surprising conclusion to a poem dedicated to the fascist leader was reaffirmed in the 1935 title of Pound's *Jefferson and/or Mussolini*, a book that attempted to show how Mussolini's innovations were consistent with American principles. Pound seems to have believed—and this is something he had in common with many thinkers on the left—that a certain amount of economic planning, along with the suppression of private money-lending, would provide the security necessary for basic American (Jeffersonian) freedoms.[5]

---

5 In spite of his support of fascism, Pound was an individualist. He argued that "Liberty is not defendable on a static theory" and explained the threats to liberty in terms of modern bureaucratization: "One has only to consider the enormous and hardly conscious sacrifices of long held immunities made during and since the war [World

Pound's economic obsession, his out-of-the-way location, and his even more out-of-the-way claim that Mussolini was heir to the political wisdom of Jefferson (and John Adams and Martin Van Buren) cost him much of his audience. As World War II approached he made up for his diminishing influence with increased vehemence, tapping into a long tradition of anti-Semitism to blame usury and its alleged results—poverty, social disintegration, perversion, bad art, war—on Jews (Pound, *Selected Prose* 269). Pound began delivering regular, mainly pre-recorded broadcasts for Rome Radio before the United States entered the war and continued until 1943, the year Mussolini was deposed and briefly imprisoned, then installed by the German army as nominal head of the Salò Republic. The broadcasts were often indecipherable, partly because of Pound's idiosyncratic blend of monetary theory and modernist aesthetics, and partly because he delivered his theories in a strange "cracker barrel" dialect that he believed would appeal to American listeners (Sieburth, *Pisan* xvi). Apparently the incoherence led some Italian authorities to conclude that Pound must have been smuggling out state secrets in code (Sieburth, *Pisan* xi). However, American monitors had no trouble deciphering the criticism of Roosevelt's fiscal and foreign policy, the encomiums for Hitler and Mussolini, and the often savage attacks on Jews. Several of the broadcasts made after 1941 were judged to be treasonous. In 1943 a grand jury indicted the poet on federal charges.

Since Pound never stood trial, the question of treason cannot be settled. However, the transcripts of the radio broadcasts, compiled by the U.S. government for purposes of prosecution, reveal how Pound's economic

---

War I], the depredations of bureaucracies, passport idiocies etc. When constitutions are not violated by legislature they are quietly subverted by departmental orders and the only defence [*sic*] against such pervasive tyranny lies in the education and discrimination of the individual. To be free he must know his law, that is his own law, the law of his country or countries, he must know his history, the supposed principles underlying it and he must fight every encroachment with every legal and ethical means his knowledge provides" (*Selected Prose 275*). However, these same state institutions must play a role in defending the economic conditions that allow individuals to work in the ways they want to: "When the state understands its duties and powers it does not leave its sovereignty in the hands of private interests that are irresponsible or arrogate to themselves unwarranted responsibilities. It is not right to say that 'work-money' is a 'symbol of work.' More exactly, it is a symbol of a collaboration between nature, the state, and an industrious population" (*Selected Prose* 297; see also 182, 184, 266). Here, for the sake of comparison, is John Dewey on the need to control the economy for the purposes of individual liberty: "Earlier liberalism regarded the separate and competing economic action of individuals as the means to social well-being as the end. We must reverse the perspective and see that socialized economy is the means of free individual development as the end" (*Liberalism and Social Action* 90).

obsessions repeatedly gave way to full-blown racist paranoia. The broadcast from March 8, 1942 is a fair example. It begins, "The ENEMY is Das Leihkapital [loan agencies and capital]. They're working day and night, pickin' your pockets." A few paragraphs later, Pound makes clear who he means by "[t]hey": "DO YOU think that there is any basic, essential difference between a committee of kikes in LONDON betraying the United States of America and a gang of kikes in New York selling up England […] ?" (Doob 55–56). The examples could be easily multiplied, but I think these suffice to show that the broadcasts show a disturbing penchant to reduce politics to economics and economics to racialized greed. Thus, Pound's early enthusiasm for Mussolini as a peacemaker mutated into a fascist argument for waging war against the phantasm of a Jewish world conspiracy.

In May 1945 Italian partisans captured Pound at his desk translating *The Book of Mencius*. He had time to pocket two books—Confucius and a Chinese dictionary—before they took him away (Heymann 154). There was apparently some confusion about what to do with the American poet. The partisans released Pound who, fearing for his safety, immediately gave himself up to American military authorities. He was interrogated about the radio broadcasts and then transferred to a Disciplinary Training Center outside of Pisa—a prison camp "for convicted rapists, murderers, and traitors who had been members of our Armed Forces," as one contemporary observer remarked (Allen 33). For three weeks he was held in an open air cage called a "death cell," resembling those more recently used in Guantanamo. The canto he first began composing in captivity would later represent the death cell as the culmination of failed efforts to quell usury, up to and including the Soviet experiment: "But in Russia they bungled […] / and went in for dumping in order to trouble the waters / in the usurers' hell-a-dice / all of which leads to the death-cells" (74/461).

Pound was in no position to write during the first three weeks of his internment. Exposed to the sun all day, the glare of spot lights all night, and unprotected from inclement weather, he slept on a bare concrete floor. Eventually he was given a pup tent to rig at night between the bars. He was allowed no contact with fellow prisoners (Allen 33–34; Wilhelm 217–18). By all accounts, the elderly prisoner suffered a mental breakdown. On the recommendation of two military psychiatrists, he was confined under better conditions in the medical section of the prison camp. It is probably at this point that he acquired the bare necessities for writing: pad, pencil, and a desk that a fellow prisoner made for him—against regulations—out of a medical crate: "and the greatest is charity / to be found among those who have not observed / regulations" (74/454).[6]

Uncertainty about his fate spurred Pound on to feverish productivity. He took up work on the next ten cantos, 74 through 84. According to his loose plan, modeled on Dante, he should have been entering the *Paradiso* section of the work in progress (Sieburth, *Pisan* xvii; Kenner, "Rose in Steel Dust" 122). Life in the detention center, however, was purgatory, which Pound (surrounded by mainly African American detainees) describes as a slave ship: "in limbo no victories, there, are no victories— / between the decks of the slaver" (77/490). Deprived of all reading material except the two books he had slipped in his pocket when the partisans came for him, a stray copy of *Time* magazine, and M. E. Speare's *Pocket Book of Verse* fortuitously "found on the jo-house seat," he concentrated on his surroundings and his memory (80/533). The conditions of confinement gave *The Pisan Cantos* the intense, lyrical quality that many contemporary critics believe represents Pound at his poetic best. The nostalgia for fascism and the anti-Semitism, evident in several passages, also suggest Pound at his political worst.

In 1945 Pound was flown back to the United States to stand trial for treason. The press was comparing him to William Joyce, alias Lord Haw Haw, who in 1946 would be executed in England for treasonous radio broadcasts made from Germany during the war.[7] A technicality may have prevented the death penalty in Pound's case, since U.S. constitutional law requires two eye-witnesses for a treason conviction, and it is unclear if any of the six Italian radio technicians flown to the United States to testify understood enough English to confirm what he had said. Nevertheless, under advice from his attorney Julien Cornell, retained through the offices of his publisher James Laughlin, Pound pleaded incompetent to stand trial by reason of insanity (Torrey 183, 185). A board of prominent psychiatrists supported the plea. The federal jury found Pound to be "mentally unsound.

---

6 Sieburth points to the importance of African American interlocutors in *The Pisan Cantos*: "All of these Africanist elements converge in what is perhaps the single most moving passage of the first Canto of the Pisans, which gratefully celebrates the *humanitas* and *caritas* of a certain Mr. Edwards, the black soldier who, in violation of camp regulations, provided Pound with a table (fashioned from a packing crate) to write on in his tent. Amid the mnemonic Babel of ghostly voices besieging the poet's consciousness in his solitary confinement, this is virtually the sole recorded occasion in the entire text when he is actually addressed, in the present tense of Pisa, by another living human being" (Sieburth, *Pisan* xxi).

7 William Joyce, alias Lord Haw-Haw, was executed in England, and Mildred Elizabeth Gillers, alias Axis Sally, served a long prison sentence in the United States (Wilhelm 265).

The verdict saved Pound from standing trial on treason charges arising out of his wartime writings and broadcasts in Italy," as *The New York Times* put it in February 1946 (O'Connor 22).

Pound was remanded to St. Elizabeths, a federal clinic overseen by one of Pound's psychiatric evaluators, Dr. Winfred Overholser. He spent his first year in the criminal ward, but Overholser was sympathetic to his plight, and with the encouragement of Pound's many supporters he extended his privileges to include a private room in a better ward, generous visitation rights, and access to books from the Library of Congress (Torrey 220). The nearly thirteen years Pound would eventually spend at St. Elizabeths, deprived of his liberty but for the first time in his life free from financial worries, were productive. In 1948, Laughlin's New Directions published the poetic record of his captivity in the prison camp, *The Pisan Cantos*.

Pound's internment in the Pisan prison camp had deprived him of a microphone, but many of the uglier sentiments expressed in the radio broadcasts spill over into *The Pisan Cantos*. Thus an early section of the opening canto quickly moves from praise of John Adams to criticism of the Jewish founder of the banking house of Rothschild to the claim that

> the yidd is a stimulant, and the goyim are cattle
> in gt/ proportion and go to saleable slaughter
> with the maximum of docility. (74/459)

The anti-Semitism rears its ugly head again in a Vichy libel in Canto 80:

> Pétain defended Verdun while Blum
>   Was defending a bidet (80/514)

The examples could be easily multiplied, but I think these suffice to show that the poetry shares with the broadcasts a disturbing penchant to reduce politics to economics and economics to racialized greed.[8]

However, *The Pisan Cantos* also strike a different note: passages depicting intense personal suffering and regret provide a counterpoint to the paranoid accusations. "When the raft broke and the waters went over me" is how Pound describes the experience of imprisonment, drawing on the Odysseus leitmotif that runs throughout *The Cantos* to depict his personality on the verge of drowning (80/533; Sieburth, *Pisan* xiv).He turned to lyrical reflection as his life raft. He had no other choice.[9] As Richard Sieburth points out,

---

8 See also pp. 449, 460, 463 for other anti-Semitic references.

9 Even the lyrical turn can be seen as making a distinct political and historical critique. The famous passage—"As a lone ant from a broken ant-hill / from the wreckage of

for the first time in years Pound was forced to write without the compendious research materials that had provided the numerous citations from Jefferson and others (*Pisan* xxiv; see also Wilhelm 221).

Pound's (partial) return to a more personal form of poetry had a number of contributing factors, but in 1949 the members of the Bollingen committee were nearly unanimous about its significance. Those voting for Pound included T. S. Eliot, Conrad Aiken, W. H. Auden, Louise Bogan, Robert Lowell, Katherine Anne Porter, Allen Tate, Robert Penn Warren, and Léonie Adams. Statements issued jointly and separately defended the Bollingen Prize on two related grounds: 1) Pound's return to more personal or lyrical poetry was understood as a retreat from or even apology for his fascist politics, and 2) poetry was understood to be primarily personal or lyrical anyway, which meant the more poetic the writing, the less propagandistic its meaning.

The committee, as I said, was nearly unanimous. There were two dissenting members. One was Katherine Garrison Chapin, the wife of Francis Biddle, the U.S. Attorney General who issued the indictment against Pound in 1943. The other was Karl Shapiro, the Pulitzer Prize-winning war poet who, as poetry consultant to the Library of Congress—a position now called Poet Laureate—had an automatic seat on the committee. In his autobiography Shapiro describes being approached by a conspiratorial figure from *The Saturday Review of Literature* to write an exposé critical of the Bollingen decision (*Reports of My Death* 44). He refused, so *The Saturday Review* turned to former Pulitzer Prize winner Robert Hillyer, who wrote a scathing two-part essay attacking what he saw as a New Critical plot against American democracy. Paul Mellon, who provided money for the prize, had asked that it be named Bollingen in honor of Carl Jung, who in later years spent much of his time in the Swiss village by that name. Making much of this fact, Hillyer claimed that members of the Bollingen committee, led by T. S. Eliot and in secret sympathy with Carl Jung's alleged Nazism, had conspired to honor a fascist poet with a crypto-fascist prize.[10]

The members of the committee issued a joint statement published by the Library of Congress and *Poetry* magazine in which they denied being influenced by Eliot (O'Connor 5–7). They had known that the decision would be controversial but insisted that aesthetic decisions must be made independently of political considerations. Judging art by political criteria, as

---

Europe, ego scriptor"—immediately follows a passage criticizing the BBC for its lies (76/478).

[10] See both of Hillyer's articles on the Pound award, "Treason's Strange Fruit" and "Poetry's New Priesthood," and also the follow-up editorial by Norman Cousins and Harrison Smith, all in *The Saturday Review of Literature*.

Hillyer demanded, "would destroy the significance of the award and would in principle deny the validity of that objective perception of value on which any civilized society must rest" (O'Connor 29–30).

In an editorial that kicked off a *Partisan Review* symposium on the Bollingen Prize, William Barrett assumed that the judges had endorsed Pound on purely aesthetic grounds, identifying the crux of the issue as follows: "How far is it possible, in a lyric poem, for technical embellishments to transform vicious and ugly matter into beautiful poetry?" ("A Prize" 347). Most of the contributors to the symposium agreed that Barrett's formulation of the issue was a fair one. Even Dwight Macdonald, whom the editors of *Partisan Review* were beginning to accuse of "ultra-leftism" (Rahv, "Disillusionment" 524), agreed with the distinction between poetry and politics, arguing that the ability "to evaluate each sphere of human activity separate from the rest instead of enslaving them all to one great reductive tyrant, whether it be The Church, The Proletariat, People's Democracy, The Master Race or American Patriotism" is what distinguished democracy from totalitarianism and gave Americans the "right to oppose Soviet totalitarianism in the name of freedom" ("Twelve Judges" 48).

Barrett would ultimately distance himself from this extreme formulation of the liberal aesthetic, which he termed "liberalism for liberalism's sake" ("Further Comment" 522). However, the basic principle of the liberal aesthetic—the separation of art from politics in the name of political freedom—was to prove decisive in a range of conflicts and issues extending far beyond the Bollingen controversy. Pound became the primary test case for those interested in defining the relation of art to politics at a critical juncture of history: at the end of WWII, in the aftermath of genocide, on the eve of the Cold War and during the great postwar expansion of mass culture in the public sphere and literary criticism in the universities (cf. Schwartz, "Our Country" III, 595). Other defining controversies would follow in rapid succession: the Rosenbergs, Hiss and Chambers, McCarthy, Korea, Vietnam. However, the Pound award was the decisive moment in the crystallization of a liberal aesthetic that would play a brief but important role in postwar culture, especially in American universities, through the late 1960s.

Why was defending Pound a liberal cause? The reactionary opinions that Pound shared with some of the committee members were clearly evident in *The Pisan Cantos*. Pound frames the poem as an apocalyptic response to Eliot's "The Hollow Men": "yet say this to the Possum: a bang, not a whimper, / with a bang not with a whimper" (74/445). Eliot had just won the Nobel Prize in Literature (1948), and he was being celebrated as a moderating voice. However, anyone who had attended his Page-Barbour lectures at the University of Virginia in 1933 or read the published version *After*

Strange Gods (1934), knew that his views could be extremely right-wing and anti-Semitic:

> The population should be homogeneous; where two or more cultures exist in the same place they are likely either to be fiercely self-conscious or both to become adulterate. What is still more important is unity of religious background; and reasons of race and religion combine to make any large number of free-thinking Jews undesirable. (20)

Hillyer's paranoid style made it easy to ignore that he had a valid point. Eliot and Tate may not have been conspiring on Pound's behalf—whatever conspiracy might mean on a committee—but Eliot's arguments did indeed bear affinities to Pound's and Tate's. Indeed, Eliot introduces his Page-Barbour lectures as an addendum to "Tradition and the Individual Talent" in the spirit of *I'll Take My Stand*. He declares himself a partisan of Southern Agrarianism because "I think that the chances for the re-establishment of a native culture are perhaps better here than in New England. You are farther away from New York; you have been less industrialised [*sic*] and less invaded by foreign races; and you have a more opulent soil" (15–17).

Karl Shapiro may have heard Eliot take his stand south of the Mason-Dixon Line. The aspiring poet dropped out of the University of Virginia the same year Eliot delivered his lectures there. Recalling his undergraduate studies in "University," published in the volume that won him the Pulitzer Prize and effectively placed him on the Bollingen committee, Shapiro wrote "To hurt the Negro and avoid the Jew / Is the curriculum" (*Selected* 17). The arguments Shapiro mustered to support his dissenting vote—as a Jew he could not vote to honor anti-Semites, and there could be no absolute distinction between poetry and politics—were more reasoned than Hillyer's conspiracy theory, but his polemic cuts in the same direction ("The Question" 518–19). Barrett, for his part, eventually endorsed Shapiro's argument that anti-Semitism was not irrelevant to *The Pisan Cantos* but central to the complex of themes or "myths" galvanizing their particular form ("Further Comment" 522). Robert Gorham Davis, who contributed to the *Partisan Review* symposium and also wrote a longer article in *The American Scholar*, made a similar argument about "a complex of ideas" which he linked to Pound and Eliot and "which made poetic sensibility, purity of language, and the integrity of art inextricably involved with ideas of authority, aristocracy and reaction, and at odds with the ethos of a liberal democracy" ("The New Criticism" 12).

Liberal critics such as Macdonald were not ignorant of the political content of Pound's verse—or Eliot's and Tate's arguments—but considered it out of bounds to factor this into aesthetic considerations. By evaluating

Pound's poetry in terms of his politics, critics like Hillyer (Davis's and Shapiro's more reasoned, scholarly arguments were not taken up) merely perpetuated Pound's basic error of politicizing art—but from a different ideological perspective. Macdonald, on the contrary, advocated erecting strong boundaries between art and politics, although with the larger political goal of demonstrating the superiority of liberal democracy. This convergence of formalism (focusing on technical achievement) and liberalism (separating freedom of expression from the content of expression) would become increasingly conspicuous in the academy and in the pages of journals like *Partisan Review*. Midcentury criticism set itself the task of bringing together high modernism—widely if wrongly assumed to be reactionary—and liberalism (Carton and Graff 296; Howe, "New York" 217). The argument it hit upon—the liberal aesthetic—stressed the allegedly apolitical nature of lyrical poetry, elevated to the status of representative art.

The pervasiveness of this argument might suggest a liberal rather than a reactionary conspiracy. A fairly recent account of Pound's time in St. Elizabeths casts MacLeish in the role of ringleader of such a conspiracy, although this is not a widely-shared view (Torrey 234–35).[11] What is clear is that MacLeish made extensive use of the valuable political experience and contacts he had acquired as assistant Secretary of State for cultural affairs under Roosevelt and as former Librarian of Congress. From earlier days in Paris MacLeish also knew the U.S. Attorney General responsible for the initial indictment of Pound, Francis Biddle, and his wife Katherine Garrison Chapin, whom MacLeish had appointed as one of the original fellows of the Library of Congress. MacLeish had connections to the Bollingen committee and to the government, and he worked on Pound's behalf. He did not, however, conspire with his friends and contacts—Chapin's vote against Pound would be hard to square with this theory, as would MacLeish's active cooperation with the FBI during the early stages of the Pound indictment.[12]

[11] James Laughlin offers a refutation of E. Fuller Torrey's conspiracy theory in the first essay in *Pound As Wuz* (21). Leick convincingly argues that only evidence pointing towards a conspiracy implicates *The Saturday Review of Literature*, which conspired to create a scandal in order to increase sales (36; on the unlikelihood of a MacLeish conspiracy see 23, footnote 13).

[12] Heymann links MacLeish's early cooperation with the FBI to Pound's savage criticism of him in some of his radio broadcasts (134). He also argues that MacLeish actively worked towards Pound's release only after visiting him at St. Elizabeths—a visit that led him to the conclusion that Pound did not belong there (216–17). On MacLeish's views of Pound and the Bollingen Award see Scott Donaldson's MacLeish biography (443). See also MacLeish's letter to the editor of *The Saturday Review of Literature* (Winnick 344–46).

MacLeish is best understood not as a conspirator but as one of the architects of the postwar liberal aesthetic. He advocated separating politics from art in a way that made it possible for modernists of all ideological stripes to support Pound. He also paved the way for the migration of literary studies to the universities. Significantly, MacLeish published his own defense of the Pound award, *Poetry and Opinion* (1950), with the University of Illinois Press.[13] A dialogue between the allegorical figures Mr. Saturday and Mr. Bollingen, the book argues that while Pound's political ideas may be reprehensible, his true loyalty is to his poetry: "With Pound, as this poem itself demonstrates and as the earlier Cantos make abundantly clear, the loyalty is not to dogmas of fascism but to the poet's vision of a tragic disorder which lies far deeper in our lives and in our time" (48). This is a surprising argument from the writer whose much-derided prewar manifesto "The Irresponsibles" describes World War II as "a war of treason: a war of corruption: a war of lies," calling upon artists and scholars to "accept[ ] responsibility for the common culture [and] for its defense" (MacLeish, *Time to Speak* 112, 113).[14]

---

[13] Under the editorship of communications theorist Wilbur Schramm, the publication list of the University of Illinois Press included, besides MacLeish's book, a spectrum of books ranging from titles in linguistics to Werner von Braun's *The Mars Project*. The publication list uncannily reflects the emerging concept of a literary world apart.

[14] Viereck cites MacLeish's "The Irresponsibles" in his initial indictment of Pound ("My Kind" 35). Matthiessen, in his contribution to a 1948 pamphlet on Pound, alludes to MacLeish when he writes, "He [Pound] did not want to be regarded as *an irresponsible*, although his political tracts [...] were a fantastic mixture of social credit and a literary man's admiration for the efficiency of the new Italian state" ("Statement" 58; my emphasis). MacLeish's own poetic responses to the war and the Pound controversy would make an important study, which unfortunately lies beyond the scope of this book. "The Irresponsibles" in fact decries the separation of the profession of letters into writing on the one hand and scholarship on the other in a way that would seem to make MacLeish suspicious of the institutionalization of literary studies after the war—an institutionalization to which he gave tacit approval by separating politics from art. However, in a slightly earlier essay on "Poetry and the Public World" (1939), in which he already decries one version of the institutionalization of modernism ("Contemporary poetry is in large part [...] a continuation of pretended revolution" [*Time to Speak* 95]), he identifies Pound as a great dismantler of academic conventions (*Time to Speak* 93). It is likely MacLeish continued to see Pound in this role even after the academy rallied in his defense. MacLeish's *Actfive* (1948), published the same year as *The Pisan Cantos*, mentions the war and the camps, but it ends on a surprisingly positive note when an image of bare life bereft of God, man, and identity—mere bones and flesh—miraculously endures and loves (*Collected* 393, 395). The prose poem "Geography of This Time," the poem on "Treason" and the one devoted to Pound, "Ezry," also demand analysis in relation to the Bollingen Award, as do some of the essays in *Freedom is the Right to Choose*, which laments postwar consumerism (19), links

Apparently the cessation of hostilities rendered Pound's irresponsibility, his opposition to common culture and his manifest commitment to "the disorder of our time," irrelevant for MacLeish (109). He consigned Pound to the realm of poetry—an extra-political territory governed by visionary truths rather than passing ideologies—while working behind the scenes to ensure adequate legal representation, engineer an insanity defense, and eventually, with the help of Robert Frost and other well-known writers, obtain Pound's release without a trial.[15]

The reactionary members of the Bollingen committee followed the liberal MacLeish's lead. Those directly accused by Hillyer confined themselves to praising Pound's poetry and left the politics to others. Eliot may have sent inquires about Pound's legal counsel through MacLeish, but he remained largely silent about the Pound case—and Pound's politics—in public.[16] The few public declarations Eliot did make, such as the single introductory paragraph added to Faber's postwar edition of Pound's *Collected Poems*, did little more than affirm Pound's importance as a formal innovator.[17] Tate, whom Jed Rasula identifies as one of the initiators of the Bollingen Prize, and whose *Reactionary Essays* echoed Eliot on the poet's job of "experiencing the past along with the present," also affirmed Pound's significance as a technician of language (Rasula 101–03; "Preface" 614). Tate did admit the political significance of prejudice in Pound's poetry, but in an impulsive way that proved to be embarrassing. In his contribution to the *Partisan Review* symposium on the award, he came close to challenging William Barrett to a duel over what he took to be a hint that anti-Semitism played a role in the committee's decision ("The Question" 520, 521). Tate's follow-up article, a partial apology, criticizes Pound's anti-Semitism and admits that

---

poetry to individualism (94–95), and opposes individualism to authoritarianism (135–36).

15 Robert Frost had his own complicated relation to Pound and played an important role in the successful 1958 bid to obtain his release from St. Elizabeths (Cornell 130–31). Frost was a political poet, although his politics were not easily classifiable in terms of party politics (three years after Pound's release Frost would recite "The Gift Outright" at Kennedy's inauguration).

16 C. David Heymann notes that Eliot continued to send MacLeish letters concerning Pound while the latter was a ward of St. Elizabeths; Eliot began to suspect that Pound did not want to be released (232).

17 The New Directions version of Pound's *Selected Poems* appeared—and still appears—without an introduction, partially because of disagreements over how to describe Pound's politics (Barnhisel 131–36); the *New Selected Poems and Translations,* edited by Richard Sieburth, finally corrected and commented on this omission in 2010.

he (Tate) had felt humiliated by his own ("Further Remarks" 667).[18] Tate remains convinced, however, that even if Pound had been convicted as a traitor, his "concern for the health of language" meant he "had performed an indispensable duty to society" ("Ezra Pound" 512–13).

Bogan, another member of the committee, also honored Pound for his contributions to language, which she separated from his ideas, deferring the evaluation of their relation indefinitely: "The future must judge whether his crude mistakes in theory and conduct entirely negate his frequent triumphs as a writer" (*Achievement* 107, 108). Marginalizing Pound's ideas was the first step in marginalizing him from the tradition, and Bogan turned to Eliot's "dark night of the soul," his discovery of religion and the lucid constructions in *Cocktail Party* (1950), as indications of where poetry would go at mid-century. Bogan makes much the same argument in "Modernism in American Literature," which appeared in one of the early issues of *American Quarterly*. The article credits Pound's technical achievements and once again touts Eliot as their rightful heir, but then locates the future of poetry in criticism rather than composition: "Interpretation, rather than exploration, however, is the task of the moment and of any imaginable future" (109–10). Judgments from such reputable critics set the critical tone for decades, saving Pound's formal innovations by attenuating their relation to his ideas, and placing poetry into the hands of its interpreters, who increasingly held positions in universities and wrote for university quarterlies.

As Bogan's dismissive remarks indicate, there is a sense in which the Pound consigned to the interpreters was not being interpreted at all. The separation of politics from poetry might have been an effective legal strategy, but in the end it also separated Pound from the poetic tradition, establishing what a *Kenyon Review* article by James Blish, later to become known as a science fiction writer, decried as the "ritual" of declaring Pound's poetry indecipherable without giving it a fair hearing (185–86). Pound did not have to stand trial for treason, but in their efforts to save the poet his benefactors denied the poetry its day in court. *The Cantos* became a verbal icon: rewarded, regarded, but rarely analyzed except in terms of its technique and the personal validity of its lyrical voice.

These were the formal terms of the postwar critical consensus. Indeed, it was a formal consensus. The critics working together as scholars in the same universities found their aesthetics to be compatible even when their politics differed. The writers on the left tended to argue that poetry was a protected

[18] In an annex to *The Case Against the "Saturday Review of Literature,"* Tate underscores his opposition to all forms of totalitarianism, whether fascist or communist, and insists that he is a non-political writer (20–21).

form of free speech; the New Critics maintained that poetry could only be evaluated according to objective, which is to say formal, criteria. These positions were never mutually exclusive, as Marjorie Perloff has pointed out, but they proved extremely compatible during the Pound controversy ("Fascism" 12). Some of the committee members may have sympathized with aspects of Pound's thinking before the war, but contrary to Hillyer they did not vote for Pound to promote his politics. It would be more accurate to say that Cold War anticommunism helped create the cultural-political context in which a self-proclaimed fascist could become a champion of free speech and aesthetic autonomy.

Pound's canonization as a repentant—and therefore democratic—lyricist is presented as an article of faith in *The Oxford Book of American Verse* (1950). This was the last book Matthiessen completed—in this case edited—before his death, and he used the introduction to argue that Pound had finally achieved poetic greatness by confessing the error of his political ways (xiii). Matthiessen argues Pound's political sins and the suffering he has gone through redeem the poetry in a Christian sense: "the lyric meditation [...] rises clear and entire above the latter fragments that Pound has shored against his ruins." After this allusion to Eliot's *Waste Land*, Matthiessen continues,

> These lines, from one of the latest volumes to be published before this anthology was made, are some of the most remarkable in the entire course of American poetry. They show Pound at last reaching a fusion between his great technical gift and a content worthy of his skills. They demonstrate that out of the aberration of his Fascist politics, he has at last experienced suffering and learned humility. They are lines to be borne in mind as we move into the second half of our menaced century. (xiii)

The lines quoted by Matthiessen—and also anthologized in the volume—come from Canto 81. This would quickly become the most famous passage in *The Pisan Cantos*, and it was absolutely central to subsequent debates:

> Pull down thy vanity
> Thou art a beaten dog beneath the hail,
> A swollen magpie in a fitful sun,
> Half black half white
> Nor knowst'ou wing from tail
> Pull down thy vanity
> How mean thy hates
> Fostered in falsity,
> Pull down thy vanity,
> Rathe to destroy, niggard in charity,
> Pull down thy vanity,
> I say pull down. (81/540–41)

Matthiessen, like many of Pound's contemporaries, detected an apology in this passage, which seems to achieve its lyrical balance by actively turning away from politics to more personal passions: "What thou lovest well remains, / the rest is dross" (81/540).

Contemporary critics are less convinced that Pound composed Canto 81 as an apology for his politics.[19] However, by 1950 the distinction between lyrical poetry (personal) and politics (non-poetical) was a critical commonplace. Evidence can be found in a guide to poetry that was even more influential than *The Oxford Book of American Verse*: Cleanth Brooks and Robert Penn Warren's *Understanding Poetry* (1938, 1950, 1960). In the postwar odyssey of English Lit., this is the textbook that launched a thousand seminar papers.

Warren was a member of the Bollingen committee that honored Pound in 1949. Twenty years earlier he had contributed to the Southern Agrarian manifesto *I'll Take My Stand*. He thoroughly repudiated the views expressed there, and some would argue he did not fit in to begin with, but an agrarian and regionalist element is nevertheless evident in *Understanding Poetry*'s introduction, which remained almost completely unchanged through all three editions. (What follows is based on the third edition of 1960.) The introduction describes poetry as a self-contained tract in the realm of culture, distinct from politics, mass culture, and from the competing academic discipline of science (21). The preoccupation with science reflects the fact that *Understanding Poetry* is a textbook, defining the place of the lyric in an academic landscape. That place is organic, or more precisely an "organic form" that dramatizes "the reaction of [...] a person to a situation, a scene, or an idea" (16, 20). The way poetry acts out meaning renders it indifferent to its context, and to authorial intent, emotional impact, and philosophical and scientific validity (8, 12–13, 14).

This is another version of the separate sphere argument I have labeled the liberal aesthetic. The lyric in Brooks and Warren is an organic entity formally independent of its context; where they differ from their more left-leaning contemporaries is in attributing to this organic form a pastoral significance. The pastoral significance of organic form is evident in the way their argument makes science bear the brunt of the problems of modernity. Brooks and Warren sum up these threats with a term from Bertrand Russell: "power-knowledge" (20–21). The excerpt they include as a counter example is enthusiastic about the potential of power-knowledge. In language that

[19] As Sieburth points out, Pound may have been criticizing the commander of the prison, or the corrupt society that would engage in another brutal war and place a poet behind bars (Sieburth, *Pisan* xxxiii).

would seem poignant to any agrarian, Russell argues that the intellect is a tool of abstraction which produces concrete results: the railway is more abstract in relation to crops than the cultivator, but it generates more profit; the stock-broker more abstract still. The most powerful figure in Russell's schema is the scientist, who not only generates value but understands how it transcends economics. Brooks and Warren locate poetic value at the other end of the power-knowledge spectrum. The lyric rejects abstraction for a concrete and deliberately non-scientific mode of acting out understanding. Another way to put this is that poetry is cultivated and returns to cultivation for the source of its value. It declares regional independence from modernity in a way the South never could.

The lyrical self in Brooks and Warren is independent because unreconstructed. I do not want to overstate this point because Brooks and Warren are not proponents of complete literary independence, nor does their textbook put forth anything like an actual political agenda. In fact, their argument is less dependent on the notion of aesthetic autonomy than is often claimed. They admit that "form [...] does not exist in a vacuum," and part of what informs it is the "historical moment" (xiv). Again: "poetry is not an isolated and eccentric thing, but springs from the most fundamental interests which human beings have" (22, 8). Like many critics of the 1950s, Brooks and Warren erect a differentially permeable boundary between culture and politics; poetry can teach us something about political rhetoric, but not vice versa. Their theory has its roots in a kind of cultural regionalism, but its implications are in keeping with the anti-political impulse Joseph Frank attributed to New Criticism in *The Widening Gyre* (1963): "In defending the autonomy and integrity of the work of art, the New Critics were repulsing the claims of the liberals and radicals to appropriate it for social or political ends; their influence was part of the wave of disillusionment with politics that marked the generation of the fifties" (254). If there is a difference between the kind of aesthetic autonomy proposed by Brooks and Warren and the kind proposed by critics on the left, it is in the tenor of their respective disillusionments. Former agrarians published in the same journals as former radicals, occupied neighboring offices in English departments, and found that they agreed with their colleagues about the importance of keeping culture separate from politics. Poetry seemed to offer the only remaining refuge from the historical catastrophes that had invalidated so many political ideologies; it hardly mattered if that refuge was figured as a golden age or a better world to come.

Thus it was not as a reactionary or a closet agrarian but as a lyricist that Pound was included in the third edition of *Understanding Poetry*. The editors selected poems that confirmed his reputation as a poet driven to despair—

and perhaps political error—by the tragedies of modernity. "In a Station of the Metro" was retained from previous editions, but "Preludes" and "Preparation for the Pyre of Patroclus" give way to "Envoi (1919)," *Mauberly*, and the famous passage from Canto 81. A new feature in the third edition was the expanded "Poems for Study" section, which grew to be a full-fledged anthology of modern poetry. Brooks and Warren describe the change in these terms: "Though not intended to provide a systematic survey, the poems are not selected at random, but have been chosen with the idea of illustrating various methods and topics in planned but unlabeled clusters, an arrangement that makes for ready comparisons and contrasts on the basis of theme or style" (xv).

The excerpt from Canto 81, separated from the other Pound poems, fits into one of these thematic clusters. It is preceded by Wallace Stevens's "Peter Quince at the Clavier," which retells the Biblical story of Susanna and the elders to show how song transcends shame: "Now in its immortality [Susanna's music] plays / On the clear viol of her memory, / And makes a constant sacrament of praise" (507). Pound's song also survives his shame; it survives his politics well. Thus Canto 81 is followed by Marianne Moore's "In Distrust of Merits," an anti-war poem that shows how even good intentions—set off in scare quotes—are suspicious: "'We'll / never hate black, white, red, yellow, Jew, / Gentile, Untouchable.' We are / not competent to / make our vows" (509). The implication is psychological rather than political; the true wars are those we fight within ourselves: "There never was a war that was / not inward." The record of these inner battles creates a beauty that goes beyond politics. Moore ends with a line that resonates with the artistic immortality suggested by Pound's "What thou lovest well remains" and Stevens's "sacrament of praise": "Beauty is everlasting / and dust is for a time" (510). Poetry, in the Canto 81-cluster, is more significant than its political and historical context. Indeed, it is poetry *because* it personalizes context as song and memory.

This notion—that the lyric is distinct from politics because it is personal—was something on which former radicals and former reactionaries could agree. And they agreed in the name of the liberal anticommunism invoked by Macdonald in his defense of the Pound award. Lyricizing Pound not only elevated art above politics; it showed that former political disagreements meant nothing in the face of the greater totalitarian threat. It would be hard to overemphasize the pervasiveness of the liberal aesthetic in the early stages of the Cold War. Much of the poetry community rallied around Pound, but he also served to crystallize a number of theories about liberalism and lyricism that were becoming prominent anyway. What is it that distinguishes open society from totalitarianism? The answer hit on again and again by cultural critics, philosophers, and even economists involved those realms of human activity (poetry, private property, free speech) that seemed secure from political instrumentalization. Art was understood to be a prominent example, perhaps the test case, for the most fundamental kind of liberal freedom: the freedom *from* government interference.

It should be noted that freedom from government interference was not the same as freedom from government support. The first Bollingen Prize was awarded under the auspices of the Library of Congress, and those of Pound's defenders who worked in public universities more or less had government jobs. Postwar scholars demanded aesthetic autonomy, but they also depended on public funding. The expanding postwar university system was assuming the role that New Dealers such as Grace Overmyer, in her influential *Government and the Arts* (1939), had envisioned for government patronage: "The state should pay the piper, but should not call the tune" (217).

As Jed Rasula points out, Pound was institutionalized at the same time literary studies was; indeed, placing the political thinker behind locked doors seemed to qualify his poetry—or at least his prosody—for entrance to the ivory tower (114). Contemporary scholars were quite open about the link between depoliticization and institutionalization. Richard Chase wrote at least two essays on the topic, both of them touching on the Pound controversy, one advocating the creation of an "institutional avant-garde" and the other his contribution to the famous "My Country, My Culture" symposium in *Partisan Review*. His basic thesis in both is that "There is no service in attacking avant-garde critics" because "their specifically polemical task of the last forty years has expired with the success of the movements they championed" ("Avant-Garde" 373). The success he refers to is a formal one, or the general acceptance of modernist technical experiments as an aesthetic benchmark. He continues,

> What has happened to the avant-garde in our "suspended" culture of the 1950s is a psychological equivalent of what has happened to it sociologically. Sociologically it has been institutionalized by the universities and the publishers, which by definition means that in its modern phase it has to come to an end. At the same time, it has been internalized, so to speak, in the flexibly dialectical mind of contemporary criticism. (375)

This tame description is actually a manifesto for cultural "suspension." The critics who internalize the values of the avant-garde, like the publishing houses and English departments canonizing its principles, make up the opposite of a movement. They are the literary establishment—an establishment devoted to the doctrine of ambiguity and irony, or what Chase calls the "dialectical mind." The dialectical mind was perfectly suited to the union-in-contradiction presented by the emergent literary establishment, whose ranks were populated by former socialists and old reactionaries agreeing on one crucial issue: the difference between poetry and politics. In effect Chase provided the constitution to MacLeish's declaration of literary independence, establishing a world apart whose boundaries were the academy, whose citizens—whatever their ideologies—agreed on the apolitical nature of art, and whose doctrines would dominate research for almost twenty years. Chase singles out Pound because he—or at least the political part of him—had to be sacrificed for avant-gardism to become official. Chase actually performs the purification ritual by placing Pound in opposition to another rejected critic, Van Wyck Brooks (who eventually also issued a statement in favor of Pound's release). Why Pound and Van Wyck Brooks? There are some curious biographical parallels, but Chase sees them both as deviating from the formal insights of avant-gardism through nationalism, one as an expatriate and the other as a super-patriot. His alternative to cultural nationalism, invalidated by the excesses of war, was not cosmopolitanism but institutionalism, or the emergence of a new class of academics who internalized the insights of the avant-garde but who were protected, by virtue of their professional location, from falling prey to ideological extremes.

The institutionalization of literary studies was essentially a border action, separating literature from politics in the same way Pound was separated from his poetry. Cold War attempts to define the form and methodology of literary studies ritualistically exorcised undesirable elements from literary consideration. Northrop Frye's justly influential *Anatomy of Criticism* (1957), for instance, begins by lamenting the infringements onto literary territory by other disciplines such as psychology and sociology: "It is clear that the absence of systematic criticism has created a power vacuum, and all the neighboring disciplines have moved in" (12). Once literature is protected from outside influences, however, it becomes a talisman of liberal freedom. Here is Frye's version of the liberal aesthetic: "Liberty can begin only with an immediate and present guarantee of the autonomy of culture" (348–49). Frye could have been quoting Macdonald on Pound here, although his purpose was to defend literary criticism as an independent academic discipline. To do so he turned to the aesthetic theory of a classic liberal thinker: "The artist, as John Stuart Mill saw in a wonderful flash of critical insight, is not heard but overheard" (Frye 5). This is a deliberate misquote. Mill was talking about the poet rather than the artist. But Mill's usefulness for the postwar cultural project had to do with his lyrical definition of culture, his equation of poetic voice with isolation and isolation with freedom.

Frye and others like Lionel Trilling and M. H. Abrams repeatedly cited John Stuart Mill's 1833 distinction between eloquence (heard) and poetry (overheard) to stress the fundamental independence of art: “Eloquence supposes an audience; the peculiarity of poetry appears to us to lie in the poet’s utter unconsciousness of a listener. Poetry is feeling confessing itself to itself, in moments of solitude” (Mill, *Poetry* 12; Trilling, *Liberal Imagination* 6, 8; Abrams 25).[20] The implications drawn from this distinction reached far beyond definitions of the lyric. Mill was an appealing figure at mid-century because he seemed to exemplify the kind of conversion attributed to Pound and performed by a number of former radicals who publically renounced their political affiliations after World War II (cf. Rosenberg, *Tradition of the New* 221–40). Jeremy Bentham and Mill’s father had raised Mill *fils* to be a mechanical monist, a utilitarian, someone who believed that personal happiness had to be subordinated to the greatest good. This education in rational selflessness led to a serious bout of depression that by Mill’s own admission could only be cured by poetry (Trilling, *Liberal Imagination* 6, 8; Sharpless 64–72, 134; Himmelfarb 7). In Wordsworth he discovered an emotional intensity that seemed to be irreducible to external causes or collectivist rationales. Many of the studies that came after Mill’s depression, prominent upon them “Thoughts on Poetry and Its Varieties” (1833 [here cited in *Essays on Poetry*]) and *On Liberty* (1859), stress the importance not only of the greatest good but of individual passion. Indeed, in keeping with the classical liberal doctrine that self-interest is the foundation of public welfare, Mill argued that the individual was useful to society to the extent that he or she was true to his own heart: “In proportion to the development of his individuality, each person becomes more valuable to himself, and is therefore capable of being more valuable to others” (*Liberty* 91–92).[21] Mill’s definition of lyrical poetry as a private voice overheard, epitomized this individualism at the cultural level.[22]

---

[20] According to Frederick Rosen’s recent study of Mill, “security *against* government was more important [...] than security under government,” although the emphasis was very different in his 1861 book on utilitarianism (Rosen 140).

[21] Adam Smith’s famous dictum in *The Wealth of Nations* (1776): “It is not from the benevolence of the butcher, the brewer, or the baker, that we expect our dinner, but from their regard to their own interest. We address ourselves, not to their humanity but to their self-love, and never talk to them of our own necessities but of their advantages” (14).

[22] According to Wendy Donner, Mill endorsed poets like Shelley because of his strong conviction that emotions were threatened and repressed in society (152–53). In the same volume Colin Heydt points to a connection between his essays on poetry and *On Liberty*: “It is through the development of interiority (“individuality”) in the language of *On Liberty*, that is, through the development of intellectual and affective resources, that we can resist the homogenizing effects of the culture of commercial modernity (including the “tyranny of the majority”)” (269). The relevance to Mill’s lyrical

Of course, the privacy of poetry is staged—a paradox that becomes clear through Mill's own choice of the term "soliloquy" to describe the utterance overheard (*Essays on Poetry* 12). Midcentury critics tended to ignore the social scripting that required poets to play individualistic roles. Walter J. Ong was virtually alone in pointing out the obvious fact that Mill's poet *had* to be excluded from society for the social good: "[Mill's] poet had to be both in exile, where he would be safe from a mechanistic world, and not in exile in order to redeem this world. The poet *over*heard is such a poet, inside and outside society at one and the same time" (344). Mill himself was perhaps aware of the constraint implicit in his model of lyrical freedom—the social imperative, as it were, to speak privately. A telling passage edited out of the 1860 American reprint of Mill's poetry essay makes the following remark about a favorite ballad: "That song has always seemed to us like the lament of a prisoner in a solitary cell, ourselves listening, unseen in the next" (*Essays on Poetry* 14; cf. Jackson 132).

Prisoner and prize winner, Pound embodied the liberal paradox implicit in Mill's definition of lyrical freedom. That is to say, Pound's actual confinement helped make his verse free: the poetry could be (mis-) read as lyrical as long as the poet remained locked in his cell. Bollingen committee members undoubtedly wanted to help Pound by honoring his postwar writing. Nevertheless, the arguments they hit upon to justify their decision—that Pound had rediscovered lyricism and rejected political polemic, or that lyrical poetry was by definition apolitical—not only ignored the obvious political, economic, and racist elements in *The Pisan Cantos*, but unintentionally acknowledged the depoliticizing effect of Pound's incarceration. The indefinite term in a mental institution, which prevented Pound from ever having his day in court, rendered his statements "merely" personal. *How* he spoke was more important than *what* he said because poets were supposed to be introspective, and introspection was politically equivalent to legal

account of liberalism to midcentury poetry, and its strange pairing of confinement and freedom, can be seen in another example from the far left, Herbert Read's *Poetry and Anarchism* (1938): "I shall endeavor to live as an individual, to develop my individuality; and if necessary I shall be isolated in a prison rather than submit to the indignities of war and collectivism" (17). Read already offers a cultural version of the anti-totalitarian argument that would become prominent after the war: "Art becomes, not a mode of expressing the life of the imagination, but a means of illustrating the concepts of the intelligence. At this point, Marxism and fascism, the prodigal and the dutiful sons of Hegel, meet again; and will inevitably become reconciled. There is not the slightest difference, in intention, in control and in final product, between the art of Marxist Russia and the art of fascist Germany" (25).

insanity. In other words, Pound's poetry was secure *from* government because the poet was secure *under* government, institutionalized and depoliticized in a manner that made incarceration strangely resonant with arguments for artistic autonomy.

If Pound embodied a paradox in liberal theory dating back to Mill, he also occupied an institutional space constructed at midcentury to secure freedom from the threat of totalitarianism. Pound's contemporaries missed this because they tended to talk about freedom in absolute terms; Gertrude Himmelfarb argues that postwar thinkers turned to Mill "in the aftermath of absolute despotism [...] to seek refuge in absolute liberty" (332). "That absolute liberty cannot, in fact, sustain itself," Himmelfarb adds, "is suggested by the disjunction in contemporary liberalism, the increasing claims of liberty and individuality in one area and the increasing demands for social and government control in another" (334). Her advice is to return to an older "temperate, humane, and capacious liberalism, a philosophy that can accommodate liberty together with such other values as justice, virtue, community, tradetion, prudence, and moderation" (xxii). This conservative argument would become increasingly significant in the 1960s as a number of (older) thinkers began to question the culture of absolute freedom that seemed to play a role in student radicalism. However, to understand the argument for personal responsibility and against absolute liberty, it is important to explore how liberty was actually secured at various institutional levels. In this I build on the work of Jed Rasula who argues that "What was crucial was the preservation of the administrative security system that had assumed custodial control of poetry (not just Pound's poetry) as surely as the man was impounded in a mental asylum" (114).

Rasula explores how the growth of the administrative security system was linked to the growth of higher education after World War II. Pound's institutionalization in a mental facility, as I have already mentioned, paralleled the institutionalization of literary studies in English and creative writing departments throughout the United States (Rasula 114). (In this connection it is worth mentioning that the Bollingen moved from the Library of Congress to Yale as a result of the Pound scandal.) Just as St. Elizabeths contained Pound's threat by making it unnecessary for his ideas to stand trial, the university contained the threat posed by other writers on the right and the left. The institutionalization of English studies facilitated a consensus in which cultural freedom became indistinguishable from professionalization. As *The Pound Era* (Hugh Kenner) led to *The Program Era* (Mark McGurl), writing became an exercise in lyrical freedom at the same time, and through the same gesture, that it was assigned a particular place in an academic setting.[23]

Another part of the administrative security system, to use Rasula's phrase, involved foreign relations. The claim that democratic culture was secure from government interference proved ideologically useful during the cultural Cold War. As the United States fought on multiple fronts to contain the Soviet threat, it exported American culture as a kind of anti-propaganda, representative of democracy to the extent that it could be shown to reflect un-coerced personal views. Pound, still "contained" in St. Elizabeths, was nevertheless an exportable symbol of artistic freedom in the age of containment. Evidence for this paradoxical role can be found in *Perspectives USA*, a highbrow quarterly originally launched by the Ford Foundation in 1952. The magazine, which contained glossy reproductions of contemporary art but no advertisements, was published simultaneously in England, France, Italy, and Germany—in the local languages. It was designed, according to its editor, not "so much to defeat the leftist intellectuals in dialectical combat as to lure them away from their positions by aesthetic and rational persuasion" (qtd. in Saunders 140).That editor was James Laughlin of New Directions, Pound's publisher in the United States and the man responsible for organizing his legal defense. *Perspectives USA* ceased publishing in 1956 when the Ford Foundation redirected its financial support to Melvin Lasky's *Der Monat*. (Lasky also served as chief editor of the CIA-funded *Encounter* magazine from 1958 to 1991.)[24] Issue 16—the final issue—can be seen as the culmination of Laughlin's efforts at aesthetic persuasion, and it is built around a defense of Ezra Pound.[25]

The final issue of *Perspectives USA* features several of Pound's poems, including the Usura Canto and the "tear down thy vanity" passage from Canto 81. These preface a long, biographical essay on Pound by Hayden Carruth, who concludes by calling for the poet's release (Pound would be freed two years later without having to stand trial). Carruth's arguments show the influence of Matthiessen, the Bollingen committee, and ultimately Mill. He admits that Pound's economics became "compulsive," "obsessive" and in parts of *The Cantos* "dominates the poem" (150–51). However, in a

---

[23] Recent work by Eric Bennett should also be mentioned here.

[24] See Macdonald's brief account in *Discriminations* (57–59) and the account by Giles Scott Smith. Thanks to Hans-Jürgen Grabbe for the latter reference.

[25] Heinz Ickstadt discusses the role of *Perspektiven* in bringing William Carlos Williams's poetry to a German audience in "William Carlos Williams and German Postwar Poetry." He argues that "being associated with the American re-education program" "did not endear [the magazine] to German intellectuals" (136–37, including footnote 16).

stunning reversal he blames Pound's use of poetry to express political ideas on "the heritage of shoddy thought which descended to him and to all of us" (159). Pound's fault, in other words, is the American fault of believing "that a poem is an instrument which conveys or arouses the ideas and emotions that are current between the poet and his readers" (129). This formulation is deliberately vague, but it suggests that writing with an audience in mind is a mistake—one that critics only perpetuate by judging Pound's poetry by his politics. Poetry, Carruth claims, is boring when it is too political: "The poem has no autonomy because it cannot speak for itself; its authority has been dissipated in hundreds of external references" (153, see also 151). Poetry is best when it is strictly personal, for instance in the more lyrical early *Cantos* and in "a number of magnificent lyrical passages" that begin to reappear in the personal sections of *The Pisan Cantos*: "The poems are given shape by Pound's genuine feeling, deeper and more complex than the merely hortatory sentiments of the middle cantos [which contain his economic and political arguments]" (129, 154). By rejecting oration—or what Mill called "eloquence"—Pound has been able "to redress in part the unfortunate bias in American cultural life which Pound himself was one of the first to disclaim" and he has "restored the integrity to the language" (158–59). By the end of the essay Pound becomes an emblematic figure whose supposed return to personal lyricism reaffirms the significance of cultural autonomy.

I might add: the significance of cultural autonomy in a liberal democracy. While Carruth's essay does little more than reiterate the standard defense of Pound as a repentant lyricist (ignoring *The Pisan Cantos*'s obvious political outbursts to do so), it is framed in a way that makes the poet's alleged retreat from politics politically significant. The last issue of *Perspectives USA* opens with the transcription of a keynote address by George F. Kennan, the author of the U.S. containment policy, which is praised by the editor for epitomizing the entire *Perspectives USA*-project (5). In his speech Kennan calls for "a revolution in the attitude of many of us toward culture activity generally as well as toward our obligations here in the international field," insisting on practical matters like giving foreign intellectuals and artists "their visas in a relatively relaxed and civilized way" without having to be "fingerprint[ed] […] like common criminals" ("International Exchange" 13). Since he is dealing with "the unhappy problem of security" anyway, as he puts it, Kennan moves on to make his own non sequitur plea for cultural autonomy—a plea consistent with Carruth's defense of Pound: "In recent years, it seems to me, there has grown up among us a most reprehensible habit, a totalitarian habit in fact, of judging the suitability of cultural contributions by whatever political coloration we conceive their creators to have acquired. I know of nothing sillier than this" (13). "After all," he adds, "cultural events are not political livestock exhibits in which we put forward human figures to be admired for the purity of their ideological features" (13–14). Kennan believes that Americans profit from their exposure to foreign ideas (8–9); he also realizes that artistic dissent is the best advertisement for a political system that claims to defend personal liberty (10–11). He sees internationalization as an opportunity to de-provincialize American culture, but also to use more complex examples of American culture (Kennan is no fan of Hollywood films) to advertise the American way.

Kennan does not mention Pound by name, but the significance attributed to Pound in *Perspectives USA* is consistent with the role he assigns culture in the age of containment. Twenty years later Kennan would seemingly modify his views when another poet, whom Kennan this time would explicitly refuse to name, used another poetry award to protest the Vietnam War. I will discuss this incident in a moment. First, I want to explore the role Kennan envisions for culture by returning to the late 1940s and the article that, following The Long Telegram, expanded on "containment" as a concept: "The Sources of Soviet Conduct," first published anonymously in *Foreign Affairs* (1947) and then in Kennan's *American Diplomacy, 1900–1950* (1951). This necessary detour will move away from the Pound controversy, but I will return to it in the context of 1960s protest culture.

Containment, as Kennan defines it, offers a check to Soviet expansion without unnecessarily challenging Russian "prestige" ("Sources" 575). Absolute opposition would be a mistake, Kennan maintains, because the Soviets believe themselves to be in a "state of siege, with the enemy lowering beyond the walls" (571). Kennan vacillates between describing this siege mentality as the product of paranoia or a "semi-myth" or "fiction" maintained for the purposes of domestic control (570–71). Either way, the siege mentality "is not founded in reality"; it is the result of Soviet security apparatuses becoming "in large measure the masters of those whom they were designed to serve" (571). It would be possible to counter Kennan's repeated claims that the Soviets had nothing to fear from the West (570–71). Rather than challenging his historical account, however, I want to explore how containment is designed to counter the siege mentality without feeding into its oppositional logic. This is where culture fits in as an alternative to security: because culture is supposed to be personal rather than ideological, because it expresses the author's opinion whatever his or her particular ideological beliefs, it models a fundamental liberal freedom without pledging any particular political allegiance, thereby countering Soviet security without feeding into its paranoid plot.

Kennan believes that the Soviet preoccupation with security tends towards an absolutism which reproduces the official party line at all levels.

He describes the absolute dominance of Soviet thinking by borrowing a metaphor from Western consumer culture: "The individuals who are the components of this machine are unamenable to argument or reason which comes to them from outside sources. [...] Like the white dog before the phonograph, they hear only the 'master's voice'" (574). This Victrola phonograph comparison expresses a fear that Kennan held in common with many Cold War thinkers, namely that mass culture was a form of creeping totalitarianism. When he describes the Soviet Union, however, the automatism of hearing the master's voice has more to do with the oppositional logic of security than with culture or ideology. Security, for Kennan, is independent from ideology, belief, and even the intentions of political leaders; its own unfettered logic makes it absolute. A government that strives towards total security from the enemy, whoever it is, inevitably sacrifices the security its own citizens should have from government itself, leaving no room for personal opinions that differ from the official recording, and therefore no room for authentic cultural expression, i.e. personal voice as opposed to the master's voice (569).

This lack of personal security, which renders virtually any personal expression illegal, also makes the Soviet system vulnerable to dissent. Security automatically radicalizes personal opinion by forbidding it. Kennan believes that, given enough room, the Soviet system will eventually destroy itself because Marxism (in a reversal of the Marxist dictum) contains the seeds of its own destruction (580). Absolute security leads to internal insecurity—in governmental structures (568), in the "apocalyptic" or "messianic" dream of world revolution (576, 582), and especially for Russian children, so dramatically impacted when families are torn apart by harsh economic programs and the punitive policies that enforce them (577). The United States should resist Soviet expansion, but it should also encourage internal dissent in indirect ways. The indirection is essential; the only alternative to the totalizing fiction of total security is not to accept its antagonistic plot. Kennan's follow-up essay in *American Diplomacy* argues that simple propaganda will not work because the change has to come from the Russians themselves (144). "Informational activity," however, is not the same as propaganda. Kennan maintains that the future will depend on "the degree to which the United States can create among the peoples of the world generally the impression of a country which knows what it wants, which is coping successfully with the problems of its internal life and with the responsibilities of a world power, and which has a spiritual vitality capable of holding its own among the major ideological currents of the time" (581). American culture is particularly suited to advertising this spiritual vitality because it demonstrates liberal individualism by refusing to tow the party line. Pound in *Perspectives USA* is a case in point.

Kennan's argument is not free from contradictions. The "disunity" that he makes the bane of Soviet leadership (580) is something he also detects in the United States (581). American security also depends on a willed (not imposed) unanimity that has its own messianic flavor: "He [the "thoughtful observer"] will rather experience a certain gratitude to a Providence which, by providing the American people with this implacable challenge, has made their entire security as a nation dependent on their pulling themselves together and accepting the responsibilities of moral and political leadership that history plainly intended them to bear" (582). However, Kennan wants to maintain a distinction between Soviet security *under* government and American security *from* government, between totalitarianism's single party rule and liberalism's balance of power, between the messy transitions of leadership in the Soviet Union and the regulated electoral revolutions in the United States, between the recording of the "master's voice" and the lyrical voice of personal dissent (573). Exporting dissent, in the form of culture, is the best way to export liberal ideology. This is why Pound fits alongside Kennan in the *Perspectives USA* roster. As long as it can be argued that Pound is free to express his own opinion, that opinion can be said to support liberal ideology by being "overheard" within its institutional framework—whatever Pound's own political beliefs. Kennan nowhere mentions Pound, although the writer he holds up as exemplary of democracy did spend a night in prison for his political convictions. *American Diplomacy* concludes with a quote from Henry David Thoreau supposed to exemplify how democratic culture shines a light that "dissipates the gloom" behind the "iron curtain": "there is no ill which may not be dissipated, like the dark, if you let in a stronger light upon it" (146).

Kennan was shocked when the youth he predicted would rise up in Moscow actually rose up on American campuses in response to civil rights abuses and the Vietnam War (579). When a speech on the irresponsibility of the student protesters delivered at Swarthmore College in 1967 generated a wave of protests, Kennan collected his manuscript, selected responses, and his reply in an edited volume called *Democracy and the Student Left* (1968). Kennan's unapologetic remarks are critical of students for everything from their lack of personal hygiene to the "compulsive character of their indulgence in the fields of sex and narcotics, as well as in various forms of political extremism" (*Student Left* 137, 145–47, 160). His main concern, however, is the draft dodgers who are "victims of that preoccupation with personal security which, curiously, is more pronounced in this age of social security systems" (165). This is a familiar line of argument against postwar liberalism that would later be picked up by Himmelfarb: The preoccupation with absolute personal freedom goes hand in hand with increased government regulation, and the security provided by such regulation encourages the exaggerated freedom of rebellion.

Emblematic for the rebellion is an incident that occurs at the ceremony for a major poetry award in 1968. Kennan, who was present at the award ceremony, does not mention the poet's name, but it was Robert Bly, winner of National Book Award in Poetry for *The Light Around the Body*, a collection featuring several anti-war poems. One of the poems, "Johnson's Cabinet Watched by Ants," ironically revises Kennan's use of Thoreau: "Tonight they burn the rice-supplies; tomorrow / They lecture on Thoreau" (5). Bly probably did not have Kennan in mind, but like many affiliated with the New Left he was wary of the kind of establishment liberalism that instrumentalized liberty as a rationale for waging war. The students appealed to a different Thoreau, the author and practitioner of "civil disobedience," to challenge policies they saw as hypocritical and unjust (Kennan, *Student Left* 214). If Thoreau could be appropriated to justify Cold War policies, he could also serve as a voice of critique. When Bly received the prize for the National Book Award for Poetry, he immediately "disobeyed" in a Thoreauvian gesture by signing over the award check to the anti-war effort. His acceptance speech concludes: "You have given me an award for a book that has many poems in it against the war. I thank you for the award, and for the $1,000 check, which I am giving to the peace movement, specifically to the organizations for draft resistance. That is an appropriate use of an award for a book of poems mourning the war. Thank you very much" ("National Book Awards").

Kennan did not support the Vietnam War; he privately criticized the policies of the Johnson administration and ultimately spoke out against them in a televised panel organized by Senator Fulbright (*Student Left* 156; Gaddis 591–92). Nevertheless, Kennan also criticized student protesters for trying to impose their own concepts of justice on the majority without regard for the structures and procedures of democratic policymaking (168–69, 200; Gaddis 609–10). Kennan claims to admire the part of their intellectual legacy going back to Thoreau, but in choosing "civil disobedience," they choose the most problematic aspect of his thinking (*Student Left* 214). Kennan, on the contrary, wants to separate Thoreau's "moving and noble vision of individual freedom" from his impatience with democracy: "His view, like that of his contemporary sympathizers, was essentially anarchical in its implications. […] He, too, did not question the correctness of his own judgment of what was right and what was wrong" (214, 212).The implications of this distinction between individualism and what Kennan sees as anarchy (the

New Left saw it as social critique) become clear in his discussion of the poetry award. Confronted with Bly's donation to the draft resistance movement, Kennan does not defend the cultural significance of expressing independent points of view, as he did in *Perspectives USA*; rather he laments the breakdown of the institutional structures that are supposed to secure the possibility of free expression:

> I had been under the impression that it was the business of Harper and Row to publish books, of the American Book Publishers Council to represent its members in their common professional interests, and of Yale University to educate young men.[…] To them, obviously, the business of all these bodies was to sit permanently in judgment over government policies, and if they found them out of line with what they themselves thought was right and moral, then to punish the government by placing in abeyance at least some of their own chartered functions and devoting themselves primarily to the manifestation of protest until such time as the government, shaken and intimidated—we must assume—by these evidences of opposition, gave in and altered its behavior […]. [I]t was plain that in the view of the new Left the corporate conscience, like the individual one, was to assume total dimensions. (190–91)

The adjective is deliberate: like many Cold Warriors, Kennan saw the student protesters—and not the American "power structures" (a term he despised as social science jargon [*Student Left* 141])—as potentially totalitarian (Gaddis 609). While he had his own list of social ills from "the commercialized mass media" to "the sickly secularism of this society" to the environmental degradation he was one of the first to decry (*Student Left* 216), he nevertheless disagreed with those students who claimed the U.S. government was totalitarian (202). However, it could become totalitarian if the New Left succeeded in dismantling those institutional structures that made democratic decision-making possible (205). It seemed to Kennan that this had already happened at the cultural level. The students had already transformed culture into propaganda by expecting everyone to support the same opinion. Thus Kennan hears in Bly not the personal voice that was so central to his earlier defense of free culture, but a collective voice that wants to be the new master. The tail is trying to wag the dog. The New Left that is in some sense the product of social security is on the verge of implementing a new form of total security against their perceived enemy the "establishment." The freedom from government students express in their personal lifestyles, coupled with the freedom under government they have enjoyed as children of the welfare state, has combined to create a new tyranny of the majority, leftist in rhetoric but totalitarian in implication.

As a representative of the establishment and *in loco parentis*, Kennan abandons his cultural defense of personal liberty to deliver a jeremiad of responsibility and restraint:

> It is superfluous to remind the reader that not just the American political system but the very organization of American life has traditionally been based on a division of responsibilities as well as powers [...]. In particular, certain duly elected or appointed officials, some legislative and some executive, were seen as sharing among themselves the responsibility for conducting foreign policy and making provision for the national defense. (*Student Left* 183)

One can detect in Kennan a generational resistance to the new youth culture (168). His biographer John Gaddis remarks that many of his anxieties about the protest movement were linked to anxieties about his own children (Gaddis 611). Kids are no longer in their place, and they expect government to bring its policies, regardless of the balance of power and mechanisms of debate, in line with their desires. That's why Kennan no longer feels compelled to defend liberty as freedom from government. The New Left has already appropriated the liberty to alter government without respect for its departments and structures. His call for responsibility was a plea to protesters to control themselves in ways befitting their age and station. But he was not beyond calling for control by external means as well.

Perhaps there was a change in Kennan: by the late 1960s he was more concerned with securing government against culture than with securing culture from government. However, there is a consistency behind this change that suggests a sinister connection between liberty and security in the age of containment—more sinister than the general defense of artistic free speech would have suggested. Just as the political threat posed by Pound had to be contained in St. Elizabeths so his poetry could be free, Kennan had always endorsed containing the threat to liberty through covert and openly coercive means. He believes that foreign relations depend on a calculus of power rather than good will (*Student Left* 170–71). In domestic terms, liberty also has to be secured *under* government to be secure *from* it. Responding to widespread criticism of CIA involvement in financing magazines such as *Encounter*, and by extension magazines funded by the Ford Foundation such as *Perspectives USA*, Kennan defended "the highly useful and constructive things the Central Intelligence Agency was once doing. The Agency was doing them largely for the simple and innocent reason that our government structure had (and still has) no federal ministry of culture to handle matters of that sort" (188). Kennan saw no contradiction between cultural freedom and the work of the CIA. Indeed, as Gaddis points out, "despite Kennan's having declined the offer of a job [at the CIA] in 1953, Allen Dulles had been using him ever since as a confidential adviser" (Gaddis 517). Gaddis also points out that during the student protests "Kennan was getting FBI reports on student and black protests [...] and at one point suggested that the government suppress them, in a manner 'answerable only to the voters at the next election but not to the press or even the courts'" (Gaddis 611). Kennan never put anyone behind bars, but his openness to covert and coercive strategies of containment, foreign and domestic, does suggest the close connection in his thinking between locking up the poet and freeing the poetry.

Kennan's book on the student left marks an epoch. The movement made it difficult to argue that culture embodied personal liberty by being free from politics. The New Left argued that the personal was political, and that meant culture was political too. It is unclear if the argument had any direct implications for government policy or university structure; however, it did break up the Cold War consensus about the role played by culture in mediating between liberty and security. It began to make more sense to think about culture not as the antidote to security but in relation to it: culture not as an instance of freedom but as an element of ideology or its critique. Critics on the right and the left who once agreed that culture should be autonomous, began to demand that culture defend traditional values by showing constraint (Himmelfarb and Kennan) or that it intervene to effect political and social change (Bly). This polarization within cultural thinking also impacted Pound directly. In 1972 Pound's editor and defender James Laughlin—the onetime editor of *Perspectives USA*—nominated him for the Emerson-Thoreau Medal of the American Academy of Arts and Sciences. This time there was a furious debate that led to his being rejected twelve to nine (Wilhelm 360–61). It is an irony of history that the name of Thoreau, which was so central to 1960s arguments about the politics of culture, should be withheld as an honorary title from the man who embodied liberal freedom while he was sitting in a cell. Pound died in Italy later that year.

Pound's poetic influence continued to grow, but his reputation was also beginning to suffer around the time of his death. Those insisting on the political significance of culture could no longer simply celebrate him as a champion of free speech while gesturing at the lyrical validity and formal complexity of his poetry. The new approach had already been announced in John Harrison's groundbreaking study *The Reactionaries* (1966), which placed political reaction at the center of Pound's poetry and Pound at the center of modernism. William Empson, in his strangely dismissive introduction to the volume, describes Harrison as the representative of a younger generation of critics genuinely (and he implies naively) shocked by the social attitudes of the modernists (12). Harrison did indeed represent a new generation in his rejection of the literary world apart. He insists that culture is political. The threats of mass hysteria and total warfare that earlier critics hoped to quarantine with Pound and criticize from the safe haven of the university, galvanize Harrison to read with an eye towards the social causes and consequences of literature (210). The reactionaries, for Harrison, provide an example of how *not* to react to the characteristic crises of modernity. Their elitist aesthetic made them anti-democratic; their shock at the violence of World War I made them bellicose (25).

Harrison's undisguised disappointment with modernism helped inaugurate a new post-liberal criticism. A decade after *The Reactionaries*, William Chace would argue that "The step from being authorities in poetry and criticism to thinking well of authoritarianism in general is the most important step Pound and Eliot took" (Chace 215). He went on to criticize the "liberal intellectuals" who are blind to authoritarianism because, while quick to condemn the abuses of power, they "live at odds with its use for their own direct benefit" (215). Numerous studies followed Harrison and Chace in looking at the way fascism and anti-Semitism helped shape the modernist aesthetic.[26] These studies are all post-liberal in their emphasis on the political significance of culture and in their insistence that criticism is political whether it admits it or not. The generation of critics coming to maturity two decades after the war were not necessarily any less institutional than their predecessors, but they considered the liberal separation of aesthetics from politics to be ideologically suspect, perhaps even complicit with the fascism it seemed to tolerate. Vietnam, for these "cultural radicals," was proof positive that liberalism had always harbored fascist tendencies; Pound was the poetic incarnation of a general trend.[27] Harrison's approach to Pound

---

[26] There are by now a number of books discussing the relation of modernist poetics to anti-Semitism. For a general discussion of the "discourse of semitism" in English literature see Bryan Cheyette's *Constructions of 'the Jew' in English Literature and Society*, which makes the important point that 'the Jew' is not a fixed or mythic character, but rather an indeterminate symbol—and a symbol of indeterminacy—which can serve as both grotesque image and object of desire and/or identification (3–4, 268). See also see Anthony Julius, *T. S. Eliot: Anti-Semitism and Literary Form*; and Christopher Ricks, *T. S. Eliot and Prejudice*. On Pound see Robert Casillo, *The Genealogy of Demons: Anti-Semitism, Fascism, and the Myths of Ezra Pound*. Casillo argues that the New Critical quarantining of Pound's anti-Semitism repeats Pound's cultural ghettoization of the Jews (17).

[27] Gene Wise coined the term "cultural radical" to describe the oppositional criticism and pedagogy practiced by many teachers of American studies beginning in the late 1960s. They assumed that dominant American culture was "bent on corrupting [...] naturally humane impulses" (185). Winfried Fluck has used the term to describe the "race for professional distinction through difference" which he sees dominating contemporary

helped inaugurate a style of post-liberal criticism that might not have moved beyond the walls of the ivory tower but was no longer content to be housed there, or for that matter to internalize contradictions as a matter of critical complexity. Culture once again became an arena in which to effect political change, and criticism a form of activism—one that parleyed debates over literary representation into struggles for political representation, largely by advocating minority literature and rights.[28] If cultural politics at the beginning of the century had been waged by communists and fascists in the name of class and nation, by the 1960s the issues involved gender, ethnicity, and what increasingly became known as identity. The identity-based explications followed Shapiro's early assertion that fascism and anti-Semitism played generative roles in modernism, giving rise not only to its characteristic ideas but also to its characteristic forms. This ultimately proved such an effective way of bringing content or ideology back in relation to literary form that by the 1990s critics like Stanley Sultan and Louis Menand felt it necessary to remind colleagues that there was more to modernism than reaction.

This book traces literary and poetic reactions to Pound's reaction from the heyday of the liberal aesthetic, which argues poetry is politically relevant to the degree that it is personal, to the emergence of the post-liberal aesthetic, which argues that poetry is relevant because the personal is political. My subject is not Pound's poetry *per se*. I am not interested in measuring his influence, positive or negative, on other poets. The lines of influence have already been delineated in studies like Christopher Beach's *ABC of Influence: Ezra Pound and the Remaking of the American Poetic Tradition*, George Bornstein's edited volume *Ezra Pound among the Poets*, Ken Goodwin's *The Influence of Ezra Pound*, and of course Marjorie Perloff's *The Dance of the Intellect: Studies in the Poetry of the Pound Tradition*. Beach et al. do the important work of compiling lists of the poets influenced directly and indirectly by Pound: starting with H. D., William Carlos Williams, Eliot, Yeats, Heart Crane, e. e. cummings, Archibald MacLeish, and extending through Zukofsky, Charles Olson, Robert Duncan, Denise Levertov, and Gary Snyder. The list should be extended to include Ginsberg, as I will argue in the next chapter. Given Pound's central role in theorizing and articulating modernist poetics and his wide circle of acquaintances, it is a relatively

American studies; political and aesthetic rebellion, in this sense, function primarily as masks for self-promotion ("Humanities" 51).

28 See Louis Kampf's and Paul Lauter's influential edited volume *The Politics of Literature*, which emerged out of professional debates at the 1968 MLA convention, on this point (39). The editors draw attention to the postwar "expansion of the education industry" (22), call on literary intellectuals to "better use our talents outside the classroom" (45), and link literary studies to "radical culture" such as "black writing" (47).

simple matter to find Poundian styles, themes, and metaphors in the poems of any number of possible epigones. Studies of influence, when they do not concern themselves with the biographical details of discipleship, isolate patterns (of rhyme, meter, and metaphor) that can be said to originate in the precursor and surface, as echo or counterpoint, in his followers. These continuities are important. However, my study is concerned with broader cultural continuities, which I argue were shaped by the Pound controversy, stretching from the midcentury argument that poetry is an expression of free speech (lyrical individualism) to the more contemporary argument that poetry represents a social and cultural position (lyricism of identity).

My approach is closer to that pioneered by Charles Molesworth in *Fierce Embrace*. Molesworth describes midcentury lyricism as a self-conscious counterpoint to the formal and almost scientific emphasis on poetic method advocated by Eliot and Pound, rendered somewhat official by Eliot's Nobel Prize for Literature in 1948 and Pound's Bollingen Award in 1949. The first decade of midcentury poetry, Molesworth argues, was formal and academic, following the modernist dictates and epitomized by Auden. The "poetry of immersion" that emerges after the 1950s rejects academic formalism to draw on the older Pound of the imagistic tradition, immersing itself in the world of objects while re-situating the lyrical self vis-à-vis the anxieties of war, the standardization of American language through advertising, and the decreasing audience for poetry caused partly by the academic turn (5, 7, 8, 20). Poets like Bishop—but also Ginsberg, Frank O'Hara, John Ashbery, Robert Bly, and Theodore Roethke—experimented with various techniques of poetic self-removal (10). Their poetry is in a sense post-lyrical; it suppresses the self to let things speak.

I find Molesworth's account compelling; however, it seems to me that the Bollingen Prize was more scandalous and disruptive than he suggests. He is correct in pointing out that many poets turned to an older Pound—Pound the imagist—partly because they were fascinated by Williams, and partly because the older style represented a prelapsarian modernism, seemingly untainted by fascism and anti-Semitism. He is also correct in pointing out that this turn impacted prevailing fashions of the lyrical self. However, the poets and writers who interest me experimented with lyricism (and anti-lyricism) not to reject an academic style associated with the older Pound, but to confront the dilemma posed by the Pound award. These writers rejected the official division between poet and political thinker. They used literary form as a tool of ideological and institutional analysis. Making sense of their work involves going beyond the patterns isolated by theories of influence—beyond stylistic correlations between poet and poet or poem and poem—to find other patterns of correlation between literary style and ideological/

institutional structures. The questions I ask are: How did postwar writers understand Pound's politics in relation to his poetics? Where did they place Pound in relation to existing cultural and legal institutions? Where was he located in the shifting political and cultural alliances of the Cold War? Where did midcentury writers locate themselves in relation to the arguments, institutions, and politics of the postwar cultural landscape?

To address these questions I focus on a select group of writers who were deeply invested in the Pound controversy. Some of them served on the Bollingen committee, others wrote extensively about the committee's decision. The group is not exhaustive, but its members—considered individually and in sequence—do illustrate what I take to be the most tangible consequence of the Pound reaction: the shift from individualism to identity in postwar literature and politics. Identity is one of the most common terms in our current critical vocabulary. However, its usage as a marker of group membership is a fairly recent innovation. My claim is that this type of identity was articulated first as a poetic trope, a structure of voice, before it became a theoretical commonplace. The writers I am interested in did not abandon the lyric. They—or the critics who wrote about them—tried to develop a style of lyricism that countered the postwar incarnation of Pound as lyricist. The lyric, in the decade or so following the Pound controversy, was transformed from a vehicle of individualism to a vehicle of ethnicity. It spoke from the subject position excluded by Pound in one way and excluded by liberalism in another.

The first chapter takes up the question to what extent Pound can be considered a lyricist at all.[29] Those who read *The Pisan Cantos* as a personal rejection of Pound's politics had to ignore blatantly pro-Fascist and anti-Semitic passages to do so. Those who mounted a free speech defense for the Bollingen Prize had to argue that the poetry could serve as a symbol of liberty even if the poet was behind bars. Both arguments are versions of the liberal aesthetic. They are based on the premise that what makes poetry lyrical is its indifference to its context; voice, to the degree that it is personal, travels beyond its surroundings through introspection, transcendence, or both. I explore the viability of the liberal aesthetic by analyzing how and if midcentury poetry can be said to travel free from its context, both in relation to the journey elements in Pound's poetry and by comparing Pound's conception of the journey to the role played by mobility in liberal conceptions of lyricism. The lyrical passages in *The Pisan Cantos*, I argue, should be considered as failures of Pound's poetic project. That project was to establish

[29] These chapter summaries do not provide page references to primary texts. Those references are, however, included in the chapters themselves.

what he called "subject rhymes" between different epochs, places, and between poetics and economics. Nothing rhymes, however, in a landscape dominated by usury, which is epitomized not by individualism in the lyrical sense but by the isolation of the death cell. Nevertheless, Allen Ginsberg, who in this regard is typical of Pound's supporters, saw Pound's isolation as a verification of his lyrical insight. Using Pound's imprisonment as a symbol for his own travel poetry, he claimed to speak for a better America because like Pound he was isolated from the mainstream. I conclude by contrasting Ginsberg's lyrical appropriation of Pound with Elizabeth Bishop's poetic account of visiting him in St. Elizabeths. Because Bishop was less sympathetic to Pound's plight, she provided a more accurate map of his location in the postwar cultural landscape—a landscape in which lyrical individuation was linked to the institutionalization of Pound (in a mental hospital) and of literary studies (in universities). Bishop's own poetry rejects the lyrical trope of individual voice by showing how identity is a product of institutional location.

The second chapter focuses on Karl Shapiro's dissenting vote as a member of the Bollingen committee. This is a two-part story, having first to do with the liberal response to Pound's reactionary politics, and then with the poetic and critical reaction to liberalism. When Shapiro voted against Pound he did so as a Jew voting against an anti-Semite, in effect violating the liberal consensus that poetry was to be understood as free expression and therefore different from politics. But he subsequently attacked identity as a poetically invalid form of personification, defining himself as "a negative Jew," or a Jew without ethnicity, at precisely the moment it became fashionable to "discover" one's identity. Shapiro, in other words, traverses the trajectory I am interested in describing in reverse. During the reign of aesthetic individualism he argued that anti-Semitism was bad form, political and poetic; but when identity gained in critical and poetic significance he insisted his Jewishness was a matter of personal choice. The chapter concludes by considering what the difference between individuality and identity means in terms of the structure of lyrical voice by looking at Shapiro's attempt to elegize another member of the committee, W. H. Auden; and by comparing Shapiro to Lowell and other poets who would soon be labeled confessional.

The third chapter explores what Shapiro disparagingly dubbed "the Age of Auden" by focusing on the verse drama that actually did name the 1950s, Auden's *The Age of Anxiety*. Seen by his contemporaries as a defense of political and literary individualism, the poem was often cited as evidence of Auden's shift to the right. The poet who had been a radical leftist in his youth seemed to have reinvented himself as a Christian existentialist. However, Auden's poem was misread by his contemporaries, and it is misread in tellingly different ways today. His subject was not the individual but the group, and he turned to archaic literary structures—such as alliterative metrics and psychomachia—to compose an allegory for displaced persons. Postwar critics saw Auden's displaced persons as archetypes of the alienated individual. Contemporary criticism argues that, moved by the atrocities of the Holocaust, Auden was actually identifying with Jews. However, this shift from individualism to identity in the critical response to Auden conceals the poet's true subject: communities of scholars who saw themselves as displaced or alienated because their homeland was international modernism. Auden was an academic poet writing for academics. Intellectuals who described themselves as alienated were actually part of a growing community and institutional structure. The importance of this community to Auden helps explain his ambiguous role on the Bollingen committee. He voted for Pound but argued that it might make sense to censor his poetry. The censorship, however, would only apply to those unequipped to deal with the implications of Pound's ideas. Auden insisted that the poetry should be available to scholars who might learn something from the moral failure he did not hesitate to call evil. He is not a lyricist of individuality or identity, but the voice of the emergent group of professional scholars.

Despite the claims of his detractors, Auden was more academic than conservative. There was, however, an author who was briefly celebrated for his political and poetic conservatism in the 1950s. Chapter four turns to the forgotten poet and polemicist Peter Viereck, who helped inaugurate the postwar conservative movement with his 1949 volume *Conservatism Revisited.* He won the Pulitzer Prize that same year for his first book of poems, *Terror and Decorum.* Viereck's poetic and political "revolt against revolt," as he described it, had oedipal dimensions. His father, a fairly well-known author in his own right, was convicted as a Nazi agent and spent five years in a U.S. federal prison. The son earned his PhD in history at Harvard with a cultural-historical study of the Romantic roots of Nazism. He enlisted in the army and served as a radio monitor, listening in on Pound's broadcasts from a shortwave station in Africa; his brother was killed fighting in Italy. The fact that Viereck's father went to prison for his support of fascism probably made the son unsympathetic to Pound's insanity defense. Peter Viereck vocally opposed the Pound award, and like Shapiro, believed this opposition damaged his career. However, his poetry fell out of favor for the same reason his politics did. He was an individualist, and he defined individualism as the conservative compromise between fascism and communism and as the lyrical compromise between formalism and avant-garde poetics.

The more radical conservatives who rallied around Joseph McCarthy described Viereck as a liberal in disguise. Poetry critics began to see his subjectivist lyrics as repetitive. Viereck sought to occupy a position between political and poetic extremes. However, he fell through the crack opening between the liberalism becoming established within the universities, and the populist conservatism gaining ground without. As the *National Review* became the trendsetting journal for conservatism and academic criticism became more interested in identity than in individualism, Viereck lost both of his audiences. Nostalgic for a time when he could shock by simply claiming to be a conservative or a traditionalist, he wrote increasingly erotic—even pornographic—verse in rigid rhyme and meter. I argue that it makes sense to consider this conservative poet as a forgotten representative of the emerging post-liberal aesthetic. His growing interest in the body is an attempt to situate the individual in biology, and he ultimately sees corporeality as the source of identity and the final measure of cultural and political responsibility.

The turn towards the body might seem surprising in a self-proclaimed conservative, but Viereck was hardly unique. Those interested in going beyond the limits of liberalism, whether on the right or the left, increasingly turned to the body and its desires—rather than the concept of the individual—as the affective ground of situated selfhood. Katherine Anne Porter and Leslie Fiedler, the subjects of chapter five, both turned to pornographic tropes and structures to articulate the social dynamics leading to racism and war. Porter was a member of the Bollingen committee. She voted for Pound, defending his poetry as a form of free speech. She did not believe him to be insane but described him as the incarnation of "unreason." What she meant by this term might be extrapolated from the novel it took her twenty years to write, *Ship of Fools*. The novel was an instant success, but like the poems of Shapiro and Viereck, and Auden's *The Age of Anxiety*, it has faded into relative obscurity. This may be due to the bleakness of its moral allegory. Nobody is immune from the sex and violence the novel associates with unreason; the implication seems to be that we are all Poundians insofar as we too are subject to irrational hatreds and desires.

Perhaps Porter was also a Poundian in this sense. The second part of this chapter begins with a semi-public argument between Porter and one of her critics, Leslie Fiedler. Fiedler was not disturbed by *Ship of Fools*'s sex or violence, which he considered standard elements in American fiction, rather by its liberal pretensions. He dismissed the novel as "ladies' magazine fiction." Porter responded, in a private letter that has been printed by one of her biographers, by calling him a "kike." There is no evidence that Fiedler knew of her response, but he was deeply concerned with the passions and hatreds—in other words, the unreason—concealed behind American ideals. He tried to show how unreason might be channeled poetically in a short story appearing the same year as Porter's *Ship of Fools*. The story (and the collection of short stories containing it) borrows its name from the famous line in Pound's Canto 81, "pull down thy vanity, I say pull down." "Tear Down Vanity" (the short story) is a campus morality tale about a Jewish poet leading a poetry workshop at a mid-western university. It shows a writer finding his subject—and his desire—in reaction to the anti-Semitism he encounters in a liberal institution. This poetic self-discovery is presented in a highly sexualized, phallocentric language that Fiedler detected in Bellow, Malamud, Roth, and Mailer. It dramatizes lyricism as the personal embrace of ethnicity—an embrace that rejects the pretensions of liberal individualism by responding to the unreason beneath its surface. This chapter will read "Tear Down Vanity" as Fiedler's rejection of the kind of liberalism Porter endorsed, a rejection mediated through a reevaluation of Pound and an embrace of sexual and ethnic identity.

Fiedler's fiction has not stood the test of time, but he was an astute observer of academic trends. He saw that ethnic literature was becoming increasingly popular in universities, and he sensed that it sidestepped the kind of individualism advocated by Porter and other supporters of the liberal aesthetic by appealing to those feelings—unreasonable because repressed—linking personal desire to group belonging. His fictional Jewish poet is the prototype of a generation of writers and scholars who would turn their back on the official battle of the Cold War—liberalism vs. totalitarianism—to declare their allegiance to marginalized groups. Fiedler heralded the cultural and institutional turn to what we now call identity, but he was also skeptical of the trend. In *Waiting for the End* Fiedler quotes a student who, apropos Mailer, asks "Do we have to become gentile Jews before we can become White Negroes?" His "yes," inflected by Pound's diatribe against vanity, suggests that the academics turning from individualism to identity did so in the spirit of impersonation.

Ethnic impersonation is the subject of my last chapter, which is devoted to analyzing John Berryman's "imaginary Jew." The phrase is the title of Berryman's first short story, which describes the experiences of a Gentile who, during a political argument, is unable to defend himself against anti-Semitic slurs. The protagonist is "made" Jewish when his opponent delivers a challenge that he cannot, in decency, rebuke: that challenge is to drop his pants and show whether or not he is circumcised. The imaginary Jew returns in *The Dream Songs*, and he was to have been the subject of the final chapter of Berryman's uncompleted autobiographical novel *Recovery*. Criticism has not treated Berryman's imaginary Jew kindly. Early critics, comparing him to poets like Lowell, saw his ethnic impersonation as uncongenial to the confessional project, although confessional poetry—for instance Sylvia

Plath's—is full of imaginary Jewishness. More recent critics see the figure as a misappropriation of Jewish identity. Berryman, however, did not want to pass himself off as Jewish; he invented the figure in response to modernist anti-Semitism. Berryman had been tapped to write the introduction to the New Directions edition of Pound's *Selected Poems*, but Pound rejected the introduction, presumably because of a footnote mentioning his politics and prejudice. This chapter traces the critical reception—and rejection—of Berryman in order to trace the growing importance of identity in American poetry—and American studies—since the late 1960s, as well as the sneaking suspicion that identity is not biological so much as impersonated or performed.

I have tried to provide a thick description of some of the neglected poems and theories of the 1950s and early 1960s, in part because I think they have something relevant to offer current debates about identity. The fact that many of the authors in this study have been largely forgotten makes them more useful for my project. Shapiro, Viereck, and poems like *The Age of Anxiety* slipped through the cracks in the paradigm shift from individualism to identity. Exhuming the artifacts buried in those cracks will help chart the tectonic shifts that have gone into creating the post-liberal, which is to say the current cultural landscape. Scholars are no longer likely to accept the liberal distinction between poetry and politics. We have been taught to regard culture as an expression of ideology or an instance of its critique. Lyrical individualism has given way to the lyricism of identity, which has less to do with the principle of free speech than with the premise that the personal is political. Voice is no longer taken to be a poetic declaration of independence but a testimony of what it feels like—in a corporeal way—to embody particular social, institutional, and political spaces. Poets who read Pound, and the second generation of Cold War scholars who analyzed him, were among the first to react against the midcentury Pound reaction. They reconsidered Pound's politics as central to his poetics, arguing that his ideology expressed itself in corporeal ways, through figures of desire and abjection. These students of Pound—one cannot necessarily call them admirers—helped signal the contemporary cultural turn to the body and identity, politicizing personality under the sign of, but not in allegiance to, Pound.

CHAPTER 1

Lyrical Freedom and Institutional Confinement: Following in Pound's Footsteps

This chapter takes up the liberal defense of Pound as lyricist by exploring the concept and context of poetic freedom. The primary issue, as I argued in the introduction, was free speech, and Pound repeatedly argued "that free speech without free radio speech is as zero" (74/446). Pound was not shy of making such non-lyrical declarations in his poetry; however he tended to represent freedom in *The Cantos* through tropes of mobility. *The Pisan Cantos* show that he dwelled on memories of traveling while incarcerated in the military detention center outside of Pisa, reminiscing in particular about two specific walking tours through France and Italy: "we will see those old roads again, question, / possibly / but nothing appears much less likely" (74/448). The spatial tropes generated by his reveries were in keeping with the journey motif that runs throughout *The Cantos*, loosely modeled, like so much modernist writing, on the *Odyssey*.

There is an intuitive parallel between mobility and poetic freedom. This may be why spatial images played a central role in midcentury accounts of lyrical form. Louise Bogan, one of the members of the Bollingen committee, described lyrical poetry as a walk without a goal, in contradistinction to prose, which is supposed to move towards a predetermined conclusion (Gilbert 4). This is a spatialized version of the classic definition of the lyric—eloquence is heard, poetry is overheard—made famous by John Stuart Mill (*Poetry* 10–11). What the two definitions have in common is the assumption that the lyric is formally independent of its context.

The Bollingen committee upheld the significance of lyrical independence in its announcement of the award. According to the official statement, the lyrical moments in *The Pisan Cantos* freed themselves from the constraints of fascist ideology and from the punitive reach of criminal indictment. Two complementary spatial metaphors were at play in this argument. One involved the symbolic freedom of lyrical mobility; the other the inner space of the self. For many of Pound's supporters, incarceration became the figure of—even the opportunity for—introspection, and Pound the prisoner was assumed to have discovered that part of himself that was universally relevant because absolutely interior. The Pound award, by invoking the linked lyrical vanishing points of transcendence and interiority, the depth of field implicit in the poetic image of mobility and the depth of consciousness in the lyrical notion of self, set the coordinates for a key Cold War argument that I have been calling the liberal aesthetic: the lyric was supposed to be immune to politics insofar as it said what it wanted to say, and went where it wanted to go, without regard for propriety or power. The liberal aesthetic transformed the incarcerated Pound into a symbol of political and poetic freedom. His example authorized a personal turn in American poetry that would lead to a postwar renaissance of the subjectivist lyric ranging from poems of isolated introspection to walk poems, which I argue are variations on the same form.

The Pound award demonstrates that the art—like the practice—of walking takes place in a highly politicized terrain. This chapter offers a provisional map of the terrain by exploring how Pound's incarceration haunted Cold War concepts of the lyric, and how constraint haunts the liberal (and lyrical) analogy between freedom of movement and freedom of speech. First I will argue that it makes sense to describe *The Pisan Cantos* as poems of confinement *and* as walk poems; it also makes sense to consider the signifycance of confinement in a form that typically links rhyme, image, and meter to unrestrained personal mobility. Next I will turn to two poets who followed Pound's footsteps, but in different ways, breaking with chronology in order to sharpen the spatial contrast in exemplary poems of mobility and constraint. Allen Ginsberg, who visited Pound after his release from St. Elizabeths, took it upon himself to forgive Pound for his anti-Semitism, arguing that his prejudice against others was significant only insofar as it was part of the poetic truth he revealed about himself. This notion of lyrical introspection, intended to exonerate Pound from political blame, paradoxically confined him in the freedom that Ginsberg thought alienated all poets from society. Elizabeth Bishop, who dutifully but unhappily visited Pound while he was still an inmate of St. Elizabeths, provided a more nuanced map of the institutional space in which confinement could be construed as poetic freedom. By forcing herself to consider Pound's place in postwar poetry instead of trying to forgive him, she gave voice to a new form of lyricism, less grandiose in its claims for freedom but more compelling in its account of the social and institutional coordinates of identity. The "lyrical I" articulated in Bishop's poetry is not the master of unconstrained mobility, or the possessor of limitless depth, but the reflective inhabitant of specific cultural and institutional spaces.

The Pisan Cantos draw heavily on two formative walks: Pound's 1912 tour through Southern France and a 450-mile trek through war-torn Italy to visit his daughter in Tirol (see for instance 74/448, 466–69). They also draw on the theory of spatial poetics Pound developed to account for how writing takes place in a cultural landscape already shaped by tradition. Pound was an advocate of peripatetic writing, translating, and editing, for instance in Canto 74, which praises a translator of the *Odyssey* who traveled the Aegean in a sailboat to get the old legends firsthand (74/446; Terrell II, 365). An earlier canto indicates Pound's interest in writing poetry from the perspective of what he calls the "periplum, not as land looks on a map / but as sea bord [*sic*] seen by men sailing" (59/324; see also Pound, *ABC of Reading* 43–44). This coinage appears throughout *The Cantos*, usually to mark passages that are neither subjectivist nor cartographic but shaped by the landscape in the way language is shaped by meter. A number of postwar poets attuned to such landmarks approached *The Cantos* like travelers exploring newly charted terrain. "Creeley," as one scholar points out, "has noted that he was 'intrigued by Olson's reference to *The Cantos* as 'a walker'—something you could take a walk into daily, and have as experience of daily possibility'" (Nicholls 141). Scholars also approach Pound peripatetically. Issue one, volume one of *Paideuma*, the journal dedicated to Pound research, contains an article by Donald Davie entitled "*The Cantos*: Towards a Pedestrian Reading," which argues that the best preparation for reading Pound is a good map (1972). Richard Sieburth, who follows Davie in maintaining that Pound's writing is accurate enough to serve as travel guide, would literally follow in Pound's footsteps when editing Pound's previously unpublished *A Walking Tour in Southern France* (1992) (Perloff, *Differentials* 42).

Sieburth argues that Pound's 1912 walking tour was central to his invention of himself as a modernist poet (Sieburth, *Walking Tour* ix–x). Poetry, for Pound, was a form of exploration. In his early work especially, "The central male figure is often an itinerant, bohemian troubadour, a rebellious artist and lover in exile" (Witemeyer 45). However, Pound wanted to do more than follow in the footsteps of the courtly singers; his aim was to show that their lives shaped the landscape in the same way their verse left its trace on metrics (Sieburth, *Walking Tour* xiv). His walking tour was a voyage of self-discovery but also an archeology of buried artifacts and forms (cf. Stark 135). As Sieburth puts it, "Pound's roving eye is only drawn to that already aestheticized (and semiotized) arrangement of place into legible contour which he calls 'landscape'" (Sieburth, *Walking Tour* xvii).[30]

In his memoirs, Pound describes the landscape in Southern France as a sestina (Albright, "Early Cantos" 82; Sieburth, *Walking Tour* 15). The rigid

---

[30] In his efforts to read the landscape Pound "transform[ed] his eye into a modernist organ of phanopoeia [a Poundian term for the visual imagination]," sensitive to the images but also the patterns he believed to be implicit in geography (Sieburth, *Walking Tour* xvi).

form originated with the troubadours who lived there in the twelfth and thirteenth centuries, and Pound's own early effort in that direction, "Sestina: Altaforte," written three years before his 1912 walking tour, is set at a castle he would visit, Hautefort, and ventriloquizes the voice of its troubadour liege, Bertran de Born, who was vassal to the kind of England (*Walking Tour* 21). Pound's walking tour had the touristic goal of visiting the specific landmarks and objects he would call "luminous details."[31] However, walking also exposed the topographical contours he understood as functioning analogously to rhyme and meter. It is this poetic *dependence* on the landscape as structuring device that Pound designates by the term periplum. Pound's art of walking is different in one significant respect from the theory that equates lyricism with unrestrained mobility: the poet's path—lead where it may—works like frottage, making visible the contours that shape poetic rhythm and the traces of poets who have been there before. If the feet can be said to pick out the lyrical melody of a walk poem, then Pound insists on drawing attention to the landscape as a musical instrument, record, or score. This double layer of description creates the characteristic density of the cantos which, as Marjorie Perloff and others point out, renders their references "hyperspecific" to the point of impenetrability (Perloff, *Differentials* 52). It is possible, with careful scholarship, to follow Pound's footsteps, but it is easier to get lost in the welter of descriptions, patterns, and names.

Pound's density is the result of a deliberate compositional strategy that can be understood as peripatetic, but not in a conventional way. The walk poem, in Roger Gilbert's description, links personal meditation to spatial sequencing, thus keeping the structure "truer to the temporal character of experience, the pure successiveness that governs human life" (9). Pound, more concerned with "the tale of the tribe" than with the lyrical evocation of personal experience, approaches space as an archive or record of cultural patterns (Wilhelm 130; Pound, *Kulchur* 194). The walk poem temporalizes space as experience; Pound spatializes time as landscape.[32] *The Cantos* are

---

[31] Luminous detail: "a field of visual particulars seized not as ineffable totality but as a sequence of detached details" (Sieburth, *Walking Tour* xvii). Marjorie Perloff argues that Pound is actually a nominalist (*Differentials* 41–42). Pound wants "to turn the signifier—the found object, citation, or proper name—into that which it signifies," and while this creates the documentary quality that allows someone like Sieburth to follow in Pound's footsteps, it also produces the surface density that renders Pound's poetry impenetrable to many readers (*Differentials* 44).

[32] As Daniel Albright puts it, "In some sense *The Cantos* […] are to history what […] landscape is to geography: a mapping of recurrence in time, *heard* as a subtle chiming, as if history were an endless troubadour song, a huge *canto*" (Albright, "Early Cantos" 82).

peripatetic, but they are also impersonal and indexical: the poet is most poetic when he cleaves to the contours of tradition in the same way that the ship follows the shore. The characteristic feature of such verse is a compound image Pound called "subject rhyme." Pound typically expressed subject rhymes in "the kind of ideogram of time and space" that superimpose, for instance, ancient Greece, modern Provence, and the Orient (Sieburth, *Walking Tour* xviii). These ideograms are highly idiosyncratic but they are not lyrical in the conventional sense of the term. What is deliberately excluded from the subject rhyme is the personal component that contemporary criticism designates by the term "subject," namely the self. Pound's spatial poetics thus poses a challenge to lyricism. They also pose a challenge to reading. As many critics point out, his subject rhymes and ideograms provide more texture than structure, demonstrating the principle that "[a]ll ages are contemporaneous" but without a unified point of view or narrative arc (Sieburth, *Walking Tour* xviii; Nicholls 147).[33]

If the lyric is to be conceived as an open-ended walk, then the subject rhyme is not a lyrical device. Pound himself conceived of *The Cantos* as an epic.[34] Nevertheless, Pound's grand design for *The Cantos* did seem to lack a clear sense of destination that suggests a lyricism of the second order. The first lines of the first Canto read, "And then went down to the ship, / Set keel to breakers, forth on the godly sea" (1/3). The *Odyssey* is the starting point, but it is unclear where the ship of the poem is sailing. Pound may have hoped that the itinerary of the poem, developing as it went along, would fall into place in the same way his tour of Southern France fell into a sestina. Thus *The Cantos* repeatedly gesture towards travel narratives that seem to be echoes of one, big journey. Besides Ming China, the Pyrenees, the America of the Early Republic, and a whole cast of characters ranging from Confucius to John Adams to contemporary politicians and artists, *The Cantos* keep returning to the worlds of the *Odyssey*, *The Seafarer*, and the *Divine Comedy*, hinting that the final subject rhyme would constitute a kind of homecoming,

---

[33] Nevertheless, critics see the early *The Cantos* especially as "a set of impersonations, as the poet's voice reels back through history and myth, trying to discover the authentic voice that can rectify the modern world" (Albright 70).

[34] Pound described *The Cantos* as an epic, which he famously defined as "a poem including history" (Kenner, *Pound Era* 360). In a letter to Harriet Monroe dated Rapallo, 14 September 1933, Pound argues that she should print the Adams and Van Buren Cantos (Canto 35 and 36) for the following reasons: "I know you hate like hell to print me, and that an *epic* includes history and history ain't all slush and babies' pink toes. I admit that economics are *in themselves* uninteresting, but heroism is poetic, I mean it *is* a fit subject for poesy" (*Selected Letters* 247).

when history would find its pattern as landscape, and Pound's extensive cast of passengers would reveal themselves to be the hero with a thousand faces.

After WWI, it seemed less likely that Odysseus would ever return to Ithaca or Dante to paradise. Pound thought war profiteering and usury were to blame for the carnage, and as I have argued in the introduction, he began arguing with increasing compulsion that only the state-controlled lending process known as social credit could curb usury, and that only a strong hand in government could institute social credit (see Pound, *Selected Prose* 276–305; Nicholls 142; Albright, "Early Cantos" 78, 88; Sieburth, "Trust" 161; Wilhelm 123). At first, Pound described usury as a non-denominational phenomenon, for instance in the widely-anthologized Usura Canto (Canto 45). But in keeping with a long tradition of anti-Semitism, Pound increasingly blamed economic problems on "the Hebraic monetary system which is a most tremendous instrument of usury" (*Selected Prose* 321; see also Doob 113–16, 427; Sieburth, "Trust" 149, 153, 158–59). Much work has been done on what Hugh Kenner calls the "rhymes" between Pound's poetics and his economics (*Pound Era* 309). Pound sought to link words to things in the same way he wanted to link value to production, eliminating superfluous verbosity and interest-bearing loans in a poetics and economics of austerity (and racial purity).[35] Social credit was supposed to connect values and commodities in the same way that imagism would connect the word with the thing (Sieburth, "Trust" 146–48).[36] Culture and economics were supposed to cleave close to the shore of the natural and the traditional in what might be termed a periplum of ordered development. Pound believed that Mussolini was capable of reorganizing the national economy in the right way, and he thought he found in "the Boss," as he called him, an enlightened ruler who had respect for the arts—including Pound's poetry (Sieburth, "Trust" 159; see also Laughlin 152; Heymann 58; Pound, *Selected Prose* 303).

The imminent collapse of fascism may explain the increasing vitriol of Pound's radio broadcasts. The actual collapse certainly impacted *The Pisan Cantos*, into which some of the uglier sentiments of the broadcasts overflow. The poem begins with an elegy for Mussolini. Pound added this after completing the main body of the manuscript, but there are other significant forays into fascist and anti-Semitic polemic, which I have already discussed in the

[35] For concise treatments see Sieburth's introduction to *The Pisan Cantos* and his groundbreaking article, "In Pound We Trust."

[36] At the center of Pound's thought, whirling like a vortex, is an ideal "collaboration between nature, the state, and an industrious population" (*Selected Prose* 297). This passage refers to money as the "symbol" of collaboration, but the same could be said of poetry or the landscape.

introduction. Pound was supposed to be entering into the *Paradiso* stage of *The Cantos*, but paradise did not "rhyme" with the place he called "the a.h. [ass hole] of the army" (74/463)—in fact, Pound had already furnished his own inferno (Cantos 14 and 15/61–67) with the scatological imagery that now confronted him as the reality of prison experience (Kenner, *Pound Era* 474–75; Sieburth, *Pisan* xvii).[37] Above the hell of the camp floats the saving vision of the beautiful lady, whose "suave eyes, quiet, not scornful" (74/445)—the original opening line—promise to console the poet like the troubadour ladies of old. Nevertheless Pound repeatedly slips back into the gruesome details of camp life (Bush, "Late Cantos" 115). This deixis marks the shipwreck of Pound's journey, but it has found a broad resonance with contemporary readers: there are snatches of prison dialogue, journalistic descriptions of disciplinary routines, portraits of the primarily African American inmates, and poignant examples of "the greatest […] charity / [which is] to be found among those who have not observed / regulations" (74/454). The birds sitting on barbed wire remind the poet of musical notes; the insects that were Pound's only company in solitary confinement move him to contemplate his own insignificance in relation to nature.

As discussed in the introduction, critics typically read *The Pisan Cantos* as the most lyrical of Pound's mature verse. Many passages are certainly the most personal. Confinement, as Sieburth points out, separated Pound from his usual reference materials, forcing him to delve into his memories and experiences, such as an encounter during his 1912 walking tour with a man near Périguex, whose name "Borr" recalled Bertran de Born (Sieburth, *Pisan* xxiv; see also Wilhelm 221; 80/528–29).[38] Many critics interpret this turn towards the personal as a turn away from Pound's previous political, economic, and historical themes. Eva Hesse, for instance, describes *The Pisan Cantos* as a "Rückwendung zur Menschlichkeit" or return to humanity (*Ezra Pound* 260). This interpretation harmonizes with the humility that early readers of *The Pisan Cantos* thought they detected in Pound's personal tone. The passage most often pointed to was the long concluding segment of Canto 81 in which the speaker seems to regret past mistakes: "Pull down thy vanity / How mean thy hates / Fostered in falsity, / Pull down thy vanity, / Rathe to destroy, niggard in charity, / Pull down thy vanity, I say pull down" (81/541–42). F. O. Matthiessen, as I have already pointed out, singled out these lines for special notice in his introduction to the 1950 edition of the *Oxford Book of American Verse* (xiii). The anthology that begins with Pound's supposed

[37] "Above the hell-rot / the great arse-hole" (Canto 14/62; see also Bush 109).

[38] Pound's presentation of his memories is to some extent modeled on Villon's *Testament* (Bush 116).

confession ends with the poetry of Karl Shapiro, Randall Jarrell, and Robert Lowell, soon to be called confessional. More important than the nomenclature is the fact that two of these poets would serve on the Bollingen committee (Lowell voted for Pound, Shapiro against him), and all three of them would write in the personal style that seemed in keeping with Pound's alleged return to more lyrical verse.

In this, the last book he saw to print, Matthiessen accurately predicts—authorizes is probably the better term—the trajectory followed by postwar lyricism: away from politics and towards the pathos of personal experience. Lowell's startling "It is I" in the concluding lines of "Falling Asleep over the Aeneid" (and the final lines of the anthology) is programmatic for the selfhood that would become style and subject matter for these postwar lyricists, all of whom would teach in universities (Matthiessen 1106). I offer a fuller analysis of this poem in the next chapter. The two poems included in the anthology that might qualify as walk poems focus on the significance of personal experience but also reflect their institutional surroundings: Jarrell's "The Soldier Walks Under the Trees of the University" (1088–89) and Shapiro's "University," in which "The entering boys […] / Wander in a maze of mannered brick" (1068–69).

I have already drawn attention to Jed Rasula's argument that Pound's institutionalization in a mental facility paralleled the institutionalization of literary studies in English departments (114). Just as St. Elizabeths contained Pound's threat by making it unnecessary for his ideas to stand trial, the university contained the threat posed by other writers on the right and the left, who accepted jobs in the same English departments and published in the same academic quarterlies and poetry anthologies. Higher education institutionalized lyrical freedom by isolating poetry from politics and rendering it "innocent" by official decree. This sometimes made actual poets uncomfortable; Jarrell for instance complained that the university was a "zone of innocence […] born in banks / And cultured in colonies the rich have sown" (Matthiessen 1088). The Bollingen committee transformed this institutionally sanctioned innocence into an ideological principle. Pound remained locked up, but his poetry provided the occasion for liberalism to enlist lyricism in the struggle for political freedom.

I do not mean liberalism in the narrow sense that came to be associated with center-left politics. The Pound award did crystallize a number of issues important to writers who had at one point called themselves socialists or Trotskyists and were affiliated with the *Partisan Review*. I discuss some of the key figures in my introduction. However, an important Pound scholar who would later become affiliated with William F. Buckley's conservative *National Review* also defended Pound as a lyricist, although he tended to understand lyricism in the "impersonal" way described by Eliot in "Tradition and the Individual Talent" (13–22). I am referring to Hugh Kenner, whose unflagging efforts on Pound's behalf did much to rehabilitate the discredited fascist as representative modernist. The spring 1950 issue of *The Hudson Review* provides the synopsis of an argument that would soon receive fuller treatment in *The Poetry of Ezra Pound* (1951). The issue features Pound's translations of *The Analects*, a selection of Pound's letters dealing with aesthetic issues, and Kenner's long article "The Rose in the Steel Dust." Kenner claims that *The Pisan Cantos* offer "a *Paradiso* in counterpoint," in spite of the fact that it was written in a prison camp; and this because there is a unity not only to *The Cantos* but to Pound's entire poetic career. The "positive" elements in the poem

> are, in ways the reader can learn to see, implied in the poem from the very first, from the first descent of the swift ship to the tenebrous home of undying intelligence. They are implicit, furthermore, in Pound's earliest researches into "what had been written and how," and his first Imagistic campaign, nearly forty years back, for the rectification of language and the excision of unnecessary words. (122)

Kenner concludes his positive reading of *The Pisan Cantos* by citing the famous Canto 81 ("But to have done instead of not doing / this is not vanity [...].") as "poetry that needs no Apologie" (123). This suggests that the "counterpoint" he is interested in establishing obtains not only between paradise and purgatory but between those who accept Pound's apology and those who see no need for one, and on a broader scale, between the proponents of progress and those of tradition. In Kenner's view, Pound in his cell suffers the passions of so-called progress, and his suffering confirms his role as amanuensis of the European tradition or, as Kenner would later put it in *The Pound Era*, the European mind. In Kenner's words, Mussolini

> (and the cage, and the madhouse) lay ahead as he assumed, in the early 1920's, the role of Odysseus and the role, simultaneously, of amanuensis for the mind of Europe, itself Odysseus, in desperate straits (wars, inflations) seeking Ithaca, questing as men always are after lost securities that lie somewhere around the rim of a great circle. (377)

Pound's quest for the eternal "lost securities" while *secured* behind bars constitutes a lyricism of the second order; his Homeric journey provides a counterpoint to the "merely" personal journeys advocated by more progresssive readers, but it follows the same basic lyrical trajectory of such journeys by declaring its formal independence from its (modern) context.

Kenner invokes the lyrical trope applied to Pound by his more liberal defenders when he describes the poet "enclosed by barbed wire in timelessness" (*Pound Era* 474). This is an affirmation of what Sharon Cameron calls "lyric time," removing the speaker from his context—and from political conflict—in order to render his experiences universal.[39] Virginia Jackson's account of "postromantic theories of lyric reading" offers another way to think about the midcentury lyricization of Pound; lyric styles of reading "convert[ ] the isolated 'I' into the universal 'we' by bypassing the mediation of any particular 'you'" (129). Jackson traces this habit of reading back to Mill's 1833 distinction between eloquence (heard) and poetry (overheard), pointing out that Mill's image for the isolated poet is a prisoner in his cell (129; Mill, *Poetry* 12).[40] The prison cell haunting the supposed timelessness or universalism of the lyric is important to keep in mind when thinking about the occasion of *The Pisan Cantos*. Pound's lyrical "you"—however we read the "tear down thy vanity" passage—was either a prisoner or a prison guard, and his timelessness was actually a prison term. Passages of *The Pisan Cantos* may indeed be lyrical, but to understand their significance we must convert the timelessness of the barbed wire back into the actual space of confinement, the European mind back into concrete experience, lyrical expression back into the fragments of Pound's disrupted cultural and political itinerary, the liberal significance of lyricism back into its institu-

[39] Cameron: "The heart of the lyric's sense of time might be specified, at least preliminarily, by its propensity to interiorize as ambiguity or outright contradiction those conflicts that other mimetic forms conspicuously exteriorize and then allocate to discrete characters who enact them in the manifest pull of opposite points of view" (23).

[40] As I have pointed out in the introduction, Jackson points to a telling passage that was edited out of the version of the essay Mill republished in the United States: quoting from a favorite ballad, Mill remarks, "[t]hat song has always seemed to us like the lament of a prisoner in a solitary cell, ourselves listening, unseen in the next" (Jackson 132; Mill, *Poetry* 14). Why was this passage deleted? Mill had felt imprisoned in the mechanistic world view endorsed by his father and Jeremy Bentham, but poetry seemed to offer a way out (Trilling, *Liberal Imagination* 6, 8). It did so by providing a model of individualism that declared its independence from social and material constraints. Mill's definition of the lyric—worth hearing so long as it was overheard—is the prototype for the definition of individualism he later offered in *On Liberty* (1859): "In proportion to the development of his individuality, each person becomes more valuable to himself, and is therefore capable of being more valuable to others" (91–92). Liberalism, as defined by Mill, makes individuals socially significant to the degree that they are socially unique. This paradox is consistent with the basic tenet of economic liberalism, which equates self-interest with the social good, but it creates unintentional ironies such as the one that became apparent when Pound was held up as a symbol of liberal democracy or the European mind.

tional context. Pound's incarceration haunts the supposed freedom of post-war poetry in the same way Mill's jail cell haunts liberal free expression. The independence of the lyric—apotheosized in the walk, journey, or quest—also tells a story of confinement.

Reading Pound's poetic journey as an expression of confinement highlights the critique of economic liberalism that is at its core. There is a proliferation of the term "periplum" in *The Pisan Cantos*, ranging in signifycance from the cosmic—"the great periplum brings in the stars to our shore" (74/445)—to the personal and disjointed—"and the cool of the 42nd St. tunnel (periplum) / […] / Towers of Pisa" (74/467). What is most notable about Pound's repetitive use of the term is the divergence it marks. Subject rhymes seem to have disintegrated into experiences and observations that no longer harmonize; there is no way to bring together New York and Italian geography with whatever coastline is designated by "the great periplum." The barbed wire, and the immobility it enforces, destroys the historical rhythms Pound once uncovered by walking through the landscape. The wire does not enclose the poet in timelessness, as Kenner asserts, but in dissonance. Those passages in Pound that are most conventionally lyrical mark the breakdown of the historical patterns once inscribed on the landscape, marking the impossibility, as it were, of going back to the sestina.

Pound, in his usual fashion, analyzes this breakdown as an aesthetic problem leading back to an economic one. In Canto 82 Pound mentions "Three birds on the wire" (82/544) then transcribes their song with notational accuracy:

> 8th day of September
> f f
>   d
>   g
>   Write the birds in their treble scale (82/545)

These birds appear in various permutations throughout *The Pisan Cantos*. Canto 75 is simply the transcription of a Renaissance musical score entitled "The Song of the Birds" (Sieburth, *Pisan* xxvii). Scholars have noted the tendency of Pound's birds to write themselves in musical notation or become the "image" of their own "sound" (Byron 164; Albright, *Untwisting* 88). Pound, however, makes clear at the end of Canto 82 that the birds embody a very different tune from the one they write or sing: "three solemn half notes / their white downy chests black-rimmed / on the middle wire / periplum" (82/547). The barbed-wire is not a musical score; the birds do not rhyme with the song they sing; subjects do not rhyme with their spaces. The prison camp is a periplum of disruption—literally a monotone or a flat scale without contours. The ultimate cause of the disruption, Pound points out everywhere, is usury—which he says leads directly to the "death-cells" (74/461). The death cell constitutes an existential threat but also a disruption of the old landscape patterns that once seemed to come together in unifying ideograms and musical rhymes. New, more disturbing ideograms announce the disintegration of subject rhyme: "the ideogram of the guard roosts" (74/448), "from the death cells in sight of Mt. Taishan @ Pisa" (74/447). Even Pound's recollection of his formative walking tour is disrupted: "But to set here the roads of France / […] / Aubeterre, the quarried stone beyond Poitiers— / — as seen against Sergeant Beaucher's elegant profile" (76/475). In a world ruled by usury, nature no longer rhymes with humanity: the landscape is threatening, institutional, carceral, and monotone.

The failure of subject rhyme is linked to a failure of subjectivity—something Hesse correctly describes as an "Identitätskrise" (*Ezra Pound* 260). In the same passage where the birds fail to embody the notes they sing, the speaker remarks "the loneliness of death came upon me / (at 3 P. M., for an instant)" (82/547). "When the raft broke and the waters went over me" is how Pound describes the experience of imprisonment two cantos earlier, drawing on the Odysseus-leitmotif that runs throughout (80/533; Sieburth, *Pisan* xiv). Solitary confinement in a cage led the nearly 60-year old poet to experience a loss-of-self similar to death by drowning.[41] Gaining access to writing materials helped him swim back to mental health, but what he writes about is the disintegration of selfhood. In the first of *The Pisan Cantos* (74) he declares "OÝ TIΣ / I am noman, my name is noman" (74/446). There is an important difference between the identification with "noman," and the loss of identity this implies, and the impersonality of earlier verse. The Odysseus myth is operative in *The Cantos*, as Kenner remarks, when it is no longer a "version of Homer" but "an exhibition of 'Homer' as a persistent pattern" (*Pound Era* 149). Here the pattern collapses and the speaker can merely identify with a version of the wanderer; he becomes the emptiness signified by the pun on the name without any hope of escaping the Cyclops's cave (Sieburth, *Pisan* xxv). Pound's verse normally runs counter to our expectations of how the lyric is supposed to work in that subjectivity is confirmed not in isolation, but when it is subsumed in subject rhyme and myth. Pound strives towards the universal, as Kenner argues, through the impersonal. What Kenner fails to point out, however, is that when the verse is "merely" personal drifts from the shore of historical-geographical meaning in the same way that Kenner's notion of "*Paradiso* in counterpoint" drifts from the actual

41 Some of the more poignant passages edited out of the final manuscript simply repeat, in the form of a lament, "alone, alone, alone, alone" (Sieburth, *Pisan* xxv).

context of the prison camp. "The muses are daughters of memory," as Pound affirms, but memory becomes detached from tradition in the same way that the dream of walking becomes detached from the landscape when the poet sits confined in his cell (74/465).

What I am arguing, contrary to Kenner, is that the *incarcerated* poet is no longer the vehicle of ancient rhythms, merely the subject of his own private recollections. For Pound the lyric is failed epic, elegizing—but not abandoning—the insufficiency of its technique. "Mere" lyricism is the point where the Odysseus myth no longer operates, and what I have called the second-order lyricism of the poem, its hope to settle into one great sestina-like journey, capsizes and leaves its passenger stranded as traumatized "no man."

The failure of Pound's poetic and political journey, his collapse into "mere" memory, authorized a lyrical turn in midcentury poetry that was consistent with liberal ideologies and institutions. It is in this context that postwar walk poems become significant. In *Walks in the World*, Roger Gilbert points to the second half of the twentieth century as the Golden Age of walk poetry. He does not claim that the era invented the walk poem. Its long history is evidenced by the fact that "many prosodic terms are derived from the act of walking: feet, iamb, enjambment, and less technical concepts like that of pace" (26). Nevertheless, the walk poem gained in popularity after the war as part of the general turn towards lyricism authorized by the Bollingen Prize. Walk poetry seemed to be non-ideological in the same way it was non-teleological: the link between verbal rhythms and bodily movement made pattern a function of geography, to be sure, but the basic trajectory of the journey seemed to be a matter of whim (8, 26). Gilbert suggests that the "present-tense immediacy" of *The Pisan Cantos*'s "particular landscape" makes the sequence a typical example of American walk poetry (15). This is true in a trivial way. What makes *The Pisan Cantos* so significant in the history of postwar American poetry is how writers turned to peripatetic devices to separate Pound the lyricist from Pound the fascist, celebrating the prison walls, paradoxically, as the confirmation of Pound's personal wanderlust and poetic freedom.

Allen Ginsberg's "Wichita Vortex Sutra" (1966), part of the long journey-sequence *The Fall of America* (1965–71), is exemplary in the way it invokes Pound as isolated traveler to authorize a poetic and political quest for freedom. *The Fall of America* is a peripatetic poem with roots in American walk poetry and links to Beat road narratives. Its structure is lyrical in Bogan's sense, describing a series of open-ended road trips across the United States. At times the poem threatens to collapse into the "pure successiveness" (Gilbert) of the journey as the speaker juxtaposes descriptions of passing landmarks with the advertisements and news reports playing on the car radio, punctuated by the occasional relief of a Bob Dylan song (Breslin 38). For all its structural insufficiency, however, successiveness is a deliberate poetic device, which Ginsberg links with Pound and contrasts with the language of advertising and politics:

> Language, language
> Ezra Pound the Chinese Written Character for truth
>   Defined as man standing by his word
>   Word picture: forked creature
> …
> Ham Steak please waitress, in the warm café.
> Different from a bad guess.
>   The war is language,
>   Language abused
>   for Advertisement,
>   language used
>   like magic for power on the planet:
> …
> handmedown mandrake terminology (400–01)

Ginsberg offers Pound's ideogram of truth as an alternative to the "handmedown" language of advertising and power. There is a difference between the "forked creature" that is the Chinese word-picture of a man standing by his word and the mandrake or "forked root" of deception; the man-ideogram enters by way of a metonymic pun into a warm café, and the mandrake of deception, perhaps because of the hallucinogenic properties of the root, comes to stand for the black magic of advertising and war. Clearly, Pound's (early) critique of war and usury helped fuel Ginsberg's own critique of politics and advertising. Pound's Chinese ideogram also provides a metaleptic link to the midcentury enemies of America—the Chinese, the Communists, and the Viet-Cong—as Ginsberg questions the language of antagonism that puts them on the other side (398). The poem argues that international aggression is linked to lying, which in turn is linked to personal repression, and that the United States has to get beyond its Puritanical hate to stop war (Breslin 32). Paul Breslin argues that Ginsberg, in his desire to free liberal society from the manipulative authority of propaganda, bows to the much stricter spiritual authority of personal authenticity (39–40). Ginsberg also bows to Pound as the unexpected guru of lyrical authenticity.

In 1966 Ginsberg visited Pound in Venice; the senior poet famously expressed regret for his "stupid, suburban prejudice of anti-Semitism," and Ginsberg, controversially, forgave him (Reck 154). He felt he could forgive Pound on everyone's behalf for the same reason that Pound, in speaking for himself, spoke for everyone. This lyrical equation between "I" and "we," timeless because apolitical, is reflected in what he says of Pound's lasting influence: "Anti-Semitism is your fuck-up, like not liking Buddhists, but it's part of the model, and the great accomplishment was to make a working model of your mind. Nobody cares if it's Ezra Pound's mind, but it's a mind like everybody's mind" (Reck 154). Ginsberg sees Pound as an individualist and a lyricist, although in some ways he is not a lyricist himself.[42] His most famous poems are series of apostrophes—addressing, in jeremiad fashion, an America on the verge of self-destruction. Nevertheless, his poems are structured around lyrical moments of identification with "the mind like everybody's," which he finds exemplified in Pound. The "you" Pound expresses through anti-Semitism does not matter; his mind is the "I" that symbolizes everybody's "we." Pound's context, in other words, is supposed to be less significant than his personal journey. Politics, landscape, the way culture inscribes itself on the landscape, even on the mind—all of these things become incidental to experience. Here is how Ginsberg expresses the same lyrical model of I-we identification in "Wichita Vortex Sutra": "not afraid / to speak my lonesomeness in a car, / because not only my lonesomeness / it's Ours, all over America" (405). Pound, amazingly, serves to authorize Ginsberg's project of lonely identification, but only because Ginsberg takes him to be a representative individual, not the vehicle of tradition.

---

[42] There is an argument to be made that Pound was always an individualist even if he was not a lyricist; indeed, that his individualism pushed him away from lyricism. Michael Levenson has argued that the modernism propounded by Pound and his group before 1914 "was individualist before it was anti-individualist, anti-traditional before it was traditional, inclined to anarchism before it was inclined to authoritarianism" (79). Auden had also suggested that modernist individualism led to elitism during his own Page-Barbour lectures at the University of Virginia in 1949, when he polemically extended the "Romantic period" through 1914 in order to argue that early modernists believed "the artist, the maker himself, [to be] the epic hero [...]. [G]reat heroic figures are not men of action but individual geniuses" (*Enchafed Flood* 147). Fen Lan argues that in the 1920s Pound was still "identifying 'Confucian' with the Western tradition of liberalism" (93). Only later did he transform his understanding of Confucianism "in an attempt to reconcile his liberal individualism and cultural elitism, eventually paving the way to a new autocracy, an authoritarian state" (110). This linking of individualism and authoritarianism occurs when Pound begins lumping together liberalism with mercantilism and usury. However, it is already hinted at in some of Pound's earlier poetry. "To Whistler, American" (1912) puts it like this: "You [Whistler] and Abe Lincoln from that mass of dolts / Show us there's chance at least of winning through" (*Personae* 235). Pound's roster is democratic but his argument is elitist. Midcentury critics lyricized Pound to make his poetry compatible with individualism, but a certain kind of individualism may have pushed him towards poetic and political forms that elevated exemplary figures over the "doltish" group.

Ginsberg follows Pound by mistaking his periplum for a personal journey, his time-space ideogram for a spiritual symbol. Pound walks to find rhythms and subject rhymes that speak through him; Ginsberg transforms these cultural patterns into an image of selfhood imprisoned in its own freedom. Ginsberg misreads Pound in a way that makes him feel closest to the senior poet when the one is isolated in a prison, and the other in a car. Pound's incarceration is the ghost in Ginsberg's machine. For all his anger at the liberal establishment, the poet on the far left misreads his predecessor on the far right in a manner consistent with the liberal aesthetic. He also reads him in a manner consistent with Kenner, seeing in Pound not the European mind but the new American mentality about to be born ("Ours, all over America").

Ginsberg, rebelling against consumer society in his car, is representative of a generation of midcentury poets and novelists who set out on journeys to demonstrate their independence from political control. The aging group of writers affiliated with *Partisan Review*, more suspicious of the new "Post-Modern" (Howe) writers than they were forgiving of the older modernists, sensed this independence might be more institutional than it seemed. Irving Howe called the new writers "veritable mimics of the American tourist" ("Mass Society" 435). Harold Rosenberg's term for the new brand of collective individualism was "the herd of independent minds" (*Tradition of the New* 244).

I now break with chronology to turn to a poet who was more sensitive to the institutional structures that could make confinement seem like poetic freedom. In 1949–1950 Elizabeth Bishop followed in the footsteps of Shapiro, Lowell, and Léonie Adams (all members of the Bollingen committee) as Poetry Consultant to the Library of Congress. She ambivalently took up the ritual initiated by Lowell of visiting Pound in the place she called Bedlam (after the infamous mental hospital in London). Her biographer Brett Millier describes these visits as "torture," arguing that "Elizabeth measured herself against him [Pound] and found herself wanting"—that is until she wrote "Visits to St. Elizabeths" six years later (220, 222). (*The Complete Poems* dates "Visits" at 1950). The poem was commissioned for *Nuova Corrente: Rivista di letteratura* (1956) by the Italian Pound scholar and translator Alfredo Rizzardi, who met Bishop while visiting the United States on a fellowship (Travisano *Words in Air* 186; cf. Pilandri). "Visits to St. Elizabeths" was published in *Partisan Review* in 1957. Lowell read the poem out loud—he said to great effect—at several events dedicated to Pound, who was released in 1958 (Travisano, *Words in Air* 597). (Pound immediately returned to Italy, where local reporters photographed him giving the fascist salute [Torrey 263]). Lowell considered Bishop's poem to be superior to a widely-circulated essay by Robert Fitzgerald ending—like Kenner's "Rose in the Steel Dust" and Matthiessen's introduction to the *Oxford Book of American Verse*—in a "trapdoorish" citation of Canto 81 (Travisano, *Words in Air* 203).[43]

"Visits to St. Elizabeths" is based on the rhymes, rhythms, and structure of the nursery rhyme "This Is the House that Jack Built." Thomas Travisano links it to other poems by Bishop deploying childhood themes and devices to explore moral dilemmas: "The pattern and rhythms of 'This is the House that Jack Built' achieve in her hands a relentless logic that, while it keeps all Pound achieved and perpetrated in balance, drives straight at the climactic word *wretched*, the one unflinching word that, after the crimes and after the glory, sums Pound up" (*Elizabeth Bishop* 173). The poem begins with the statement "this is the house of Bedlam" and adds a line per stanza, identifying first "the man / that lies in the house of Bedlam" and then other figures who might be fellow inmates: a "sailor," "the Jew in the newspaper hat," and "the soldier home from the war" (134–35).

The original nursery rhyme is a cumulative tale that adds details stanza by stanza while leaving preceding lines intact. Bishop was adept at using rigid structures—like Pound she was an admirer and practitioner of the sestina—to force herself to say things that were difficult to admit. The most cited example is the villanelle "One Art," which concludes with the insight it has been denying all along: loss is a "disaster" (Bishop 178). (Helen Vendler: "Her art, wrung from loss, paradoxically becomes her life principle" [111]). "Visits to St. Elizabeths" does use the repetitive structure of the nursery rhyme to powerfully link "poet" with "lies." However, the poem strays significantly from its model. The base-refrain changes with each iteration, allowing Bishop to insert details excluded in the initial descriptions. The accumulating lines alter the substance of their predecessors as if by geological compression so that gem-like amendments shine out from underneath the new semantic strata: that time is passing in Bedlam, that the Jew is in mourning and perhaps in mortal danger, and—in the final stanza—that the sailor is crazy, the poet wretched. The resulting texture is extremely Poundian and decidedly not lyrical—at least not in the liberal sense meant by mid-century critics. Indeed, Bishop is more Poundian in her descriptions of incarceration than Pound, the prisoner, could be himself. Her inmates move

---

[43] Robert Fitzgerald's 1948 review of *The Pisan Cantos* for *The New Republic* anticipates Kenner's 1950 argument. Like Kenner, Fitzgerald argues that Pound "would mount to a *paradiso* as his master, Dante, did," claiming that his post-orthodox version of paradise provides "more exhilarating poetic sketch books [...] than can be found elsewhere in our literature" ("What thou Lovest Well" 363). The review concludes with the "Tear down thy vanity" passage from Canto 81.

through their institutional landscape, a periplum of confinement; they do not remember old walks or escape down the paths of memory. There is no *Paradiso* to be found because the asylum is not exactly hell; it is an institutional space that shapes character and produces cultural meaning.

"Visits to St. Elizabeths" was a popular poem, but it has received little sustained attention. In *Becoming Canonical in American Poetry* Timothy Morris argues this is because it never deserved recognition in the first place. When it appeared in *Questions of Travel* (1965) it helped establish the reputation of that volume, but "the poem is a permanently embarrassing feature of Bishop's work" because it "normalizes" Pound in a way typical for the decade: "the late 1960s saw not so much a rehabilitation of Pound [...] but a renormalization of his work" (114–15). I disagree that a poem so preoccupied with the institutional conditions of Pound's confinement can be read as normalizing the poet. Indeed, it is significant that the piece Bishop and Lowell referred to as the "Pound poem" in their correspondence never mentions him by name (Travisano, *Words in Air* 597). Instead it indirectly names the author by designating the institution in the title: St. Elizabeths. This has led other critics to assume that the poem is personal, or political in a personal way. Its significance is supposed to lie in what Bishop learned about herself during her visits to the asylum; this is presumably revealed in the changing descriptors and in the poem's accumulation of detail. Robert Dale Parker argues that "Visits to St. Elizabeths" confronts a "Pound Era" "where the world still sputters in the shadow of Pound's once-triumphant literary Modernism and the cataclysm it got swept up in, sweeping Pound along with it" (117). What Bishop offers in response to modernism is personal experience (117). Siobhan Phillips offers a variation of this reading, describing the poem as "a defense borne of identification" (S. Phillips 131).

These interpretations—normalization and personalization—are two sides of the same coin. Both assume that "Visits to St. Elizabeths" is to be read as a lyric. Either Bishop's poem fails by depoliticizing Pound, or it succeeds by personalizing her encounter with him. The crux of the poem is supposed to be linked to the arc of the visitor's impressions, and its effectiveness hinges on the appropriateness of those impressions to Pound's situation. This line of interpretation makes intuitive sense. We can imagine the germ of the poem lying in a kind of impersonal "I told you so." It is unfortunate Pound is confined to an institution, Bishop might have thought, but after all this is the house he built for himself. Pound, however, did not build St. Elizabeths, nor did he choose his company there. The mental hospital is an institution, and Bishop's relation to it, as Poetry Consultant, was institutional. Bishop's turn to the anonymous, folk-art structure of the nursery rhyme reflects the institutional quality of her experience; it allows her to remain impersonal.

The impersonal form protects her from lyricizing Pound or her speaker. This is not a poem that leads to an epiphany or a judgment. It refuses to "resolve" the dilemma posed by Pound by seeing him as a victim or a criminal or a poetic authority. Contrary to Travisano, I do not think the "wretched" sums Pound up. Instead of judging Pound, who never stood trial, the poem invokes an impersonal but deliberately non-epic form to describe his institutional location and significance.

The nursery rhyme proves useful for this task because it complicates responsibility in the same way it complicates the notion of individual authorship. Jack built the house. Is he also the architect of what transpires in his yard? The original nursery rhyme provides an inventory of property but no information about the owner. The title of the poem is parodied by the plot, which mocks the ordered progression of a causal chain. Two unnamed but rhyming characters whose relation to Jack is unclear—"the man all tattered and torn" and "the maiden all forlorn"—do end up marrying. This is as close as the nursery rhyme comes to establishing character or narrating plot. Bishop's poem is also better at sketching out digressive subplots than exploring the theme named in the title. The main subplot involves the other inmates in the asylum, mainly the sailor and the Jew:

> These are the years and the walls and the door
> that shut on a boy that pats the floor
> to feel if the world is there and flat.
> This is a Jew in a newspaper hat
> that dances joyfully down the ward
> into the parting seas of board
> past the staring sailor
> that shakes his watch
> that tells the time
> of the poet, the man
> that lies in the house of Bedlam. (Bishop 134–35)

At first glance, Bishop seems to deny the incidental union of the nursery rhyme's marriage subplot. The mental asylum is pathologically individualized. Nobody "watches" as the Jew walks a plank we later learn is a coffin board; nobody seems to be responsible; even the victim is emotionally detached from his plight. The exception, a significant one, is the "with" in the final stanza: the Jew is last pictured "walking the plank of a coffin board / with the crazy sailor." Bishop converts Jack's house into a ship of fools where everybody goes overboard, passengers and crew.

This is probably what bothered Morris. Victims and perpetrators seem to suffer the same fate. But alternate readings are possible here. The chain of tropes—more strongly linked than the poem's chain of events—suggest that the literary denial of difference can lead to murder. The "roadstead all of board" becomes in a subsequent stanza the "sea of board," waltzed over by the Jew, who is then made to walk the plank, and finally in the last stanza, "the plank of a coffin board." The universe constructed all of boards is without difference in the same way it is without depth. The only place for difference—in this case the Jew—is the plank. Ultimately, however, I think the poem does not depict the incarcerated poet as an author of destruction so much as a figure hardly distinguishable from his own creatures. Bishop's poem suggests a kind of circus animals' desertion in which Pound's metaphors turn on him and "watch."[44] Pound has been reduced to the status of his symbols. He is himself a symbol, an occupant of somebody else's house.

The anonymity and ambiguity of the nursery rhyme are linked lines of defense against the temptation of lyricizing Pound. Another line of defense involves an allusion that, as far as I can tell, has gone unremarked in Bishop scholarship. There was an original poet in Bedlam: Nathanial Lee was incarcerated for five years in the infamous Bethlem Royal Hospital, popularly called Bedlam, near the end of his life (1653–92). He was the subject of a poem by William Wycherly, and more significant for my argument, a famous anecdote in Coleridge's *Biographia Literaria* (1817): "'I asserted that the world was mad,' exclaimed poor Lee, 'and the world said that I was mad, and confound them, they outvoted me'" (148–49). Coleridge relates this anecdote in the context of a philosophical argument. He quotes Lee to epitomize a relativist impasse in the debate between idealism and realism, but also, by siding with "poor" poet, to suggest a higher philosophical synthesis. The mad poet is in some ways more lucid than his captors, and idealism, as Coleridge asserts, is "the truest and most binding realism" (148). It is typical for a Romantic thinker to locate the synthesis between self and world, imagination and empiricism, in a mad poetic insight. The Romantic drama is a phenomenological one that might resolve itself negatively when the poet fades into the forest dim, or positively through the "egotistical sublime," but it is always the private drama of the poet that establishes the significance of the outside world. In Coleridge's anecdote the asylum walls provide lyrical isolation, but the "mad" monologue is nevertheless important enough to be overheard. The pathos of this situation—the individual telling the truth about the world because he is separate from it—inspired Mill to turn to the

[44] David Moody reports that Pound incurred the wrath of his supervisors at Hamilton College by taking out a large tin watch during lectures and comically winding it (23–24, 28–33). I do not know if Bishop was aware of the anecdote, but it certainly fits the sailor's antics.

Romantics (including Coleridge) to define the lyric.[45] It also provided the coordinates for the poetic form that M. H. Abrams famously defined as the "greater Romantic lyric." Abrams was concerned with nature poetry, often structured around a journey, but the mad poet in the asylum is the prototype for all sorts of lyric speakers: "In the course of this meditation the lyric speaker achieves an insight, faces up to a tragic loss, comes to a moral decision, or resolves an emotional problem" (427–28). The link between depth of soul and depth of field forged by isolation allows the speaker to achieve a higher, personal synthesis between self and world.

This type of lyrical resolution is not possible in Bishop. Her allusion to Lee is a negative one. Her institution has no walls, but not because she concludes that the world is an asylum that has declared itself sane by referendum. Rather, the world is continuous with the asylum; they are both part of the same system. Self is not opposed to world in Bishop's nursery rhyme; there is no pathos of individuation; dramatic monologue is foreclosed by the anonymous form. The nursery rhyme, deliberately impersonal and digressive, has become the blueprint of an institutional structure. Remarkably silent about Bishop's own experiences and hesitant to judge Pound, the poem offers a clinical assessment of the conditions of his confinement—and his fame. Bishop's wretched poet, in other words, does not epitomize the world, but he has a specific place in it. His position no longer enables the liberal/lyrical fantasy of independence; the separation between self and other and the resulting illusion of emotional depth, is flattened out like the surface of an abstract expressionist painting.

One telling detail is the reference to "a boy that pats the floor / to see if the world is there, is flat," which replaces the rhyming line, two stanzas earlier: "This is a world of books gone flat" (Bishop 134). The flat earth denies the depth of lyrical reflection—the correspondence between depth of field and depth of consciousness—reducing everything to a common compositional element. As Lowell pointed out in a letter to Bishop, the boards pick up on a powerful metaphor from "The Monument" (*Words on Air* 591). In that poem "A sea of narrow, horizontal boards / lies out behind our lonely monument," also made of wood, which "holds together better / than sea or cloud or sand could by itself" (Bishop 24). The common material shared by object and backdrop flattens out the landscape; ekphrasis in Bishop's hands collapses the distinction between monument and surroundings. This deliberately abstract description resonates with midcentury arguments for abstract

---

[45] The artificiality of seeing exclusion as independence might also explain why G. E. Moore turned to the same anecdote in *Principia Ethica* to refute what he described as Mill's hedonism (75).

expressionism, which demanded that pictorial art sacrifice the illusion of depth in order to be true to its own media: flat canvas and paint. However, Bishop's monocoque construction offers an alternative to the pictorial vanishing point in the depth of its cryptic interior:

> But roughly but adequately it [the monument] can shelter
> What is within (which after all
> Cannot have been intended to be seen).
> It is the beginning of a painting,
> A piece of sculpture, or poem, or monument,
> And all of wood. Watch it closely. (Bishop 25)

The parenthetical evocation of what the monument secretes inside—its secret—dramatizes the mechanisms involved in the social production of monumentality. The monument is not posterior to what is remembered; rather it produces significance as an artifact of its own composition (hence the implied rhyme in the passage describing beginnings of "wood" with *would*).

Bishop's poetic analysis of the production of cultural significance suggests a moral that has nothing to do with individualism or genius. The secret of St. Elizabeths, to borrow the subtitle from E. Fuller Torrey's study of that institution, is quite simply what it contains. Bishop describes the institution as another wooden construction (reinforced by the rhyme: ward/ board), one that produces a monument to modernism by turning Pound into a secret. The institutional Pound is a poet without depth; his poetry earns accolades while his ideas are dismissed as insane. By simultaneously evoking and denying Pound's significance, by applauding him and locking him up, midcentury American culture creates the illusion of depth. The space between the two Pounds, confined in different institutional locations, became the field on which American culture constructed a monument to individualism. But it was a monument that made confinement the precondition of freedom.

"Visits to St. Elizabeths" confronts Pound's legacy by denying the kind of individualism that turned him into a lyricist. The poem is not the lyrical expression of Bishop's personal encounter with Pound, but an evocation of the institutional structures involved in Pound's monumentalization. "Elizabeth" may be a "saint" for visiting Pound in captivity, but his institutional status—at the margins of society but never quite disappearing—is a visitation in its own right. Pound is a haunting presence, a melancholy figure who refuses to be integrated or dismissed. Voice seems to emerge in the echo chamber between the two Elizabeths—the visitor and the place. We are left not with depth but with the blueprint of an institution designed to separate art from politics, monuments from criminals—an institution that makes the redeeming confession impossible or irrelevant. Later, Bishop would personify this institutional structure in poems like "In the Waiting Room," which transforms the graduated, institutional spaces between dentist office and waiting room into spaces of identification:

> What took me
> Completely by surprise
> Was that it was *me*:
> My voice, in my mouth.
> Without thinking at all
> I was my foolish aunt,
> I—we—were falling, falling,
> Our eyes glued to the cover of the *National Geographic*,
> February, 1918. (160)

Poetic voice here emerges as in an echo chamber, establishing correspondences between the speaker, her aunt, and the ethnographic images she looks at in the magazine. These spaces do not offer the privacy or the intimacy implicit in Mill's model of lyricism. They situate the speaker in relation to other racialized and gendered identities. Bishop's encounter with Pound, and her refusal to monumentalize him according to the dictates of the liberal aesthetic, pushed her own writing beyond the limits of lyrical individualism towards a new lyricism of identity. I will provide a more precise definition of what I mean by the lyricism of identity in the next chapter.

CHAPTER 2

Liberalism and Lyricism, or Karl Shapiro's Elegy for Identity

What happened to Karl Shapiro? He returned from active duty in WWII the Pulitzer Prize-winning author of *V-Letter* and was shortly thereafter appointed poetry consultant to the Library of Congress (a position now termed Poet Laureate). He left Washington, D.C. to accept the first tenured professorship for creative writing at Johns Hopkins and later taught at other major American universities, including the University of Chicago. He was editor of the prestigious *Poetry* magazine from 1950 to 1956, and of the *Newberry Library Bulletin* for part of that time, and in 1956 he became editor of *The Prairie Schooner* and a professor at the University of Nebraska. In 1968 he accepted a professorship at the University of California at Davis, and in 1969 he shared the Bollingen Prize with John Berryman. In light of these successes it is striking that the arc of Shapiro's career describes a narrative of declension. His influence diminished considerably as he migrated westward, and his poetry disappeared from major anthologies by the 1970s. At a low point in his fame, after living in California for several years, he was forced to challenge (once legally) obituaries identifying him as a suicide.

The second volume of Shapiro's autobiography is tellingly entitled *Reports of My Death*, and in this book and elsewhere he maintains that it was his dissenting vote against Pound in the Bollingen controversy of 1949 that cost him his standing among fellow poets, marking him as "just another refuser" and a Jew (43; "Scapegoat" 83). The autobiography also evidences the lifelong contrariness that probably impacted Shapiro's career more dramatically than did his opposition to the Pound award.[46] However, there is something in Shapiro's assessment that bears further scrutiny. Even if we do not credit his perhaps paranoid view that the literary and cultural "Establishment" turned its back on

[46] Shapiro repeatedly calls attention to what he calls his "aggressive defensiveness." Describing himself in the third person in his autobiography, he says "He was busy learning not only technique but how to dissent from dissent"; he later calls this deliberate polemical stance anticriticism (*The Younger Son* 32, 166). See also his statement, "I hated majority opinion" ("American Poet?" 238). Peter Viereck also claimed that his vocal opposition to the Pound award cost him his reputation (Rasula 113). I explore this in chapter four.

him for his disloyalty to *il miglior fabbro*, it is significant that a group of influential poets and critics responded to Pound one way and Shapiro responded in another (*Reports* 43).

The controversy surrounding the first Bollingen Prize—awarded to a Pound facing treason charges for his pro-fascist and anti-Semitic radio broadcasts from Italy during World War II—powerfully impacted the location and form of midcentury verse. By 1957, Richard Chase was already calling for the institutionalization and internalization of "the avant-garde attitude," partially in response to the Pound controversy ("Avant Garde" 375). Recent accounts confirm that this is precisely what happened with much of the poetry of the period. Jed Rasula has argued that the Pound controversy led to the institutionalization of midcentury poetry, i.e. its cordoning off in universities as the Bollingen Prize moved from the Library of Congress to Yale and Pound was incarcerated in St. Elizabeths (113–22). Alan Filreis has argued that the subjectivist lyric emerged as the midcentury alternative to the more self-consciously politicized verse of the 1930s (xi–xii, 183–85). Shapiro's career helps illuminate the paradigm shift that underwrote this institutionalization and individuation of poetic voice and what came next, namely efforts by influential poets and critics to re-politicize poetry by identifying lyrical voice with marginalized social groups and causes. This is a two-part story, having first to do with the liberal response to Pound's reaction, and then with the poetic and critical reaction to liberalism.

Liberal critics defended the Pound award by characterizing poetry as a form of free expression. Separating politics from poetics, they justified even anti-liberal sentiments by appealing to the liberal principle of individualism, understood to be the foundation of political and cultural value in a democracy. Such arguments enjoyed broad consensus for a decade, but they began to lose ground when individualism came to be seen as an ideological blunt object in Cold War debates, and poets and critics—especially those affiliated with the New Left—began to look to those constituencies (race, class, gender) whose specific concerns were ignored or masked by individualism's universal claims. By 1960, the poetry and criticism that would have lasting influence was beginning to abandon the liberal discourse of individualism for the more group-specific language of identity. Shapiro is interesting here because his development both participates in this shift and differs from it. When Shapiro voted against Pound he did so as a Jew voting against an anti-Semite, in effect violating the liberal consensus that poetry was to be understood as free expression, i.e. as personal rather than political. But he subsequently attacked identity as a poetically invalid form of personification, defining himself as "a negative Jew," or a Jew without ethnicity, at precisely the moment it became fashionable to "discover" one's identity.[47] Shapiro, in other words, traverses the trajectory of the liberal aesthetic in reverse. During the reign of aesthetic individualism he argued that anti-Semitism was bad form, political and poetic; but when identity gained in critical and poetic significance he insisted his Jewishness was a matter of personal choice. His final reckoning with the Pound controversy occurs in an elegy for another member of the committee, W. H. Auden, but it is also an elegy for identity, attempting to separate Jewishness from any notion of group membership, and to redefine lyricism in terms of individual voice.

Trial of a Poet

Shapiro confronted the Pound dilemma before serving on the Bollingen committee. In the title poem of *Trial of a Poet* (1947), a book that received mainly negative reviews, he imagines a poet clearly modeled on Pound brought to trial for treason, but ultimately confessing to the aesthetic crime of being "a dull poet and the lapdog of his age" (*Trial* 78). The long poem is a verse drama whose *dramatis personae* include a Public Officer, a Doctor, a Priest, a Chorus of Poets afraid that all poetry may be "stained" by the crime of the accused, and the accused poet himself (69). The poet responds to the verse accusations of the others in a prose monologue commencing in gibberish and ending in romantic irony when he describes his own predicament by explicating the poem's Miltonic epigraph (77). Robert Fitzgerald, who panned the poem but would later repeat Shapiro's aesthetic criticism of Pound ("I think that Pound at twenty or thirty would have thought hanging an entirely appropriate reward for the author of those radio scripts!" ["Gloom and Gold" 22]), correctly identified Pound as the subject of the verse drama and its form as Audenesque ("Present State" 26).[48] Auden would be Shapiro's constant companion in his reckoning with Pound's anti-Semitism, although Shapiro's rather one-sided argument with Auden tended to put him at odds with another member of the Bollingen committee, Robert Lowell. I will return to this point later.

The dramatic form of "Trial of a Poet" surely owes something to verse dramas like Auden's *The Age of Anxiety*, which I analyze in the next chapter,

---

[47] Shapiro coins the phrase "negative Jew" to describe how identity is imposed from the outside but consented to by the self. He compares this process to military induction ("The Jewish Writer in America" 300).

[48] Robert Phillips makes similar claims in his Afterword to the new edition of *Essay on Rime with Trial of a Poet*. Noting that there is "little doubt that the poet on trial [...] is based on Pound," he goes on to point out that "the poet whose work Shapiro's most resembles is Auden's" (112, 115).

but its most Audenesque feature may be the authority it grants the character of the Doctor. Shapiro would repeatedly criticize Auden for "intellectualizing" emotion in a way more consistent with psychology than poetry ("Retreat" 77, 80). In later remarks on the Pound controversy, he would claim that "psychology [...] was born out of the ruins of literature" ("Poets and Psychologists" 184). But in this early poem it is the psychologist who gives the most compelling diagnosis of the poet—a diagnosis that implicitly rejects the poet's confessed crime ("dull") to focus on the hierarchies and structures implicit in the poet's notion of "genius" (60). According to the Doctor, it is this avant-garde conception of genius that leads the poet to apotheosize his heroes and consign everyone else to hell, and criticism must confront the political implications of this hierarchy to "bridge" the gap between the poet's act of imagination and his actual crime:

> Out of his new-found phrases and dead footnotes
> He wove a critique of life, a bad world history,
> With a Cloud-Cuckoo-Land for his heroes
> And a hell in minute detail for the rest.
> I think we must find the bridge between
> This harmless sublimation and his consummate crime. (61)

The Pisan Cantos, published the year after Shapiro's *Trial*, must have confirmed the younger poet's intimation of the link between Cloud-Cuckoo-Land and hell. Canto 74, the first of the series, begins with an elegy for Mussolini and his mistress, followed a dozen pages later by a libel of Rothschild, and then these explicitly anti-Semitic lines:

> The yidd is a stimulant, and the goyim are cattle
> in gt/ proportion and go to saleable slaughter
> with the maximum of docility. (74/459)

The anti-Semitism rears its ugly head again in a Vichy libel in Canto 80:

> Pétain defended Verdun while Blum
> Was defending a bidet (80/514)[49]

What Shapiro euphemistically called "the ideas in Pound," evident everywhere in *The Pisan Cantos*, led him to confirm his Doctor's diagnosis in the later "Ezra Pound: The Scapegoat of Modern Poetry" (65). In this essay Shapiro argues that criticism has to consider the social implications of Pound's poetry because the relation between art and society is Pound's subject matter:

---

[49] See also pp. 449, 460, 463 for other anti-Semitic references.

"As far as a social order goes, Pound has a vestigial idea of a kind of hierarchy based upon the good-ruler-art-patron equation [...]. Pound's lifelong problem has been to establish an equation between poetry and society, between the esthetic and the politick" [*sic*] (68). Contemporary criticism also supports the diagnosis of Shapiro's Doctor. Pound's problem was, to paraphrase Bob Perelman, a problem of genius. In his radio broadcasts as in his writing, Pound idolized strong figures who were supposed to fight modern decay, embodied in both the abject figure of the Jew and in decadent language (45–46, 60). The interpretive bridge invoked by Shapiro's Doctor is necessitated by Pound's reactionary avant-gardism, which forges a fascist alliance between poetic and political "genius" in the name of social and linguistic purity. Many of Shapiro's contemporaries denied this bridge in the name of liberalism. In the introduction I describe the symposium kicked off by William Barrett's editorial on the Pound award in *Partisan Review*. Barrett charitably assumed that the Bollingen judges endorsed Pound on purely aesthetic grounds, identifying the crux of the issue as follows: "How far is it possible, in a lyric poem, for technical embellishments to transform vicious and ugly matter into beautiful poetry?" ("A Prize" 347). Most of the contributors to the symposium upheld the separation between poetry and politics, arguing, in the words of a subsequent editorial written by Dwight Macdonald, that the ability "to evaluate each sphere of human activity separate from the rest instead of enslaving them all to one great reductive tyrant, whether it be The Church, The Proletariat, People's Democracy, The Master Race or American Patriotism" is what distinguished democracy from totalitarianism and gave Americans the "right to oppose Soviet totalitarianism in the name of freedom" ("Twelve Judges" 48).

Barrett would ultimately distance himself from this extreme formulation of the liberal aesthetic, which he termed "liberalism for liberalism's sake" ("Further Comment" 522). However, the basic principle of the aesthetic—the separation of art from politics in the name of political freedom—was to prove decisive in a range of conflicts and issues extending far beyond the Bollingen controversy. The Pound award was the decisive moment in the crystallization of a liberal aesthetic that would play a brief but decisive role in the postwar cultural landscape, especially in American universities, until the 1960s.

Shapiro, perhaps buckling under pressure exerted by senior members of the Bollingen committee, first cast his vote for Pound (Leick 25). After a sleepless night he changed his mind to become one of two dissenting members of the committee, the other being Katherine Garrison Chapin, whose puzzling appointment may have had something to do with her marriage to Francis Biddle, the attorney general responsible for indicting Pound (Torrey 235; Leick). In his opposing statement, published in the *Partisan Review* symposium, Shapiro stated that his primary reason for voting against Pound "was that I am a Jew and cannot honor antisemites." The second reason was his belief that "the poet's political and moral philosophy ultimately vitiates his poetry and lowers its standards as a literary work" (518–19). Shapiro deliberately articulated these rationales in opposition to what he took to be the *pons asinorum* of contemporary criticism, namely the division between art and politics, or form and content, which had been erected by the New Critics in their attempt to isolate the literary text as an object of critical analysis.[50] The Latinate phrase may be an indirect reference to the bridge in Shapiro's recently published *Trial of a Poet*. Shapiro, like his character the Doctor but in contradistinction to his contemporaries, demands that criticism bridge the gap between political anti-Semitism and poetic form in order to confront the relation between Pound's cloud-cuckoo-land (inhabited by genius) and his hell (where he consigns Jews). It is in the interest of building this bridge that he lays claim to his Jewish identity.[51]

Criticizing Pound from an explicitly Jewish perspective put Shapiro into obvious conflict with modernist anti-Semitism but also, as Shapiro himself pointed out, with the politics-poetry distinction of the liberal aesthetic. Later poetry collections such as *Poems of a Jew* (1950) (*CP* 143–52) and Shapiro's essay on "The Jewish Writer in America" were intended to be provocations, and were taken as such. But contrary to what some contemporary critics assert, Shapiro was outspoken about his Jewishness from the very beginning of his career, and many of the poems collected in *Poems of a Jew* originate in *V-*

---

[50] Shapiro returned to the relation of the Bollingen Award to New Criticism in a later essay, "The Critic in Spite of Himself": "Giving that honor to Pound was an act of intellectual arrogance which has no parallel in literary history [...]. Eliot had popularized the term *autotelic*, which made it possible for critics to ignore the views of the poet, however unsavoury, while commending the technique. Thus, the intellectual critic has it both ways: he can dictate to society about its ills and he can regard a poem as a pure exercise of language, at his convenience" (325–26).

[51] Peter Viereck, like Shapiro, draws attention to the poetic significance of Pound's anti-Semitism in "Pure Poetry, Impure Politics, and Ezra Pound." This line of criticism would not be raised again until the 1960s, and not with any resonance until the 1990s. The first book to systematically take on the modernists, including Eliot and Pound, for their anti-Semitism and fascism was John Harrison's *The Reactionaries*. Significant is also Leslie Fiedler's pamphlet, dealing however with the prose tradition, *The Jew in the American Novel*. In the early 1970s Hugh Kenner claimed that Pound had been unaware of the racial implications of Nazism and fascism, and he dismissed "Pound's political judgment" as irrelevant to the understanding of his poetry (*Pound Era* 410, 436). For a more modest defense in the Kenner tradition, see Ben Kimpel and T. C. Duncan Eaves in "Two Notes on Ezra Pound's 'Cantos,'" which takes the rather surprising line of argumentation that *The Cantos* are not as anti-Semitic as one might expect.

Letter (cf. Flanzbaum, "The Imaginary Jew" 22–24). Shapiro's Jewishness was no secret to the Pulitzer Prize committee, and his early success should be considered in relation to the immense postwar popularity of Jewish American literature whose primary representatives were novelists like Malamud, Bellow, Mailer, and Roth (M. Hoffman). There may be some truth in Shapiro's assertion that his vote against Pound, articulated in terms of identity, played a role in his rejection by the poetry "Establishment," but this argument does not exactly square with his early fame. It also fails to account for the present lack of a Shapiro revival (he appears nowhere in the *Norton Anthology of American Literature*, edited by Nina Baym). Shapiro was not a poet made invisible by his ethnicity and later discovered because of it. The reverse is true: he was extremely visible and then slowly disappeared, outliving his fame.

Individualism and Identity

It makes sense to think about Shapiro's fame in relation to identity, or more specifically, in relation to the changing significance of identity as it began to challenge the poetic autonomy carved out by the liberal aesthetic. Shapiro was inconsistent on matters of identity, but he was consistently contrarious, deliberately adopting what one critic calls a "middlebrow American" stance in opposition to prevailing intellectual trends, or what Shapiro repeatedly referred to as his "dissent from dissent" (Flanzbaum, "The Imaginary Jew" 24; *The Younger Son* 32). When his contemporaries defended Pound on the grounds that art was separate from politics, Shapiro self-identified as a Jew to reject Pound the anti-Semite, although it should be pointed out that he never sought to muzzle Pound; he just disagreed with the award. Later, when identity caught on as a critical and political concept, Shapiro rejected racial and ethnic identity as a "wound" inflicted by modernity, and urged poets to strive for individual expression rather than group allegiance ("American Poet?" 252).

Insufficient attention has been paid to the history of identity, a concept that revolutionized literary and cultural studies, and arguably politics, in the second half of the twentieth century. Identity tends to be associated with liberal and progressive causes today, but in the immediate aftermath of World War II it was seen as a threat to liberalism, classified as a "fable" or "myth" (in keeping with Northrop Frye's usage in *Fables of Identity*) and approached primarily through the literary and psychological vocabularies of personification, prejudice and projection.[52] The primary vehicle of postwar liberalism

[52] See Walter Benn Michaels's argument that identity is a crypto-conservative idea (13).

was not identity but individualism, and in fact identity was seen as a curtailment of individual freedom.

Arthur Schlesinger's *The Vital Center*, published the same year as the Pound controversy, influentially defined "Mid-twentieth-century liberalism" as "an unconditional rejection of totalitarianism and a reassertion of the ultimate integrity of the individual" (ix). Schlesinger's commitment to individualism also entails the rejection of identity, which remains unnamed as a concept in his book but is clearly associated with the anti-democratic personality he calls the "totalitarian man." The totalitarian man deludes himself into believing he has an identity by pretending to embody the will of a class or a party (56). Adorno, a year later, would describe the similarly conceived "authoritarian personality" as someone who stereotypes Jews and targets them as "personalizations" of threatening social forces (*Authoritarian Personality* 627–37, 653, 663). "Totalitarian man" and "authoritarian personality" are analytical abstractions but also deliberate caricatures, deployed to illustrate how identity—whether positively or negatively conceived, whether assumed or projected—limits human freedom, reducing individuals to stereotypes that are anti-democratic not only because they are false, but because they are predefined. Identity is not individual; it is the personification and/or projection of a social role.

Adorno's terminology in particular suggests how the rhetoric of identity, whatever its basis in theories of biological or cultural inheritance, almost always depends on the figure of personification: the individual is supposed to personify certain characteristics of race or class, just as race and class are supposed to embody specific historical and political principles. The dominant trend in postwar criticism was to separate culture from politics in the name of free speech; in keeping with this argument identity was seen as a misplaced literary figure, i.e. as an unwarranted aestheticization of politics. Midcentury critics argued that to reduce politics to identity was to mistake history for literature, and to look for salvation in heroes and scapegoats rather than through public debate and legislation. Hannah Arendt warned against thinking about history on the analogy of stories or biographies: history has actors but no author, and its actual protagonist is "mankind," which is not a character but an abstraction (*Human Condition* 184). Harold Rosenberg argued that identity is a constant, but personality changes, and to ignore this is to reduce history to morality play or myth (*Tradition of the New* 141–53, 159, 168). This kind of separate-sphere thinking led at least one influential critic to the conclusion that Pound's avant-gardism went astray by mistaking politics for literature. Alfred Kazin makes the following connection between personification and violence in his assessment of Nazism and Pound: "It was his witchlike instinct for the hate buried in the age, coming to the surface in the Warsaw ghetto and the ovens of Treblinka [...]. He had his mad gift for personalizing history and for making other persons speak as History" (*New York Jew* 33).

Liberalism depersonalizes politics in the name of individualism and equality; it rethinks history as a space of political negotiation rather than as the dramatic conflict between ideas or principles cast as social types.[53] Philosophical liberalism can be understood as trying to drive a wedge into the identity of what the medievalist Ernst Kantorowicz, a refugee from the Nazis, called the king's two bodies—the body politic and the physical body—by attacking the theological arguments binding them together. Postwar liberalism would attempt to drive a wedge between the racial and national bodies of fascism by attacking the cult of "the folk" binding them together, and between the proletariat and the worker's state by attacking the myth of the workers' council or soviet. The basic article of faith of postwar liberalism is that no individual or group—whether king, Aryan or proletariat—personifies a political principle. Politics was understood to be different from personality and personal expression in the same way form was held to be different from content; the value of art might be a function of its form, but its meaning was supposed to be a matter of personal expression or content.

In identifying himself as a Jew to reject Pound the anti-Semite, Shapiro refuses to separate the king's two bodies or the aesthetic from the political sphere. (He does, however, accept the argument that identity is misplaced personification—something I will return to later.) At this stage—but only for a brief moment in his career—he adheres to a principle of identity recognizable from a contemporary perspective. In fact, Shapiro's refusal heralds what would become the New Left response to liberalism's belief that it had rationalized politics and "ended ideology."[54] The New Left position, popularized in the 1960s, may be epitomized by the following question: if American-style liberalism solves the major problems of the twentieth century, then what

[53] Daniel Bell: "These theoretical foundations of modern liberal society were completed by Kant, who, separating legality and morality, defined the former as the 'rules of the game' so to speak; law dealt with procedural, not substantive issues" ("Passion" 61). See Habermas for the classic statement on the rules of discourse implicit to the theory of the public sphere.

[54] The "end of ideology" arguments put forth by Daniel Bell and others in the late 1950s and early 1960s lumped together fascism and Stalinism under the rubric of totalitarianism. Bell argued that the old twentieth-century ideologies, fascist and communist, led to the end of history in the form of the concentration camps and the gulag; he also believed that the unprecedented economic expansion fuelled by American capitalism had solved most of the social problems targeted by Marxist ideology and fascism anyway. Hence, right thinking people, i.e. liberals, were supposed to be technicians of improvement, beyond ideology and beyond millennial or apocalyptic thinking ("End" 88).

are we to make of racism at home and imperialism abroad? To expose the gaping oversights of those preaching the separation of the political from the personal, and to reorient itself in relation to liberal anti-Communism, the New Left began to abandon old class-based arguments and the official "war on poverty" to rally around issues of race, gender, and sexuality—or what we today call identity politics.[55]

One of the factors distinguishing postwar affirmations of identity from their "reactionary" precursors is the notion that identity is itself a reaction. This way of thinking about identity is related to W.E.B. Du Bois's pioneering work on race, but in the 1940s it arrived on the American scene with the cachet of French existentialism.[56] Shapiro would later describe himself as a "negative Jew" in terms that are recognizably Sartrean. As Paul Lauter put it in a 1958 *New Republic* review: "'Jew' thus becomes for Shapiro, as for Sartre, a reflection of non-Jewish attitudes" (18). Many influential American writers besides Shapiro were strongly influenced by Sartre in the first decades following WWII. The essays comprising Sartre's *Anti-Semite and Jew* were published in *Partisan Review* and *Commentary* in the late 1940s, and then almost immediately as a monograph by Schocken. It is probably a coincidence, but nevertheless significant, that Sidney Hook's essay-length review of *Anti-Semite and Jew* appeared in the issue of *Partisan Review* featuring the symposium on the Pound award. Sartre's essays and the responses to them established the terms in which identity and individuality would be discussed for at least the following decade, and they provide a helpful context for considering the issues involved in Shapiro's rejection of Pound.

Anti-Semite and Jew builds on the dyadic models of identity as negative projection developed in *Being and Nothingness*.[57] "If the Jew did not exist, the

---

55 For a brief account of the emergence of identity-based thinking on the left see Hobsbawm. For an early account of the "white supremacist culture" in the United States and the link between American racism and the war in Vietnam, see Frank Joyce (133, 141). See also Peter Irons for an early account on the link between racism at home and imperialism abroad.

56 See W.E.B. Du Bois's reflections on "the veil" and "double-consciousness" in *The Souls of Black Folk*. His *Dusk of Dawn*, originally published in 1940, reformulates "the veil" in the more contemporary metaphor of "plate glass" and discusses the relation of identity to individuality in a way that directly anticipates Sartre: "Practically, this imprisonment within a group has various effects upon the prisoner [...]. He thinks of himself not as an individual but as a group man, a 'race' man" (132).

57 Sartre famously argues that the Other is implicit in the constitution of the self: "Here the appearance of the Other is indispensable not to the constitution of the world and of my empirical 'Ego' but to the very existence of my consciousness as self-consciousness [...]. The equation 'Myself=Myself' or 'I am I' is precisely the expression of this fact" (*Being and Nothingness* 319).

anti-Semite would invent him" (*Anti-Semite* 13). However, Sartre goes to great lengths to point out that anti-Semitism, unlike individual passions of hate or love, cannot be reduced to an isolated interaction between self and other. In order to address the collective nature of anti-Semitism, he confronts the materiality of what he calls the "identity of situation" (85, 145). Jews, no matter what their individual qualities and achievements, are subjected as a group to systematic insult and exclusion. It is the systemic nature of anti-Semitism that constitutes Jews as a group apart and deprives them of the equality—really a form of anonymity—that is supposed to be the right of individuals in a liberal society (101). Those anti-racists Sartre calls democrats or liberals miss the collective nature of this identity, and the common situation that produces it, because they can conceive of people only as abstract, equal individuals (55–58). Sartre's definition of the "identity of situation" is an attempt to navigate between the extremes of racism and liberalism—the anti-Semite denying the common humanity of his victim in order to excoriate the Jew, and the liberal denying Jewishness in order to promote universal rights. Identity does not stem from common nature but from a common situation (67). Jews are "overdetermined" as Jews, condemned to be members of a subordinate group by social, historical and political forces beyond individual control (78–79).

Few during the Cold War accepted Sartre's concluding argument that a classless society would alleviate anti-Semitism, in the end rendering inconsequential and perhaps even non-existent the difference between Gentiles and Jews (149). Sartre was also resoundingly criticized for his negative model of identity, which reduces Jewishness to a mere reflection of anti-Semitic stereotypes (although Shapiro, for one, would embrace negative Jewishness).[58] However, Sartre's insistence on the social significance of identity as an index of inequality resonated with liberal thinkers trying to grapple with the reality of genocide, and with the possible links between the European catastrophe and racism in the United States. Contemporary definitions of identity—whether derived from models of interpellation, discipline or performativity—have by and large remained true to the Sartrean principle of overdetermination or extrinsic group derivation. Identity, as the term is currently applied in cultural and literary studies, is less a matter of self-discovery than it is an expression

[58] In her preface to the 1967 edition of *The Origins of Totalitarianism*, Hannah Arendt remarks on the popularity of Sartre's definition, at the same time commenting on its unfortunate propagation of the "myth" that "Jewish self-consciousness was ever a mere creation of anti-Semitism" (xv). She does, however, admit the reverse dynamic when she points out that the "tribal nationalism" of the early national socialists merely inverts a misconception of Jewish "chosenness" (242–43).

of external social and cultural relations. Another way to put this is that identity is not individual, not an expression of the "I"; it is the personification of socially determined plural constructions such as "they" and "we" (cf. Simpson 217).

In sum, identity and individualism are convenient nomenclatures for two intersecting sets of beliefs that come into recurrent conflict in the second half of the twentieth century, revealing what appears to be one of the fundamental problems of liberalism.[59] I want to stress that identity and individualism are not opposing concepts, but placeholders for overlapping assumptions that are polarized in moments of political crisis. Individualism can, of course, be constitutive of identity-claims, as in the exceptionalist argument that Americans are more individualistic than Europeans. However, if, like Dwight Macdonald, you believe in the separation of art from politics, form from content, you do not believe that identity should be a significant political, and perhaps not even a cultural, factor. If, like the early Shapiro, you believe that identity is an important cultural and political factor, then you do not believe in the separation of form from content, and Pound's poetry is an expression of his anti-Semitism. Individualism is a principle of personal or expressive freedom guaranteed by a framework of political equality. Identity is a metaphor expressing how individuals, as social beings, are made to embody structures of political and cultural inequality overlooked by individualism. Individualism's conception of freedom is negative in relation to the group and positive in relation to the self; it leaves room for personal expression, regardless of its content, by insisting on the formal and procedural significance of free speech. Identity's conception of freedom is positive in relation to the group and negative in relation to the self, demanding the recognition of differences between social groups that are personified in their individual members. Individualism is the basic tenet of postwar liberalism, which separates the political sphere from the cultural sphere, believes in oppositional culture and supports Pound in spite of what he stands for. Identity is what might be called a full-blooded abstraction, attempting to make visible those complex social and cultural relations that determine individual lives without being reducible to individual choices. The liberal intellectual trend in the second-half of the twentieth century would move from individualism to identity. Shapiro dissented.[60]

---

[59] On the overlapping theories of individualism and identity, see Johannes Voelz's book, *Transcendental Resistance,* especially chapter three.

[60] My reflections on the relation of individualism to identity in this paragraph derive from several sources. For the classic formulation on how political liberalism attempts to regulate the competing demands of liberty and equality see John Rawls. David Riesman attempts to define individualism as limited liberty, recognizing as early as

Identity as Confession

Would it be possible to see Shapiro as a trendsetter? More famous poets such as Lowell, Plath, and Berryman wrote "as Jews" in the postwar years—even though they were not Jewish. These more successful cases of assumed identity, which I explore at greater length in the final chapter, should give us pause. It is difficult to think of Shapiro as exerting the kind of influence exercised by these poets; the literary history of midcentury poetry has the torch passing from the modernists to the confessionals, skipping the man who is remembered—if he is remembered at all—as a war poet. This genealogy says a lot about the emerging structure of identity in postwar verse and its troubled relation to the modernist legacy.

After WWII, anti-Semitism and fascism had a proper name in American poetry: Pound. Many poets writing in the 1950s felt indebted to Pound's style but rejected his politics, identifying with the victims of modernity and not with those high modernists who seemed to condone political cruelty. These problems of divided allegiance are usually described in terms of a generational struggle. Lowell rebels against the poetic impersonality of Pound and Eliot by discovering his personality, and it is precisely in the way this personality is at odds with received values that we see what is wrong with contemporary politics and modernist aesthetics.[61]

Personality, in this formulation, is understood to be the victim of history rather than the author of a tradition. Thus early explicators of confessional poetry picked out victim-identification as one of the distinguishing features of confessional voice. What might be called the standard narrative of confessional poetry treats voice as a symptom of history. A. Alvarez, M. L. Rosenthal and Robert Phillips (now literary executor for Shapiro's work) were already making this psycho-historical argument in the 1960s and 1970s, and

1954 the emergence of the concept of "cultural conditioning" that modulates individualism in terms of identity (38). Charles Taylor recognizes that identity depends on difference, or the incommensurability of the needs and values of disparate social groups, but he tries to reconcile this difference with the concept of a more fundamental equality: "To come together on a mutual recognition of difference—that is, of the equal value of different identities—requires that we share more than a belief in this principle; we have to share also some standards of value on which the identities concerned checked out as equal" (52). This is tantamount to redefining identity not as the limit of individualism but as the basic principle of individualism.

61 Diane Wood Middlebrook in "What Was Confessional Poetry?": "Confessional poetry was not overtly political, but it participated in the protest against impersonality as a poetic value by reinstating an insistently autobiographical first person engaged in resistance to the pressure to conform" (635). Others, such as Alan Williamson, argue that it is precisely the personal that is public or political in Lowell (3–4).

it has been picked up more recently by scholars like Hilene Flanzbaum and Susan Gubar, who approach confessional poetry from the perspectives of Jewish studies and trauma theory.[62] The victim-centered approach is useful for explaining why Lowell "discovers" his identity in *Life Studies* (*CP* 109–92), a book including "91 Revere Street," a long prose passage speculating on his possible—but distant—Jewish ancestry. Sylvia Plath, his most famous student, would later and even more famously begin to dissect her relationship with her father using figures of Nazis and Jews. John Berryman, certainly a member of the "middle generation" if not necessarily a confessional, was preoccupied for much of his career with the figure of the "imaginary Jew," as I explore in the final chapter. A significant strand of postwar poetry discovers its identity when it begins to identify with Jews, and especially Jewish victims. In terms of the liberal tension between individualism and identity, this poetry moves away from subjectivism towards group affiliation, in spite of the fact that its primary authors are not Jewish. At its extreme, in poems by Berryman and Plath—Randall Jarrell might also fit here—the poetry is elegiac, forging its distinctive voice through a form of prosopopoeia, the identification with those murdered in concentration camps (Gubar 181–89).

I think the standard account of confessionalism as victim-oriented poetry is correct, but it does not tell the whole story. Confessional poets identify with the victims of history without completely rejecting the authors of the modernist tradition. This double alignment often expresses itself in troubled relations to politically abhorrent figures, as when Plath locates Nazis within her poetic family tree. It is also worth considering the example of William Snodgrass, whose "Heart's Needle" is often cited as inaugurating the confessional style, and who spent decades writing tortured lyrics depicting the final days of the Third Reich, finally collected in *The Fuehrer Bunker*. Those who knew Lowell remarked on his ambivalent fascination with victims and perpetrators. Alfred Kazin reports that Lowell had mixed feelings about Jewish refugees, and Lowell's biographer Ian Hamilton writes of his obsession with Nazism during his early manic phases, an obsession which produced

---

[62] M. L. Rosenthal's influential 1967 definition of the confessional poet is the "individual as a *victim*" (*New Poets* 15). For Rosenthal and his contemporaries, the act of poetic confession forges the link between the individual "experience of reality" and "symbolic embodiment of national and cultural crisis" (13). Robert Phillips takes the personal trauma of the victim-poet to be symptomatic of larger social dynamics. Society is sick, in other words, but only poets can admit it (*Confessional* xi–xiii). A. Alvarez is interested in how the assault on individuality by totalitarianism and mass society makes "men and women […] as equal and identity-less as objects on an assembly line," producing an "anonymity of pain" ("Plath" 65). Plath and the other confessionals write from this position of damaged subjectivity.

an uncollected and virtually unreadable parody called "Adolf Hitler von Linz (Siegfried)," which Lowell may have enclosed in a letter to Pound (Kazin, *New York Jew* 191; Hamilton 210–12).[63]

Confessional poetry identifies with the victims of history, but it also confesses its indebtedness to the modernist avant-garde. It is this split allegiance or double determination that produces its characteristic voice. In confessional poetry, as in the theories of identity emerging after WWII, identity is plural before it becomes singular, articulating first social groupings and then the "I" as its expression, symptom or personification. This double or plural structure is evident not only in confessional poetry's ambivalence towards high modernism, but in its relation to a fundamental crisis of postwar liberalism. Kazin suggests as much when he remarks that Lowell's "'confessional' mode" suited "an age merciless with guilt," by which he means the alleged guilt of liberals suspected of harboring communist sympathies in the 1950s (*New York Jew* 205).[64] This link between confessional verse and the "confessions" of former communists is based on more than a terminological convergence. What Kazin points towards, without fully explaining, is an emerging structure of postwar identity, one pegging identity to social and historical forces beyond individual control. Harold Rosenberg offers a contemporary account of this emergent identity, arguing that the "liberal we" of repenting ex-communists was actually a Cold War fabrication, most often articulated by those with the least to confess (*Tradition* 228). Rosenberg's point is that the real or imagined misdeeds of supposed ex-communists were never as significant as the defunct groups they served to stigmatize (radicals) and the new groups they helped to define (liberal anti-communists) (224). The "I" is secondary and articulates positions already outlined by the "we"; the confessional speech act voices the creed of a confessional community.

Midcentury modernists identified with the victims of modernity in the same way, although for different reasons, that ex-communists became anticommunists. This is not to imply that confessional poetry has a particular political orientation; at issue here is its articulation of a common political problem. Confessional poetry responded to the crisis of liberalism by articulating liberalism's guilty conscience. This is true in the trivial sense that poetry—including the poetry of political conservatives—played a key and often dissenting role in liberal publications like *Partisan Review*, a dissent that

63 Hannah Arendt's assessment of Lowell in a private letter to Mary McCarthy: "Cal: No, I don't think either that he is manic. The Hitler-thing is bad precisely because it never was just sickness" (Arendt and McCarthy, *Between Friends* 260).

64 Norman Mailer says that Lowell, during the anti-Vietnam War march on the Pentagon, seems to bear with him the guilt of his ancestors (*Armies of the Night* 99).

could easily be mobilized for the purposes of Cold War propaganda.[65] However, it is also true in a profounder sense linking liberalism and lyricism in the politics of culture and form. Stretched between Pound's technique, the gift that midcentury poets could not refuse, and the anathema of Pound's politics, confessionalism identifies with victims without abandoning the tradition that excluded them. The confessionals were not right-wing poets (Lowell, the scourge of Yaddo, also protested against Vietnam): their emphasis on identity also laid the groundwork for the New Left response to the limits of the old left, a response replacing the class rhetoric compromised by anticommunism with the discourse of identity.[66] It would be exaggerated to claim that confessional poetry invented identity, but it is one of the first places where the liberal reevaluation of identity emerges as voice. In other words, confessional poetry appears to be the switching point where individualism, with its commitment to unique personality, metamorphoses into identity, understood as the personification of historically defined groups.

An early example is Lowell's "Falling Asleep over the Aeneid," a poem telescoping real and mythical conflicts, from the implied context of WWII to the Civil War to the Trojan War, in an attempt to highlight the element common to all of them: violence. In what is possibly an extended reference to Simone Weil's "The Iliad, or the Poem of Force" (published in Dwight Macdonald's *Politics*, one of the few journals during WWII serving as a forum for conscientious objectors), the poem isolates violence as a force capable of transforming subjects into objects (soldiers into corpses) and objects into subjects (swords into bloodthirsty avengers). At the crux of the poem Dido's sword "tries to speak" (Lowell 91). This near-personification is preparatory to the speaker's finally waking up to his own identity after the poem's central caesura: "It is I" (93). The object—it—here literally becomes the subject, and while the poem deliberately blurs the pronominal reference (does "it" refer to war? The grandfather? His picture? The boy in the dream?), this seems part of the larger project of tracing the genesis of the "I" as the product and personification of various historical forces. Identity is not a matter of self-discovery in this poem; it is a subject position generated by war, and by the

[65] Robert von Hallberg has argued that the lyric was the privileged form of Cold War poetry because it was taken to demonstrate the individualism supposed to be at the heart of democratic freedom, even—or perhaps especially—in its criticism of the mass society of which it was a part (25–26). Also see Edward Brunner.

[66] Alan Brinkley points to the literature of alienation of the 1950s as inspiring the protest movements of the 1960s, which focused on those problems deemed "irrational" by an earlier generation of leftists, such as race and ethnicity (100, 228). The decisive role Brinkley assigns to the literature of alienation I attribute to confessionalism, the poetry of identity.

centrality of war and classical fantasies of violence in modernist and contemporary verse. Other poems in *The Mills of the Kavanaughs* (1951) (*CP* 71–107) also signal that the "I" is the personification of various historical, social, and cultural forces. Hence the insistent questioning throughout the volume: "Who am I?" "This I […] it is not I" (83, 93, 103).

This volume is generally underestimated in Lowell criticism, perhaps because it does not confirm the prevailing consensus that *Life Studies* marks the emergence of Lowell's more personal voice (cf. Williamson 8). I would argue, however, that a closer reading of *Mills* shows that identity emerges as a historical or social structure before that structure is filled by voice, in much the same way that the first poem of *Life Studies*, "Beyond the Alps," depicting the "berth" or birth of the speaker, takes its title from a phrase in "Falling Asleep" (*Collected* 114). Personality, in Lowell, is the personification of history, or what one critic calls "history's autobiography" (Corn). It is into this structure of historically determined identity that Lowell would later pour speculations about his Jewish ancestry; poets following him would identify with various minority groups as actual or surrogate members. This poetry of identity preceded and helped pave the way for identity politics, which mobilizes the collective structure of lyrical voice for the purposes of protest.

Shapiro's Elegy for Identity

"Falling Asleep over the Aeneid" is the final poem in *The Oxford Book of American Verse* (1950), indicating what editor F. O. Matthiessen saw as the future direction of American poetry. The introduction to the anthology plots the course of the new verse by orienting itself in relation to Pound. Matthiessen's basic editorial principle is not to excerpt from longer poems, but he deliberately breaks his own rule to include the famous lyrical passage from Canto 81 of *The Pisan Cantos*, which appeared shortly before his anthology went to press ("What thou lovest well remains, / the rest is dross […]. Pull down thy vanity, I say pull down" [81/540–41]). Matthiessen misread this passage as a confession (xiii). I say misread because nowhere in *The Pisan Cantos* is Pound apologetic for his numerous pro-fascist and anti-Semitic utterances, although Matthiessen wanted to see him as having learned from past mistakes.

Even if Matthiessen's assumption is wrong, the trajectory he draws from Pound's wished-for confession to the poetry that would soon be called confessional does establish the major players and concepts in what would rapidly become the standard genealogy of midcentury verse. Richard Ellmann's revised edition of 1976, *The New Oxford Book of American Verse*, describes the relation between the high modernists and Lowell (whom he links to Ginsberg) in this way: "If Eliot and Pound were covertly autobiographical when they pretended not to be, their more autobiographical descendants were covertly archetypal, as if the universe were confessing through them" (xxix–xxx). This claim about universals and archetypes can be translated into the slightly scaled-down language of history and types: Pound's tradition confesses personality in the same way Lowell's personality confesses history. The point of intersection anchoring this chiasmus is personification—a figure establishing a lyrical relation between personal voice and the larger whole.

Matthiessen allotted more pages to Shapiro than to Lowell. Ellmann's anthology dropped Shapiro entirely. This revision of a major anthology is useful for dating Shapiro's fall from fame; and in fact shortly before the appearance of the Ellmann anthology Shapiro published a poem titled "My Fame's Not Feeling Too Well" (*Selected* 158). While the difference between the two anthologies undoubtedly points to a general reassessment of Shapiro's work, I think it also hints at a change in Shapiro's style. It seems to me that Shapiro's later poetry was at odds with the kind of personification favored by Ellmann, who consequently cast a more critical eye on his earlier work. The early poems anthologized by Matthiessen (and many other midcentury editors) do suggest a model of lyrical identity compatible with archetypes and larger historical forces.

Shapiro's widely anthologized "Elegy for a Dead Soldier" is a case in point, one that offers a useful comparison to Lowell's "Falling Asleep." Shapiro's elegy, like Lowell's poem, pushes the highly individuated voice into an expression of impersonal or collective identity—only what for Lowell is clearly a confession of identity is for Shapiro an expression of hope. Shapiro's hope would soon be disappointed by the liberal defense of Pound. Ironically, when he turned away from identity it was to turn back towards the individualism of his opponents, first as a matter of prosody—largely through a critique of personification—and only later as a matter of politics.

The unknown GI mourned in "Elegy for a Dead Soldier" is not a hero but an accidental casualty who may have been a suicide (*Younger Son* 237). The speaker supplements his ignorance of the circumstances surrounding the soldier's death by imagining his character. He feels justified in speaking "for" him based on their common situation and above all their common fear: death could befall any soldier in the field, the poet included. Speaking for the soldier is an attempt to redeem his death from statistical irrelevance. However, since Shapiro did not actually know the man, speaking for him also involves speculation and even impersonation, implicating the poem in a pronoun Shapiro rarely used ("we") and a figure he always mistrusted (personification): "We too are ashes as we watch and hear / The psalm, the sorrow, and the simple praise / Of one whose promised thoughts of other days / Were such as ours" (*V-Letter* 42). Although the poem—as Shapiro insists—is not gung-ho, the portrait it provides of the soldier is hardly more personal than the image on a recruiting poster (*Younger Son* 237). Shapiro wants to commemorate the dead soldier as "one," but to do so he has to imagine him as a type of the "we" (*V-Letter* 43). What he buries in his verse is a personification of this type.

However, the type he imagines is not exactly somebody with whom he can identify. There are positive "American" qualities such as self-reliance, but also a willful political ignorance and a penchant for violence, as evidenced by the dead man's sporting interest in gang warfare (*V-Letter* 45). The soldier, as the poem imagines him, was not fighting for world peace so much as generalized self-interest: he goes to war to bring prosperity to the United States in what the poem accurately predicts will be a period of postwar economic expansion (44). The image describing progress is a geographical one in keeping with the peripatetic poetry I analyze in the previous chapter: "the Lincoln Highway of a land / Remorselessly improved." The ominous adverb suggests that the highway of progress may be less than ideal; indeed, it may very well be segregated as the soldier-driver is also a racist: "He hated other races, south or east, / And shoved them to the margins of his mind" (45). The speaker may feel solidarity with him in the field, perhaps even sympathize with his American dream, but he can hardly identify with his prejudice, which Shapiro angrily criticizes in the other poems of the period such as "University."

Nevertheless the soldier's efforts, no matter how self-interested, could play a role in bringing about "Whole toleration or pure peace," and the poem, in keeping with elegiac conventions, invokes this kingdom-come in its vision of the future (45). The poem is laden with Christian imagery, but it distances itself from dogmatism, deliberately contrasting the architecture of belief with the absurdities of war. It draws attention, for instance, to the makeshift altar made out of a tailgate; it invokes the architrave of an imaginary cathedral only to collapse it into "columns" of soldiers who "come together through the mud"; and it openly questions the doctrine of "rebirth" (42). This theological doubt leads, however, to a cautious political utopianism. The concluding epitaph is conditional, addressed to visitors who might come upon the grave at a time of "peace kept by a human creed." It is this peace that has the potential to redeem the soldier from having "died in vain"—the emphasis of this final line underscored by its rhyme with "Remember that this stranger died in pain" (46).

The military grave has no tombstone, so the epitaph does double duty as a crypt. Shapiro was always fascinated with crypts and with what he called the "cryptic sayings on the crypt" (*Younger Son* 93). The structure of the elegy plays upon the double meaning signaled by Shapiro's parallelism: a crypt as something buried and cryptic as something secret. It does so by locating the meaning of life in a series of spaces or termini inaccessible to the deceased but open to the poet-hierophant. The first of these is the peaceful world the soldier may inadvertently help bring about but which he will never see. The second space is the inside of the tomb, whose significance is revealed not by the dead man, who cannot speak, but by the poet who speaks for him. The lyrical voice is a composite of these spaces or a kind of echo chamber of the past and future. That is to say, the poem speaks from the locus where the conceptual axes formed between the two sets of cryptic spaces intersect: the first axis between the present world and the world-to-come, and the second axis between poetic interiority and the interior of the tomb. The first axis makes personification possible as a form of utopianism, and the second as a form of haunting or possession. The poet, in speaking for the dead, also channels him in a process of identification and internalization Freud linked to mourning.[67] As I have already pointed out, Shapiro cannot completely identify with the soldier as he portrays him, so the poem has difficulty moving from the "it might have been me" that authorizes speaking for the soldier to the "he died for me" implicit in the epitaph. But the conditional quality of the elegiac voice allows the speaker to identify with the soldier provisionally, and to address the hypothetical tourists as fellow citizens in the peaceful world of the future.

"Elegy for a Dead Soldier" approximates identification in the same way Lowell's sword in "Falling Asleep Over the Aeneid" almost speaks. The poem approaches what would soon become the conventions of confessional voice, the speaker merging his own "I" with the "I" of the soldier in a tolerant, postwar "we." The poem expresses a liberal longing for a world in which identification is possible because irrelevant. Sartre, in his Marxist phase, thought the redistribution of wealth would end prejudice; Shapiro, the soldier, hoped that allied victory would make it possible for even a racist to die for a Jew. The cryptic structures of the poem work to transform soldierly solidarity and the conventions of remembrance into equitable social space; later, Shapiro would remark that self-identifying as a Jew was similar to being inducted into the army ("Jewish Writer" 300). What is distinctive about "Elegy for a Dead Soldier" is the way it puts lyricism to work for liberalism in precisely the manner denied by liberal critics mounting a free-speech defense of Pound. Shapiro speaks for the dead soldier, a racist and perhaps a suicide, in order to be able to speak as a Jew. The interpretive bridge Shapiro would demand as a reader of Pound is here realized in the cryptic space of identity—a space

---

[67] For the "Identifizierung des Ichs mit dem aufgegebenen Objekt" see Sigmund Freud, "Trauer und Melancholie" (203).

opening up at the intersection of past and future, racist and Jew, war and tolerance.

Shapiro decrypted his identity when he spoke out as a Jew against the Pound award. He had not made a secret of his Jewishness before, but the liberal defense of Pound moved Shapiro from speculations about tolerance to identity-based criticism and protest. However, the need to protest identity seems to have rendered Shapiro's cryptic speculations about tolerance irrelevant. Thus he begins to doubt the significance of identity after speaking out as a Jew: As Leslie Fiedler put it in *Waiting for the End*, "his [Shapiro's] awareness of himself as a Jew is reaching a vanishing point, when the gesture of rejection seems his last possible connection with his historical past" (65–66). Within a decade of the Pound award Shapiro began to attack identity in essays like "American Poet?" and "The Jewish Writer in America." He was particularly skeptical of the way his students began to "discover" their identities in the 1960s, famously disparaging such notions in the essays "To Abolish Children" and "The Poetry Wreck" and in his roman-à-clef, *Edsel* (1971), to the extent of calling hippies and black militants "Nazis."[68] This shift is useful for reading literary history against the grain, but how to explain it in terms of Shapiro's career?

Shapiro's late rejection of identity seems pegged to an article of liberalism he never challenged, namely the argument about personification as a misplaced literary figure. Shapiro used personification in some of his early poems, but in a cryptic and provisional way; and in fact he always viewed lyrical voice as "sublimely" indifferent to history and politics, an attitude he began prescribing for American poetry as early as his 1945 verse essay, *Essay on Rime* (30). It is in this exploration of contemporary poetry that Shapiro first criticizes Auden for personifying history and geography in an unsuccessful attempt to make up for his lack of an "authentically" personal or individual voice (42).[69]

---

68 In "The Poetry Wreck" Shapiro says, "There is no question in my mind that the identity crusaders are the villains of the cultural upheaval and can be held accountable for the dissolution of educational standards and values in this country" (261). In "To Abolish Children," he accuses both "Negro looters" and "WASP children in posh suburbs" of "play[ing] Nazi" (337). *Edsel* repeatedly parodies a poet clearly modeled on Ginsberg.

69 See also the passages on how style is an index of personality, how Auden separates personality from style, and how the modern malady is one of multiple personalities (*Essay* 33–35). Shapiro claims that the absence of personality or style leads to national or epic verse (66–67). Many critics were impressed that Shapiro would attempt such a comprehensive assessment of contemporary poetry while stationed on an island in the Pacific, far from any library. Shapiro's mentor William Van O'Connor, who would later co-edit *A Casebook on Ezra Pound*, quotes Shapiro's *Essay on Rime* at length on the problems of national or epic verse, and shares his preference for the personal as opposed to the personified in modern poetry (*Sense* 29–30). However, the opinions expressed

Shapiro respected Auden and would later write two Auden elegies, which I will turn to in a moment. But he felt that Auden succumbed in his struggle against the high modernists, Eliot and Pound, when he consented to employ their trademark trope of personification or what Shapiro consistently called prosopopoeia.[70] Why the vehemence about a literary trope? I would argue that when Shapiro objects to the personified poetry he sees as impersonal, he is actually rejecting modernist impersonality; i.e. the convention of speaking for the tradition and at the expense of those excluded from it (Eliot's Bleistein, Pound's Blum, etc.). This argument against personification as a misplaced or dangerous literary figure is similar to the one articulated by Harold Rosenberg, and in fact Shapiro cites Rosenberg in his attempt to explore the complex relation between personification and racism ("Jewish Writer" 300). The anti-Semite sees the Jew as the personification of evil; Shapiro affirms his Jewishness but rejects personification. This is the dynamic at work in his concept of negative identity—a concept that would eventually lead him to embrace an individualism virtually indistinguishable from that of the liberal critics who defended Pound.

The negative model of identity was widespread in the 1950s. Rosenberg can again serve as a guide here—particularly his "Jewish Identity in a Free Society," published in *Commentary* in 1950.[71] Rosenberg understands fixed group identity, or what he calls "the super-personal collective 'I,'" to be fundamentally orthodox and totalitarian—terms that he views as roughly synonymous. He lumps together Stalin, Eliot and—even more provocatively—conservative Jewish leaders in his general indictment of all demands for individuals to commit to stable identities, whether communist or Anglican or Jewish (509–10). What Rosenberg understands as "authentic" Jewishness (the term comes from Sartre) is more personal and contingent than collective Jewish identity. His example of the authentic Jew is the refugee from Nazism, who is forced to adopt a contingent sense of self Rosenberg calls the "*naturalized* ego": "it is not native to him; he has acquired it as an immigrant acquires citizenship in the country of his option" (508). Jewish refugees serve a double function in Rosenberg's argument, providing a concrete example of immigrants undergoing naturalization, but also serving as allegorical figures for how authentic identity emerges generally. In this liberal definition of the ego,

---

in the verse essay met with mixed reviews. Delmore Schwartz, for instance, dismissed the volume as an extended exercise in anti-intellectualism ("Karl Shapiro's Poetics" 498).

70 See also Shapiro's essay, "The Retreat of W. H. Auden," and his blurb on Auden in *Prose Keys to Modern Poetry* (200).

71 See also Sidney Hook's description of negative identity in his review of Sartre (475) and Irving Kristol's definition of Judaism as an "existential religion" (28).

Jewishness is a metonymy for the process by which all identities are actually acquired through compromise and adaptation; Jewishness is not a metaphor for a particular identity. The naturalized ego is a migrant, alienated but also free, whose membership in any given society depends not on remembering traditions or embodying ideals, but in consenting to live according to basic principles.

What Shapiro means by negative Jewishness would increasingly resemble Rosenberg's notion of the naturalized ego. This concept of Jewishness as metonymy for individualism rather than as metaphor for fixed identity was common at a time when certain Bellow and Roth characters were seen as synonymous with modern alienation; but it was eclipsed as poets began to "confess" their identities, almost always in idioms carried over from modernism. Ethnic identity, sexual identity and gender identity would all find their poets and theorists, who despite considerable phenotypic and experiential differences were "super-personal" in their orientation. Shapiro might be seen as one of the initiators of this trend, but after the Pound controversy he would swim against the stream, returning to a more classically liberal definition of selfhood as a set of individual choices. What underwrites Shapiro's shift from identity to individualism is a negative model of Jewishness that activates identity as a polemical position, and a utopian one, but only fleetingly makes it available as a subject position or origin of voice. Shapiro rejects identity in the name of Jewishness, which he understands as a metonymy for individualism.

Shapiro's Jewish individualism is non-dogmatic to the point of apostasy. Many of the poems in *Poems of a Jew* describe moments of declension or near-conversion, as when "The Crucifix in the Filing Cabinet" concludes by storing a cross in a tefillin bag (*Collected* 152). Such outrages quickly become pro forma and polemical, and if they indicate a dead end in terms of lyrical innovation, they also hint at the future stations in Shapiro's career, namely his prosody textbooks and angry essays.[72] His prose poems in particular—written throughout his career but especially featured in *The Bourgeois Poet*—point toward the polemics that would increase his notoriety as his fame was fading. But in fact all his formal experiments can be understood as props in arguments, from the sonnets in *White-Haired Lover* meant to demonstrate that quinquagenarians can fall in love, to the rigid structure in "Sestina: of the Militant Vocabulary," which deploys formal repetition to show how anti-establishment discourse leads lockstep to a new establishmentarianism (*Collected* 323–24).

To explore the lyrical structure of this negative form of identity, and its increasing estrangement from the model of identity prevalent in what Shapiro

[72] Two of Shapiro's many studies on prosody: *English Prosody and Modern Poetry* (1947); *A Prosody Handbook* (1965).

called the poetry "Establishment," I will conclude by considering Shapiro's late elegy "At Auden's Grave." This elegy has the last word in the final volume of his autobiography *Reports of My Death*, and thus can be understood as Shapiro's elegy for himself (as signaled by the title of the book) and as a personal commentary on his disappearance from the anthologies. Shapiro did not write many elegies, but he valued the mode and considered it particularly appropriate to modernity, which he believed to be indifferent to poetry (*Reports* 265). In *Younger Son*, the first volume of his autobiography, Shapiro argues that "Poetry was all elegiac" and that "That was what Auden meant when he said poetry makes nothing happen" (51). This is a curious assessment because Shapiro uses the same phrase to condemn the supporters of Pound in the second volume of the autobiography: "It was all right for poets to hate Jews, because they were poets and said that poetry makes nothing happen" (*Reports* 43). In both instances, the reference to Auden's "In Memory of W. B. Yeats" converts a poet's elegy for another poet into poetry's elegy for its own irrelevance. Juxtaposing Shapiro's two elegies shows how the poet lived up (or down) to his diagnosis. He began by writing activist verse employing lyricism for the purposes of liberalism; but by the end of his career he resigned himself—and poetry—to permanent exile and insignificance, inadvertently affirming the cultural autonomy that Pound's defenders had maintained all along, and retreating from the dream of utopian identity (when a racist soldier could die for a Jew) to resigned individualism.

Shapiro's outrage over the Pound controversy did not diminish over his lifetime. It was still foremost in his mind when in the 1980s he traveled with his wife Sophie Wilkins, the translator of Robert Musil's *The Man without Qualities*, to the small Austrian town Kirchstetten to visit Auden's grave, not far from the house where the older poet summered for the last sixteen years of his life. Auden detested Pound's politics but voted in favor of the Bollingen Award. Shapiro would later claim that Auden urged him to do likewise with the rationalization "Everyone is anti-Semitic sometimes" (*Reports* 266). Shapiro's recollection of this incident moves him to apostrophize Auden in the following lines:

> I call you Wystan, as I did then
> In the days of the terrible Bollingen Prize
> In the days of the moral dilemma we never solved. (266)

These lines are metrically uninteresting, but they form the kernel of the elegy "At Auden's Grave" as Shapiro describes writing it in *Reports of My Death*. The final version of the elegy, which has the last word in the autobiography, excises this passage and all mention of the moral dilemma, but without solving it. Instead, the elegy refigures the silent argument Shapiro has been having with Auden for forty years by focusing on another, related argument—the one about prosopopoeia. Shapiro revives his old critique about Auden's dependence on the figure in his introduction to the elegy, in part because he was confronted with a surprising fact when visiting Kirchstetten (*Reports* 266). The town named a street after the poet: *Audenstraße*. The speaker of the poem is fascinated by this commemorative "mating" of English and German (repeated in a sense by Shapiro's own marriage) and even more so by Auden's "becoming" eponymous, which he designates with the verb made famous in Auden's elegy of Yeats (275). Auden has made something happen. He has lent his name to a place: "now the mask outworn / The geographical visage consummated" (276). This shift from the modernist persona or mask to geographical consummation suggests, at first glance, that Auden's use of prosopopoeia—his tendency to "personify physical areas" (266)—has been vindicated by history. Thus the poem ends by "blessing" the "Poet who made poetry whole again," and it takes advantage of enjambment to capitalize—and personify—History as an agent: "over his grave / A cross, a battle monument, and a name / History will polish to a shrine" (277).

But whose name? A shrine to what? The answers to these seemingly obvious questions are left deliberately vague. Part of the problem is that Auden does not seem to belong in this village. Although he summered there during his final years, he remained in his lifetime a "country man / Without a country" and "urban bard / Without a city" (275). There is a sense of exile in death as well, not only because Auden's grave seems out of place in this country churchyard, but because it is within sight of a cenotaph for the lost Austrian soldiers of WWI. Another cenotaph is mentioned: Auden's own in Westminster Abbey, next to Eliot's. The discursive field of the poem opens in the cenotaphic space between memorial and grave, a space of exile and alienation where loss is compounded by distance.

It is because of the cenotaphic convention of separating memorial from crypt that we do not know whose name will be turned into a shrine by "History." The cab driver who chauffeurs the speaker to the cemetery certainly does not know where to find Auden's grave, so the speaker begins by asking for directions at a *Gasthaus* (277). Asking for directions is the mundane version of the central problem of the poem, which restates the partially repressed "moral dilemma" in geographical terms. *Quo vadis*? The poem does not seem to know where it is going. In a way "At Auden's Grave" is more peripatetic than elegiac; *Audenstraße* does not name a shrine so much as a trajectory that only accelerates as the poem progresses. The speaker begins on a train, shifts to a taxi and concludes by mentioning the Autobahn and a NATO fighter. "Elegy for a Dead Soldier" stresses points of intersection, the cryptic structure of identity bringing together politics and poetry in a tolerant space of the future. The vectors in "At Auden's Grave" are overlapping but non-intersecting; they exacerbate the distance between poetry and politics, with the slightly ominous geopolitical implications signaled by the jet plane.

Shapiro's ongoing discussion with Auden over the political significance of poetry—the bridge between poetry and politics—has become a problem of endless trajectories and impossible mourning. The NATO jet executes the final word of the elegy, and the autobiography, with all possible expediency: "gone." This does not signal dismissal or closure, except perhaps as wishful thinking. The poem is full of figures of exile and displacement, and they have no end in the way Shapiro's argument with Auden never seems to end, despite the death of the interlocutor. In his earlier Auden elegy "W.H.A.," Shapiro had argued that Auden's death "enhanced" other poets, leaving a space in which they could write (Shapiro, *Collected* 281). Here the space left behind is pathological, empty and endlessly traversed by figures, structures and arguments that are themselves displacements and displacements of displacements. To point to one other example: Shapiro transforms Auden's "valley of [poetry's] making"—where it "makes nothing happen" in the Yeats elegy—into the "vale" where Auden lies (Auden, *Collected* 248). This is also, of course, the Latin "vale" of farewell—but one that has "no exits" because Auden cannot return, and because Shapiro, who never seems to stop writing Auden elegies, can never say goodbye (Shapiro, *Reports* 277). "At Auden's Grave" is not cryptic but cenotaphic; it does not perform an act of mourning, by which the dead are internalized and buried in the self, but remains suspended in what Freud called melancholia, traversing, with increasing speed and elevation, a landscape permeated with loss (Freud 199).

This problem of endless mourning also marks a retreat from the kind of identity provisionally affirmed in "Elegy for a Dead Soldier" to an individualism compatible with existential alienation—something already signaled by the reference to Sartre in the vale with *No Exit* (cf. Malin 17). The cenotaphic preoccupation of "At Auden's Grave" is worlds apart from the cryptic structure of "Elegy for a Dead Soldier." The cryptic relations of interiority that motivate prosopopoeia and make identification possible are here replaced by a displacement so extreme that death ultimately seems like another form of exile or alienation. This conflation of death and alienation, typical of existentialism, is not far removed—theoretically or historically—from the version of individualism articulated by the liberal defenders of Pound. Shapiro seems, in this poem, to have come full circle. Presented schematically, the arc of his career might look something like this: Shapiro affirms identity provisionally, as a function of tolerance, but when he is forced to identify himself as a Jew to protest the liberal defense of Pound, he loses hope in finding a space for positive identity and becomes increasingly alienated from poetic and political conventions; in the end his alienation is indistinguishable from the individualism he initially rejected. This poem, in recognition of his alienation from "Establishment" conventions, is actually a cenotaph in reverse: not an empty tomb but a voice speaking from what is not a tomb, i.e. the false "report" of a forgotten poet's death.

Shapiro cannot bury Auden, nor can he put to rest the issues of identity raised by Auden's role in awarding the Bollingen Prize to Pound. His flight from personification and identity in this poem recasts the fight he has been having with Pound, via Auden, all along. Shapiro's brief mention of personification in his introduction to the poem is actually a bit of a red herring: *Audenstraße* is eponymous, it does not personify the poet. Even the model of identity that emerges negatively in the poem—identity as a fantasy of self-unity denied by the cenotaphic structure of displacement—is different from the problem of group membership that preoccupied Shapiro for much of his career. But what is displaced through these reconfigurations, and half concealed in Shapiro's record of his revisions, is the poet's own flight from group identity. I do not believe this flight involves a reversal of principle. The shift from affirming his Jewishness during the Bollingen controversy to repressing it in this poem remains true to the conception of negative Jewishness that led Shapiro to provisionally accept the roles he felt were thrust upon him while rejecting the personification doing the thrusting. He called this his dissent from dissent, but the formulation is too vague. Shapiro was haunted by identity, and in a way that shows how current preoccupations with identity are haunted by modernism. He polemically gave the name "the age of Auden" to the "period of re-examination—of forms, of vocabularies, of ideologies" that began in the 1950s and arguably extended through the second half of the twentieth century ("Retreat" 83–85). It would perhaps be more accurate to call it the age of identity.

CHAPTER 3

Individualism, Auden's *Anxiety*, and the Liberal Unconscious

> Civilization must be saved even if this means sending for the military, as I suppose it does. How dreary [...]. I've tried to be good. I brush my teeth every night. I haven't had sex for a month. I object. I'm a liberal. I want everyone to be happy. I wish I had never been born.
>
> — Herod's speech, "The Massacre of the Innocents," in Auden's *For the Time Being: A Christmas Oratorio* (*Collected* 116–17)

Karl Shapiro's ongoing struggle with W. H. Auden reflects his sense of the senior poet's centrality to the age, or what he called "our age of moral expediency and intellectual retreat—the age of Auden" (85). For Shapiro "the age of Auden" began with the Pound controversy, but his charge deliberately invokes the title of a poem that preceded the first Bollingen Award by almost three years.

Auden published *The Age of Anxiety* in 1946, the same year he was naturalized as an American citizen. The verse drama dared to name an age; as a reward for its presumption it was made eponymous, but at the price of being misunderstood. The title became a talisman for individualism during a decade that was widely described in terms of repression and conformity. Totalitarianism was the external threat; the internal one was mass culture. Both seemed on the verge of producing cookie-cutter citizens who towed the party line or consumed themselves into submission. Auden, however, had proved he was an individual by rejecting his earlier radicalism. His support of Pound seemed to be a vote for freedom of opinion; art, at least, should not have to pursue a political or a commercial agenda. Shapiro was suspicious of Auden's change of course, as were a few other poets and critics. The Herod-as-liberal speech, cited above, was often invoked as evidence that Auden, and indeed the entire age, had overcorrected for youthful radicalism and was veering dangerously towards jaded conservatism. However, both Auden's supporters and his detractors missed the poet's actual and persistent concern. Auden was not an individualist, nor was he inconsistent; his concern had always been the group.

The Age of Anxiety is an eclogue that represents group dynamics in dramatic form. Postwar critics had trouble seeing this because their political bias was simultaneously a genre bias. They opposed collectivism in the name of liberalism and made the lyric paradigmatic for individual expression. More recent criticism reads Auden in terms of identity rather than individualism, but its bias is still lyrical. Individualism and identity-based criticism dissolve Auden's drama into a series of competing soliloquies. Auden, however, saw genre as an almost sociological tool for describing, and in a modest way correcting, social structure. That structure needed correcting because it was producing displaced persons on an unprecedented scale. Intellectuals were apt to describe displacement as individualism because they mistook alienation for authenticity. That was part of the problem. Auden wanted to keep communities together, not dissolve them into factions, and his eclogue dramatizes how the feeling of togetherness can become first a symbol and then a place of association—a public sphere.

This chapter will begin by exploring how *The Age of Anxiety* was misread to authorize an individualism that had little to do with Auden's concerns. The next section will analyze the verse drama in terms of the forms and figures Auden developed to represent group dynamics; it will also explore the affinities between his group poetics and the political theories of Hannah Arendt and Eugen Rosenstock-Huessy, who became key figures for Auden at midcentury. The final section will approach the Pound controversy as an example of the kind of group dynamics Auden saw as typical for an anxious age. His vote for the award reflected a deep-seated belief that poetry, even wrong-headed poetry, could build community, although he did not think that everyone in the community should read it.

An Age Takes a Name

1945 brought an end to hostilities but not to wartime anxieties. The battles were over, but the individual seemed to be under siege. This formulation is as vague as it was pervasive. Individualism played a key role in the first act of the cultural Cold War, although there was only a loose consensus about what the term meant. John Dewey argued that it was impossible to consider the individual in isolation from society, and that if anything "society" was the concrete and "individual" the abstract term ("Crisis" 2–3). The majority of intellectuals, however, considered Dewey to be a left-over from the radical

1930s; even if they could not define "individual" precisely, they were convinced that subordinating individuals to the group led to communism or fascism, considered more or less equivalent under the emerging theory of totalitarianism.

The American left was particularly adamant about individualism because many of its members felt guilty for erring on the side of collectivism in the 1930s. Harold Rosenberg, who was critical of the flood of ex-radical confessions following Whittaker Chambers, nevertheless touched a nerve when he criticized Auden (and Stephen Spender) for the collectivist fallacy of deriving the lyrical "I" from the abstract "we" (*Tradition* 248). Rosenberg undoubtedly had in mind Auden's *Spain*, and probably poems like *Letter to Lord Byron*, which named the age in an ironic way—"Our age is highly educated"— in order to come to "the rather tame conclusion / That no man by himself has life's solution" (Auden, *Collected* 89, 112).[1] Such calls for solidarity did not seem so tame by the end of World War II. They seemed "innocent" in the pejorative way Leslie Fiedler used the term in his notorious indictment of the Rosenbergs.[2]

The Age of Anxiety was typical of Auden's "ageism" (he showed a proclivity for naming ages throughout his career), but it seemed to represent him in a new, more mature phase.[3] Jacques Barzun announced the verse drama's contemporary relevance with his enthusiastic review in *Harper's* (1947): "It is the fate of certain poems to become shorthand notes on history. I have not the slightest doubt that when books analyzing our plight are read only by

[1] Mendelson argues that Auden had major doubts about communism after his experiences in Spain, and these emerged as contradictions in the poem at the metaphorical level. The poem emphasizes the importance of personal choice, but at the same time it suggests the volunteers are pulled into the civil war by unconscious, natural processes. This is not so much a "we," as Auden's critics would suggest, but a "divided geography" on which "the war projects our mental division" (*Early* 318).

[2] Fiedler's article appeared in the first issue of the new magazine *Encounter*, ironically co-edited by Rosenberg's other bête noir, the sometime Auden-collaborator Stephen Spender. Fiedler: "For the true believer believes above all in his own unimpeachable innocence. Precisely because the Rosenbergs could have committed espionage as they did, they could not ever confess it" (19). See Filreis on the midcentury link between aesthetic innocence and political guilt (56).

[3] Auden was a compulsive name-giver of ages. Perhaps his most famous early poem, "Consider this and in our time" (Poem XX), from 1930, describes an "Age of Ice." By 1939 Cleanth Brooks was already claiming, "The advent of the new age of ice, a 'polar peril,' supplies the background for his [Auden's] finest poetry" (Auden, *Collected* 18). Decades later Auden would name an "Age of Care" in "Eulogy," although the usage here is more modest than the epochal gestures of his youth (*City Without Walls* 17). By the end of Auden's career "age" tended to designate biographical rather than historical periods.

candidates for degrees, Auden's eclogue will be quoted, in bits, as a sufficient token of our times" (back matter). Barzun's prediction about the poem's exemplary historical status has not been borne out by scholarship, but *The Age of Anxiety* did become the 1940's token to itself. The title was on everyone's lips when the poem won a Pulitzer Prize in 1948. (Leonard Bernstein, for instance, paid homage to Auden by calling his second symphony *The Age of Anxiety*). The age was anxious because individualism was at risk—this is what Barzun meant by "our plight." Auden described anxiety as a general social condition, to be sure, but this seemed to be society in aggregate, as the sum total of individual symptoms, rather than imagined as a collective "we."

Critics were nearly unanimous in acknowledging Auden's turn to individualism, although what they made of it had more to do with their politics than with Auden's poetry. Randall Jarrell thought Auden had abandoned psychological and social concerns for an empty rhetoric of religious guilt (Jarrell, "Freud to Paul" 450). Robert Gorham Davis accused Auden of betraying liberalism and feared his shift to the right was indicative of a general trend ("The Question" 514). The conservative poet Peter Viereck, who will be the subject of the next chapter, embraced what he saw as Auden's midcentury turn towards religion and conservatism (285). Joseph Warren Beach and Frederick Buell dwelt on Auden's rejection of his earlier ideological commitments, the former skeptically and the latter (20 years later) enthusiastically.

I am not convinced Auden changed as much as the critics thought he did. However, he was useful for marking a cultural turning point. The 1950s told a story about the 1930s—Alan Filreis calls it "the 50s 30s"—that represented modernism and radicalism as partners in crime (xi, 27, 40). Avant-gardism was taken to be a telltale sign of communism and/or fascism, and midcentury critics, shocked into moderation by the war, turned to the subjectivist lyric as a restrained and individualistic alternative.[4] The early Auden stood for the collectivist 30s. The midcentury Auden stood for lyricism and individualism. He was so central to the arguments being articulated on behalf of democratic culture that a number of influential thinkers borrowed the title *The Age of Anxiety* to describe what they saw as the fundamental Cold War plight.

---

4 Northrop Frye, defining the lyric as "subjectivized decorum," traces its emergence back to an act of rhetorical emancipation, when the personal rhythms and associations of poetic voice freed themselves from the semi-official forms of the epos (Frye, *Anatomy* 273).

I now turn to three appropriations of Auden's title—anti-communist, existential, and New Critical—to sketch out the contours of postwar individualism. The next section will turn to Auden's poem. Arthur Schlesinger's foundational statement of Cold War liberalism, *The Vital Center* (1949), begins with a chapter entitled "Politics in an Age of Anxiety." The age is anxious, Schlesinger argues, because social reform has not kept up with industrial progress. "The liberation of the individual [...] set the Industrial Revolution in motion [...] [but] industrialism drives the free individual to the wall" (4). Corporate capitalism and communism, the two most developed forms of industrial economy, threaten individual freedom. Both are "impersonal" systems, marshaling vast materials and energies, and both are indifferent to the personal relationships that once formed the basis of traditional societies (5, 8). It is natural for individuals to feel anxious under the conditions of industrial modernity, or guilty for wielding power they cannot control (6). It is also common for many to seek refuge from their feelings in the false security offered by totalitarianism, in either its communist or fascist versions (9, 58). Schlesinger argues that "the flight from anxiety [...] at the bottom of the totalitarian appeal" has transformed "the twentieth century, which began as the century of democracy" into "the century of the totalitarian revolt against democracy" (58, 59). Nazism and communism replace the "anxious man" with the "totalitarian man" who refuses—violently—to face the uncertainties characteristic of the modern condition (59). Schlesinger's attempt to steer a middle ground between unbridled capitalism and communism, against totalitarianism and for free society, places anxiety at "the vital center" of liberal thought. Anxiety marks the precarious place of the individual in a vast, impersonal system whose velvet glove is the false security of mass conformism and whose iron fist is political repression.

Schlesinger does not mention Auden directly, but a long footnote in a subsequent chapter provides a clue to the role played by *The Age of Anxiety* in the genesis of his argument. The footnote contains an excerpt from Samuel Greenberg's review of Auden's poem for *Masses and Mainstream* (June 1948) and is meant to illustrate the dangers of turning away from anxiety to the false certainties of totalitarianism (53). Greenberg's argument is that Auden is an existential, and therefore a bourgeois, poet; he contends that "The City of Man will be built by those who speak with the voice of Maxim Gorky, not with the whine of W. H. Auden" (qtd. in Schlesinger 57, footnote). Greenberg was wrong about the glorious communist future, but he was right about Auden's appeal to the existentialists. One of the dominant trends in Auden criticism, from the 1940s through the 1970s was to describe the poet as an existentialist or Christian existentialist.[5]

Auden himself was ambivalent about existentialism, as I will explore below, but the title of *The Age of Anxiety* did provide a stage for the American encounter with the philosophy. In 1947 William Barrett, who would two years later kick off the Pound symposium, published a "Dialogue on Anxiety" in *Partisan Review*.[6] It begins with an imaginary Heidegger saying to an imaginary Freud, "It is now the Age of Anxiety, I have read somewhere" (151). Barrett uses Heidegger to represent the position that anxiety is a basic human experience. One must face it to be authentic. This is why the Freudian model of working through anxiety is misguided: "Perhaps the more neurotic the individual (more clinically neurotic, that is), the more definite becomes his delusion and its accompanying anxiety, and the less capable he is of that generalized anxiety that I find to be of the human essence" (156).

Barrett gives the final word to Freud, who advocates reducing anxiety by tracing it back to its origins in family life (159). His career, however, would move in the other direction, "On the Way Toward Heidegger," as he titled the last chapter of *What Is Existentialism?*, the book that grew out of a series of essays on the topic. Barrett became existentialism's great promoter in the United States, in part due to his growing skepticism that psychoanalysis could adequately account for the anxieties that drove one man to become "a Nazi functionary" and another "a Stalinist official" (Cotkin 144–47; *Existentialism?* 108–09). Psychoanalysis seemed to trivialize totalitarianism by reducing anxiety to family drama; it was only by exploring the ontological basis of anxiety that one could begin to understand the human urge towards complete control.

Barrett never addressed Heidegger's own links to Nazism, but those who followed him on the way towards existentialism voted with their feet and turned to Sartre and Camus instead. Existentialism in the United States was primarily a "French affair" (Leitch 166). It was seen as a philosophy of resistance, and through Sartre and Camus as the philosophy of the French resistance (Rice 201). The French existentialists, however, understood themselves to be individualists first and partisans second; the primary problem was not the occupation but self-deception (Barrett, *Existentialism?* 67). Most

---

5 Indeed, the poem was interpreted as an allegory of the crisis of individualism until the 1970s, when one critic claimed "The figures in *The Age of Anxiety* [...] represent a variety of individual expressions of universal *Angst*" (Bahlke, *The Later Auden* 145–46). For similar statements see Buell (67) and Bayley.

6 The first page of the dialogue faces the first printing of Peter Viereck's early poem "Don't Look Now But Mary Is Everybody," which I will analyze in the next chapter as an example of the conservative critique of mass culture.

people denied their own freedom and this made them susceptible to coercion (Rice 211). Sartre argued that the individual is "condemned to be free," and anguish, in the words of Sartre's translator Hazel Barnes, was "the reflective apprehension of the Self as freedom" (*Being and Nothingness*, 799–800; see also Sartre's definition on 51 and Leitch 171). Anxiety, in existential terms, is not an emotional response to an impersonal economic or political system; it is a fundamental expression of the human condition.

Despite its fundamentally apolitical definition of anxiety, the existential emphasis on individual freedom, apprehended through anguish and dramatized through choice, resonated with Cold War fears about communism and the atomic bomb. It also proved useful for defining the difference between totalitarian and free societies, and for articulating the ambivalences of a rapidly professionalizing American intellectual class. Sartre was interested in communism and wrote two books trying to reconcile freedom with dialectical materialism, but most of his American readers argued that communism denied freedom by forcing people to subordinate their desires to those of the class or state.[7] Existentialism, against Sartre's will, became the philosophy of anti-communism, and anxiety, through figures like Barrett and Schlesinger, the anti-red badge of courage.[8] Indeed, the philosophy provided an entire pallet of related terms (ranging from authenticity to alienation) that proved useful for updating the classic American rhetoric of independence and self-reliance. One defender of the American origins of this line of thinking went so far as to argue that the French existentialists were "parvenus to absurdity" (Rice 219).

Whatever existentialism's pedigree, its vocabulary helped bring together the hopes of intellectuals with the disappointments of the downtrodden, as in Norman Mailer's accounts of the white Negro and the existential hipster.[9] Anxiety replaced class consciousness as the binding element in the old avant-

---

7 Sartre in *Search For a Method*: "As soon as there will exist *for everyone* a margin of *real* freedom beyond the production of life, Marxism will have lived out its span; a philosophy of freedom [existentialism] will take its place" (34, italics in original).

8 Rosenstock-Huessy's *Die europäischen Revolutionen und der Charakter der Nationen* (1951), revised after he took up a permanent teaching position at Dartmouth, contains the following statement: "Der Existentialismus hat nämlich das ewige Fortschreiten des Denkens nach links abgestoppt […]. Sartre ist der erste atheistische Intellektuelle von Rang, der nicht Kommunist geworden ist." ["Existentialism has stopped the intellect's eternal drift towards the left. Sartre is the first atheistic intellectual of rank who has not become a communist." My translation (399). In fact, Sartre endorsed Marxism although he never became a member of the communist party.

9 Mailer in "The White Negro": "Any Negro who wishes to live must live with danger from his first day […].The Hipster had absorbed the existentialist synopses of the Negro, and for practical purposes could be considered a white Negro" (273).

garde dream of a coalition between intellectuals and outsiders. That this coalition existed only on paper was hardly a deficit in an age worried about the totalitarian potential lurking behind all groups.

Former radicals like Barrett turned to existentialism for their anti-communism. But the philosophy also proved surprisingly compatible with the more conservative assumptions of the New Criticism. Sartre and John Crowe Ransom both believed that "the disengagement and alienation of criticism and art were the keys to their cultural centrality" (Carton and Graff 313–14). Ransom is an interesting figure in the context of my argument because he too appropriated Auden's title without attributing it. In a lecture at the Library of Congress in 1958, "New Poets and Old Muses" (itself an allusion to Cleanth Brooks's *Modern Poetry and the Tradition*, which also contains a chapter on Auden), Ransom praised contemporary poets for turning away from avant-garde innovation—his negative example is Pound's "Make it New"—towards traditional meters and metaphors (10–14). He likens regular meter to "the reading of an ecclesiastical service by the congregation" (13). Metaphor he describes as a species of anthropomorphism that works by attributing moral order to nature (9–10). It too is religious. Ransom invokes Auden's title to explain how poetry can serve as the modern proxy to religion. The ritualistic rhythms and moral metaphors "lend us morale; it is an excellent effect in the Age of Anxiety; and so far as we know every age is an age of anxiety. The poets are responsible public functionaries for doing this service" (*American Poetry* 11).

Ransom saw poets as modern priests, but he did not really believe that every age was anxious. Like Schlesinger and Barrett he diagnosed anxiety as a modern phenomenon, which he likewise linked to industrialism and modern technical developments. He differed from his liberal counterparts, however, in seeing the root of the problem in the modern lack of faith. The origins of this argument go back thirty years earlier to his *God without Thunder*, which attacks science for setting itself up as a new religion.[10] The only alternative to the anxieties produced by science and industrialism is the kind of transcendence enabled by poetry (*Thunder* 140, 324, 327–28).[11] This is a post-religious concept of faith. Ransom wants to bring his readers the good word, but the closest he can come to faith is the willful suspension of

---

[10] Ransom: "when we conceived God in the image of a Scientist, whose purposes and technique we as little scientists could understand and emulate, we undertook to play a part which was beyond us [...]. Under industrialism, which we conceive to be our divinely appointed mission, we scourge ourselves like true fanatics" (*God without Thunder*, 185–86).

[11] See also Ransom's restatement from 1938: "It is the poet and nobody else who gives to the God a nature, a form, faculties, and a history" (*World's Body* 140).

disbelief.[12] Poets tell stories they know to be false in order to reveal that all stories we tell about the world—including scientific ones—are false. Ransom thinks poets tell better stories than scientists. An anthropomorphic divinity like the Old Testament God is preferable to a chaos of colliding atoms. The problem is that most people lack the aesthetic judgment to recognize the better stories (*Thunder* 87).

Ransom was not ignorant of the fact that many people do believe in the God of the Pentateuch. However, he was careful to distinguish his Old Testament aesthetics from Judaism, which he dismisses as "secular and commercialized" (*Thunder* 326). The prejudice seems gratuitous but it is not. Ransom projects his suspicion of collectivism onto Judaism as an organized religion. He is neo-orthodox in the same way Eliot is a classical modernist, and in fact "New Poets and Old Muses" invokes Eliot as the alternative to Pound in a way that would become increasingly common in the postwar years. Pound wants to innovate; Eliot wants to preserve, but what he preserves turns out to be more individual than avant-garde innovation, which is just an artistic version of technical innovation anyway.[13] Ransom's poet-priest and Eliot's classicist are not members of a congregation, and certainly not of a *minyan*, but lone defenders of a lost cause. They offer a conservative version of individualism, one articulated not through struggles for political or metaphysical independence but in the equally bitter fight to preserve a disappearing tradition. Ransom, like his liberal counterparts, invokes Auden's title in the name of the individual. His religious individualism is compatible with liberal anti-communism in its application, but shows traces of anti-Semitism in its derivation.

Auden's *The Age of Anxiety* was a constant reference in the emerging discourse of postwar individualism. Ransom's conservative individualism had some affinity with reactionary modernism; but what brought together the New Criticism, existentialism, and liberal anti-communism was not a common culture but a common principle. Auden's title was appropriated to dramatize the struggle of the individual against totalitarianism, or with his own metaphysical freedom, or towards the personal leap of faith that would give that freedom meaning. Auden's name, however, was hardly ever mentioned. This may have indicated a lingering suspicion that he was not as individualistic as his poetry was made out to be.

---

[12] Lentricchia describes existentialism as making the same argument, which he calls "conservative fictionalism" (50).

[13] Eliot in "Tradition and the Individual Talent": "the most individual parts of [a poet's] work may be those in which the dead poets, his ancestors, assert their immortality most vigorously" (14).

Auden's *Anxiety*

The Age of Anxiety is a strange poem full of deliberate anachronisms and incongruities. It was Auden's last verse drama (except for the *libretti* he wrote with Chester Kallman) and his final effort to represent group dynamics in dramatic form. Auden had been interested in groups since his involvement with the Oxford Group Movement in the 1930s (Mendelson *Early* 24–26). *Paid on Both Sides*, the "obscure charade" that established his reputation when Eliot published it in *Criterion* in 1930, was the first in a series of poetic experiments intended to dramatize the conflict that Auden saw as part and parcel of group cohesiveness (*Early* 15–16). That verse drama, as Mendelson points out, reports its off-stage murders in the alliterative style of old English prosody (*Early* 48). *The Age of Anxiety* is composed almost exclusively in archaic meter: accentual, alliterative, and four-beat. The alliterations are often deliberately bathetic ("Come, peregrine nymph, display your warm / Euphoric flanks in their full glory / Of liberal life; with luscious note / Smoothly sing the softer data" [*Collected* 483]), but the cadences are meant to evoke Anglo-Saxon verse. These were not new devices for Auden; in fact the poem shows a great deal of continuity with his earlier work, especially in its group theme and its archaisms. Most contemporary critics ignored the former, and some saw the latter as a betrayal of Auden's earlier style.

Jarrell, for instance, described the poem's repetitive consonant sounds as a kind of automatic poetry machine:

> the man who, during the 1930s, was one of the five or six best poets in the world, has gradually turned into a rhetoric-mill grinding away at the bottom of Limbo, into an automaton that keeps making brilliant little jokes, extraordinary little plays on words, unbelievable little rhetorical engines, as compulsively and unendingly and uneasily as a neurotic washes his hands. (Burt 60–61)

Jarrell's argument is simply the obverse of those made by Barzun, Schlesinger, Barrett, and Ransom. They see Auden as the diagnostician of an anxious age, and Jarrell sees *The Age of Anxiety* as "the best example of the disease that it diagnoses" (63). Almost all midcentury critics agreed that Auden had changed in a way that was representative (or symptomatic) of the times. The mainstream thought Auden had become more of an individualist; Jarrell thought he had become less of one. There was no significant ideological difference between the camps. They agreed about the overarching significance of individualism and differed only about such details as where the individual was supposed to reside in the self. Schlesinger et al. subscribed to the existential credo that individuality is a matter of conscious choice. Jarrell, locating individuality in the unconscious, believed Auden's poem was too controlled to be personal, which meant too repressed and neurotic. Such disagreements could stir up the proverbial tempest in a teacup, but they did not challenge the reigning political and poetic paradigm. Lyricism was commonly accepted to be the poetic expression of liberalism, and liberalism the political guarantor of individual freedom.[14]

It is my contention that *The Age of Anxiety* runs counter to the paradigm; it is not about individuals but their roles in the collective. Indeed, I would agree with Mendelson that—midcentury critics to the contrary—the group remained Auden's great theme throughout his career, although his ideas changed radically about how groups functioned (*Early* 16–19). In his youth he was fascinated with strong leaders, then with the rigid fairness of communism; later he developed a theory of social love or "agape," which plays an important role in *The Age of Anxiety*, as do his mature speculations about the freedom to be achieved through the structure of the polis and its poetic correlates, genre and form (Auden, *Dyer's Hand* 85). The repetitive cadence that Jarrell criticized for sounding automatic was in fact intended to suggest the standardizing effect of social pressure, but also the archaic cultural resources that can "forbid automatic responses, / force us to have second thoughts, / free from the fetters of Self" (qtd. in Mendelson, *Early* xiv–xv). Groups can be oppressive but they can also be liberating. Auden tends to focus on the way they open up roles, relations, and possibilities to characters who would otherwise be imprisoned in routines, such as the midcentury routine of individual rebellion.

The Age of Anxiety is a drama, and it emphasizes its theatricality in the subtitle: "A Baroque Eclogue." Criticizing an eclogue for its artificiality, as Jarrell does, is like impugning nobles in shepherds' garb for only pretending to care about sheep. The prose stage directions and commentary, added by Auden after he completed the verse dialogue, suggest that acting is the essential human characteristic:

> only animals who are below civilization and the angels who are beyond it can be sincere. Human beings are, necessarily, actors who cannot become something before they have first pretended to be it; and they can be divided, not into the hypocritical and the sincere, but into the sane who know they are acting and the mad who do not. (518)

[14] The assumption that *The Age of Anxiety* is about individual anxiety, usually coupled with the criticism that the poem is not individualistic enough, persists. Glyn Maxwell repeats Jarrell almost verbatim when he complains, in a recent article in *The Guardian*, that the characters cannot be sufficiently distinguished by their dialogue (Burt 61).

This is a performance theory of identity. Sincerity is self-deception; the theater an allegory for life. Elsewhere in the poem Auden deliberately draws on Shakespeare's *As You Like It*, and in this passage on Jacques's famous monologue "all the world's a stage," to stress the scripted nature of all social roles.

The setting is a New York City bar (the low pun on "bar" probably explains one meaning of the "baroque" in the subtitle). The characters who gather there are outcasts, but the poem makes clear that displacement is a general condition:

> in war-time, when everybody is reduced to the anxious status of a shady character or a displaced person, when even the most prudent become worshipers of chance, and when, in comparison to the universal disorder of the world outside, [the barkeeper's] Bohemia seems as cozy and respectable as a suburban villa, he can count on making his fortune. (449)

Anxiety is a personal feeling but it is also the status marker of the social group. Auden would echo this language of general exile in his introduction to the first English language anthology of Kierkegaard's writings. "The ubiquitous violence of the present age," he wrote, has produced "an amorphous, despairing mass of displaced persons and paralysed Hamlets" (*Kierkegaard* 16). The *Age of Anxiety* begins with an amorphous mass and dramatizes its transformation into a collective. The poem does not follow Kierkegaard's advice that individuals change themselves first ("the association of individuals who are themselves weak is just as disgusting and as harmful as the marriage of children" [*Kierkegaard* 41]), nor does it follow a representative Hamlet through the pathetic steps of his tragic downfall. Instead it represents Hamlet as a class, bringing together four variations on the type.

Malin, Quant, Emble, and Rosetta are solitary drinkers with vaguely allegorical names. Contemporary critics tend to see them as embodiments of Jungian archetypes who—as archetypes—work counter to the existential anxieties they articulate. Malin is the intellect of the group, a medical researcher with the Canadian air force who is often described as a stand-in for Auden. Quant is the civilian, an aging widower who is overqualified for his job as a clerk and drowns his cynicism in alcohol. He is said to represent intuition. Emble is a young sailor who is proud of his attractiveness to both sexes but afraid he will amount to nothing and therefore overly-critical of other people's failings. He is sensation. Rosetta is a buyer for a department store who grew up in England. She is often taken to represent compassion (Mendelson, *Later* 247).

To my mind the Jungian coordinates of the characters are of secondary importance. Their *coordination* is the central theme. The characters begin as interchangeable members of the most loosely defined kind of public—an audience listening to the radio (*Collected* 454). The "matter and manner" of reporting, and its seamless continuity with the advertising, moves them to common disgust and Malin to buy the first round (462). Facing each other over drinks, they cease being members of an anonymous public and constitute themselves as a collective; their first common act is a linguistic one, agreeing to talk about something more meaningful than the radio broadcasts.

Very little happens in the drama beyond conversation, and the progression of topics, which are as allegorical as the characters' names, provides what amounts to the dramatic arc. The conversation commences with a collective lament of aging entitled "The Seven Ages of Man" (borrowed from Jacques in *As You Like It*). The fifth age, roughly corresponding to Auden's at the time of writing, epitomizes the characters' existential concerns: Malin talks about success in the eyes of the "Generalized Other"; Emble voices his fear about "Not [being] wanted at all"; Quant worries about becoming a commodity in a consumer society; and Rosetta "refuse[s] to accept / Your plain place, your unprivileged time." Her protest against the regimentation of the workaday world is the poem's most convincing manifesto for the lyrical individualism that Auden's contemporaries took to be his message. Ordinary people, she says, are "Driven like Danaids by drill sergeants / To ply well-paid repetitive tasks […] In cosy crowds. Till the caring poet, / Child of his chamber, chooses rightly / His pleased picture of pure solitudes" (474–76).The critics who emphasized the poem's individualism (Schlesinger et al.), or its individualism manqué (Jarrell), were echoing Rosetta's plea for an isolated artist to redeem the lonely crowd.

After the "Seven Ages" runs its course to dust and death, Quant asks Rosetta, as the only woman present, to lead them on a return journey from tomb to womb (cf. the "Come, peregrine nymph" passage cited above). This is an infantile fantasy, a "regressive road to Grandmother's House," but it enables the kind of group rapport which Auden had been describing in poetry and prose since the 1930s and which he would denote with the term "agape" (Mendelson *Early* 164–76).

> For it can happen […] that members of a group […] establish a rapport in which communication of thoughts and feelings is so accurate and instantaneous, that they appear to function as a single organism.
> So it was now as they sought that state of prehistoric happiness which, by human beings, can only be imagined in terms of a landscape bearing a symbolic resemblance to the human body. (*Collected* 484)

This passage leads into the section entitled "The Seven Stages," in which the characters dream a common dream of exploring, and becoming parts of, an anthropomorphized geography or somatopia. The temporalized body of "The

Seven Ages" and the spatialized body of "The Seven Stages" are complementary aspects of the same "single organism"; this organism exists through the characters and can only be said to extend itself in space and time as a function of their interaction. The body is the personification of their interaction, and they are its members and its explorers. This seems like a strange innovation, but it is actually anachronistic. "The Seven Ages" and "The Seven Stages" constitute an example of dream-psychomachia. Auden had turned to the device before, but it puzzled critics.[15] The linked sequences are the heart of the poem, bringing together the performative aspects of identity with a drama of incorporation and dispersal. I will return to them in a moment.

After the characters awaken from their collective dream, which lingers only as a vague memory, Rosetta invites them home, half hoping that the older men will decline. They accept, however, and become spectators to the flirtation that constitutes "The Masque." "In times of war," the stage directions tells us, "even the crudest kind of positive affection between persons seems extraordinarily beautiful, a noble symbol of the peace and forgiveness of which the whole world stands so desperately in need" (*Collected* 519). What passes for affection in Rosetta's apartment is the parody of a fertility ritual, which goes unconsummated when Emble passes out drunk in her bed. Alone with her unconscious hero, Rosetta soliloquizes about her loneliness, juxtaposing reflections on her inability to fit into a Christian society with what one critic argues may be the first poetic reference to the extermination camps in English (*Collected* 529; Gottlieb 19). Rosetta is Jewish, living isolated from the Jewish community, and she ends her monologue by invoking a central Jewish prayer, the *Shema Yisrael*, which apostrophizes that community with its opening "Hear O Israel." Earlier Rosetta called for the lyrical protest of lonely poets, but she responds to her own loneliness, and locates it in relation to genocide, by invocating the scattered community of the Diaspora.

The moment of sublime lyrical reflection is reserved for Malin, who seems to both redeem and contradict Rosetta's earlier call for a poet of "pure solitudes." His final thoughts reveal him to be a Christian struggling with faith:

---

15 Mendelson describes how Auden decided to add dream-psychomachia to *Paid on Both Sides* (*Early* 58). Greenberg is a good example of the perplexed critic. After admitting he is at a loss to explain Auden's "Seven Ages"/"Seven Stages" sequence and putting forth his "efforts of explanation" in "humility," goes on to hypothesize that the "Stages" are "Ages" and do little more than add detail to what Auden has already stated (163–64).

Yet the noble despair of the poets
Is nothing of the sort; it is silly
To refuse the tasks of time
And, overlooking our lives,
Cry—"Miserable wicked me,
How interesting I am."
We would rather be ruined than changed,
We would rather die in our dread
Than climb the cross of the moment
And let our illusions die. (533)

Early critics saw Malin's concluding reflections as central to the poem's existential theme. The age is anxious, the poem seems to suggest, but a leap of faith, poetic and religious, can provide meaning.[16] This reading takes cognizance of the Kierkegaardian link between anxiety and belief that Auden had begun to explore in *For the Time Being*.[17] It likewise resonates with

---

[16] The early critics disagree about whether or not *The Age of Anxiety* should be taken as a statement of faith, but they are unanimous in asserting that the poem articulates the *need* for personal faith. John G. Blair: "Like St. Augustine's *Confessions*, Auden's poem demonstrates that human beings are perpetually restless unless they can find a faith in the Timeless, but unlike that work, it suggests no path by which one could reach a spiritual home" (50). Monroe K. Spears: "The anxiety with which the poem deals is, in Auden's view, essentially a religious phenomenon. […] Though felt by all men in all times, anxiety is intensified in our civilization with its failure of tradition and belief, its atomism which leaves the individual isolated, without aid or support in his terrifying responsibility for his own ultimate destiny" (*Poetry of W. H. Auden* 231). John Fuller: "The 'Epilogue' […] demonstrates that although Rosetta's recognition of a paternal deity may reflect an emotional need for God, it is left to Malin (and therefore to the intellect) to make the Christian choice. […] Malin's last words stress the irresponsible childishness of men, but Auden's poem is such a subtle and generous effort of understanding that this speech, with its appeal to the traditional Judeo-Christian God, paternal and inscrutable, seems like an historical pose suited to the years of Belsen and Hiroshima" (200–01). Herbert Greenberg: "Malin summarizes Auden's Christian conception of man, who must live his life partly in nature and time, as self, and partly transcending it, as ego" (157–58). "Malin has only 'negative knowledge,' the knowledge that faith is necessary and of how and why, but not the faith itself" (167). Cotkin: "After the death of communism, only religious truth mattered for Auden" (55).

[17] *The Age of Anxiety* can be considered a sequel to *For the Time Being*, which connects biblical themes to contemporary events through passions or feelings that are ahistorical in their universality. Jesus learns anxiety in Mary's womb, but the character of Simeon prays that the coming of the Christ child will allow believers to "depart from our anxiety into His peace" (*Collected* 379, 390). The rest of the poem demonstrates, however, that departure from anxiety is illusory and nevertheless comes with a cost. Right after Simeon's prayer, Herod tries to kill the infant Jesus through the wholesale

Schlesinger's anti-communism, Barrett's existentialism, and Ransom's concept of individualized religion. The drama becomes the frame for a moment of hard-won transcendence that replaces automatism with personal anxiety, and perhaps with faith. Faith is individual but it is supposed to be more than lyrical, defining itself against the solipsism of the poets. However, it expresses itself through an alternate lyricism—that of prayer—which is marked by Malin's shift in diction. The lines ending "poets" and "moment" distribute their stresses in iambs and anapests and just miss a feminine rhyme. Most of the poem sounds anachronistic, but this recalls Hopkins and his struggle for belief.

This reading is in some ways persuasive, although it simply assumes that Malin's sprung rhythm reflections differ from the self-absorbed poetry he criticizes. It also soft pedals Auden's oft-repeated reservations about existentialism's suspiciously articulate despair. In fact, in a poem read at Harvard the same year he published *The Age of Anxiety*, Auden echoes Malin's lines to criticize not the poets but the existentialists who are in despair "yet go on writing."[18] Malin's confession might be little more than a religious variation

---

massacre of innocents (393). He is authoritarian for liberal ends (see epigraph), rationalizing the use of violence as an attempt to save "Reason" from "Revelation" (393). The murder of the innocents resonates with the equally disturbing policies of Caesar, who has rounded-up all aliens and free thinking Jews, and registered all citizens who live "contrite but without anxiety" because they are convinced that his policies are reasonable (373). The final, depressing lines of the poem seem like a relief compared to this parody of Nazi means-ends rationality. The audience is invited to return from the Christmas play to the work-a-day world ("we had forgotten / The office was as depressing this" [399]). One of the many tasks beside paying bills, fixing machines, and learning irregular verbs is redeeming the "Time Being" from insignificance, and this involves "Seek[ing] Him in the Kingdom of Anxiety," which all too obviously endures (400). This search for a Messiah who continues to tarry, the discovery of a kingdom of heaven inside rather than instead of anxiety, may be the closest the poem comes to salvation. The goal is not Kingdom Come but a society that leaves space and time for charity and love (385).

18 Auden's "Under Which Lyre: A Reactionary Tract for the Times," presented as the Harvard Phi Beta Kappa poem the same year *The Age of Anxiety* was published, provides a version of Malin's monologue but without the pathos:

Behind our battle-line, in swarms
That keep alighting,
[The] existentialists declare
That they are in complete despair,
Yet go on writing. (338)

The battle lines are those of the humanities versus the social sciences. Auden places the existentialists on the side of the latter. The tone of the poem is best captured by the academic Decalogue it ends with, including the commandment "Thou shalt not sit / With statisticians nor commit / A social science" (*Collected* 339). Auden's objections

on the existential theme: Miserable, wicked me, how unregenerate I am. Piety is not always distinguishable from self-pity, and it is even harder to disentangle from the customs of the tribe. Malin's leap of faith seems to parody the academic trend that would explain itself in terms of Auden's title: the postwar turn to existentialism, individualism, and religion.

The Christian-existential reading also has some uncomfortable political implications. It suggests that only Malin's personal struggle with Christianity can redeem Rosetta's Jewish exile. Auden's introduction to *Kierkegaard* does invoke a parallel between crucifixion in the ancient world and genocide in the twentieth century, in effect turning Jews into the types of Christ and Calvary into the antitype of Auschwitz (*Kierkegaard* 12–13, 16). Auden was capable of making this kind of argument in prose. However, his poetry seems to me to be more nuanced. The crux of Malin's soliloquy is the "cross of the moment." Is Rosetta, in her lyrical expression of Jewish suffering, stuck in a precarious collectivism that only Malin's personal appeal to the universal can resolve? More pointedly: Is Malin's Christian leap of faith the answer to Rosetta's Jewishness in the same way Ransom's Pentateuch poetry is the answer to Judaism?

Contemporary critics do not think so (Mendelson, *Later* 259). Anxiety has become less individual and more communal, less a symptom of "the human condition" and more the expression of concrete political repression. Susannah Young-ah Gottlieb's *Regions of Sorrow* (2003), typical of the newer trend, links Auden's anxiety (and Arendt's) not to personal alienation, or the pathos of belief, but to the collective experience of the Holocaust (31–32). Poetry speaks for the victims of modern atrocity; it does not afford personal transcendence or invoke the divine but "stutters" displacement (128) from "holes of oblivion" (67). Gottlieb's reading places Rosetta's Jewishness at the center of the poem (122), and concentration camps at the center of modern experience (21). The poem is not a prayer in any doctrinal sense, but it expresses an "anxious hope" for a weak messianism that would offer a literary space, and a voice, for the victims and witnesses of genocide (22, 135). This reading turns Auden back into a social poet whose own exile

to existentialism are indicative of his reservations about individualism generally. Although he recognized existentialism's personal emphasis as a "laudable protest against systematic philosophers, like Hegel or Marx, who would reduce all individual existence to general processes," he argued that existentialists "invented an equally imaginary anthropology" that over-dramatized the finality of choice (*Dyer's Hand*, 102–03). "In a reflective and anxious age," wrote Auden, "it is surely better…to minimize rather than to exaggerate the risks involved in a choice." Placing individuals "in an existential relation to life without intermission" does not make them free—it turns them into automatons (102–03).

enables him to formulate an elegy for the dispossessed. The Christian-existential reading of Auden links anxiety to personal belief; Gottlieb attempts to re-territorialize anxiety as a post-national space of trauma, memory, and diasporic identity (66).

I think both interpretations—the Christian existential and the traumatic—are wrong, but juxtaposing them reveals how criticism has shifted its emphasis from individualism to identity over the past fifty years. Anxiety used to be a marker of individuality; now it is taken to express the experiences of people denied individual rights, including—at its most extreme—the right to exist. Individualism is a form of humanism that is at least potentially pre-national; being true to oneself is more important than being true to one's country. Identity is post-humanist and post-national, testifying to the experiences of those groups denied a place in the nation-state for reasons of race, gender, ethnicity, or creed. Identity was widely hailed as the radical corrective to liberal individualism, which can be blind to the systematic denigration of minority groups. A few dissenters have begun to argue that if identity politics is post-liberal, its agenda is actually a conservative one, gesturing towards multiculturalism in the same way multinational corporations sponsor heritage festivals (Michaels, *Shape of Signifier*).

Perhaps the rise of identity over individualism marked a shift in literary politics. However, it did not challenge the reigning conception of what makes literature political. Both individualism and identity are committed to a lyrical conception of voice, understood to be the authentic expression of an individual or group. Kenneth Burke's analysis of the lyrical bias of individualism is helpful here, and it illustrates the difference between lyrical models of individuality and identity on the one hand and Auden's dramatic rendition of community on the other. Individualism, according to Burke, adheres to a romantic script of rebellion, but it is so invested in its own performance that it tends to forget it is playing a role. Similarly, the lyric believes in the originality of its own voice, which actually emerges in relation to the multitude of voices that make up the literary tradition. Burke argues that voice is dialogic, lyricism a species of "monodrama," and individuality part of the larger theater of social roles (306–07). In other words, individualism is identity that ignores itself as such, if identity is defined as a performance that situates itself in relation to a group (306, 310–11).

Burke is primarily interested in corporate identities that reinforce the myth of individual self-determination by aligning themselves with ruling interests. Criticism would take a different turn, pursuing identity politics in the name of disadvantaged minorities. This approach would seem to be closer to Auden's concerns, but it is has led to a surprising theoretical chiasmus. The marginal group has taken on the familiar role of the rebellious outsider, expressing its experiences—and its anxieties—through the more broadly defined subjectivity of ethnic lyricism. The 'fifties responded to the 'thirties by opposing individualism to collectivism. More recent criticism treats the collective—and especially the disempowered collective—as if it were a composite individual, i.e. a coherent locus of experience and a unified voice.

Midcentury criticism made Malin a figure of individualism; recent critics make Rosetta a figure of identity. Both reveal their lyrical bias by reducing the *dramatis person æ* to a roster of competing voices. But does Auden the dramatist give us any reason to believe that he favors Malin over Rosetta or vice versa? *The Age of Anxiety* is not a song contest but an eclogue; it embodies the broader drama of social relations in its form.

It also adapts formal devices, and the verse drama's assessment of wartime society has much to do with Auden's innovations (or anachronisms). The most obvious of these is the setting. The eclogue does not follow its characters through arcadia; it incorporates them into a universal body and then turns them loose in a dreamscape reminiscent of the human anatomy. The temporalization and spatialization of what the characters have in common—a body politic—allows for the kind of telescopic satire invented by Swift but not unknown to modernists; cf. the mock-heroic giant of *Paterson* (Auden, *Forwards* 207). It also invites the allegorizing characteristic of medieval morality plays. "The Seven Ages" is a secular version of psychomachia, with individual characters personifying chronological periods rather than virtues and vices. "The Seven Stages" is psychomachia in reverse, transforming the personifications back into actors by turning them loose in the allegorical topos that in a sense generates their roles. This is allegory turned into itself, personification transformed into place, and it suggests the metafictional device of characters talking back to their authors. It also suggests a complicated form of metalepsis, in which the dramatic form, meant to embody social structure, generates a series of related figures that represent their own generating matrix. The effect is abstract, but the impulse is historicist. Elsewhere Auden complained that "[t]he allegorical morality plays are concerned with history, but only with subjective history; the social-historical setting of any particular man is deliberately excluded" (*Dyers Hand* 181).[19]

---

[19] Auden's solution in this same essay is a "return to Shakespeare, as an attempt once again to present human beings in their historical and social setting and not [...] either as wholly private or as embodiments of the social manners of a tiny class" (*Dyers Hand* 179). It would be possible to describe *The Age of Anxiety* as the medieval morality play filtered through *As You Like It.*

The social-historical setting of this poem is the midcentury group, which emerges as a symptom of but also an alternative to displacement.

Can a society of displaced persons form a group? Displacement renders individualism, with its stark division between self and other, obsolete. As Auden put it in 1948: "The division of which we are aware is not between Reason and Imagination but between good and evil will, not between objectivity and subjectivity but between the integration of thought and feeling and their dissociation, not between the individual and the masses but between the social person and the impersonal state" ("Yeats" 110). This argument is constructed around a modernist commonplace ("dissociation of sensibility"), and Auden, like many modernists, is nostalgic for a unified community that would encourage more integrated ways of thinking and feeling. He does not, however, subscribe to the conservative nostalgia for a prelapsarian collective, nor does he pursue the liberal utopia of confederated individualism. Rather, Auden is a proponent of the more ad hoc solution of neighborliness. Mendelson says that *The Age of Anxiety* began as an exploration of isolating guilt but evolved, during its composition, into an expression of "an almost instinctive wish for a shared community we can imagine but never achieve" (*Later* 242). Adam Gopnik argues that Auden "travels the cosmos to come back to the dinner table" (xiv).

The Age of Anxiety does achieve temporary community, but while Auden could wax eloquent about the pleasures of the table, this poem cannot be reduced to a simple encomium of the board and good company.[20] In fact, it is formally irresolute. The eclogue is neither tragic nor comic; it passes through the section entitled "Dirge" but does not end in elegy, nor does it reverse itself in an epithalamium. The characters often talk past one another, and in the end they all go their separate ways. Instructive here is the relationship between Rosetta and Malin, who are the only two characters not to pair up in their journey across the somatopia of the "Seven Stages." Why does Auden keep these characters apart? There are several indications that Malin is gay (*Collected* 503–04). This may have encouraged midcentury critics to identify his voice with Auden's and to describe Malin's struggle with faith as Auden's own. However, the biographical evidence suggests otherwise. While writing *The Age of Anxiety* Auden entered into a sustained

---

[20] Auden did write many such poems. See "Thanksgiving for a Habitat," a series of poems composed in honor of close friends in 1963 and 1964. The poem written for M.F.K. Fisher (author of *The Gastronomical Me*) praises small gatherings ("For authentic / comity the gathering should be small / and unpublic") and insists that the importance of hospitality is as important, and old, as the most fundamental human rituals: "The right of a guest / to standing and foster is as old / as the ban on incest" (*Collected* 709).

heterosexual relationship with Rhoda Jaffe, a Jewish friend who served as his sometime secretary and, apparently, the model for many of Rosetta's traits (*Later* 265). The affair lasted over a year and ended amicably, and Mendelson claims it led Auden to re-think his homosexuality as a choice rather than a curse (*Later* 267). He began to rethink religion as well and—in letters to the poet Alan Ansen, who helped him iron out modern rhymes and rhythms such as those still evident in Malin's soliloquy—toyed with the idea of converting to Judaism (259).

Malin and Rosetta do not enter into a lasting relationship, but they have more in common than is generally acknowledged. Malin's leap of faith is not a corrective to Rosetta's Jewish tribalism, nor is Rosetta's identity an alternative to Malin's Christian individualism. In fact, their religious gestures imply each other and overlap: both invoke God as a witness to community, and both privilege belonging over personal faith. Rosetta's final lines, as I have already pointed out, invoke the scattered community of the *Shema Yisrael*. She addresses "His Chosen, / his ragged remnant" after realizing that the "Momma Earth" she has briefly impersonated for the "boys" (in support of their regression fantasy) is "His stone still." She also realizes that she will never have the "Christian luck" of belonging to the "Who's-Who" but only the "anxious hope" of being classified, in Christian terms, as a "What's-Not" (*Collected* 529, 528).

The passage that is consistently (mis-) read as Malin's monologue of redemption proceeds from the diatribe against poetic solipsism ("the cross of the moment") to a general critique of religious narcissism: "Yet the grossest of our dreams is / No worse than our worship which for the most part / Is so much galimatias to get out of / Knowing our neighbor, all the needs and conceits of / The poor muddled maddened mundane animal / Who is hostess to us all" (534). The neighbor mentioned by Malin is not the customer on the nearest bar stool but the biological human substratum. He is invoking Momma Earth, but he fails to see the Rosetta behind her. It is ironic that he turns her into the "What's-Not" while stressing the importance of recognizing ourselves in others and in nature. His solution to this dilemma is not to look for Rosetta but to invoke a "Him," who "Condescended to exist and to suffer death [...] scorned on a scaffold" (535). Only the capitalization of his phenomenological vocabulary—the "Self-So" and "Always-Opposite," which echo but subtly invert Rosetta's "Who's-Who" and "What's-Not"—helps prepare the way for the abrupt emergence of the Messiah. The syntax and the argument would point to the emergence of a "her"—Momma Earth—who a few lines earlier is identified as our common matrix. The job of the "He" is to voice the "Always-Opposite" part of ourselves that is common but also commonly denied: "it is where we are wounded that is

when He speaks / Our creaturely cry [...]. As they wait unawares for His World to come" (535). This cry has already been voiced by Rosetta but goes unheard because she remains doubly obscured, behind the Momma Earth role she temporarily agrees to play and behind the redeemer who is supposed to speak for her.

Unheard by Malin that is: the similarities between his invocation and Rosetta's constitute one of the commonalities of the play, which is all about naming and inhabiting what drives the characters apart. The cast of displaced persons are caught in a symbolic centrifuge. Almost everything tends towards dispersal; the common dream is forgotten, and the dialogue often dissolves into synchronous reflections and unheeded soliloquies. Something coordinates the characters, however, and it is not simply the arbitrariness of dramatic form. The displaced persons come together by thematizing their displacement, by making the isolation they have in common the basis of community.

Malin thinks he is praying to Christ, but he may be praying to Rosetta, or both could be praying to the anthropomorphic figure behind their divergent allegorizing. Given the abrupt emergence of He in both of their soliloquies—*Deus ex machina*—it would be reasonable to interpret the capitalized pronoun as one in a series of masks or roles assigned to the shifting psyche behind the psychomachia. The verse drama makes no effort to harmonize its gods. It is not a conversion narrative or a play of sacrifice or exclusion. Auden's early verse dramas like *Paid on Both Sides*, *The Ascent of F6*, and *The Orators* explored the anthropological theme of ritual scapegoating. His first dramatic communities constituted themselves through sacrifice and common guilt. Displaced persons, who are all potential scapegoats, must resort to other means. It is not common guilt but common vulnerability that is the foundation of their community. One way they express this vulnerability is through prayer, which offers a serial extension of their dialogue at a theological level. Prayer has a group-allegorical function like the temporal and spatial versions of psychomachia. It creates a community of concepts in this poem of ideas, achieving for an academic audience what T. S. Eliot was self-consciously striving for at a popular level in his best-seller and Broadway success *The Cocktail Party* (1949).[21] Auden's play self-consciously

[21] It is productive to compare Auden's drama of ideas to Eliot's successful attempts to penetrate the popular market. *The Cocktail Party* is a drawing room comedy, which nearly conceals the fact that it is a verse drama; it tries to involve the audience in the way he argues music halls once did, and in the way he argues literature should do in the fight against "Secularism": "I incline to come to the alarming conclusion that it is just the literature that we read for 'amusement', or 'purely for pleasure' that may have the greatest and least suspected influence upon us" ("Religion and Literature" 396).

demonstrates how ideas can constitute an intellectual or academic community.

Two exiled German intellectuals influenced Auden's thinking on exilic communities, both through their theories and through the examples of their lives. The lesser-known of the two is Eugen Rosenstock-Huessy, a Protestant thinker born to Jewish parents in Germany. Rosenstock-Huessy converted in his youth, but the Nuremberg laws made him a "racial" Jew. When Hitler came to power he fled to the United States, where he taught philosophy at Harvard and then Dartmouth. After the death of his first wife, he married Freya Gräfin von Moltke, who was involved in the anti-Nazi Kreisau Circle during World War II. (Her first husband, Helmuth James Graf von Moltke, was executed by the Nazis for treason). Auden would eventually write the preface to a collection of Rosenstock-Huessy's writings (*I Am an Impure Thinker*), and in 1972 he commemorated the theologian's death with the poem "Aubade." Mendelson argues that *The Age of Anxiety* takes place on All Soul's Day—the celebration of the spiritual communion between the dead and the living—because Rosenstock-Huessy's book on European revolutions identifies it as the Christian source of the democratic idea (*Later* 260). This is an interesting—if bizarre—detail, but I think the real significance of the book lies in its thesis, namely that revolutions produce national (or group) character through the violent collectivization of new patterns of thought.[22] Violence comes first, the "we," second, and the "I" as a variable of the "we." While this formula does not preclude individualism, it does suggest that the individual defines him- or herself through roles made possible by the collective.

World War II produced new forms of collectivism, but also exile on a vast scale. Rosenstock-Heussy was an exile, as was the great theoretician of displacement, Hannah Arendt, who taught that mass violence is not only a forge for collective identity but also its opposite: dehumanization. Auden and Arendt became close friends in New York. He even proposed to her after his wife Erika Mann (they married so she could get British citizenship in 1933) and Arendt's husband Heinrich Bluecher died.[23] Arendt's early essay "The Concentration Camps," which would later form one of the core sections of *The Origins of Totalitarianism*, appeared in *Partisan Review* two years after

[22] Rosenstock-Huessy: "Die Revolutionen […] sind eine Krise, ein Einschmelzungsvorgang, der alle Anschauungen, Einzelzüge und Sitten des Volkes in Weißglut versetzt. Einen Volkscharakter prägt nicht ein Staatsstreich um, sondern nur eine Leidenszeit, durch die *alle* Zeitgenossen in die Hohe Schule genommen werden" (22).

[23] On Auden's proposal to Arendt, see the letter exchange between Arendt and Mary McCarthy, 22 Nov. 1970–1 Dec. 1970 in *Between Friends: The Correspondence of Hannah Arendt and Mary McCarthy*: 1949–1975 (269–72).

Auden published *The Age of Anxiety*. It argues that the Nazis pursued a systematic program of dehumanization, first denying their victims the juridical rights linked to citizenship, then the space or opportunity for moral decision-making, and finally the attributes of humanity itself. The actual murder, Arendt argues, was designed to be anti-climactic; the victims were denied their place in society—their social being—in order to reduce them to the status of living corpses (761). The defenselessness of the individual in the face of this massive onslaught made Arendt skeptical of the concept of universal rights: "From the beginning the paradox involved in the declaration of inalienable human rights was that it reckoned with an 'abstract' human being who seemed to exist nowhere" (*Origins* 291). Equality in the age of concentration camps turns out to be the undifferentiated anonymity of corpses in a mass grave.

This line of argument takes Arendt closer to Tocqueville's concerns than to the individualism he named and analyzed. Modern equality only pretends to support individualism; it actually masks a deeper conformism, whether the relatively benign forms characteristic of democracy or the statistical equality of mass murder. True individuality is possible only in a public realm, like the ancient Greek city state, where acts can be witnessed and remembered by peers (Arendt, *Human Condition* 41).[24] Auden, whose enthusiastic response to Arendt's theory is still one of the blurbs on the back of *The Human Condition*, thought poetry was structured like the public realm (he called it the city), with different rhymes, rhythms, and figures of speech

---

[24] Tocqueville coined the term "individualism" to describe the diminished sense of personal obligation that he perceived as a potential danger in democracies. He defines it as a "misguided judgment," which he contrasts with (1) the extended sense of family responsibility characteristic of traditional societies and (2) "egoism," defined as an exaggerated but instinctive self-love possible in all societies (506). It is instructive that he does not contrast individualism with a term denoting group identity such as "collectivism." The chapter "Of Individualism in Democracies" is less concerned with describing the structure of society than the way people think about personal relations. Nevertheless, his discussion does touch on the structural paradox that is central to my argument. Individualism is committed to individuals in the abstract and indifferent to personal needs or beliefs. Tocqueville describes this paradox in terms of obligations rather than rights, feelings rather than principles: "In democratic ages…the duties of each to all are much clearer but devoted service to any individual much rarer. The bonds of human affection are wider but more relaxed" (507). Auden explicitly follows Tocqueville in arguing that the poetry of democracy will necessarily be lyrical, which is to say it will "prefer the delineation of passions and ideas to that of persons and achievements." Auden sees this kind of lyricism as quintessentially modern because the experience that acquaints Americans with democracy also gives them an early taste of the "dehumanized nature and the social leveling which a technological civilization was about to make universal" (Auden, *Dyer's Hand* 367–68).

distributed hierarchically according to function and location. He insisted that the analogy between political and poetic order was a weak one. Trying to make society as coherent as a poem led to fascism, and trying to model poetry on democratic structures led to banality. Nevertheless, the job of poetry is to convert crowds of experiences, feelings, and memories—and the rhymes and rhythms that are the linguistic correlates of memory—into communities of meaning.[25] The lyric was not Auden's aesthetic standard, nor did he consider voice to be a matter of individual expression. Drama, with its multiple characters and social complexity, was his genre paradigm. In this too he was similar to Arendt, who argues that theater is the most political genre because it is the literary analogue of the public sphere (*Human Condition* 186–88).

For Auden the city was more than a metaphor for thinking about poetry. He believed there were two dominant modern sensibilities—with two corresponding mythopoetic structures—and two opposing perspectives on human activity: "If we think of [man's] ever-open future, then the natural image is of a single pilgrim walking along an unending road into hitherto unexplored country; if we think of his never-forgettable past, then the natural image is of a great crowded city, built in every style of architecture, in which the dead are as active citizens as the living" (*Dyer's Hand* 278–79). Elsewhere he would label these sensibilities the Utopian and the Arcadian (*Dyer's Hand* 409). Auden saw individualists as pilgrims marching towards an egalitarian utopia; he was more apt to think in Arcadian terms, although his garden often resembles an urban landscape. The city can function as an Arcadia because it offers spaces of relative freedom (like bars and apartments); it also embodies the kind of tradition that makes freedom possible, not as a function of the equality of formal rights, or as the sum product of ethical behavior, but through concrete prerogatives carved out against the realm of necessity,

---

[25] Auden: "The subject matter of a poem is comprised of a crowd of recollected occasions of feeling, among which the most important are recollections of encounters with sacred beings or events. This crowd the poet attempts to transform into a community by embodying it in a verbal society. Such a society, like any society in nature, has its own laws; its laws of prosody and syntax are analogous to the laws of physics and chemistry. Every poem must presuppose—sometimes mistakenly—that the history of language is at an end" (*Dyer's Hand* 67). Auden was careful to maintain that the relation between poem and society was one of analogy rather than identity: "A society which was really like a good poem, embodying the aesthetic virtues of beauty, order, economy and subordination of detail to the whole, would be a nightmare of horror for, given the historical reality of actual men, such a society could only come into being through selective breeding, extermination of the physically and mentally unfit, absolute obedience to its Director, and a large slave class kept out of sight in cellars. Vice versa, a poem which was really like a political democracy—examples, unfortunately, exist—would be formless, windy, banal and utterly boring" (85).

which in human beings is the realm of compulsion. Freedom, for Auden, is not a private right or a matter of public indifference; it is a process of conscious reflection that grows out of social structures and ultimately dialogue.[26] The complex geography of a city is analogous to and enables the moral physiology of conscious reflection. In the poem he wrote to commemorate Rosenstock-Huessy's death in 1972, Auden alluded to the relation between consciousness and urbanity in the concluding stanza: "Human Time is a City / where each inhabitant has / a political duty / nobody else can perform" (*Collected* 882).

Auden's assessment of displacement does not lead him to side with individuals or identify with a specific group of outsiders. He is a partisan of the social drama that constantly redefines its boundaries and its membership, drawing those who are excluded into a dialogue that continually redefines the center. The age is anxious because it is an age of displacement, but drama—and literature in general—can help make up for the violence of nationalisms inflicted and denied. Auden described his ideal in a 1951 interview as a "beneficent anationality" that reflects "a social longing, a desire to join with other men to form associations" (Griffin, "A Dialogue" 578). One place this institutional "anationality" would be realized—as the future Chancellor of the Academy of American Poets perhaps guessed—was the academy. The postwar city, in Auden's writing, has more of an institutional than a geographical presence. In a poem to the Niebuhrs—Reinhold Niebuhr may have introduced him to the work of Rosenstock-Huessy—Auden talks about there being "little [...] left standing / But the suburb of dissent" (*Nones*, n. pag.).

Pound beyond the Pale

After WWII Auden tried to invent a poetics that would bring the damage done by the public, or in its name, back into the public sphere. "Memorial for a City" (1951), an elegy narrated from a historiographic perspective, breaks with the dramatic conventions but preserves the repetitive quality of *The Age of Anxiety*, transforming its alliteration into an assonance that some

[26] Auden: "Man has a real history; having come into being, he has then through his choices to become what he is not yet, and this he cannot do unless he first chooses himself as he is now with all his finite limitations. To reach 'the age of consent' means to arrive at the point where the 'given' Ego-self relationship is changed into a contractual one. Suicide is a breach of contract" (*Dyer's Hand* 111).

critics still find unnerving. (Anthony Hecht finds the poem virtually unreadable because of the "congestion" of its internal rhymes [332]). The poetic rendition of urban history provides snapshots of representative cities, culminating in a description of the war-torn Europe that Auden visited in an official capacity for the U.S. military. (Beyond this poem, he never wrote about his experiences in the bombed-out cities of Europe.) The bombed-out city is also a space of DP camps and concentration camps. Auden wants to let the victims speak, but he can only do so by invoking the structures that exclude them:

> Behind the wire
> Which is behind the mirror, our Image is the same
> Awake or dreaming: It has no image to admire,
> No age, no sex, no memory, no creed, no name,
> It can be counted, multiplied, employed
> In any place, at any time destroyed.
> Is it our friend?
> No; that is our hope; that we weep and It does not grieve,
> That for It the wire and the ruins are not the end:
> This is the flesh we are but never would believe,
> The flesh we die but it is death to pity;
> This is Adam waiting for His City.
> *Let Our Weakness speak* (*Nones* 43)

The italicized line at the end of this stanza shows Auden trying push this poem further than Malin's "it is where we are wounded that is when He speaks." The last section of the poem channels the voice of "Weakness" in Whitmanesque, long-breath lines providing variations on the sentiment: I was the man, I suffered, I was there. The "I," however, is a bit of a misnomer because it does not refer to an individual or an identity. The locus of articulation simply does not exist. The speaker represents his role in history as a shadow presence: "I was the missing entry in Don Giovanni's list; for which he could never account" (44). The "I" is actually an "It"—the vulnerable flesh that is not allowed identity or individuality—a lyricism deprived of its "I."

It seems likely that Auden identified Pound with this "it"—especially the Pound incarcerated first in a cage in a U.S. Army prison camp and then in St. Elizabeths. Like many contemporary critics, he might have also believed that Pound was expressing remorse in the "pull down thy vanity" passage in Canto 81 of *The Pisan Cantos* (81/541). But while Auden's vote for Pound harmonized with the majority opinion, his rationale—like his verse—could hardly have been more different. Most contemporaries defended Pound on the grounds of individualism and the individual right to free speech. David

Riesman's *Individualism Reconsidered* (1954) offered a concise version of the argument: "There are violently anti-Semitic writers, such as Ezra Pound or Louis-Ferdinand Céline, who have the right to say what they please [...]. [O]ur tradition of civil liberty is the best defense we have for individuals and for minorities; and Jews have every interest, as Jews and as Americans, in seeing that this tradition remains strong and vital" (144–45). Riesman's civil libertarianism dovetailed nicely with the formalist argument also widely employed in Pound's defense. In a *Partisan Review* editorial reviewing the decision, William Barrett—already leading his readers on the way towards existentialism—entertained the claim, associated with the New Critics, that technical innovation should outweigh content in matters of aesthetic judgment ("A Prize" 347).

Auden voted with the majority of the Bollingen committee to honor Pound, but in his response to Barrett he made it clear that neither formalism nor civil libertarianism was his primary concern. Indeed, Auden admitted that Pound's ideas were dangerous and censorship might be in order ("The Question" 512–13). It is hard to know how seriously to take his remark about censorship since he distanced himself from Random House in 1946 when his editor, Bennett Cerf, made a point of excluding the allegedly treasonous Pound from an anthology of American poetry (Mendelson, *Later* 262, footnote).[27] This debate involved Pound's earlier work and not *The Pisan Cantos*, but the contradictions in Auden's position were hard to overlook. Shapiro, for one, found them intolerable. In his autobiography he recalled Auden rationalizing his vote on the Bollingen committee with the remark "everybody is anti-Semitic some time." Shapiro assumed this comment had more to do with Auden's ambivalence towards his unfaithful Jewish lover Chester Kallman than with Pound (Auden, *Reports* 42–43). However, Auden's commentary in *Partisan Review* suggests that his reflections on prejudice went deeper than a lover's quarrel: "Antisemitism is, unfortunately, not only a feeling which all gentiles at times feel, but also, and this is what matters, a feeling of which the majority of them are not ashamed. Until they are, they must be regarded as children who have not yet reached the age of consent" (513).

Auden's sin-and-ignorance vocabulary treats anti-Semitism like a Christian rite of passage, in effect ignoring historical specificity of genocide and fascism. It does not, however, dismiss anti-Semitism as irrelevant to *The Pisan Cantos* in the manner of aesthetic formalism, nor does it defend it as a

---

[27] One of the editors of the anthology was Conrad Aiken, who would also serve on the Bollingen committee and vote for Pound. Like the majority of his contemporaries, he also objected to Cerf's censorship (Barnhisel 105–06).

protected form of free speech. Auden felt obligated to recognize the importance of Pound's work although he believed it to be potentially dangerous. He offered by way of analogy the hypothetical effect Baudelaire's *La Charogne* might have on a "necrophilist." Barrett points out it is unclear what bearing this might have on the Pound case as necrophilia was never a political movement, but Auden's argument is less political than moral-psychological. Indeed, it resembles the arguments of the psychologist Fredric Wertham, an outspoken opponent of Pound both during his trial and after the Bollingen Award, and soon to become infamous for his opposition to comic books in *The Seduction of the Innocents* (1953) (Torrey 281, 235). Auden, unlike Wertham, supported the award, but like Wertham he believed that some art can be bad for some readers, who should be regarded as minors to the extent that they are vulnerable to aesthetic seduction (522).

To make sense of Auden's seemingly contradictory position, it is useful to contrast it with both the moral condemnation voiced by the conservatives who adopted Wertham as one of their standard-bearers; and the range of liberal positions represented by Shapiro, Riesman, and Barrett. The postwar conservatives were anti-modernists who insisted that art be evaluated in terms of its clarity and moral content. The more widely accepted liberal argument was content-neutral as a matter of principle; it viewed art as free speech, free speech as an individual right, and society as a forum for balancing competing rights. This is what I have been calling the liberal aesthetic. The moralism of the conservatives made them post-reactionary for the same reason they were anti-communist; their ultimate yardstick of value—moral and aesthetic—was a standard of decorum antithetical to the excesses they associated with the avant-garde. Liberalism's commitment to equal rights made it more accommodating to both the expressive individualism opposed by conservatives and the aesthetic formalism they averred was a cover for avant-gardism anyway. Although liberals and their allies were often sympathetic to the modernist cultural project, they supported Pound not for his ideology but for reasons of principle. The civil libertarians defended the fact of Pound's utterance; the formalists honored its structure; and while few people condoned his ideas, many considered them irrelevant for purposes of judgment.

Auden was neither a conservative moralist nor a liberal individualist, although his contemporaries mistook him for both. His minority opinion—in favor of the award but entertaining the possibility of censorship—was in fact of a different order from the range of political-aesthetic responses anathematizing Pound on the one hand or defending his rights on the other. Unfortunately Auden's Pound commentary does not do justice to his views.

At a key point his argument collapses into a theory of mimesis which obscures the distinction between representing evil and endorsing it: "An art which did not accurately reflect evil would not be good art" (513). This is a red herring. It was not in his conception of mimesis but in his model of society that Auden differed from most of his contemporaries. Auden did not begin with the individual—or with a standard of moral rectitude measured in terms of personal behavior—but with the group (Mendelson, *Early* 100, 102, 116, 183). He tended to describe the difference in more traditional terms—individualism stresses equality over virtue, *romanitas* stresses virtue over equality—but it is clear that he saw himself as the representative of an archaic notion of community that puts group considerations before individual rights (*Dyer's Hand* 318–19).

Robert Gorham Davis saw Auden's emphasis on duty over liberty as typical of the reactionary modernism he thought was being honored with Pound. In his contribution to the *Partisan Review* symposium, he points to Auden's "Herod-as-liberal speech in *A Christmas Oratorio*" (see epigraph) as emblematic of a modernist belief "that living language, literary sensibility and poetic values are supported by the traditional, the Catholic, the regional, the mythic, the aristocratic, and by a sense of the tragic, of transcendental absolutes, of sin and grace" ("The Question" 514). Davis missed the irony in Auden's version of "The Massacre of the Innocents," but the Pound response did provide a much-needed refuge for one self-proclaimed reactionary and representative New Critic. Allen Tate, who also voted for Pound, felt personally insulted by Barrett's editorial. He believed Barrett's form/content distinction implied that the committee had purposely ignored Pound's anti-Semitism, and he responded in aggressive language that Barrett understood—rightly or wrongly—as a challenge to a duel ("The Question" 520). Tate toned down his rhetoric in a letter printed in the following issue of *Partisan Review* by citing Auden on the universality of anti-Semitism and the moral importance of shame: "Mr. Auden says all Gentiles have felt [it] (I have felt it, and felt humiliated by it)" ("Further Remarks" 666). Contrary to what Davis contended, Auden was not part of the Eliot, Pound, Tate tradition, but his argument enabled Tate to reformulate his passionate indictment as a crisis of conscience, and to insert (in parentheses) his own shame as a personal solution to an aesthetic and political dilemma.[28]

My argument is that the role Auden played for Tate he played for the age. He became the conscience for the New Critics, but (despite Davis's protestations to the contrary) also for liberals who aligned themselves with anti-

[28] Charles Altieri describes Auden as cultivating "a spiritual attitude capable of rejecting modernism" (149).

communism and existentialism. Reactionaries like Tate went to him for confession and religion; liberals went to him for individualism. But individuality, for Auden, was not something given but achieved, and achieved only with difficulty in a society (of which Pound was sadly representative) increasingly bent on total domination. Auden articulated a poetics of individuation (not individualism) for the age he named. He became a bastion of affective inwardness for liberal politics and poetics because of his ostensibly conservative sensibility.[29] He did not convert anyone—in fact he was already being dismissed as "academic" by the end of the 1950s, in part because of this poem—but his anxiety articulated the collectivism denied by liberalism as a matter of principle.[30]

Auden's group poetics marks the space of what might be called the liberal unconscious. I mean this in the sense of the "socially symbolic act" that Fredric Jameson calls "the political unconscious" (Jameson, *Political Unconscious* 20). *The Age of Anxiety*, consistently misread as an individualistic (or more recent identitarian) endorsement of lyrical voice, actually articulates the historical conditions that make that voice possible, or give it its dual significance of confinement and freedom. Since the end of World War II criticism has been haunted by a vision of community just beyond the horizon of its political commitments. This vision is a literary chimera, but the postwar years made it an institutional fact. Universities became safe havens for the ritualized individuation Harold Rosenberg attributed to "the herd of independent minds," but also for the kind of intellectual community that makes individualism its badge of membership. *The Age of Anxiety* was mistaken as individualistic because it articulates the social conditions that could make individualism a common—and regulated—good. The poem is not an example of the conservative poetics that will be the subject of the next

---

[29] On this point, see Buell's disagreement with Jarrell: "If anything, then, Auden's later 'conversion' to existentialist Christianity is not a submission to authority, but the acquisition of an authority that allows a more inclusive and congenial arena for essential playfulness. […] [The poetry is] confident of divine approval for this least of all possible human wickednesses ["comic exravegance"]" (67). Buell is taking issue with Jarrell's assertion that Auden's enfant terrible rebellion is fundamentally conformist ("Freud to Paul" 449).

[30] Albert Gelpi's contribution to Robert Shaw's edited volume, *American Poetry Since 1960*, gives a concise version of the academic-Auden argument. Auden's selections for the Yale Younger Poets Series in 1951 "substantiat[e] Eliot's prediction that poetry should take a turn to a stricter formalism than was needed in the 'teens and 'twenties" (123). Out of the straightjacket of the restrictive Eliot, Auden, Tate, and Lowell tradition emerges Adrienne Rich, whose seemingly unassuming poems usher in a revolution in poetic diction and political aims.

chapter; rather, it offers an intoxicated and ironized version of the kind of literary discourse that would constitute the academic establishment.

CHAPTER 4

"When conservatism was still a dirty word …": Modernism, New Conservatism, and Peter Viereck's "Poetry of Ideas"

Tales of "the tranquillized *Fifties*," in Robert Lowell's phrase, have fallen out of fashion (Lowell 187). The conservatism and conformism supposed to characterize the decade are now widely held to be artifacts of consensus-oriented history, and recent scholarship has concerned itself with uncovering those subversive forces—racial, sexual, generational, ideological—simmering under the deceptively calm surface of the Eisenhower years (Higham 464–65).[1] The 1950s did, however, witness the birth of the first "genuine American conservative movement," and little attention has been paid to the unapologetically conservative literature that helped announce it (Allitt 159). The research gap is so great that it is difficult to recall the names of conservative authors active after WWII, with the exception of those who had made their reputations before the war such as Faulkner, Eliot, and Pound, whose indictment for treason did much to dampen the appeal—but also change the concerns—of writers on the right. Michael Kimmage, one of the few literary historians to devote attention to what he calls "the conservative turn," argues that "The conservative emphasis on precedent and experience, the anti-utopian cast of the conservative mind, leads conservative authors to autobiography, to a nonfiction reckoning with the dilemmas of history, politics, and the self" ("Plight" 949). Since prewar conservatism was often the provenance of literary figures such as Tate, Ransom, and the Southern Agrarians, and literary scholars such as Babbitt, More and the New Humanists, the "nonfictional" orientation of postwar conservatism is curious. Could it be that the political ideology that has become agenda-setting in the United States had its biographers and pundits but no literati?

There are of course some likely candidates among novelists and critics. Kimmage points to Saul Bellow ("Plight" 950), and he makes the case that Lionel Trilling, who in 1950 famously claimed "In the United States at this

[1] For recent accounts of 1950s subversion, see T. Jackson Lears's *The Culture of Consumption*, Larry May's edited volume *Recasting America: Culture and Politics in the Age of Cold War*, and David Halberstam's *The Fifties*.

time liberalism is not only the dominant but even the sole intellectual tradition," influenced the conservative turn as decisively as did Whittaker Chambers, who had been Trilling's classmate at Columbia in the 1920s (Kimmage, *Conservative* 7, 10; Trilling, *Liberal Imagination* 5).[2] Allan Bloom, the model for Bellow's *Ravelstein* and author of the bestselling *The Closing of the American Mind* (1987), is another obvious candidate. William F. Buckley, founding editor of *National Review*, wrote novels. The New Criticism, in its postwar incarnation, provided refuge for conservative humanists (and also former socialists) in an increasingly liberal academic setting (Rasula 77–84, 86, Carton and Graff 313; Guttmann 157; Schryer 674–75).[3] And many conservatives rallied around Peter Russell and later Hugh Kenner in their attempts to rehabilitate Pound.

While it would be possible to expand this list of novelists and critics, it is worth noting that one of the major conservative voices of the 1950s expected the literary tradition to be maintained by poets. Russell Kirk's groundbreaking *The Conservative Mind* (1953), which helped establish the intellectual credentials of the postwar conservative movement, was subtitled (in later editions) *From Burke to Eliot*. Kirk struck a hopeful note in the concluding chapter: "From the beginnings of European literature to this century, the enduring attitude of serious poetry has been—so far as one may apply a modern term of politics to abiding questions of the human condition—what is now called 'conservative.' After some decades of the verse of protest and negation, twentieth century poetry has returned to an affirmation of this permanent truth" (456).[4] "Conservative," as Kirk points out, was a recent coinage, and the most authoritative history of the movement, George Nash's *The Conservative Intellectual Movement in America Since 1945*, deliberately begins with the end of the war. Nevertheless, poetry seemed a safe bet for those seeking the "permanent truth" behind the twentieth century's violent transformations. Eliot himself had famously argued that poets were most traditional when they were most individual, and his two contributions to conservative cultural theory—*The Idea of a Christian Society* (1939) and

---

2 Trilling, as Kimmage points out, always considered himself to be a traditional liberal, but he had a profound impact on conservative thinkers such as David Horowitz, Irving Kristol, and Gertrude Himmelfarb (12–13).

3 Rasula: "New Criticism discovered the ideal corollary of utopian regionalism in the figure of the 'text itself'" (74).

4 Kirk's *Eliot and His Age*, published the year before Kenner's *The Pound Era*, further promotes the link between Eliot and postwar conservatism. Kirk's is clearly a minority position, but in more recent years the argument has been taken up by Donald Stanford in *Revolution and Convention in Modern Poetry*.

Notes Towards the Definition of Culture (1948)—are mentioned approvingly by Kirk (Eliot, "Tradition" 14–15).

However, Kirk's prediction that conservative poets would return to tradition in the manner of Eliot was wrong, and in a double sense. First, it was the left that rallied behind Eliot in influential journals such as *Partisan Review*, which—after arguing that "Only the blind would hesitate to call Eliot a fascist" in 1934—printed an early installment of "Notes Towards the Definition of Culture" in 1944 (and "East Coker" in 1940 and "Dry Salvages" in 1941) in its efforts to unite modernist aesthetics with leftist social critique (Phelps 52; Carton and Graff 296).[5] (Eliot, for his part, cites Dwight Macdonald approvingly in the introduction to the book version of *Notes*—the same Macdonald who left the editorial staff of *PR* in the 1940s to pursue an agenda that Philip Rahv described as "ultra-leftism" [Rahv, Disillusionment" 524–25; Eliot, *Notes* 9]). Second, the conservative poetry that emerged at midcentury did not follow high modernism but rejected it. Emblematic for this shift is the work of the largely forgotten writer Peter Viereck, who considered avant-garde aesthetics to be a conduit for political extremism, and pursued what he saw as the alternative program of formalism in prosody and conservatism in politics.

The modernist legacy presented a problem for the literary right in general, and Viereck in particular, in the figure of the unregenerate fascist Ezra Pound. The controversy surrounding the Bollingen Prize was "seismic"—as Jed Rasula puts it—in its impact on the cultural landscape (113). Pound created a major fault line in the new postwar cultural geography, where conservatism defined itself as post-reactionary and anti-modernist; and modernism installed itself as the professional discourse of the "literary

---

5 Wallace Phelps's 1934 review of *After Strange Gods* begins by quoting that book's most infamous remark: "And reasons of race and religion combine to make any large number of free-thinking Jews undesirable" (52). Nothing could be more illustrative of *Partisan Review*'s political shift than the difference between this review, published during its John Reed Club phase, and Robert Gorham Davis's review of *Notes Towards the Definition of Culture* in 1949. Davis was no friend of what he saw as the conservative drift of postwar criticism, and he does not share Eliot's conclusions about the cultural importance of Christianity. Nevertheless, he praises Eliot for developing a holistic model of culture that does not restrict itself to literary texts: "[Eliot's essays] ought to give the academic mind an uncomfortable sense that a verbal analysis of a poem by Marvell cannot be ultimately separated from whatever may be on the radio at the moment. Because of Eliot's prestige these essays ought to stimulate a general discussion of what cultural responsibility in a democracy really means" ("Culture, Religion, and Mr. Eliot" 752).

establishment."[6] The literary establishment, Rasula argues, emerged out of the original cadre of Pound supporters to fend off attacks against the award (Rasula 114). Former fascists joined forces with former communists in their defense of *il miglior fabbro* (Guillory 165, 172). The ideological debates once raging between these former antagonists had already been rendered obsolete by the Cold War. However, the Bollingen controversy was not simply a footnote to anti-communism. The establishment did not defend Pound as a fascist or as an anti-communist but as a modernist, and by 1949, the modernism that had originated as a series of avant-garde movements began to establish itself as an institutional fact (Trilling, "Modern" 264; Guillory 171–72).

Pound's supporters from the right and left contributed to the same journals and sometimes occupied neighboring offices in English departments. They put forth the argument—one harmonizing with the basic assumption of New Criticism—that art had to be kept separate from politics in a free society (Carton and Graff 305). This separate sphere argument rendered Pound's alleged treason inconsequential in terms of the aesthetic value of his poetry. It also marked a reversal from prewar avant-gardism, which—and Pound is an example here—mobilized culture with the express purpose of changing society (Bürger 90–91). The separation of culture from politics served the anti-communist agenda of distinguishing art (produced in an open society) from propaganda (produced for political ends); it also mirrored the increasingly significant division between the ivory tower and the public sphere.

The modernism that established itself in universities soon began to seem more bureaucratic than revolutionary. Harold Rosenberg coined the phrase "the tradition of the new" to describe the paradoxical quality of institutionalized rebellion; Rahv spoke of the "*embourgeoisement* of the American intelligentsia" ("Our Country" I, 306), and Louise Bogan of "the bohemianization of the outlands," by which she meant suburbs but also college towns ("Our Country" III, 565). Irving Howe conceded that "the academy" was the "best bet" for intellectuals without independent means, but with the

---

6 In his contribution to the famous "Our Country, Our Culture" symposium in *Partisan Review*, Delmore Schwartz suggested that universities and the mass culture they officially opposed had to be seen as existing on a continuum, arguing that only a critical intelligentsia—presumably one outside of universities—could prevent the New Criticism from transforming literature into "a set of courses in the departments of English and comparative literature" ("Our Country" III, 595). Karl Shapiro, who voted against Pound on the Bollingen committee, describes being shut out from the literary "Establishment" in the same way that Jews were excluded from country clubs (*Reports* 43).

proviso that "no one who has a live sense of what the literary life has been and might still be, either in Europe or this country, can accept the notion that the academy is the natural home of intellect" ("This Age of Conformity" 150). Eventually, the academic home of the intellect spawned its own filial rebellions. The predictability of modernist revolt became an impetus (or rationalization) for postmodernism's revolt against revolt, its traumatized rejection of official narratives (Lyotard 1612–14) and its histrionic recycling of outmoded fads (Jameson, "Postmodernism" 1967, 1971; Harvey 63–63). There was, however, an earlier revolt against revolt, one that weighed the intellectual appeal of fascism and communism and came to the conclusion that avant-gardism in aesthetics led to extremism in politics. I am referring here to midcentury conservatism, which in addition to being the sworn opponent of what was already being called "the liberal establishment" was highly suspicious of the modernist leanings of the literary establishment (Schneider xii).

This is in a sense surprising. Today it is widely assumed that there is no such thing as conservative literature. At midcentury, however, conservatism was understood to be "*an essentially literary phenomenon*," as Allen Guttmann put it in *The Conservative Tradition in America* (1967) (11; italics in original). Some political scientists took this to mean conservatives were detached from reality. Morton Auerbach's *The Conservative Illusion* (1959) made this argument in its very title, and Philip Chapman indicted the impracticality of conservative thinkers in *Political Science Quarterly* in these terms: "As cultural critics, as literary men, as poets, novelists and doctors of literature, their interest in political theory per se has been slight; and this fact has reflected itself in the quality of their commentary" (24). Auerbach and Chapman considered the literary traditionalism of Babbitt and the regionalism of the Southern Agrarians to be synecdochic for all forms of conservatism. There were, however, many examples of conservatism at midcentury including isolationism, libertarianism, a classical liberalism antagonistic to New Deal reforms, regionalism, white supremacy, evangelicalism, and above all anti-communism (Allitt 159). The various conservative ideologies were not always compatible, and many of their proponents refused to line up behind the Republicans, especially with Eisenhower at the helm (Galbraith 100–01). The disunity was convenient for those seeking to make the conservatism of some literary figures symbolic of the general ineffectiveness of the right.

However, liberal commentators—and even many conservative insiders—were caught off guard by the emergence of the populist conservatism rallying behind McCarthy and later Goldwater and Reagan. The new conservatives aligned themselves with the Republican Party and built themselves up as a viable political force parallel to, but defining itself in opposition to, the emerging liberal—and literary—establishment. The mainstreaming necessary to bring conservatives together was undertaken largely by Buckley's *National Review* (founded 1955), and particularly by contributing editor Frank S. Meyer, who popularized the term "liberal establishment" and collected some of his articles in a book called *The Conservative Mainstream* (90–94; Allitt 179–80; Kimmage, *Conservative* 94). *The National Review* rallied conservatives of various stripes behind the banner of anti-communism, which had a foreign policy component but also fostered a home-grown distrust of "big government," especially after the Hiss hearings touched off anxieties about communist infiltration (Allitt 175).[7] The new conservatism was, in fact, fundamentally anti-establishmentarian, and its populism had much to do with the surprising fact that many leading figures of the movement—like Myers and James Burnham and Chambers—were ex-communists, "men who had left the discipline of the party but had not lost the habit of the party's thought," as Archibald MacLeish put it (*Freedom* 135). The rhetoric of midcentury conservatism was adamantly opposed to communism but also owed something to its romance of the common man. The elite were supposed to be untrustworthy; average Americans were on the side of freedom. The pathos of parochialism, stylizing itself as closer to "the people" in inverse proportion to its distance from the centers of culture and political power, signaled a paradigm shift from the older, more literary conservatism, which was sometimes parochial (or agrarian) but almost always elitist (Schneider 51–60, 67–70, 76–77; Allitt 203).

Postwar conservative writing, like Chambers's *Witness*, was testimonial and anti-elitist. There was an art to its artlessness—Chambers mentions Shakespeare and Beethoven in the introductory letter to his children—but the children and what they represent, namely uncorrupted common sense, are the vehicles of the autobiography's populist appeal. The anti-elitism of midcentury conservatism should be juxtaposed with the professionalism of the literary establishment to provide a picture of how the cultural landscape was developing around and beyond obvious Cold War parameters: literature became officially rebellious, and rebellion a matter of aesthetic expertise, at

---

[7] Communist infiltration was the premise of Burnham's *The Web of Subversion*: "During the 1930's and '40's an invisible web was spun over Washington. Its interlaced threads were extended to nearly every executive department and agency, to the military establishment, the White House itself, and to many of the committees of Congress. Through the records of the Congressional investigating committees and through the trials of Alger Hiss, the Communist leaders and the atom spies, part of the pattern of this web can now be traced" (15).

the same time conservatism became testimonial, non-fictional, and (in its own stylization) commonsensical.[8]

Pound was a cultural test case for both the emergent literary establishment and the new, post-reactionary conservatism. The establishment defended him despite his politics, and the conservatives rejected him for the modernism that marked him, in their eyes, as elitist and revolutionary. Mary McCarthy reports that Arthur Miller was questioned about his attitude towards Pound during the anti-communist hearings conducted by the House Committee on Un-American Activities (24). The incident marks the postwar fault line between two contrary ways of thinking about politics and culture. The conservative assumption was that communists like Miller were more likely to support a fascist. The literary assumption was that extremists like the committee members were more likely to attack an artist.

This chapter will explore the midcentury shift in the cultural landscape by focusing on Peter Viereck, the poet and conservative publicist who did not fit into either camp and who, in his eccentricity, embodies the institutional and rhetorical divisions between them. Alan Filreis describes Viereck as "for a few crucial years a major player in defining a new kind of modernism" (Filreis 44–45). Actually, Viereck's writing is best described as anti- or even post-modernist, an orientation he defined through his opposition to avant-gardism in general and Pound in particular. He believed that his antagonism towards Pound damaged his career. While the story is more complicated than this, his poetry and political writing did fall into obscurity for linked but contradictory reasons having everything to do with the changing shape of the postwar cultural landscape. Viereck was literary at a time when conservatism was defining itself as populist and conservative at a time when literary studies aligned itself with a domesticated version of modernist revolt. His inability to fit in, however, was actually a self-conscious attempt to find the golden mean; he advocated this compromise position not only in his political writing but in the didactic style of versification he called his "poetry of ideas" (Ciardi 22).

If Viereck is remembered at all today, it is as a publicist—not as a poet. He christened the "new conservatives" in his 1940 manifesto in *The Atlantic*, "But—I'm a Conservative!" striking the middle ground in a manner that would become characteristic for Viereck's poetry as well as his political

8 Chambers in *Testimony*: "Faith is the central problem of this age. The Western world does not know it, but it already possesses the answer to this problem—but only provided that its faith in God and the freedom He enjoins is as great as Communism's faith in Man" (17).

prose, the article criticized Popular Front liberals for being soft on communism, but it also rejected isolationist or "ostrich conservatives" for being indifferent to or even covertly supportive of fascism and anti-Semitism (538, 541). (A month earlier *The Atlantic* had published an example of "ostrich" conservatism in Charles Lindbergh's subtly pro-German appeal for isolationism, "What Substitute for War?" [306]). Reiss, in a 2005 *The New Yorker* article, identifies Viereck as the forgotten founder of the new conservative movement. In *Up from Conservatism*, a book dedicated to Viereck, Michael Lind praises his poetry but describes him first and foremost as "one of the most accomplished, and unjustly neglected, American thinkers of the twentieth century" (50). In *The Conservative Intellectual Movement in America*, Nash has this to say of Viereck's groundbreaking *Conservatism Revisited: The Revolt Against Revolt* (1949): "This was the book which, more than any other of the early postwar era, created the new conservatism as a self-conscious intellectual force [...]. [I]t was this book which boldly used the word 'conservatism' in its title—the first such book after 1945. At least as much as any of his contemporaries, Peter Viereck popularized the term 'conservative' and gave the nascent movement its label" (67–68).

Viereck wrote extensively on conservative issues, but he considered himself "a poet and a professor—in that order," as Marie Hénault puts it in the only book-length study of his writing (17). He taught history at Mt. Holyoke for half a century and wrote verse for most of his life. It is in fact difficult to separate his poetry from his prose—his art from his politics—and at the beginning of his career especially he tended to package them together, using his own poems as epigraphs and credos ("Crass Times Redeemed by Dignity of Souls" fronts *Shame and Glory of the Intellectuals* [1953]) and his essays as commentary ("The Poet in the Machine Age" appends *Strike Through the Mask!* [1950]). His early efforts met with success. He was awarded a Pulitzer Prize in 1949 for *Terror and Decorum*, his first book of poetry, and he received two Guggenheims, one for poetry and one for history (he is the only writer to be doubly honored in these fields). His early poems appeared in *Atlantic*, *Horizon*, *Harper's*, *Poetry*, and *The American Scholar*, and his prose ran the gamut from wide-circulation newspapers like *The Christian Science Monitor* and the book review section of *The New York Times* to academic publications like *American Quarterly*. Disappointed over the populist and pro-business orientation of conservatism, Viereck more-or-less stopped writing political tracts in the 1960s, but he remained active as a poet and to a lesser extent as a critic until his death in 2006, publishing a biological theory of iambics in *Critical Inquiry* (1978), the last of many indictments of Pound in the *New York Review of Books* (1985), and poetry in journals like *The Massachusetts Review* (2003). His book-length poetry cycle *Archer in the Marrow* appeared in 1987; *Tide and Continuities* (with a rhymed introduction by Joseph Brodsky) in 1994; his final collection of poems *Door* in 2005; and a book of essays on and translations of German poetry entitled *Transplantings* appeared posthumously in 2008. This is far from a complete list.

It is essential to consider Viereck's poetry in relation to his prose to make sense of the arc of a career that I want to argue is not only conservative, but symptomatic of the way conservatism reinvented itself after WWII, turning away from a literary tradition both reactionary and elitist towards an anti-communism so popular that, in Viereck's analysis, it crossed the line to populism (*Unadjusted*, 167–78). This is actually a double story. Conservatism was propelled by anti-communism in the direction of populism, while literary criticism moved to the academy without abandoning its avant-garde aspirations. The widespread belief that there is no postwar conservative literature of note or that it is nonfiction is wrong. Conservative literature simply had little institutional purchase in the cultural landscape that took shape after the seismic event of the Pound scandal. A major proponent of this forgotten literature was Peter Viereck. Like Osiris in his poem "To My Isis," he embodied but was also torn apart by diverging discourses: the conservatism defining itself as post-reactionary and the "lit. crit." defining itself as professionally radical (Viereck, *New and Selected* 50–52). Viereck is like Osiris but he is also the missing piece, reminding us that postwar conservatism has a literary tradition—one opposed to modernism and committed to formalism. It is this premature post- or anti-modernism, rather than any specific political philosophy, that puts Viereck's poetry at odds with the literature taught in universities; it is his literariness that puts him at odds with conservative "nonfiction."

A brief remark on conservative post- or anti-modernism: Viereck understood literary forms to be analogous to rules of decorum, and he embraced traditional prosody as a rubric of literary but also personal restraint. Nevertheless, the deliberate provocation of being a formalist in what he understood to be an age of poetic license led him to conceptualize conventional poetics as a "revolt against revolt." This revolt was poetic and political as long as conservatism remained a "dirty word"; but as the movement gained in popularity, and Viereck became disgusted with its populism, he increasingly turned from politics to humanism, and from humanism to a specific idea of the human, ultimately depicting his ideas about convention and decorum in descriptions of the body that became for him the locus of an order older than politics, older even than culture. The poetry of ideas became corporeal and exhibitionistic; the golden mean, illicit. It is in this sense that Viereck's literature, like his literary career, is emblematic. Finding no place in the institutionalized rebellion of literary studies, or in the deliberate artlessness of conservative populism, the literary conservatism that was once common enough to be taken for granted, became obscene.[9]

What follows is divided into three main sections and a conclusion. The first will describe how the battle surrounding Pound encouraged modernists from the left and the right to lay aside their ideological differences and endorse a theory of culture that separated aesthetics from politics. The next section will take up the conservative response to modernism and explore Viereck's initial alliance and growing disillusionment with the nascent conservative movement. The third section will link Viereck's conservative politics, and his growing isolation from both the conservative mainstream and the literary establishment, to the poetry of ideas that became increasingly "dirty" or corporeal as his formalism lost its brief appeal.

The Pound Reaction and the Liberal Aesthetic

Viereck's third book of poetry, *The First Morning* (1952), might be usefully read as a book of preemptive "mourning" for his own obsolescence, precipitated by conservatism's move towards populism on the one hand, and by modernism's march through the institutions on the other. The poem "Birth of a Fascist: The Bankclerk's Vision of Frustration" registers Viereck's growing alienation from a conservative movement he felt was betraying its origins by catering to provincial, middle-class resentments (68). The bitterly ironic "Chorus of the True Unnoticed Poets" takes up the cause of writers who, savaged by the literary establishment, expire in a blood bath of red ink (35). This battle on two fronts was already well underway in 1952, having been brought to a head by the Pound controversy three years earlier. This controversy is the subtext of "Like a Sitting Breeze," which Hénault identifies as Viereck's poetic testimonial to the moral and aesthetic dilemmas posed by Pound (Hénault 48). Parenthetically subtitled "goodbye l'art-pour-l'art," the poem traces the speaker's rejection of his early and, as Viereck suggests, immature wish that art "Suspend me in this choiceless Now." Opening with clearly marked references to A. E. Housman's "Loveliest of Trees, the Cherry Now" and Eliot's "Ash Wednesday," the poem represents the moral dilemma posed by the Pound award as a rite of passage. The stanza form tends toward the heroic, but the rhyme scheme is disrupted for the

[9] I am following Linda Williams's definition of obscenity as a cultural performance that takes place at the margins of society, hidden in plain view or "off-scene" (3).

purposes of establishing a chain rhyme; this compromise between two forms dramatizes both the resolve and the compulsion involved in the speaker's rejection of aestheticism. He has no choice but to move from the luxury of aesthetic indecision to the sternness of moral judgment, but the necessity is also a sign of poetic maturity. The repetition of "again" in the final stanza, called for by the progression of the chain rhyme, indicates that the speaker's personal struggle against aestheticism will be ongoing: "I'm off to the lonely duel by the water's edge again" (98).

Viereck makes his fight personal, but it was more of a melee than a duel. The struggle was not against an individual or even a school but against modernism and its mainstreaming—a mainstreaming that did not condone fascism but may have turned a blind eye to it, in both its international and domestic versions. The academic implications of the battle become clear in the section of *The First Morning* subtitled "1912–1952, Full Cycle." Forty years later the old avant-garde has become "the new rearguard," as Viereck puts it in the final line of "Inscribed for Your Bedside 'Glossary of the New Criticism'" (86). (William Elton's *Glossary of the New Criticism* appeared as a three-part series in 1948 and 1949 issues of *Poetry* magazine, simultaneously with the Bollingen controversy and in the same issues as two mixed reviews of *The Pisan Cantos* and Paul Goodman's crushing review of Viereck's *Terror and Decorum*). Viereck made the New Criticism stand in for the forces opposing him, personalizing his fight against the Poundians as the fight against a particular school of critics. "Epitaph for the Noveaux New Critics, Hugh Kenner, E Tutti Questi" directs its rancor not so much against Pound, ironically invoked as "O miglior fabbro and O mandarin," as against his epigones, and especially Kenner, who would become Pound's staunchest defender. A remark by Louis Rubin in his *Hopkins Review*, provided in a footnote to the poem, explains what is at issue between the New Critics and Viereck: "He has twice criticized the award of the 1949 Bollingen Prize to Pound's *The Pisan Cantos*, on grounds both of form and content. Either he must repent, and publicly, or resign himself to a prominent and permanent position in the Index Prohibitorium [*sic*] of the New Criticism" (88).

Viereck's disagreement was not with the New Critics per se, but with a group of writers and critics who vigorously promoted the argument that art was separate from politics, and literary form more important than content or context in determining aesthetic value.[10] The issue came to a head, as Viereck repeatedly points out, in the Bollingen decision of 1949, when a broad

[10] In his early prose Viereck was clearer about the issues at stake. In "Pure Poetry, Impure Politics, and Ezra Pound," published the year before *The First Morning* (and referred to in the Rubin footnote), Viereck still names the New Critics as his opponents but

coalition of writers argued that aesthetic judgments had to be kept separate from political considerations in a free society.

This argument effectively silenced many critics, but ironically it also undermined the Bollingen committee's purview. The controversy surrounding the decision would soon convince the Library of Congress to get out of the business of giving awards for the artistic achievement that the majority of committee members argued was not political anyway. The Bollingen Award moved to Yale, where it has remained ever since. Viereck, like many following him, blamed literary studies' migration away from political and moral issues and into the universities on the New Critics, who were busily developing specialized methods and terminologies to define their particular area of expertise (Carton and Graff 296). However, the reorganization of the cultural landscape involved more than simply the ascendancy of a particular critical school.

In fact, the rationale for separating Pound's poetry from his politics was as liberal as it was New Critical. Critics from the left and the right agreed, for different reasons, that "absolutism adheres between the poet and his poem, between the reader and the poetry, not between them and the world," as "The Glossary of the New Criticism" puts it in the entry on "form, absolute" quoting Tate ("Glossary" II, 232–33). Literary form demarcated the object of analysis for the New Critics; it also offered an analogue to the quasi-independent, organic, and homogeneous region longed for by the agrarians among them.[11] For liberal thinkers, on the other hand, cultural

---

clearly points out that the issue is not a particular critical methodology but the separation of aesthetics from politics: "For us [those opposed to the award] the issue is whether, as some "New Critics" believe, form and technique can be considered apart from content and meaning. The sympathies of the committee were not with Pound's politics. Judging by their much debated press release, their sympathies were with the widely held belief—a belief I consider unhistorical and psychologically false but not at all 'fascist'—that artistic form can be considered apart from its content and moral meaning" ("Pure Poetry" 342).

[11] Instructive on this point is John Crowe Ransom's *The World's Body* (1938), and especially the essay "Forms and Citizens." In it Ransom identifies himself as a reactionary, and expresses an affinity for Eliot's "In politics, royalism; in religion, Anglo-Catholic; in literature, classical" (41–42). He sees art as one of the primary means for a society to achieve its primary purpose, which is "to instruct its members how to transform instinctive experience into aesthetic experience," or to elevate them above the animal and merely economic levels (41–42). Literature, in other words, is the form that makes them citizens, and it establishes a realm that is strangely territorial but ultimately more decorous than political: "The knowledge attained there [in a poem or painting], and recorded, is a new kind of knowledge, the world in which it is set is a new world" (45). Rasula makes the compelling argument that the New Critics emphasize form as an alternative to a fallen world: "The fundamental tenet of the New

autonomy was proof positive of the personal freedom essential to an open society.

Conservatism and Literature: Viereck contra Pound

The most prominent critic of the liberal and New Critical separation of art from politics was Karl Shapiro, who as consultant in poetry to the Library of Congress was automatically a member of the Bollingen committee. As I described in earlier chapters, Shapiro stated flat-out that as a Jew he could not honor an anti-Semite. He also rejected the form/content distinction upheld by Pound's liberal defenders, insisting that bad ideas made for bad poetry ("The Question" 518–20). In his autobiography, Shapiro describes being approached by someone from *The Saturday Review of Literature* who asked him to write an exposé critical of the Bollingen Award (44). He refused, so *The Saturday Review* turned to Robert Hillyer, who wrote a scathing two-part essay attacking what he saw as a New Critical conspiracy led by Eliot to undermine democracy through the honoring of a fascist poet (Leik 26).

Hillyer claimed that the award was the result of a New Critical conspiracy to undermine democracy through the honoring of a fascist poet. The talk of conspiracy eerily prefigured the witch-hunts of the 1950s, and indeed Hillyer and some of his allies would use similar arguments to lambaste suspected communist writers, partly because they associated modernist experimentation with political rebellion, and probably because the Pound decision was defended by prominent leftists like Macdonald (Filreis 174, 191). Alan Filreis usefully places Hillyer in a movement he designates "anticommunist antimodernism": a middlebrow revolt against revolutionary poetry—revolutionary in politics and form—endorsed by organizations like the League for Sanity in Poetry and the Conservative Poetry Society of America (161). Hillyer had contacts with the former and served as president of the latter (see Leick).

Hillyer's attacks received a great deal of publicity but did not exert much influence, except perhaps to motivate modernists to circle the wagons and defend the exclusive authority of their own literary sensibility. Peter Viereck wrote the follow-up piece on Pound in *The Saturday Review of Literature*, "My Kind of Poetry." He had won the Pulitzer Prize for his first book of poems, *Terror and Decorum*, the same year Pound received the Bollingen

---

Critical worldview is the degeneracy of the modern age; so its impulse to formalism is necessarily conservative" (86).

(1949). Viereck had also been one of Hillyer's students at Harvard, and like his teacher he called for an end to modernist obscurantism and New Critical aestheticism ("My Kind" 7). However, he distanced himself from Hillyer's speculations about a fascist conspiracy, warning against its analogue in red-baiting ("My Kind" 7–8). Viereck considered fascism to be akin to communism; he coined the term "communazi" to underscore their similarities and would later compare Pound to the alleged communist spy Alger Hiss ("But I'm a Conservative" 538; *Shame and Glory* 304). However, his primary interest in this article—and indeed the number of articles he devoted to Pound over the years—was not the "web of subversion" infiltrating the State Department and the Library of Congress but the moral example set by Pound himself ("My Kind" 35). Viereck provided a concise formulation of his ethical-aesthetic principle: "What dehumanizes, de-lyricizes" (*Unadjusted Man* 288).

Viereck's early arguments echoed—and in fact quoted—the dissenting statement issued by Karl Shapiro. Both poets underscored the fundamentally anti-Semitic nature of Pound's poetry, and put forth the argument—unpopular at the time—that bad ideas make for bad poetry.[12] Both disagreed with the theoretical separation of form from content and poetry from context ("My Kind" 7). And both poets would later claim that their opposition to Pound damaged their careers (Rasula 113). However, Viereck's argument was actually closer to the moral opprobrium expressed by George Orwell (who also contributed to the *Partisan Review* symposium) than to the identity-based critique voiced by the young Shapiro, and as time went on he would cite Orwell rather than Shapiro in his numerous references to the Pound controversy ("Pound at 100" 3). Viereck was sensitive to anti-Semitism but treated it as a synecdoche for all sorts of prejudice ("Catholic baiting is the anti-Semitism of the liberals"; *Shame and Glory* 45). He felt it was more important to judge Pound according to universal moral principles than to dwell on the particular objects of Pound's hatred.

At the middle of the century, however, Viereck and Shapiro were united not only in their rejection of Pound but in the belief, shared by a number of young poets, that traditional rhyme and meter offered the only adequate aesthetic response to political and poetic extremism. The new formalism

---

[12] Viereck says of *The Pisan Cantos*: "fascism and anti-semitism compose one of the essential 'myths'" ("Beyond Revolt" 52). Elsewhere he says the poem is "98 per cent incoherent, 2 percent lovely, and persistently fascist and anti-Semitic" (Ciardi 28). Hénault cites these statements and provides a good summary of Viereck's attitude towards Pound (49). Both of Shapiro's and Viereck's essays are included in William Van O'Connor's *A Casebook on Ezra Pound*, which as Blish exasperatedly pointed out, established itself as the standard college textbook on Pound the controversy.

began to take shape in John Ciardi's *Mid-Century American Poets* (1950), an anthology important not only for its early recognition of the poets who have come to stand for the age such as Lowell and Bishop, but for its rationale for grouping them with those who have been forgotten such as Shapiro and Viereck. Randall Jarrell, also featured in the anthology, described Lowell as a "post- or anti-modernist": "In a day when poets wish to be irresistible forces, he is an immovable object" (Ciardi 164, 163). This early use of "post- or anti-modernist" as a synonym for anti-avant-gardism comes from a review of *Lord Weary's Castle* for *The Nation*, included as the introduction to Lowell in Ciardi's anthology. (Lowell was the only poet not to write his own introduction; he requested that Jarrell's review be included instead.) Jarrell's phrase accurately describes the orientation of the entire volume. Indeed, Ciardi virtually paraphrases Jarrell in his introduction: "For pre-eminently this is a generation not of Bohemian extravagance but of self-conscious sanity in an urbane and cultivated poetry that is the antithesis of the Bohemian spirit" (xxix).[13]

Viereck proved a good fit for Ciardi's anti-Bohemian roster. He revised his article on Pound for *The Saturday Review of Literature*, "My Kind of Poetry," to serve as his introduction. The essay begins by underscoring the link between his politics and his poetics: "I must disappoint many readers by the unexciting conservatism of my poetic techniques" (Ciardi 16). It then goes on to elaborate the importance of formal restraint: "Just as political liberty is not based on a radical smashing of traffic lights but on law and traditional established institutions, so poetry must be subjected to the challenge of form, the more rigorous and traditional and conservative the better, to bring out the response of beauty" (17).

Viereck's self-conscious return to the "challenge of form" was hardly a novelty; leading critics like John Crowe Ransom embraced the new traditionalism, arguing that "The chances are not so bright now for poetries which are radically new" (*American Poetry* 12).[14] However, what Ransom characterized as a period of consolidation, when postwar poets would develop the innovations made by the modernists, Viereck understood as a rejection of modernism *tout court*. He was a new conservative rather than a traditionalist, and what interested him most about formal constraints, at least at first, was the analogy they offered for self-discipline and political moderation.

---

[13] See Rasula on the Ciardi volume: "Ciardi's propositions revealingly implicate the roots of formalism in a fear of the avant-garde" (182).

[14] This from a series of lectures on *American Poetry at Mid-Century* published by the Library of Congress in 1958. The other contributors, Delmore Schwartz and John Hall Wheelock, echo Ransom on midcentury poetry's post-experimental phase (20, 46).

Viereck's anti-modernism, in other words, was an expression of his anti-fascism, and his advocacy of strict rhyme and meter had more to do with the postwar political context than with the formal debates that had always been central to modernism. He concentrates almost exclusively on Pound's break with iambic pentameter (reaffirmed in *The Pisan Cantos*), ignoring the background arguments—really foundational arguments for modernism—about poetry's relation to speech, meaning, and modern conditions. [15] This made for a rather loose account of strict form—one that became looser the longer Viereck maintained it. Indeed, his opposition to Pound would eventually lead him to a wholesale advocacy of iambics grounded in a biological theory of meter: "List at random the natural functions of your own anatomy, and what do they turn out to be? Inhale and exhale of breath, systole and diastole of heart, pound and pause of pulse, in and out of coition, ebb and flow of tide: all are iambics" ("Strict Form in Poetry" 211). Pound's trochees, according to this characterization, are inhumane because they are inhuman. The meter of a fascist is, by definition, monstrous.

The traditionalist Yvor Winters had long been challenging Pound, but on formal rather than political grounds. Indeed, there is no better illustration of the growing schism between prewar traditionalism, which was primarily literary even when politically conservative, and postwar conservatism, which is political even when it is talking about literature, than the surprising enmity between Winters and the Bollingen-opponents. Winters had been an early follower of Pound, and John Crowe Ransom identified him as a New Critic (in spite of his one fault: "moralism") in the volume that coined the term (*New Criticism* xi). The infatuation with Pound ended long before the Bollingen controversy, but Winters felt personally insulted by Hillyer's broadside against the New Critical "conspiracy," demanding an apology in an angry letter eventually published as the final statement in *The Case Against "The Saturday Review of Literature."* The disagreement was not over literary matters *per se*. A decade earlier Winters had argued that Pound was the "apotheosis" behind Eliot's masks, describing his nefarious influence in these terms: "Pound's relationship to tradition is that of one who has abandoned its method and pillaged its details—he is merely a barbarian on the loose in a museum" (501, 480). The analogy between modernist forms and modern conditions most famously expressed by Pound in "Hugh Selwyn Mauberley"—"The age demanded an image / Of its accelerated grimace" (*Personae* 188)—Winters dismissed as a species of the mimetic fallacy. Eliot's traditionalism he saw as mere eclecticism. Winters identifies himself

[15] See Canto 81: "To break the pentameter, that was the first heave" (81/538). See also Canto 98: "And as for those who deform thought with iambics" (98/707).

as a "reactionary" in the essay; he does not take issue with the politics of the modernists but with their use of symbolist techniques (460). Pound and Eliot, he argues, are too concerned with the "effect" of symbols; the true task of poetry is to perform moral or evaluative work by articulating common dilemmas through forms that help clarify them (Stanford 193). Winters begins with method and arrives at politics and morality by implication. Viereck and Hillyer, in contrast, were more interested in Pound's fascism than in his metrics, except insofar as the latter could be used to indict the former.

Indeed, although Viereck brings up Pound's form repeatedly as evidence of his political and moral degeneracy, he rarely discusses the prosody of modernism without slipping into a historical critique of its genesis. Modernism, for Viereck is less a technique than an idea—one in a long train of bad ideas having their origin in the French revolution. The characteristic shift in register from formal analysis to the history of ideas is evident in the language Viereck employs in a subsequent manifesto (he was a compulsive writer of manifestos):

> As a result of this revolt against revolt, American and British poetry—and often philosophy—have moved from their storming of every possible Bastille (including the decapitation of all those royalist capital letters) to a Bourbon restoration in both credo and technique. In credo, American and British poetry has often evolved from a semi-Marxist radicalism of the 1930's to a Christian liberal-conservatism of the 1950's. In technique, the same poetry has often evolved from free verse to rigorous strictness of form. For example, the representative evolution, in both credo and technique, of W. H. Auden. (*Unadjusted Man* 285)

Viereck's characteristic irony masks what is actually a historical narrative linking e.e. cummings's typography to the French Revolution. Viereck draws a trajectory from 1789 to the modernist avant-garde, arguing that modernism is the heir to romanticism, and fascism an incarnation of Jacobinism. Irving Babbitt laid the groundwork for this sweeping argument in the first part of the twentieth century; it was taken up by Russell Kirk and can be found as late as George Steiner's *Bluebeard's Castle*. The belief that modern political and aesthetic excesses can be laid at the feet of the French Revolution is, in fact, one of the tenets of the twentieth-century Burkean revival among conservative thinkers (Babbitt, Guttmann, Kirk, etc.). Viereck, proud of this heritage, claimed Edmund Burke's *Reflections on the Revolution in France* dated the "birth of a deliberate international conservatism [...] in the same way that the birth of international Marxism is dated by the communist Manifesto" (*Conservatism from John Adams to Churchill* 10). From Burke, Viereck derives the argument that the revolution did not liberate so much as impose equality on the procrustean bed of the guillotine (*Metapolitics* 32; *Shame and Glory* 259; Burke 214). From Babbitt's reading of Burke he derives the argument that romanticism (especially in its Rousseauian strain) is the literature of revolutionary excess (Babbitt, *Laokoon* 193–200; Babbitt, *Democracy and Leadership* 101, 116, 133; Viereck, *Metapolitics* 28–29; Viereck, *Conservatism Revisited* 83–84).[16] Modernism he understood to be a belated form of romanticism. Of course, modernists like Pound and Eliot were avowed anti-romantics, but Viereck believed their experimentalism to be, at root, a romantic defiance of convention that ultimately led the way to despotism and enslavement.[17] He believed the contrary to be true as well: respect for traditional forms is the precondition of freedom in art and politics—a paradox he would come to describe as "strict wildness."

Viereck's formalism is conservative, but also anti-modernist and post-reactionary. While he might have been over-hasty in declaring alliance with Auden, whose affinity with classical and even archaic forms extends back to his earliest poems (see the previous chapter), he was correct to point to parallel developments in philosophy and the social sciences. Even prominent liberal thinkers (who were by no means Burkean) endorsed comparable programs of moderation. Daniel Bell, for instance endorsed an "end to ideology," arguing that ideological extremes led to the extremes of modern warfare, and declaring instead the importance of separating passion—especially chiliastic passion—from politics (Bell 88). Bell's calls for an institutional class of decision-makers, insulated from the vagaries of party politics, had much in common with Chase's manifesto for an institutional avant-garde, which I discussed in the introduction. The manifestos for moderation from the left and the right made for strange bedfellows, and while some critics, like Chase, welcomed the influence of "our famous con-

---

16 This is a Burkean notion. *On the Revolution in France* explicitly links sound poetic principles with those of national identification and good government. Contrasting the rationalistic philosophy behind the French Terror with Horace, Burke says: "On the principles of this mechanic philosophy, our institutions can never be embodied, if I may use the expression, in persons; so as to create in us love, veneration, admiration, or attachment [...]. These public affections, combined with manners, are required sometimes as supplements, sometimes as correctives, always as aids to law. The precept given by a wise man, as well as a great critic, for the construction of poems, is equally true as to states:—*Non satis est pulchra esse poemata, dulcia sunto* (Burke 214).

17 Other conservative critics—even those largely supportive of the modernist project—shared the view that it was a belated form of romanticism. For an example see Donald Davidson's "A Mirror for Artists," his contribution to *I'll Take My Stand* (41).

servatism" ("Our Country" III, 569), others like Joseph Frank, Robert Gorham Davis, and more famously C. Wright Mills wondered if establishment liberalism was not simply conservatism in disguise.[18]

But if liberals did adopt a deliberately moderate tone, there remained an essential difference between postwar liberalism and conservatism, namely their attitude towards the establishment itself. Chase and Bell thought that institutions could provide the same moderating influence that Viereck envisioned for form, but through the structural separation of art from politics—or even passion from politics—rather than through an ethic of restraint. Viereck, like many conservatives, remained skeptical about specialization and functional separation, seeing this "managerial revolution"—to use the term coined by James Burnham at the beginning of his long march to the right—as a bureaucratic solution to what was essentially a moral problem, depriving individuals of control over their actions and relieving them of responsibility for their decisions. Viereck argued that "The task of the new conserving of ethics is to remove freedom from the realm of collective and outer economic determinism and restore it to the realm of individual and inner moral responsibility. That responsibility is not to be shifted exclusively to the big, brotherly shoulders of impersonal forces" (*Unadjusted* 277). Such arguments were in keeping with Babbitt's emphasis on the inner check: "No amount of devotion to society and its supposed interests can take the place of [the] inner obeisance of the spirit to standards" (*Democracy and Leadership* 257). While Viereck held no truck with Babbitt's racism and isolationism, his emphasis on form and self-restraint, coupled with his distrust of institutional solutions, did amount to moral "Babbittry" (*Democracy and Leadership* 210, 267–68). This was not, of course, the middle-class Babbittry parodied by Sinclair Lewis (in fact Viereck extended the fictional Babbitt genealogy in *The Shame and the Glory of Intellectuals* to show how the narrow-mindedness of the mid-western middle class could produce a younger generation of equally narrow-minded modernists and progressives). Viereck was instead interested in upholding aristocratic standards of decorum that linked good behavior to good form, as the title of his debut book of poems—*Terror and Decorum*—suggests (*Unadjusted* 31).

The nature and genealogy of the terror indicated by the title had been the subject of Viereck's first book *Metapolitics* (1941, enlarged and reissued

---

[18] On the academic shift to the right in the 1950s, see Joseph Frank's essay on Lionel Trilling in *The Widening Gyre*, Robert Gorham Davis's essay in the *American Scholar*, "The New Criticism and the Democratic Tradition," and Mills's famous "Letter to the New Left," collected in *Power, Politics, and People*. For a later account of the conservative drift in academic criticism see Robert Scholes, "The Illiberal Imagination."

1961, 1965 and again in 2003), the published version of his PhD dissertation. *Metapolitics* was one of the earliest studies in English to make the argument that Wagner's romanticism—or at least the romanticism of the "Wagnerites"— led directly to Hitler (*Metapolitics* 130; *Unadjusted* 22).[19] Central to the argument was Wagner's own change of heart from an admirer of the French Revolution and a supporter of the revolutions of 1849 to a reactionary (*Metapolitics* 103–06). Viereck believed that the radical egalitarianism aspired to by the French Revolution is rationalism's impossible dream; when this dream collides with reality, as it must, it always derails into the opposite, irrational belief that the true task of politics is to further "metapolitical" concepts such as racial superiority or the "will" of the "Volk" (105).[20] The Nazi reaction against egalitarianism, resulting in the horrible equality of corpses in the death camps, Viereck held to be an extreme but in no way unique example of revolution turning into its opposite.[21] A later summary of the argument gives it a polemical edge that emphasizes the importance of Burke to understanding not only the French Revolution but romanticism, modernism, and totalitarianism:

---

[19] "To them [the Wagners] Hitler was not demagogue but demigod. He was that Siegfried-Barbarossa reincarnation for whom Wagner had yearned to save Germany from Wagner's three abominations: democracy, finance-capitalism, and the Jews" (*Metapolitics* 148). In *The Reactionaries* Harrison would similarly argue that the French Revolution led directly to the proto-fascist Action Français (Harrison 22–24).

[20] Viereck—like Schlesinger, Arendt, and others—downplayed the ideological differences between Nazi Germany and the USSR in order to stress the commonalities leading to the concentration camps and the gulag: "the Nazis denounced the Soviet's 'bolshevism,' 'godlessness,' and 'terror' not because the Nazis are any less state-socialist, anti-Christian, or violent, but because Russia is a rival and Marx a Jew" (*Metapolitics* 66). What justified lumping together communism and Nazism under a common heading, Viereck argued, was their anti-individualism, manifesting itself in the politics of violence and dehumanization.

[21] See Babbitt's early formulation of the egalitarianism-mass murder analogy: "If the Rousseauist set up an ideal of universal brotherhood that led actually to universal conscription, the utilitarian for his part has put prime emphasis on material organization and efficiency and so, with the aid of physical science, has gradually built up an enormous mass of interlocking machinery which was, in theory, to serve humanity and promote the greatest good of the greatest number, but has in practice been pressed into the service of the will to power of individuals and social groups and nationalities [...]. The chief victims have been the very masses whom both Rousseauist and Baconian have professed themselves eager to benefit" (*Democracy and Leadership* 133).

> Reread the 'reactionary,' classicist, post-1789 critics of Rousseau to see why the romantic idyll of spontaneous self-expression and 'natural goodness of man' was switched somehow. The romantic idyll of self-expression could not be bothered with the ethical discipline of a universal value-framework. So the arcadian pastoral was switched—by an almost imperceptible Caligari-tilt of the mirrors—into Belsen-Buchenwald-Kolyma-Katyn. (*Shame and Glory* 131)

The sidelong reference to Caligari, like the earlier allusion to cummings's decapitation of letters, is an essential part of the argument. With a likely nod towards Sigfried Kracauer's *From Caligari to Hitler* (1947), Viereck identifies modernism as the final rail switch between romanticism and the death camps.

In a review of *Metapolitics*, Jacques Barzun criticized Viereck's habit of making romanticism shoulder so much historical responsibility, arguing that ideas do not survive unchanged through the ages, nor do they simply cause political events (*Metapolitics* 350).[22] (Viereck included this review and his response in the 1961 and subsequent editions of the book). The truly transhistorical idea in Viereck, however, is not romanticism but the contrasting concept of individualism. Romanticism, in his several studies, becomes merely a placeholder for extremism, and more important than its content (rationalism or irrationalism, egotism or collectivism, nostalgia or utopianism) is the pendulum-swing in which it is implicated, always resulting in its opposite. The only exception to the cyclical history of *les extrêmes se touchent* is the individual, "the unadjusted man," whose self-restraint makes him a rebel against all mass movements, whether totalitarian or, in the 1950s, consumerist (*Unadjusted* 25, 192). Viereck admitted the individual was a historical invention, which he traced, through Burke, back to feudal prerogatives; but like contemporary social contract theorists he argued that the historical concept had to be elevated to a universal moral principle (*Unadjusted* 28; cf. Burnham, *Managerial Revolution* 26). What he calls "the dignity of lyricism" has precisely this ethical meaning: "As ethics is the restraining function of the inward frontier, so lyricism is the unleashing function" (*Unadjusted* 279). The poet is an individual whose "strict wildness" expresses the paradox that self-restraint is voluntary and therefore exceptional in the age of extremism. Individualism is the lyrical expression of a universal moral principle; it is the golden mean enunciated as voice.

---

22 Clement Greenberg makes a similar argument in his review of the book: "The term 'romanticism,' in the lower case, is an over-simplification. As Mr. Viereck uses it, it implies something that persists beyond historical limitations, a permanent category of human behavior, i.e. 'romanticism' is the way human nature shows in general its impatience with reason, tradition and external norms" (510).

Viereck's deliberately moderate ideas about ethical and lyrical individualism should be understood in light of his family history, and particularly his father's conviction as a German foreign agent during World War II. George Sylvester Viereck—nicknamed "Swastika" by his many detractors—was an American citizen of German ancestry who believed himself, with good reason, to be related to the Kaiser's family through illegitimate descent (Johnson 8–9). He was a fairly well-known poet and journalist who opposed American intervention in World War I, rejected the Treaty of Versailles as unjust to Germany, and visited the Kaiser in his exile publishing an authorized interview and later a biographical defense called *The Kaiser on Trial* (Johnson 20, 203). George Viereck was not a straightforward monarchist, nor did he subscribe, in any simple way, to the anti-Semitism playing an increasingly central role in German nationalism. In fact, he considered himself to be a progressive and was an enthusiastic supporter of Robert La Follette (who also opposed the Treaty of Versailles). With Paul Eldridge he published *My First Two Thousand Years: The Autobiography of the Wandering Jew* (1928) and two other fictions on the wandering Jew theme, all of them slightly erotic in character. He acquired a reputation as an interviewer of the influential men he characterized as artists and geniuses, and among his interlocutors were prominent Jewish intellectuals such as Freud and Einstein.

In 1923 George Viereck became the first American to interview Hitler. He described him as an artist—the term of ultimate respect in his lexicon—but nevertheless remained skeptical about Hitler's ability to influence German politics (Johnson 117–19). His enthusiasm grew in step with the Nazi leader's power, and in the 1930s George Viereck established himself as an active—and well paid—propagandist for the German government in the United States. Most of his energy went into writing and publishing, with the help of secret funds from the German Foreign Office. He also appeared as a speaker at a large Madison Square rally organized by the precursor to the German-American Bund, the purpose of which was to protest the Jewish boycott of German goods (184). It is only fair to George Viereck, but not flattering to his perspicacity, to point out that he believed Nazism could be separated from anti-Semitism (175, 187–88; 254). Nevertheless, his Jewish friends and acquaintances distanced themselves when he became a vocal supporter of the Third Reich (94–95; 261). The House Committee on Un-American Activities and then the Justice Department became suspicious of his activities. Several trials ensued, and while he was ultimately cleared of sedition charges he was convicted as an undeclared foreign agent of Germany, serving five years in a federal penitentiary until his release in 1947 (237–50). His incarceration effectively ended his career as a writer, except for a sensationalized account of his experiences in prison, *Men into Beasts*

(1952), which went through two editions and obtained some notoriety as a work of gay pulp fiction (251).[23]

The conviction also led to the dissolution of the Viereck family. George Viereck's wife divorced him while he was in prison and donated his money to Jewish and Catholic charities (Johnson 251). His two sons joined the army, the youngest dying a hero's death fighting the Germans in Italy, and Peter Viereck manning a radio-listening post in Africa and Italy. Peter Viereck earned his PhD from Harvard before enlisting, but with a convicted German agent for a father, he could not be promoted to officer's rank (which would have given him access to classified information), and instead performed the enlisted man's task of monitoring radio transmissions. It is probably in this capacity that he first encountered Pound's broadcasts for Rome Radio.[24]

Pound was transported back to the United States to stand trial while George Viereck still had over a year left to serve on his prison term. The young Peter Viereck, newly demobilized and busy launching his career, must have been struck, as others were, by the similarities between the two cases (Johnson 170). Both poets became fascists. Both believed conventional morality was for other people. Both were willing to defy American politics and popular opinion for the men they thought displayed genius in politics or art (Johnson 262–64; Perelman 29). Peter Viereck never fully reconciled with his father, who for his part never admitted his past mistakes, but the father did spend his last decade in his son's house in Hadley, Massachusetts, where he died in 1962 (Johnson 252).

It is possible that Peter Viereck transferred the unresolved argument with his father to Pound, who unlike the father was never formally convicted. At some basic level this is doubtless true. However, this simple version of the "father complex" misses the significance of what Peter Viereck was already identifying as totalitarianism's political-aesthetic complex. The arc of the father's biography illustrated what the son had begun to accept as a general historical truth even before Pound was charged with treason: political radicalism leads to radical art, which in turn inspires political reaction. The pendulum-swing of this complex is not oedipal but institutional, and its

[23] George Sylvester Viereck still had a reputation—probably a scandalous one—in the late 1950s. In his "Sixth Advertisement for Myself," Norman Mailer reports sending Viereck a copy of the editorial that would grow into "The White Negro" in order to solicit comments. He also sent copies to William Faulkner, Eleanor Roosevelt, W.E.B. Du Bois, and Murray Kempton.

[24] See Alfred de Grazia's self-published play on his experiences with Viereck at the radio listening station in Africa, "Poet-Traitor Ezra Pound," 10 Mar. 2015 <http://www.grazian-archive.com/poetry/plays/poet.htm>. See also Viereck's references to encountering Pound as a soldier in "Parnassus Divided" (67).

resolution—if that is the right word—involves not the revolt against the father but against the political and aesthetic principles involved in mass movements. Peter Viereck's revolt against revolt was an attempt to defend conventional form, individualism, and moderation. It acquired new urgency in the face of the Pound controversy, when former radicals and reactionaries entered into what must have seemed like an unholy alliance to save Pound from judgment and ordain his poetry as the verbal icon of the new literary establishment.

Viereck opposed the establishment, but he also opposed the anti-establishmentarians, such as those members of the later House Committee on Un-American activities who treated sympathy for Pound as a litmus test (surprisingly enough) for radicalism. The individualist strain in his thinking made this self-proclaimed new conservative fundamentally contrarian, a non-joiner who cleaved to movements that never really took off—such as poetic formalism—and refused to countenance those that did—such as postwar conservatism in its strong anti-communist form. Viereck tended to seek allies among dead statesmen like Washington and Gouverneur Morris—Federalist protagonists of what he liked to call "the American Conservation of 1776" (*Shame and Glory* 203). Modern conservatives, in his opinion, were not interested in conserving moral values but in promoting classically liberal economic values. He had this to say, for instance, about the Eisenhower years:

> the present Eisenhower-era complacency, currently denounced as 'America's creeping conservatism,' is not conservative at all. It is a liberalism, a nineteenth-century *laissez faire* liberalism, grown too successful, too stodgy, too fat. [...] Hence, the philosophical conservative in America (in the Melville-Hawthorne tradition) has nothing in common with so-called 'right-wing politics' (nationalist isolationism), which is really not so much right of center as Midwest of center (*Unadjusted* 312–13).

Viereck was not the only conservative to oppose Eisenhower (e.g. Clinton Rossiter [Nash 452]), although his outspoken support of Adlai Stevenson must have set him apart from other critics on the right (*Unadjusted* 231–62).[25] Conservatism became popular at midcentury, but Viereck's revolt against revolt increasingly meant going it alone.

---

[25] J. K. Galbraith had this to say of "Eisenhower and the Conservative Revolution" shortly after his election in 1953: "Nearly everything the government is doing, it has been doing long enough for the activity to seem commonplace and conservative, especially to those who benefit from it [...]. As a result, government under Eisenhower will be about as big and have about the same range of functions as government under Truman. This does not mean that the new administration will endear itself to liberals

Viereck's isolation grew during the McCarthy years. He was strongly anti-communist but also anti-anti-communist, and he used the status-resentment arguments then popular among liberal thinkers like Schlesinger, and evident in the "Midwest of center" comment above, to criticize McCarthyism as a form of regionalist populism (*Unadjusted* 129–213).[26] Viereck first published these arguments in the famous Daniel Bell collection that, in its revised edition, would appear under the title *The Radical Right*. Viereck was unique among the critics of the right in pointing out the obvious—but easily overlooked—fact that the McCarthy constituency was made up of old La Follette supporters, who propagated their anti-elitism on both sides of the political spectrum (both La Follette and McCarthy were Wisconsin republicans) ("The Revolt against the Elite" 163).[27] Viereck cited as parallel examples Senators Wheeler and Nye, who moved "from 'liberal' Progressives to 'reactionary' America Firsters. But basically they never changed at all; throughout, they remained passionately Anglophobe, Germanophile, Isolationist, and anti-eastern-seaboard, first under leftist and then under rightist pretexts" (163–64). Clearly Viereck is describing the arc of his father's biography here, but in a way that characterizes the radical right as pseudo-conservative and irrational, implicated in the pendulum-swing of extremism that Viereck sought to avoid (cf. *Conservatism Revisited* 150–51).

This did not amuse the writers of the *National Review*, who were busy cobbling together anti-communism and laissez-faire liberalism into a viable political force. Frank S. Meyer, who would collect some of his contributions to the *National Review* in a book called *The Conservative Mainstream*, had this to say in 1956: "Viereck is not the first, nor will he be the last, to succeed in passing off his unexceptionably Liberal sentiments as conservatism" (69). Viereck had already taken on the founding editor of that journal when he negatively reviewed William F. Buckley's first book, *Man and God at Yale*. Buckley argued that the best way to make Harvard representative was to bring it in line with the market forces that encouraged political freedom as a function of free trade; his proposal was to let those donating to the Harvard

[…]. But the liberals did not vote for Eisenhower. The conservative idealists did and they will have much more legitimate grounds for complaint" (103).

26 See Auerbach (175) for a helpful list of Viereck's ideal conservative attributes.

27 In his Pulitzer Prize-winning *The Age of Reform* (1955), Richard Hofstadter formulates a theory that is largely in agreement with Viereck's and relevant to the Pound controversy: "It is not too much to say that the Greenback-Populist tradition activated most of what we have of modern popular anti-Semitism in the United States. From Thaddeus Stevens and Coin Harvey to Father Coughlin, and from Brooks and Henry Adams to Ezra Pound, there has been a curiously persistent linkage between anti-Semitism and money and credit obsessions" (80–81).

endowment vet the Harvard faculty (*Shame and Glory* 295). Viereck supported academic freedom, and he insisted that free ideas should not be made subservient to free trade (*Shame and Glory* 299–300). He accused Buckley of "exalt[ing] laisser faire in economics as conservative" but "denounce[ing] laisser faire in ideas and in academic freedom as subversive and pink" (294). This critique of laissez faire economics, coupled with a polemic against populism, became Viereck's standard objection to the emerging right. Thus he would describe Goldwater as "a laissez-faire Manchester liberal" (*Conservatism Revisited* 142), and in a revised edition of *Metapolitics*, link his populist rhetoric to extremism (371). By 1962 Viereck was so disappointed with the new conservatism he had named that he concluded the new edition of *Conservatism Revisited* with the following question: "What is it, triumph or bankruptcy, when the empty shell of a name gets acclaim while serving as a chrysalis for its opposite?" (151).

Viereck was not the only name-giver of the new conservatism, but neither was he the crypto-liberal that the *National Review* made him out to be. He was alienated from liberals just as he was alienated from the new conservatives, but in ethical, rather than political, terms. Contrary to Buckley, Viereck believed the university should be an ivory tower, but contrary to the literary establishment he did not believe that poetry occupied a separate sphere. This earned him the dubious distinction of being an exile from the literary "world apart" and from the emerging movement of anti-establishmentarian conservatives. His position was internally consistent, but it was also consistently contrarian. He believed that laissez faire economics were as prone to extremism as *vers libre* poetics. The new cultural landscape, however, designated these concepts the sancta sanctorum of opposing camps: laissez faire dominated the pages of *National Review* and the arguments of the conservative mainstream, and free verse—or the freedom of verse from politics—dominated the pages of *Partisan Review* and the aesthetics of mainstream modernism.[28]

---

[28] There is a sense in which Viereck was right about the similarity between laissez-faire economics and the liberal aesthetic advocated by Pound's supporters. Both argued that certain spheres—be they aesthetic or economic—had to be kept free from political control. Friedrich A. von Hayek, widely considered to be the father of modern laissez-faire economics, had this to say about the erection of separate spheres in a liberal democracy: "The various kinds of collectivism, communism, fascism, etc., differ among themselves in the nature of the goal toward which they want to direct the efforts of society. But they all differ from liberalism and individualism in wanting to organize the whole of society and all its resources for this unitary end and in refusing to recognize autonomous spheres in which the ends of the individuals are supreme" (100).

Not fitting in anywhere, Viereck increasingly turned away from politics and toward his own poetry, which was also increasingly out of step with the times.[29] Viereck never wrote another book as well-received as the Pulitzer Prize winning *Terror and Decorum*. This partly had to do with his politics, and partly with his voice. The lyricism of the golden mean was a poetry of ideas, deliberately philosophical and, despite his repeated claims to the contrary, didactic.[30] Hénault describes his early poems as having only a loose connection to history: "They have, rather, as Viereck states, ideas as their protagonists" (73). Even before *Strike Through the Mask!*, his second book of poems, appeared in 1950, reviewers like Paul Goodman—taking issue with the poem "Incantation" and its description of "tall ideas dancing"—were complaining that his verse was all argument and no feeling (*Terror and Decorum* 82 and epigraph; Goodman 289–91). This was not because of the subject matter. The topics were often risqué and the treatment highly ironic. But the poetry always seemed to be balancing options—like the political extremes of right and left—to establish the individualism of the middle. The dominant trend was moving in the other direction, towards the confessional verse featured in Donald Allen's *The New American Poetry, 1945–1960* (which did not include Viereck) and the principled spontaneity of the Beats. At the same time, the New Left would re-politicize passion by arguing, in the manner of C. Wright Mills, that the personal was political, or in the manner of Marcuse, that political repression was linked to sexual repression. Moderation would also be rejected by the right, as the line in Goldwater's famous nomination acceptance speech, adapted from Cato by the speechwriter Harry Jaffa (shortly before his collaboration with Allan Bloom in *Shakespeare's Politics*): "Extremism in the defense of liberty is no vice. And

[29] Viereck describes his transition from politics to poetry in the following passage, which is unwarranted in its optimism about the durable appeal of strict form: "The greatest psychological change in America between the 1930's and 1950's has been the revolt against revolt. In politics this change has been sometimes salutary, sometimes dangerous. Salutary by discrediting the lure of communism and fellow-traveling; dangerous by often lending itself to temporary misuse by nationalist thought-controllers, thereby necessitating in those particular cases a revolt against the revolt against revolt. But if the change has been only a mixed blessing in politics, it has been almost entirely salutary in philosophy, art, poetry" (*Unadjusted* 284–85).

[30] Viereck: "The coming return to communication between poets and readers will communicate, among other things, an ethical content. But never, never by explicit sermonizing; rhymed editorials, even on the side of the angels, kill lyricism. And lyricism is the one great function left to the poet, now that the inroads of science and of prose have deprived him of his earlier, non-lyrical roles of law-giver, philosopher, prophet, seer" (*Unadjusted* 290).

moderation in the pursuit of justice is no virtue" (Nash 347). Viereck persisted in his revolt against revolt, continuing to man the barricades of moderation long after the 1960s made passion the proof of political and artistic authenticity. His "tall ideas" became a footnote to the success story of postwar conservatism, and his poetry was forgotten.

Remembering Viereck: "When conservatism was still a dirty word"

Viereck anticipated his fate. Several of his most important poems are written from a posthumous perspective, enjoining readers to literally re-member him, put him back together, like the Osiris of Egyptian mythology who serves as the speaker's identification figure in "To My Isis" (*The Persimmon Tree* [1956]; *New and Selected* 50–52). The postmortem enjoinder that is the poem's opening gambit makes memory a function of form. The impossibility of speaking from beyond the grave motivates the irony of the conclusion ("I'm just as real as you are [...] merely scattered") but also the apostrophes that structure the voice and the variably rhymed quatrains that maintain its balance. Strict form is central to the poem's commemorative project, but there is also a sense in which the specificities of form are irrelevant. Memory, in the poem, is less a function of tradition—continuity or identity over time—than of regularity and repetition. The poem is strangely anonymous and appeals, apparently indiscriminately, to any number of conventions. On the one hand form constitutes the materiality of memory; it is the structure that prevents Osiris from being "scattered," protestations to the contrary. But on the other hand form is not a piece of Osiris, and thus in a sense may be the part of him that is missing. The poem does not assert the identity of the speaker but the relevance of the patterns and rituals that bring him repeatedly into being.

The structure of Viereck's poem—and I would argue many of his poems—can be understood as a variation of the lyrical form that Northrop Frye defines as "subjectivized decorum" (Frye, *Anatomy* 273). Frye traces the emergence of the lyric back to an act of rhetorical emancipation, when the personal rhythms and associations of poetic voice freed themselves from the semi-official forms of the epos (273). Viereck's lyrics are also situated between the personal and the official, but they almost always move in the other direction, from mere association—a randomness that always threatens to "scatter" or disassociate—towards the decorum of strict form (Frye 273). The emphasis is on the individual, but the urge is towards compromise rather than liberation. This is clear in the first poem of the first book, "Poet," which appears under related titles in subsequent collections and, in a condensed form and under the title "Not Worms," also fronts *Transplantings*, the collection of German poetry Viereck was working on when he died (n. pag.). "Poet" subtends and bookends Viereck's poetic career; it is also perhaps his most succinct verse statement of poetic principle. The epigraph, from Baudelaire, already presents the theme: form is a human invention but nevertheless immortal, and independent of the matter through which it is realized (*Terror and Decorum* 3–5). This is significant given the plot of the poem, which is a posthumous variation on Yeats's "Circus Animals Desertion" (Viereck borrows the "rags and bones" from the Yeats poem for a section heading in *Strike Through the Mask!*). The words that once "begged favor at [the poet's] court in vain" have revolted after his death: "Lush adverbs, senile rhymes in tattered gowns— / Send notes to certain exiled nouns / And mutter openly against his reign." The words are merely material, however, and therefore immaterial to the poet's memory; he "lives on in Form, and Form shall shatter / This tuneless mutiny of matter." By the end of the poem it turns out that form is not merely metric but nomothetic, even divine: "And all things are because he willed them so."

This poem is another variation on the theme of lyrical immortality, but what makes it central to Viereck's œuvre, and in fact qualifies it as his personal anthem, is the way immortality—once again—is a function of form rather than identity. This form is explicitly anti-Poundian. The "terror" of the song—the first of many references to the book's title—is the "Tyrannic metronome" form imposes on creation, in explicit rejection of Pound's famous third principle of imagism: "As regarding rhythm: to compose in the sequence of the musical phrase, not in sequence of a metronome" ("A Retrospect" 3). It is worth noting that the pairing "Terror and Decorum" often receives an opposite valence in Viereck's poetry than in his political writing. Elsewhere Viereck would describe tradition as "decorous," reserving the term "terror" for attempts to break with it. Lyricism, however, has a duty to terrify and transgress—within limits.[31] Viereck repeatedly

[31] An epigraph in his second book of poetry—whose title *Strike Through the Mask!* locates it squarely in the midcentury Melville revival while expressing Viereck's antagonism to the modernist persona or mask—hints at his growing isolation by providing a gloss on the title of *Terror and Decorum*. The order necessary for "classic song, beautiful song […] is outwardly terrifying as much as inwardly decorous" (*Strike through the Mask* 46). This inversion of the Burkean emphasis makes decorum a matter of sincerity rather than tradition, and it places Viereck in a line of conservative thinking that has more to do with the libertarianism of Thoreau (announced for instance in the first epigraph of *The Unadjusted Man* 2) than with classic traditionalism. The re-reading of his title registers his alienation from all movements—the fact that he does not fit in anywhere, either in institutional modernism or anti-

makes the post- or anti-modernist argument that observing formal conventions is rebellious precisely because it is decorous. The argument, however, is also post-traditionalist; the particularity of form is less relevant than its regulative presence. Viereck is an anti-modernist and a post-traditionalist. His verse is unapologetically iambic, but he experiments with different rhyme schemes and stanza structures, from the haiku-like imagism in "Castel Sant' Angelo" that would develop into a twelve-year project called "Five Roman Cadences" (*Strike Through the Mask!* 42–43; *New and Selected* 159–65) to the "Hexameters, Pentameters" announced in the title of an elegy simply dedicated "for her" (*New and Selected* 115). With the exception of *vers libre*, Viereck's "strict wildness" seems capacious enough to include any number of possible inventions and traditions—as long as they engender regularity on the page.

It is this formal regularity that aspires towards immortality in Viereck's verse. Form is an idea rather than the extension of a particular poetic tradition, and it retains its shape through history in a dialectical balancing act, like the ideas in Viereck's historical narratives, consistently occupying the middle ground between scattered words and political extremes. This is evident in the poem "Incantation," an excerpt of which serves as the epigraph to *Terror and Decorum* (also 82–83). The last of three elegies occasioned by Viereck's visit to the crypt of St. Francis in Assisi, while he was still in the army and after learning of his brother's death, this poem responds to doubts about violence, death, and murder (expressed in the first two elegies of the series) with a prayer that literally embodies what it commemorates. The image developed in the following passage is that of hands folded in prayer:

> Here abstractions have contours; here flesh is wraith;
> On these cold and warming stones, only solidity throws no shadow.
> And wrists seem echoes of the chimes they ring.
> (Listen, when the high bells ripple the half-light:
> Ideas, ideas, the tall ideas dancing.) (n. pag.)

The folded hands, graphically inscribed in the opening and closing of the parentheses, perform and thereby embody the ritual named in the title. This ritualized gesture of supplication is how the body acts out abstractions in the

---

institutional conservatism—and thus is terrifying to everybody. The final poem of the volume, "Some Lines in Three Parts," stresses the individual rebellion involved in poetic creation—including breaking through an "inward mask." See also "Decorum and Terror: Homage to Goethe and Hart Crane," which praises both the classicism of the one and the non-conformism of the other, and ends by rhyming "lyric" with "Viereck" (*New and Selected* 93–96; *The First Morning* 41).

flesh; it is the performance of memory and the materialization of an idea, realer—according to the speaker—than the materiality or solidity that "throws no shadow." The transformative power of ritual finds expression in the catachresis that has wrists "echo" the ringing church bell. The abstractions are the ideas dancing inside the parenthetical hands, and their immortality—their immunity from the decay of mere matter—is reinforced by their alignment with the formal "but he is not dead" convention of the elegy. There is a sense in which "Incantation" is a dramatic poem acting out the immortality of ideas; it takes the form of a prayer, but the prayer is also a performance, realizing memory through a choreography that is irreducible to but inseparable from the hands performing it. Form, for Viereck, is not a particular stanza structure or rhyme scheme; it is the way poems act out ideas in the flesh and embodies them through a lyrical situation or voice. What he calls his "poetry of ideas" involves a process of formal embodiment (Ciardi 22).

The alignment of form and idea, however, remains incomplete in Viereck and tends to disaggregate at precisely the locus of subjectified decorum. At the personal level form is a matter of self-discipline and individuation; but at a public level it is wedded to control, even domination. This is evident in the important poem—one of the best of his first book—that offers a counterpoint to the somber tone of the Assisi elegies: "For Two Girls Setting Out In Life (a morality-play)." A comic variation on the Marquis de Sade, the poem begins with an epigraph from *Justine* in which the author sends his heroines on their way, one following the path of virtue, the other the path of vice, and both joined in a dance of libertinage that demands victims and perpetrators alike. The speaker is a reader of Sade who assumes the critic's privilege of offering advice to his "girls": "Justine, by all means do be virtuous / But not in so provocative a fashion." "And you, Juliette: have fun while doing ill" (10). The heroines, of course, cannot profit from this advice, but the didacticism (prominent in much of Viereck's poetry) that misses its mark in the characters addresses itself in a different way to the readers. One lesson is presented as a parenthetical aside, this time through a variation on the figure of apophasis: "(promise me you'll stay / A pretty little girl who'll never spell 'Chthonic' nor learn her Freud too sadly well)" (11). The fictional characters cannot deviate from their prescribed roles, but the speaker (with a knowing wink) informs the readers that these roles conform to Freudian and even archetypal models. This aside has the effect of establishing a knowing complicity between speaker and readers; at the same time, it personifies the formal rigidity of genre conventions in the ignorance of the heroines. The bodies of Justine and Juliette embody forms and rituals as surely as the hands in prayer, but in a way that guarantees they know not what they do. This ignorance is the essential counterpoint to the repetitiveness of pornographic narratives, in which outrage follows outrage, and orgasm orgasm, and the object of desire is "not eroded by whole cataracts / Of fondlers groping through—beyond—your body / To sate in flesh the spirit's old distress" (10).

The speaker, however, knows, and his knowledge is what liberates him from the endless repetition of pornographic rituals and forms. However, he also depends on—even enjoys—those forms, and his personal transcendence is linked to their persistence. Here the image is not hands clasped in prayer but, in what reads like a deliberate travesty of "Incantation," lips performing fellatio: "Your lips [Juliette] raise shrines as mystic as Assisi / From whiteness they so piously caress" (11). Form realizes itself through ritual but also, evidently, arousal; what Osiris might be lacking in "To My Isis" here unveils itself to be the phallus as transcendental signifier.

The mystical significance of arousal is established by the tenor of the metaphor linking the erection to Assisi's shrine. But again this has less to do with tradition than with repetition defined as a recurring idea. The "girls" personify ideas in this poem of ideas through their performance of patterns and forms. Thus Viereck, following Blake, transforms his "'Girls of mild silver or of furious gold'" into materializations of opposing but linked principles (11). The moral of the morality play, once again directed over the heads of the characters, is composed in the form of a file-folder stanza (that would later be adapted by Karl Shapiro in *The Bourgeois Poet*):

> Two truths, two sisters. An obsessive pair:
> Serene in their unalterable roles
> Whether their frantic author flog or kiss them.
> And either truth rebukes our limbo where
> Girls are not Bad but merely Indiscreet,
> Girls are not Good but merely Very Sweet,
> And men are filed in their own filing-system
> With frayed manila-folders for their souls—
> Once labeled GOD'S OWN IMAGE: USE WITH
> CARE
> But now reclassified as OBSOLETE. (11)

The sadistic play of virtue and vice forms a contrast to the "limbo" of modern life, in which euphemism has replaced moral judgment and classification systems have rendered ecstasy obsolete. This contrast is central to the poem's didactic project: recognizing that Sade's "girls" move like marionettes in their prescribed roles is the first step towards freeing modern men from their filing systems. It is thus an act of liberation for the speaker to give away the ending of modernity's plot in the same way he tells the two girls what awaits them on their adventures: "Two opposites will find each other / And sob for half a day together; / For heaven and hell are childhood playmates still" (11). The reader, like the speaker, is supposed to "get" what Justine and Juliette do not: the parenthetical aside, the moral for contemporary life, and the erection.

Viereck is not a sadist, but there is a sense in which he improves on the master. Horkheimer and Adorno, in their roughly contemporary analysis of Sade as an enlightenment rationalist, point to the strangely dispassionate nature of Sade's heroes, who replace love with rational exploitation, systematically violating bodies in geometrically arranged torture chambers like so many scientists in laboratories (96, 116). Sade is so repetitive that he is as boring as an operating manual; Viereck recovers pleasure by aligning it with knowledge or ideas, the ability to trace forms and patterns and find the recurring compromise between them. His poems are passionate, but their passion is for moderation. This moderation, linked to self-liberation at the lyrical level, is structurally dependent on the didactic tone and the "girls'" unquestioning performance of their assigned tasks.

The pornographic quality of the poem, and its recuperation of pleasure as knowledge or idea, provides a key to what makes form so conservative in Viereck's poetry. Viereck once described conservatism as a "dirty word" (*Unadjusted* 98). What he meant by the remark was that conservative ideas seemed obscene in the 1940s when the dominant American intellectual attitude was liberal. However, Viereck's poetry suggests that conservatism has a pornographic structure that has everything to do with the play of transgression (or transcendence) and form (decorum, genre, pornographic conventions, or bureaucratic structures) so evident in "Two Girls." Viereck's rewriting of Sade is the allegorical version of the basic plot he sees repeated over and over again in history: two extremes implying and turning into their own opposites, thereby alerting the speaker to the importance of the golden mean, which embodies immortal truths and allows for personal liberation, in turn providing a contrast to the oppressive structures of modern life. The golden mean is the locus of individualism and lyrical voice; but it is structurally dependent on didacticism and even domination. Viereck's didactic mode constitutes the conservative limit of lyricism, whose liberal or progressive limit would later manifest itself in language poetry, or the disappearance of voice into discourse.

The diminished role allotted to women may reflect Viereck's resentment at being pushed from center stage to a teaching position at a women's college; it is certainly central to the didactic project of his conservatism. This is evident in what is perhaps the most widely discussed poem from *Terror and Decorum*, "Don't Look Now but Everybody Is Mary," in which the allegorical heroine "long by Boss's kisses bored / Quit desk and stole his yacht and jumped aboard" (34). Mary, whose name evokes the pursuit of happiness described in the first lines, would seem to be following the speaker's advice to the readers in "Two Girls." She leaves the office behind and follows her passion. However, her passion is not for tradition but for novelty, suggested by the New Testament implications of abandoning her capitalized "Boss" for her pet lamb ("for purer were his kisses"). The anti-Christian implications of the poem are unmistakable, but more important than the non-redemptive theology is the way Mary's plans misfire in the same way this poem just misses (by one line) becoming a sonnet. She sinks her boss's boat, is assaulted by the lamb she brings along for company, and ends up shooting herself with her boss's pistol, probably in the groin (Filreis 275–76). Comparing this poem to "Two Girls" suggests a double standard is at work in Viereck's account of individualism. Men are supposed to liberate their souls from filing cabinets, but women are better off with the Boss.

Viereck elaborates his idea of individualism through other recurrent themes, which are usefully enumerated in the table of contents to his *New and Selected Poems* (1967). One grouping, which I have already broached, is "The Girl Menagerie"; another is "The Tree Menagerie" including some of the more important poems from his second book of poetry, such as "The Slacker Apologizes," "The Slacker Need Not Apologize," and "To My Playmate, with Thanks for Carefree Days Together." The first two poems dramatize the predicament of a tree-poet who risks life and limb to write lyrics in a time when trees have declared war on humanity. "Playmate" is a series of ironic apostrophes addressed by a personified tree to the body suspended from its limb, the victim of a lynching. What seemed to interest Viereck most about trees was their longevity, the way their durable form enables them to embody the past in a way difficult to achieve through human memory: "Humans (I almost envy you your peace) / are free of this gnarled urge for Absolutes / Which sweetens and saddens all my fruits" (*New* 3). The two menageries intersect in a number of Viereck poems, such as "Forward: Walks and Trees," which fronts *New and Collected Poems* and asks, "And who—speak, skeleton—inside his skin / Is not a walker, not a walking tree" (n. pag.). Another example would be the verse drama *The Tree Witch* (1961), in which a sylph, forced to abandon her tree when it is chopped down due to road construction, takes up residence in a suburban home.

Focusing on gendered bodies, rather than trees, provides better insight into Viereck's development as a poet and a political thinker. Viereck turned increasingly towards corporeal themes the more alienated he became from mainstream conservatism and establishment poetry, perhaps in an attempt to dignify his isolation as transgression and turn conservatism, once again, into a dirty word. The "dirtiness," however, becomes less carnal and more biologically corporeal. In a 1977 essay for *Critical Inquiry*, "Strict Form in Poetry: Would Jacob Wrestle With a Flabby Angel?," already mentioned above, Viereck argues that the basic form of lyrical poetry is the iamb, and he links the differential stress of the metrical foot to the footfall of the human biped, the systole and diastole of the heartbeat, and the rhythm of coitus (211). Sex remains central to his lyrical form, but this biological conception of the iamb goes beyond the gendered bodies of his earlier poetry, linking "strict wildness" to the human as such, and not to the male transcendence of fixed female choreographies. Poetry becomes the ultimate conserver of traditions because it is pre-cultural, natural. This formulation is the *reductio ad absurdum* of a lyrical voice whose individualism collapses into the existential parameters of being, and of conservatism, which turns out to be so old-fashioned that it is not even scandalous, merely biological.

Biology is ultimately where Viereck turns to find a way out of the pendulum-swings of history; it is also his final alternative to the didacticism and domination that haunt his lyrical voice. This becomes clear in his late poem, "Vaginolatry," published in *The Massachusetts Review* in 2003, only three years before his death. The poem is structured as a sort of vagina dialogue, alternating the "*Male author's voice*" with a "*woman's voice in italics*" (670, italics in original). The speaker, apparently fascinated with the relation of metrical feet to actual feet, lets his gaze travel up the legs and under a skirt, linking for once and all his lyrical voice to the male gaze. He admits the voyeuristic aspects of the project in some of the more ribald passages, such as: "No jeans. Skirts have a life-affirming flare. / Life, come to me glass in hand; ass in skirt" (673). The initial spondee and subsequent trochees, however, suggest that such lines are at odds with his iambic humanism.

In fact this is a poem that pokes fun at his earlier representations of women by framing the dialogue between the opening and closing parentheses of the woman's voice. While the female voice is clearly identified as the interlocutor rather than the author, she nevertheless frames the discourse and (unlike Juliette) also participates in it. What she criticizes is everything from representations of femininity in "*westciv*" (670), to the speaker's desire, moralizations, and poetic form: "*Your fem cult, your rhyme cult, they're both antiquated*" (the female voice is always italicized in the poem). The male author's voice responds, sounding once again the theme of lyrical conservatism: "What lasts is always outdated. / The rhymes resound, connect, contrast, compare. / Fem bears both meanings of 'to bear'" (673). And yet, the dialogue forces him to bear with his inability to define or instruct the woman, or for that matter to reduce her to her anatomy. The male voice admits that around the "fulcrum" of what his interlocutor calls "*she-ness envy*" "loves and seasons swarm," and he asks her to grant him "Her tragic seesaw equilibrium" (673–74). The woman in the poem has assumed the nomothetic, divine role of the poet, and she no longer simply embodies tradition but "bears" it or gives birth to it. This characterization, as such, does not escape from structure of oppositions (for instance the tomb-womb brought up several times in the poem) that have always defined femininity as the deficient—or natural rather than cultural—opposite of masculinity. However, the Juliette-Justine opposition has become her feet, her legs, and just as she redefines the rhythm of the poem, she refuses to let the male author locate his "transcendence" between them. The poem ends in a sort of impasse, one rejecting the masculinist form of individualism just as it rejects coitus.

In "Vaginolatry" the body corporealizes the pendulum swing of conflict, but it refuses to personify ideas. The posthumous thrust in Viereck's "poetry of ideas" recuperating individuality by linking it to the trajectory of male desire, here becomes dialogic and irresolute. The form that ultimately proves to be immortal is biological, which is to say inherited rather than remembered, and the poet's invocation to "Launch us beyond the flesh, bow of lap's arch,—" is revised by his interlocutor "—to beyonds only flesh can reach" (675). This late poem regards death with existential resolve. At the same time, the conservative thrust of the poem—its appeal to old forms—becomes non-political, even pre-cultural; it is the trace of the human, the rhythm of life. The speaker feels himself to be a part of biological forces without having to master or moralize about them. Or rather, these impulses—everywhere evident in the poem—are corrected by dialogue and interlocution. The revolt against revolt is unmoored from the individual and scattered in the reprise of endless banter. What remains of the old fighting spirit is a politically incorrect premise that refuses, in the end, to be masculinist or feminist, or for that matter conservative or liberal.

For most of his career Viereck defined lyricism and individualism as equivalent compromises between political and archetypal extremes, between his father's infatuation with LaFollette and Hitler, between Pound and Hiss, Juliette and Justine. But in this late poem there is no golden mean, and the individualism that once seemed to partake of the immortality of form, here collapses into the mortality of the body and the eternal rhythms of nature. Conservatism is no longer a dirty word because it is no longer what happens in private after the marriage of opposites; it is simply the "tide and continuity" alluded to at the end of "Vaginology" and taken as the title of one of Viereck's last books. The late poetry, more interested in nature than in politics, seems to concede the point made by early reviewers like Paul Goodman: Individualism is an important political principle, one that may even offer a compromise between political extremes, but individualism is not the same as an *individual*: it is not a locus of experience, feeling, or voice.

Forget Viereck

Viereck's poetry performs the disappearance of the conservative literary voice, but it had already disappeared in the flurry of debate surrounding the Pound controversy. Faced with the challenge of redeeming the political right from charges of fascism, "mainstream" conservatism rejected reaction as a form of literary elitism. Faced with the difficulty of preserving avant-gardism from charges of political irresponsibility, modernism moved to the academy in the same way the Bollingen Prize moved from the Library of Congress to Yale, quarantining politics as Pound was incarcerated in St. Elizabeths. These divergent stories tell something about the changing relation of poetry to politics over the past half century. Politics has undergone a conservative turn that is post-reactionary in the same way it is anti-modernist; but the humanities have remained resolutely modernist, and—arguments about liberal academia notwithstanding—the habits of avant-garde provocation have proven more significant than the changing fashions of left or right. Politics are supposed to be anti-elitist and poetry provocative—this despite the influence wielded by political insiders and the impact of academia on what midcentury critics were already calling the bureaucratization of the intellect.

In this chapter I have tried to show that the relation between literary modernism and conservatism is more complicated than one of simple antagonism—that the institutionalized rebellion practiced by tenured "radicals" and the anti-institutional rebellion endorsed by conservative "outsiders" are in fact linked. They are linked not only in their opposition but in their mutual suppression of a voice that is no longer heard because it is not supposed to exist: that of a postwar literary conservatism opposed to modernism but also to populism. The spokesperson for this new and forgotten conservatism was the poet, historian, and political theorist Peter Viereck, who enjoyed some notoriety in the 1950s before falling into relative obscurity.

There was a momentary Viereck revival in 2005 when journalist Tom Reiss dubbed him the deposed father of the new conservatism in the *New Yorker*. John J. Miller responded in the *National Review* by quoting Meyer's earlier charge that Viereck was a liberal in disguise, going on to argue that Reiss's faux-conservative praise of Viereck was just a veiled attack on

Bush.[32] There is an archaic quality to the recurring arguments about Viereck's right to assume the mantle of conservatism. Battles over the conservative inheritance are constitutionally archaic; they have the feel of a family struggle and are concerned less with strategies and trends than with titles and lineage.

But Viereck's own family struggle, and his ongoing struggle with Pound, convinced him to turn away from issues of legacy to a form of compromise he defined as lyrical individualism. It would be exaggerated to say that Viereck invented the new conservatism, but he did more than name it—he attempted to activate a political subject position as lyrical voice. Viereck sought out a middle position between political extremes. Form was supposed to embody political compromise as metrical regularity; the lyrical self was to be a subjectivized expression of decorum. This notion of lyrical individualism proved problematic. The formal restraint that was supposed to enact self-discipline showed signs of didacticism and domination. Viereck's dissatisfaction with his poetry, or perhaps his dissatisfaction with having it ignored, eventually led him to modify both his theory and practice of versification. What began as an attempt to embody political compromise as form ended in biological humanism, or the attempt to link form to an idealized rhythm of humanity. In his final poems, Viereck moved from formal individualism to a notion of embodied selfhood as he celebrated a staunchly masculine identity.

It seems unlikely that Viereck will find his Isis. His memory will remain scattered, and the rhyme and meter he hoped would bring immortality will remain footnotes to the formalism briefly in vogue after the war. In his obscurity, Viereck does however embody the space between two discourses—conservative and literary—that diverged at midcentury. And if he fails to find readers, it may be because his anti- or post-modernism remains anathema to a scholarship that is professionally avant-garde.

---

[32] See also Claes G. Ryan on the ongoing significance of Viereck's political thinking.

CHAPTER 5

"Pull Down Vanity": Porter, Fiedler, and the Pornographic Imagination (A Prosaic Interlude)

Katherine Anne Porter was the only writer whose primary genre was fiction to serve on the first Bollingen committee. Like most members of the committee she voted for Pound, stating on several occasions that she never considered him to be insane (*Collected Essays* 212, footnote; 300). Neither did she believe *The Pisan Cantos* to be "high poetry, and certainly not the best of Pound's poetry" (210). Her letter to *The Saturday Review of Literature* is a masterpiece of diplomacy, managing at once to ridicule Robert Hillyer's theories about a New Critical conspiracy (described in the previous chapter) and to remove herself from the ranks of Pound's supporters. A misdirected invitation prevented her from participating in the initial deliberations. When she finally cast her ballot the committee had already narrowed the list of candidates, so Porter "voted for Ezra Pound precisely within the limits set by the conditions of the award: of the four final candidates who had volumes of poetry published in this country in 1948, I considered Pound's the best" (210). Porter "abhor[s] his treason and detest[s] his emotional perversities, for they cannot be called ideas, in politics" (210–11). Nevertheless, Hillyer's accusations are emotional perversities of a related sort. He is hunting for scapegoats, blaming Pound and his supporters for a whole host of political and cultural problems that are more widespread than *The Saturday Review of Literature* cares to admit (212, 214). Porter insists that Pound's artistic "light" cannot be dismissed, in part because his benighted politics are sickeningly familiar (212, 214). He is a representative figure whose failings are typical even if his successes are sometimes exceptional. A subsequent note offers a more concise, but still vague, assessment of Pound's cultural significance: "He was just a complete, natural phenomenon of Unreason" (*Collected Essays* 300).

What is unreason? How does it differ from insanity? Porter does not define her terms, but she spent decades dramatizing them in her only novel, *Ship of Fools* (1962), the very title of which suggests a voyage beyond the limits of rationality. I will argue that the border of rationality, for Porter, is also the border of individualism. The 500-page narrative depicts a voyage on a German ship from Veracruz, Mexico to Bremerhaven, Germany in 1931 as most of the passengers and crew sink into the mass irrationalism that Porter associated with the catastrophe of World War II.

Porter had voyaged on such a ship from Mexico to Europe the same year. Her unhappiness in one European city, Berlin, is memorialized in "The Leaning Tower," an 80-page novella linking an expatriate American artist's self-discovery to his rejection of German culture—a timely rejection given the 1941 publication date, which coincided with the American entry into World War II (Givner 319).[1] The novella can be described as a *Künstlerroman* in the form of a political allegory. The protagonist Charles Upton goes to Berlin to practice drawing, but to discover his own style he must first reject overwrought European art, symbolized by stucco cupids adorning building facades and a model of the Leaning Tower of Pisa that he inadvertently breaks when inspecting a room-to-let in a private apartment (166, 68). He ends up renting the room, partially because he feels guilty for breaking the fragile memento. This accident puts him in close contact with the overwrought political passions of his German flat-mates. These passions ultimately confirm what might be described as Upton's porcine view of German culture. Focalized through his gaze, the narrative repeatedly describes Berliners as pig-like figures who are fascinated with pigs, staring up in wonder, for instance, at the anthropomorphized animals advertising butcher shops (159). Upton's rejection of bestial politics and art, as well as the bestialized Germans, allows him to discover his artistic individuality, which is a metonym for his American individualism.

The novella proved popular, probably because it fulfilled wartime expectations about American art. Cleaving to a pattern that had already been delineated by Van Wyck Brooks and Malcolm Cowley, "The Leaning Tower" dramatized what was taken to be the constituent paradox of aesthetic individualism: the artist is most American when he is most alienated, which means he has to leave home to discover it.[2] This is a spatialized version of

---

1 After writing "The Leaning Tower" Porter said that in wartime it was the writer's duty not to go mad (Givner 322).

2 In *The Ordeal of Mark Twain* (1922), Van Wyck Brooks argued "If the great artist is the freest man, if the true creative life is, in fact, the embodiment of 'free will,' then it is only he that is born for greatness who can feel, as Mark Twain felt, that the universe is leagued against him" (262). Answering Brooks directly, but also giving a geographical twist to his notion of alienation, Malcolm Cowley argued in the 1934 edition of *Exile's Return*, a study that lists Porter as a member of the "lost generation," that "the generation belonged to a period of confused transition from values already fixed to values that had to be created" (11). The transition, he explains later, involved being

the liberal aesthetic, which links self-expression to isolation in the strangely related figures of the journey and the prison cell, as I have explored in chapter one. The political analogy in Porter's story suggests interventionism is like individualism: the war against fascism becomes an accidental gesture, like the breaking of the already precarious tower, less an expression of national ambition than simply a collateral effect of good-natured American clumsiness.

Porter jettisoned some of this patriotic complacency, along with the strictly individualistic perspective, when she returned to this period of her life in *Ship of Fools*. When the novel finally appeared after a twenty-year gestation, it was a popular and to some degree a critical success; it won the Pulitzer Prize and made Porter's fortune when director Stanley Kramer turned it into a major film (1965). It is a kind of a prequel to "The Leaning Tower," focusing on the interlude before ship reaches shore. The novel defers its destination in order to generalize the short story's moral, expanding the anti-German sentiments into a universal indictment of humanity. The evil is no longer localized in a single nation, nor is the narrative focalized through a character whose patriotism coincides with his self-discovery. The realist unities of place and point-of-view that define, as paired contraries, the individuality of the novella's artist-protagonist Charles Upton, are fractured into a series of anecdotes that seem to illustrate, again and again, the pervasiveness of a basic human trait. The passengers can hardly stand each other but they have something in common: they are all unreasonable, emotionally perverse, prone to compulsive acts of sex and violence. Sex and violence are the basic elements of what Porter clearly intended as a universal allegory of unreason, as she indicates in a note acknowledging her debt to Sebastian Brant's fifteenth-century *Narrenschiff* or *Stultifera Navis* (n. pag.).

It is my argument that Porter's generalized account of emotional perversity has everything to do with her refusal to set Pound apart, either as a scapegoat or a hero. Her passengers are all Poundians, not because they are Americans or artists—although such figures are represented on the passenger list—but because they are driven by desire and aggression. Indeed, we are all Poundians, the allegory suggests, since unreason is what propelled the

---

"wrenched away [...] from their attachment to any locality or local tradition" and "adhering to a theory of art which held that the creative artist is absolutely independent of all localities, nations or classes" (215). The 1934 edition concluded that the best of the returning exiles would devote themselves to the class struggle; the 1956 rewrite suggested a renewed faith in America that was more appropriate for the Cold War.

ship of the world towards the catastrophe of World War II.[3] Unreason is passion's part in politics, the baseness that puts everyone in the same boat, the limit of individualism as a political factor.

This is a plausible, if misanthropic, basis of allegorical generalization, but what does it have to do with Pound? As early as 1960, M. L. Rosenthal was drawing attention to the "intellectual eroticism" implicit in Pound's political and poetic defense of "the procreative cycle that is the source of all life's innocent ceremony, all its joys and values" (*Modern Poet* 69–72).[4] More recently scholars and poets such as Robert Casillo, Charles Bernstein, and Bob Perelman have argued that Pound's intellectual eroticism is solidly corporeal, and that his imagery is most erotic—and most violent—when he defends the integrity of his imagined body against ambiguity, indeterminacy, and pollution (Bernstein 123–24; Perelman 44–46, 60–61). One name Pound gave to the threat to bodily integrity was usury, which he linked to perversion and decay, but also to flaccid and decadent writing.[5] Pound's repugnance for usury was also intimately related to his distrust of Jews. He seemed to believe that whatever interposes itself between symbol and object (clichés), value and product (credit), or culture and society ("the yidd" in Pound's spelling), is an interloper, bringing about dissipation, pollution, miscegenation. Ultimately, the purity Pound sought in finance (social credit as a way to eliminate interest), aesthetics (imagism to eliminate clichés), and politics (fascism to impose unity and anti-Semitism to keep out the undesirable elements) could only be effected through the cleansing domination of the poet or dictator, who guards the integrity of the body politic/body of a poem with the unforgiving stringency of a jealous lover.

Some scholars claim that even the more lyrical passages in *The Pisan Cantos* demonstrate an elegiac longing for the integrity lost with the Axis defeat in World War II:

---

3 Porter also uses the term "unreason" to describe Dylan Thomas's widow Caitlin, who in Porter's opinion displayed an affinity for compulsive sexuality and violence [*Collected* 128]).

4 See also Eva Hesse: "Die Liebe im weitesten Sinn ist der eigentliche Motor der *Cantos* unter der Selbstverwirklichung Ezra Pounds" (*Ezra Pound* 280).

5 Rosenthal: "[Pound's] conception of sentimentality as a fraudulence of feeling and expression that destroys standards of value and therefore abets Usura is brought out with all his virtuosity at the beginning of Canto 30. The goddess Artemis is heard complaining [...] that the soft-mindedness of our professedly humanitarian age prevents all correction of abuses and genuine purification of society" (72). According to Rosenthal, Pound provides his rationale against usury in the Cantos on the Founding Fathers (30–41); the sexualized and sometimes scatological imagery shows up mainly in the Usura Canto (Canto 45) and the Hell Cantos (Cantos 14–16).

> What thou lovest well remains
>   the rest is dross
> What thou lov'st well shall not be reft from thee
> What thou lov'st well is thy true heritage
> ...
> Pull down thy vanity, it is not man
> Made courage, or made order, or made grace,
> Pull down thy vanity, I say pull down. (81/540–41)

These lines can be understood as attempting to restore through memory the integrity that fascism failed to realize in politics (Bush, "Modernism" 73; Perelman 40–41). That they stem from a time when Pound was undergoing extreme psychological stress in a U.S. Army detention center outside of Pisa only adds to their pathos. The poet who survives the war is an Orpheus victorious against the invading maenads, re-membering his heritage as if it were himself, and dismissing the external world as vanity. The famous passage in Canto 76—"As a lone ant from a broken ant-hill / from the wreckage of Europe, ego scriptor" (76/478), which immediately follows a passage criticizing the BBC for its lies—would seem to confirm Pound's sense that self-expression is the last refuge for culture once society has been destroyed, implying at the same that his own broadcasts for Rome Radio were acts of personal (even lyrical) integrity.

Porter had already portrayed an artist who embodied a cultural tradition and who, in his isolated self-sufficiency, defended it from outside influences: those influences were German and the artist was the liberal individualist Charles Upton of "The Leaning Tower." Her wartime protagonist is the anti-Pound, and he rejects fascism in terms as uncompromising, and images as abject, as those appearing in Pound's Usura Canto (Canto 45). After the war, however, this quest for cultural purity began to seem as perverse as its antithesis; in fact it became the trademark of anti-Poundians like Hillyer.

Ship of Fools is Porter's plague on both houses. The characters, whatever their politics, are unreasonable, and the body politic—like the bodies of the characters—is a site of emotional perversion. Her allegorical indictment is so broad that it is not, strictly speaking, allegory at all, but borrows from the conventions of a genre that received serious intellectual attention after World War II, probably because of its suitability for representing emotional excess and violence. That genre is pornography, which according to Susan Sontag concerns itself with "the extreme states of human feeling and consciousness [...] so peremptory that they exclude the mundane flux of feelings and are only contingently linked with concrete persons" (Sontag 42). Pornography, in the sense I will be using it in this chapter, does not refer to the industry that has grown to enormous proportions over the last half century, although there are certainly some thematic continuities. What I mean by pornography is an "imagination" or representational strategy that isolates passion as the key psychological and historical force, degrading traditional agents of social change—such as the individual or the nation—to secondary status. Pornography is a genre of unreason, pushing allegory beyond the limits of its symbolic matrix: characters are abstract, but not because they personify ideals or ideas; they are placeholders for the passions coursing through them. Porter's fictional ship—the *Vera*—is not a floating insane asylum; it is the vehicle of a much deeper pathology, one drawing individualism, patriotism, and even art into the ebb and flow of an eroticized violence that is more basic than personality, more basic even than history. All of humanity, in her dramatization, is susceptible to unreason; we are all passengers on the ship of fools.

While Porter's novel is no longer widely discussed, it was a middlebrow and—to a slightly lesser extent—critical success; and its rise to bestseller status, selection by the Book-of-the-Month Club, recognition by the American Academy of Arts and Sciences, and adaption as a Hollywood film registered the growing significance of sex and violence as cultural factors. Porter owed part of her success to titillation, perhaps, but her novel is a serious attempt to come to terms with a cultural legacy that seemed complicit with the ravages of total war. Politically Porter identified herself as a liberal all her life; but her novel goes beyond the limits of liberal individualism to show characters caught in an impersonal dance of love and death.

In this Porter was representative of a general trend. By the 1960s love and death had become key terms in a widespread reevaluation of the cultural legacy that would soon undermine the influence of the liberal aesthetic. The most famous—or infamous—example is Leslie Fiedler's *Love and Death in the American Novel* (1960). The critical study appeared almost simultaneously with *Ship of Fools*, and it came as close as literary criticism comes to middlebrow success, with two editions in six years, a (negative) front-page review by Malcolm Cowley in *The New York Times Book Review*, and talk show appearances by the author, who settled comfortably into the role of what Richard Chase, referring to the photo on the book's dust jacket, described as "a darksome Ezra Pound plus Peck's Bad Boy" ("Leslie Fiedler" 9). The patronizing tone of Chase's review bears grudging tribute to Fiedler's notoriety. A tenured professor at the University of Montana, Fiedler seemed beyond the pale of the conservative modernists at *Kenyon Review* and their liberal counterparts at *Partisan Review*; nevertheless he published in both journals and became the chief proponent of a style of criticism that assumed the mantle of avant-garde provocation. Fiedler became the epitome of the tenured radical. This had something to do with his public posturing, but also with his insistence on the central role played by passion in culture.

Fiedler's arguments, like Porter's novel, have fallen into relative obscurity. This is not because they have been rejected; on the contrary, many of his insights have been rendered anonymous as critical commonplaces (Winchell, *Fiedler* 44). Fiedler claims that the archetypal narrative in American literature is one in which the protagonists (male) flee civilization and domesticity to live out perverse and violent fantasies at the frontier or on the open seas (*Love and Death* xx–xxi). In its basic contours this could be a précis for *Ship of Fools*. Fiedler takes the argument a step farther, insisting that the classic American novels also mourn the violence they direct outwards, begging forgiveness "at the breast" of the ethnic sidekicks—Queequeg, Chingachgook, the escaped slave Jim—whose job it is to bear the brunt of the protagonists' homoerotic affection, which is the displaced form of their society's guilt ("Come Back to the Raft" 671; *Love and Death* xxii; *Waiting for the End* 114–16). Fiedler's narrative is historical—he describes the main current in American literature as an offshoot of the gothic tradition—but his thematic, as Chase points out, can be understood as responding to a problem in "modern morality" (*Love and Death* xxiii; Chase, "Leslie Fiedler" 16). Chase describes the problem as the "subversion [...] [of] the passional self" (16). It would be more accurate to describe it as the subversion of the self *by* passion. Passion is the primary actor in Fiedler's cultural drama, and individual characters—and texts—are variations on a basic theme.

That theme is identical to Porter's: unreason, emotional perversity, betrayal. Fiedler's turn to passion, like Porter's, is pornographic, tending to subordinate the individual to affect, and it can be understood as a reaction to the difficulties raised by the Pound controversy. Fiedler established the Poundian coordinates of passion in the title of his 1955 short story "Pull Down Vanity," which went on to name the collection that would contain it in 1963. The title is an allusion to Canto 81, cited above, but the story mentions Pound only once. The protagonist, a Jewish American poet visiting a Midwestern university, makes an offhand remark about how much he resents having to answer questions about Pound after poetry readings. It is not audience queries, however, but the philo-Semitic advances of a beautiful *shiksa* and the anti-Semitic aggression of her drunken husband that provide the conflict of the story. The plotline is a dramatization—and travesty—of *Love and Death in the American Novel*. The poet is the mythical dark lover ("black, black—my gypsy—my black Jew!" [157]) forced to serve as the projection screen for the other characters' passions; to escape their loving and dangerous embraces he must extricate his self-image from their stereotypes (161). His battle is cultural—against the anti-Semitic myths generated by Pound and the scions of "a realer, a gentile America" (128)—but his victory is physical, even vulgar: an erection pointing his way from the house of his antagonists towards his poetic future (167). In "pulling down" the myth of "the Jew," in showing it to be "in vain," Fiedler's Milton Amsterdam also takes Pound's name "in vain," invoking his decidedly non-liberal poetics to authorize a new lyricism of ethnicity. The short story rebels against Pound *and* against the individualism that made him an unlikely champion of free speech by showing how liberalism can repress (without correcting) the anti-Semitism that was central to Pound's poetics. It answers the unspeakable (liberal anti-Semitism) with the crude or the obscene (an erect Jewish penis), situating an identity marked poetic, masculine, and Jewish at the locus of two intersecting forms of unreason: social prejudice and personal desire.

The passionate turn signaled by Porter and Fiedler was part of a paradigm shift away from the individualism that had characterized earlier political and cultural thinking towards more current conceptions of identity. The previous chapter touches on a related thematic in the writing of Peter Viereck, who flirted with pornography to dramatize his individuality as well as his discipline—a paradox he termed "strict wildness." The flirtation may have seemed surprising in a self-proclaimed conservative, but Viereck was hardly unique. Postwar literature turned to the body as a reaction to the "vanity" of ethnic stereotyping, but also to go beyond the limits of liberalism that dismissed stereotyping as free speech. The liberal commitment to individualism could provide a political rationale for defending Pound's right to speak; Porter herself subscribed to such an argument in a 1950 review of Pound's letters for *The New York Times Book Review* (*Days Before* 78). However, individualism could not begin to account for Pound's complicated cultural significance. He had a right to speak, perhaps, but something more basic—and base—seemed to be speaking through him. It gradually became a matter of consensus that what made Pound representative was not the lyricism that made him unique but the unreason that made him human.

This line of thinking tended to dissolve the individual into something pre-political, even pre-conscious, but it also gave birth to a new notion of selfhood, lodged in the body as the seat of affective—and ultimately ethnic—significance. Identity, situating selfhood at the intersection of personal feelings and social forces, scandalized liberalism's notion of the independent self. The postwar self would move from individualism to identity, a voyage that passed beyond the limits of individualism by situating selfhood in emotional dynamics that liberalism considered irrational and even obscene. This chapter will map this voyage in relation to Pound's unreason, which motivated Porter to develop narrative techniques that in some ways betrayed her political convictions, and convinced Fiedler of the cultural necessity of embracing ethnicity and desire.

Porter: The Passionate Limits of Individualism

Porter's politics evolved in a way typical for liberal intellectuals of her generation. She flirted with radicalism in the 1920s, experiencing revolution at close quarters during several sojourns in Mexico (*Never-Ending* 56). By the end of the decade, however, the bloom was off the rose, and her fictional farewell to Mexico—"Flowering Judas"—suggests that the ultimate fruit of revolution is not class solidarity but personal betrayal (*Flowering Judas* 114–16). In spite of her transformation "from radical to moderate," Porter remained true to leftist causes—but for personal rather than class reasons.[6] Her poignant 1977 essay *The Never-Ending Wrong* takes up the case of Sacco and Vanzetti a half-century after their execution in order to exhume the human beings from beneath the political principles battling it out at their trial. Porter always despised the prosecutors, but she extends her rancor to the communist defenders who turned Sacco and Vanzetti into symbols while remaining indifferent—even inimical—to their lives (5–6, 9, 11–12, 57). Communism is authoritarian, in substance no different from Nazism, which after Porter's trip to Berlin would remain her ultimate political epithet (7, 12, 17, 18, 20–21). Porter is interested in Sacco and Venzetti not as members of a class but as individuals; she is a "liberal idealist" whose principles are "Jeffersonian" (13).

Porter had made virtually the identical "Jeffersonian-Democrat" argument in her 1948 article "Communism in Hollywood," which sides with members of the Screen Actors' Guild against the "Anti-American Activities Committee [*sic*]" using what she identifies as Nazi tactics to incite a red scare (*Collected Essays* 206, 208). She is particularly angry at George V. Denny, the radio talk show host of America's Town Meeting of the Air, for providing the red baiters with a platform from which to launch their attacks (206). Porter was "concern[ed] with the threat to free expression posed by Communist ideology," as one biographer puts it, and evidence suggests that she supplied information to the FBI (against Josephine Herbst), but she was a liberal anti-Communist who saw Stalinism and Hitlerism as two sides of the

6 "From Radical to Moderate" is the title of Stout's chapter describing Porter's political development. Others, such as Robert Brinkmeyer, argue that her "obsession" with totalitarianism enabled a much more radical shift to the right, in which Porter gave full vent to the racism and anti-Catholicism she had long harbored (182–221).

same coin (Stout 162; Brinkmeyer 188–89, 191–92; Givner 360). Individualism—and especially free speech—was the democratic alternative to totalitarianism in both its left- and right-wing versions. Porter's liberal individualism was polemical, but it conformed nicely to official policy. She was one of six authors sent by the U.S. State Department as delegates to the Congress on Cultural Freedom in 1952 (Stout 164).

Porter stood up for Pound on the same grounds that she defended Sacco and Vanzetti and the beleaguered members of the Screen Actors' Guild: "Pound was one of the most opinionated and unselfish men who ever lived, and he made friends and enemies everywhere by the simple exercise of the classic American constitutional right of free speech" (*Days Before* 78). If she was inconsistent in her application of the First Amendment to the Pound case, as one of her biographers maintains, it was an inconsistency she shared with other Cold War liberals like Dwight Macdonald (Givner 359–60). One of the most remarkable aspects of the Pound controversy was how a poet who made no bones about being a fascist could, in the context of Cold War, become a champion of free speech.

Porter's interest in Pound went deeper than her commitment to free speech, however. In 1952 she visited the poet at St. Elizabeths. Porter was so pleased with their conversation that she sent Pound a gift package with an inscribed copy of *The Days Before*, containing the review article praising his outspokenness (Unrue 227). Although Pound did not respond the way she evidently hoped, the article was in one way calculated to please (227). The free-speech passage is followed directly by two paragraphs defending Pound's anti-Semitism on the grounds that it is really "anti-monotheism, which I have always believed was the real root of the difficulty between Judaism and the West" (*Days Before* 78). "'Anti-Semite' is a stupid, reprehensible word," Porter argues, "in that it does not mean what it says, for not only Semitic peoples have taught the doctrine of the One God, and it is used now largely for purposes of moral blackmail by irresponsible people" (79).

This is a strange point to make only five years after the liberation of the death camps, and it completely misrepresents Pound's remarks about Jews in *The Pisan Cantos*, which have little to do with monotheism and clearly adhere to the standard racist repertoire of anti-Semitic stereotypes:

> the yidd is a stimulant, and the goyim are cattle
> in gt/ proportion and go to saleable slaughter
> with the maximum of docility. (74/459)

Why does Porter feel compelled to defend Pound against charges of anti-Semitism? The civil libertarian position would be the one attributed to Voltaire: I disagree with what you say, but I'll defend to the death your right to say it. But Porter did seem to flirt with some of Pound's "emotional perversities," to use her term for his ideas. Her biographer Janice Stout argues that Porter exhibited some of the prejudices typical of the more reactionary, male modernists of her generation (Stout 160–61, 179). She describes Porter as "undeniably anti-Semitic"—although this in a parenthetical aside—as well as anti-Catholic and homophobic (Stout, 162; 163–64). Robert Brinkmeyer makes similar claims (220). Porter was an anti-fascist, but she was also drawn to fascism with a curiosity that could be described as erotic. Almost twenty years before the Pound controversy she met Hermann Göring at a dinner party in Berlin. He invited her out for drinks, tried to kiss her in his limousine, and then called on her the next day (Stout 102; Unrue 136–37). As Porter said later of a dubious acquaintance in Mexico, there can be "something strangely compelling" about a scoundrel: "a certain sinister magnetism that [makes] him hard to resist" (Unrue 260).

Porter did resist Göring—she made sure to be out the next day when he called—and she always despised Nazism. Whatever her attraction to the emotional perversities of fascism, she did not abandon her liberal convictions. However, those convictions may have gotten in the way of exploring the meaning of political perversion—at least in her essays. With the exception of her telling digression on anti-Semitism, Porter tolerates Pound's sentiments by dismissing them as personal opinions, protected by the basic right to free speech. This is solid liberal principle but it misses the significance of political passion. What is disturbing—and perhaps enticing—about prejudice is the way it goes beyond the limits of individualism both in expression and motivation. Prejudice denies its objects any claim to personal distinction; "the Jew," "the Catholic," "the homosexual" are little more than personifications of the "typical" characteristics of the despised group. The bigot who indulges in stereotypes does so, in part, to establish his own membership in a more desirable group. The collective structure of affect may be unreasonable, even perverse, but it can have very real political consequences. By defaulting to the free-speech argument, Porter renders the feeling of prejudice irrelevant and—except for her digressions—virtually invisible.

Porter's own contradictory feelings were also difficult to reconcile with her liberal principles. She often expressed anti-Catholic sentiments, but she converted to Catholicism to marry her first husband and received the last rites before her death (Givner 508; Unrue 295; Brinkmeyer 194–99).[7] Homophobia is widespread in her letters, but she actively sought out the company of gay men (Stout 101).[8] It would be a mistake to simply ignore these contradictions, or to dismiss her work as insincere or incorrect on their account. Any discussion of prejudice in Porter must move beyond the conceptual confines of individualism to analyze the emotional perversities of the sort she identified in Pound.

Porter undertakes this project herself in *Ship of Fools*. Her essays are individualistic, at least in intent, but her novel exhibits what Stout calls Porter's sensitivity to the "erotic surface" of right-wing movements. The phrase is Sontag's, and it is meant to describe the emotional appeal of fascism, which forges group coherence through the collective worship of a phallic leader (Stout 94). In Porter's novel fascism is highly erotic but at the same time slightly ridiculous. A version of Göring named Herr Rieber—corpulent, lewd, and virulently anti-Semitic—plays a sinister but comic role (421). His flirtation with the loud flapper Lizzi Spöckenkieker is obscene, but not because of any sexual improprieties (he never gets that far). Their endearments, when they are not slapstick, are genocidal. The following exchange is reported by Lizzi in the approving presence of Rieber, shortly after the ship takes on a load of displaced Spanish workers in Havana:

> "Oh, what do you think of this dreadful fellow? Can you guess what he just said? I was saying, 'Oh, these poor people, what can be done for them?' and this monster—" she gave a kind of whinny between hysteria and indignation—"he said, 'I would do this for them: I would put them all in a big oven and turn on the gas.' Oh," she said weakly, doubling over with laughter, "isn't that the most original idea you ever heard?" (59)

Lizzi is attracted to Rieber precisely because he is a political monster. In many respects Lizzi and Rieber are a mismatched pair, but they have one thing in common: their passion for anti-Semitism (421). The displaced workers are not Jewish, but Rieber's pleasantries about gassing and ovens clearly evoke the Holocaust, which is a decade in the novel's narrative future and two decades in its compositional past. In fact, most of Rieber's hatred is

---

7 Porter converted to Roman Catholicism when she married her first husband in 1906; however it was an unhappy marriage which she abandoned after a few years. According to one of her biographers, her famous and widely anthologized story "The Jilting of Granny Weatherall" "incorporated" her "feelings of betrayal" by first husband and Catholicism (Unrue 116).

8 Porter spent a contentious time with Hart Crane in Mexico shortly before leaving for Berlin and "was writing long diatribes against him months after he had killed himself" (Stout 65–66, 178–79).

directed against Jews. He is a rabid anti-Semite who holds Jews responsible for all the problems in German intellectual and economic life, and Lizzi responds to his sentiments with what can only be described as arousal (212–13). "Time to stop all Jew watches"—said in response to a Jewish passenger asking the time—is a witticism she finds particularly amusing (207).

Lizzy repeats the joke while singing Rieber's praises to her cabin mate Mrs. Treadwell, an American divorcee who is often seen as one of the novel's many stand-ins for Porter (Unrue 256). Mrs. Treadwell despises anti-Semitism, but her self-absorption makes her unreliable. She inadvertently betrays the confidence of fellow passenger William Freytag when she mentions his Jewish wife back home in Germany; this gets him expelled from the Captain's table (214). Treadwell is herself the target of passionate prejudice, in this case directed against Communists rather than Jews. The American William Denny—the namesake of the anti-Communist talk show host lambasted in "Communism in Hollywood" and a stand-in for Porter's first husband—calls the displaced persons "poor devils" who do not deserve to be kicked out because "They're not dirty Reds, the papers said so" (*The Days Before* 206; *Ship of Fools* 60; Unrue 257). Mrs. Treadwell responds, as guilelessly as she reveals Freytag's secret, "Why always 'dirty' please [...] and why always 'Red' and what do you really know or care about it?"

> "Are you a Red?" he asked. Without removing his folded arms from the rail he slid along toward her, turning sideways and inspected her as if she were a horse he was thinking of buying. His gaze ran like a hand to her ears, her neck, over her breasts, down her thighs, and his mouth was tight as if he did not like what he saw, but could not control the roving of his eyes. [...] "I know what I'd do to them if I were running the government," he said, in a heavy rage, peering into the front of her blouse. (61)

Mrs. Treadwell is the victim of collateral passion. By the end of the journey Denny tries to rape her, mistaking her for one of the Spanish Zarzuela dancers moonlighting as prostitutes on board (she has made herself up like a dancer in the privacy of her cabin). Treadwell fights back with a passion that surprises her, and true to her name, beats Denny's face into a bloody pulp with the metal heel of her high-heeled sandal. She continues to beat him long after he loses consciousness, acting out what the narrative makes clear is her own violent fantasy: "In her joy and excitement, she snatched off her blood-stained sandal and kissed it" (466; see also 462 and 480–81).

These violent and erotic impulses are examples of the emotional perversities Porter describes as unreason in her note on Pound. The novel's choreography of sex and violence breaks with the principled individualism of the essays to demonstrate the historical and personal significance of affect.

Lionel Trilling famously argued that liberal principles do not make for compelling fiction. A more suitable subject for novels is those "dangers which lie in our most generous wishes" (*Liberal Imagination* 7, 214). Porter's political imagination is liberal. The imagination at work in *Ship of Fools* is dangerous because it is pornographic, representing individuals as the vehicles of passions that cannot quite be called their own.[9]

Indeed, the novel took so long to write, and was interrupted by so many other projects, that it provides an emotional gauge for Porter's more reasoned arguments, some of which are embedded in the plotline. William Freytag, for instance, indulges in Porter's etymological quibble about anti-Semitism, reflecting that the term means nothing since it should logically apply to Arabs as well as Jews (412). Freytag's rejection of the term is unconvincing, however, because it is the product of a guilty conscience. The novel goes to great lengths to undermine his logic with his emotions. Freytag whets his polemic against the pretty, young American artist Jenny Brown, who takes "the high ground that racial prejudice or any sort of prejudice was the symptom of psychic and moral disease, especially anti-Semitism, which was inexcusable and unpardonable on any grounds" (412). Jenny would seem a natural ally for Freytag after his expulsion from the Captain's table for having a Jewish wife. The problem is that the potential defender of his wife is also his wife's competitor. Freytag is attracted to Jenny and courts her in the casual way of a shipboard romance, but his guilty conscience leads him to disagree with her sentiments—at least in his own mind. (He never voices his opinion because he does not want to alienate her as a dance partner.) With whom does Porter side? The would-be adulterer who voices one of Porter's more suspect arguments although his wife is Jewish or the naïve artist whom many critics identify as a version of the young Porter (Unrue 256)? The novel offers little guidance beyond the significantly schizophrenic quality of this strange dispute.

The matter is complicated by Porter's depiction of the only actual Jewish passenger, who is a caricature of anti-Semitic stereotypes. Herr Löwenthal could have stepped from the pages of the *Stürmer*-like magazine that Rieber is said to edit in Germany: "He retired into the dark and airless ghetto of his soul"; "his thick curly lips and heavy-lidded eyes"; "hair crisped in tight waves and standing up in a ridge at the crown of his head" (95, 96, 98). Even

---

[9] Trilling actually advocated individualistic literature. Liberal American novels, he thought, were not populated by individuals because the characters embodied abstractions commonly taken for reality, like social class (*Liberal Imagination* 209–10). In Porter, characters cease to be individuals when they are embodied *as* body, i.e. as an unreasonable bundle of passions and drives.

Löwenthal's vocation is suspect: the Jewish businessman makes his living selling religious paraphernalia to Catholic churches ("it's just straight business" [96–97]). As a passenger Löwenthal is the victim of prejudice, as a creature he might be its product, and his own emotional perversities reveal him to be as racist as the other characters: "He had heard plenty of times that shiksas were good stuff if you took them in the right way, that is, you didn't have to think of them as people, the same as Jewish, only just live meat, but he never had been able to buy that argument" (471). Löwenthal shies away from *shiksas*, but not because he considers them fully human. He disapproves of miscegenation on the grounds of racial purity. At the first opportunity he berates the German Freytag for the impropriety of taking a Jewish wife (241).

Taking the negative portrayal of Löwenthal as his cue, Theodore Solotaroff of *Commentary* criticized the novel for the indiscriminate universalism of its moral rancor (278, 283). The novel's fans—such as Mark Shorer of *The New York Times*—make the mistake, Solotaroff claims, of taking Porter's preface at its word; they describe the novel as "a 'parable of a corrupt faithless world,' as 'a great moral allegory of man's fate,' and so forth" (278). The novel's opprobrium is meant to be universal, but this according to Solotaroff is the problem. Porter's outrage is too diffuse to offer the kind of moral comparison at work in parable or allegory. The absence of a moral standard accounts for the novel's formal shortcomings: the fragmented, anecdotal structure; characters who are "caricatures of moral infirmity"; and naturalistic gestures that offer little more than "an overdetermined simulation of real experience" (281). Solotaroff sees in Porter the atrophied literary and moral sensibility that he finds typical for the age. Part of this has to do with her view of human sexuality:

> Miss Porter's versions of political action, artistic creation, religious belief, teaching, and so forth are no less skewed and embittered than her versions of copulation. […] [T]his clammy connection between sex and evil appears to rule out any feelings toward her characters other than a nagging exasperated irony, and to remove the possibility of any struggle toward deeper insight. (286)

The bleak eroticism is symptomatic of her pessimistic view of human beings generally. Solotaroff compares Porter to Hannah Arendt who had earned *Commentary*'s rancor the same year (1962) for arguing, in *Eichmann in Jerusalem*, that the European Jews had gone like sheep to the slaughter.[10]

[10] Norman Podhoretz ends his review of Arendt's *Eichmann in Jerusalem* with the following remark: "The Nazis destroyed a third of the Jewish people. In the name of all that is humane, will the remnant never let up on itself?" (208).

Porter too suggests that victims and perpetrators are equally guilty. This "creates not only a feeble portent of Hitler's Germany but in time a brutally indiscriminate one" (283). *Ship of Fools* perpetrates an allegory so indiscriminate that it borders on animalism.

This is a powerful criticism, in part because Porter's depiction of sex and violence is at least partially animalistic. Indeed, she introduces elements of beast allegory in the opening pages of the novel, foreshadowing human violence in the antics of a monkey, a parrot, a cat, and a dog fighting over scraps of food (5–6). Their comic battle sets off a cartoon-like chain of events that eventually propels the dog into the feet of a slumbering Indian, who "with perfect swiftness and economy swung his leg from the knee and planted a kick with the hard edge of his sandals into the dog's lean ribs" (6). Some local businessmen watching the scene from a hotel veranda yawn—such battles occur frequently—and open their newspaper to the picture of a disemboweled corpse: the victim of last night's bombing (6). There is little difference between so-called civilization and the animal kingdom; whatever threshold might exist between the veranda and the dusty ground is traversed by the violent kick of the peasant's leg.

The beast allegory established in the opening pages is borne through the narrative by Ric and Rac, the children of members of a Zarzuela dance troupe deported from Mexico for theft, prostitution, and racketeering.[11] Ric and Rac, a boy and a girl, are pure products of the dance troupe's criminal energy; they are twins

> of one mind and spirit, and lived twined together in a state of intense undeclared war with the adult world—or rather, with the whole world, for they did not like other children, or animals, either. […] [T]hey had renamed themselves for the heroes of their favorite comic cartoon in a Mexican newspaper: Ric and Rac, two lawless wire-haired terriers whose adventures they followed day by day passionately and with envy. (71)

The twins, like the cartoon dogs whose names they assume, are brutally innocent. When not attempting to drown shipboard pets, they engage in petty mischief and incestuous play. For instance, they rob an exiled noblewoman, La Condesa, of her jewels, then simply throw the priceless heirlooms overboard to escape discovery. For this they are beaten by the older members of the troupe, not for doing wrong but for spoiling an opportunity to make off

---

[11] The dance troupe is responsible for much of the thievery and prostitution on board; they organize a raffle, which takes place at an apocalyptic party and dance, where many of the tensions that have been brewing throughout the voyage blow up in an orgy of sex and violence. It is in the aftermath of this party that Denny mistakes Treadwell for one of the dancers and tries to rape her.

with the booty. After the beating "Ric and Rac crawled into the upper berth looking for safety; they lay there half naked, entangled like some afflicted, misbegotten little monster in a cave, exhausted, mindless, soon asleep" (360). The violence of the beating reduces them to their quintessence. They are actually one being split in two, "twined together" because they are the twin embodiments of a single, unreasonable force. Ric and Rac are imps of the perverse, materializations of the pure passion motivating and resulting from violence. They are not exactly personifications: the novel goes to great lengths—in the device of twinning itself—to deny them individual personhood. It would be more accurate to call them anti-individuals stationed at the threshold of personality, where they thread together the human-animal poles of Porter's beast allegory and materialize the unreason excluded from her essays. Ric and Rac, in other words, embody the de-individuation already evident in Porter's dispersal of her own opinions and experiences among conflicting characters, such as in the disagreement over anti-Semitism between Freytag and Jenny.

The novel's anti-individualism would seem to confirm Solotaroff's charge of moral relativism. Ric and Rac are both perpetrators and victims, and all perpetrators and victims—from Rieber to Löwenthal—have elements of Ric and Rac inside of them. However, the anti-individualism also necessitates formal innovations that may offer a generic answer to Solotaroff's moral objections. *Ship of Fools* diverges from individualism in the same way it diverges from allegory, not because allegory is the genre of individualism—that pride of place is reserved for realist narratives such as "The Leaning Tower." Rather, individualism is the allegory of liberalism. Porter's essays demonstrate how political controversy can be reduced—at least rhetorically—to the differences of personal opinion that are the liberal proof positive of equality. Everybody has a right to free speech, and politics means agreeing to disagree. The novel, however, is more interested in what individuals have in common than in what makes them equal or equivalent. Its theme is interpersonal; its plot a choreography of passions; its conflict dramatized by bringing bodies together rather than by keeping opinions equal by keeping them apart. *Ship of Fools* pushes beast allegory beyond the limits of liberalism towards the post-individualistic literary imagination I have been calling pornography.

Angus Fletcher defines allegory as a symbolic parallel between two orders of meaning or worlds, one concrete and the other hidden or abstract. The protagonist who inhabits the space between these worlds may be violent or daemonic, i.e. compulsively driven to live his life according to the invisible order (287). However, his psychology is characterized by anesthesia (367) or the withdrawal of affect (288). Emotions, if they play a significant role in allegory, are confined to the apocalyptic ending, when a new order triumphs over the old, sometimes in imagery referring to a mythical body (334, 355, 357, 358). Porter's narrative employs the corporeal and apocalyptic elements typical of allegory, but it works in the opposite direction, abstracting from concrete symbols to materialize the emotional miasma just below the surface of daily life. Passion, rather than anesthesia, defines the consciousness of the characters, most of whom are daemonic; the apocalypse is general rather than climactic; the body plays a central role throughout. Allegory evokes a higher order of meaning by positing a one-to-one correspondence between symbols and concepts. *Ship of Fools* pushes this matrix to the limits of its symbolic capacity by showing how signs and concepts are placeholders for feelings. This subordination of the conceptual to the passional is a defining feature of the pornographic imagination. *Ship of Fools* is not a novel of ideas but a choreography of life and death that plays itself through—but not because of—individual characters.

The primary object of popular pornography is audience absorption or arousal. Formal complexity and mechanisms of identification are useful only insofar as they facilitate the direct transmission of affect. Porter, however, does not write to "turn on" her readers. She mimics the transmission of affect through a narrative device that is formally one of the most innovative features of the novel. The narrative does not have a unified point of view. Characters serve as alternate and sometimes conflicting focalization points for intersecting scenes ("they all saw the same thing, each with his own different way of seeing" [388]). What is new is how the focalization gets passed from one character to another like a contagious microbe or a baton in a relay-race. This only happens intermittently—the technique would doubtless be difficult to maintain for the duration of a long novel. When it happens the scene is "obscene" in the sense of coming too close—to the point of compromising the barrier between participants and observers.[12] One example I have already cited: the boarding of the displaced persons which leads Rieber to flirt with genocide, Denny to accost Treadwell, and Freytag to fear for the safety of his wife.[13] The masses are obscene because they embody de-

[12] Hal Foster proposes the following distinction based on an analysis of aesthetic distance: "Might this be one difference between the *obscene*, where the object, without a scene, comes too close to the viewer, and the *pornographic*, where the object is tagged for the viewer who is thus distanced enough to be its voyeur?" His follow-up question suggests the difficulty of maintaining this distinction: "In a sense this is the other part of the question: can there be an evocation of the obscene that is *not* pornographic?" (153, 156).

[13] "He [Freytag] could not feel fated, destined for catastrophe; actually he could not imagine himself being driven out of a place, or in peril of his life; surely he and Mary

individuation in a way that is related to but politically more pressing than the twinning of Ric and Rac. Another example: Denny and David converge separately on their cabin to find one of the bunks already occupied by Herr Glocken, an impoverished and malodorous hunchback who takes opiates and reads pornography (26). The abject body of the hunchback serves the same function in this exchange as the de-individuated masses in the previous one, calling into question the corporeal boundaries of identity. The narrative perspective follows Denny into the cabin, crosses over to David when they exchange glances, then gets carried by David out to his meeting with Jenny. This passing of the narrative baton has a subtle effect. It does not by itself call into question individual points-of-view, which are preserved as discrete—if serial—entities. However, the narrative structure evokes a deep emotional connection between individual characters who share feelings across their psychological and political differences.

This narrative innovation works counter to the animal allegory. The biological metaphor suggested by the serial point-of-view is not zoological but affective. Porter is not concerned with what turns humans into beasts but what de-individuates them, makes them vehicles of the social passions coursing through them. It is not instincts but feelings that the characters have in common, not hunger but passion that drives them to sex and violence.[14] Sex is Porter's metaphor for violence because, like violence, it is obscene, diminishing the distance between participants and observers and occurring at that moment where the boundaries between individuals break down. Solotaroff criticizes her pessimistic depiction of human sexuality as evidence of moral abdication, but he misses the work performed by the sex-violence nexus in her novel. Porter's pornographic imagination materializes passion as the racist/fascist political factor, a force rendering individuals aesthetically and politically obsolete.

Passion resembles instinct but it is not exactly natural. Porter signals her dissatisfaction with the naturalistic implications of the beast allegory in the naming of Ric and Rac. They borrow their monikers from cartoon figures, not actual dogs, and this suggests that the coordinates of their de-individuation are cultural rather than natural. Their horrible innocence is not something they inherit from the animals; unreason is a social plague.

---

would never be put on a ship, penniless, prisoners, to be thrust into still another country that did not want them either—like that unbalanced Spanish countess prisoner with her wild tale of terror. [...] Leaning over the rail, he looked again to the steerage deck" (*Ship of Fools* 135).

14 As Arendt put it in her essay "On Violence," "Neither violence nor power is a natural phenomenon [...]; they belong to the political realm of human affairs" (*Crises of the Republic* 179).

Porter depicts de-individuation from below in Ric and Rac and from above in the fascist officer Captain Thiele. The Captain, responsible for order on the ship, is also fascinated by mass culture, but precisely because he hates the masses:

> That was his true world, of unquestioned authority, clearly defined caste and carefully graded privilege, and it irked him grievously to be forced to concern himself with any other. He knew well what human trash his ship—all ships—carried [...] the gutter-stuff of the steerage moving like plague rats from one country to another, swarming and ravening and undermining the hard-won order of the cultures and civilizations of the whole world. (425)

In the Captain's mind, the Spanish dancers are hardly better than the displaced Spanish workers: they represent those forces undermining order from below. But he is more like Ric and Rac than he would like to admit; his fantasies of control and extermination borrow from what he hates: "The Captain was fascinated by American gangster films [...] though he could not imagine himself as being on any side except that of established government, he had in fact noticed that it was nearly always the gangsters who were shown operating the machine guns" (426). The captain is a gangster opposed to gangsterism, the consumer of American culture opposed to Americanism (427). He is all bluster, ineffectual except against those who are already powerless against him, but it is precisely the emptiness of his character that shores up his authoritarianism (487).[15] Doubling and repetition are the psychological symptoms of authority constructed around an ego-deficit; they are also the figurative versions of what the narrative performs as contagion or the passing of the perspectival baton. The Captain turns himself into what he despises in order to destroy it. He is a sadist.

Dr. Schumann was seen by many of Porter's contemporaries as the moral conscience of the novel, probably because he saves a cat from Ric and Rac and feels justice has been served in Treadwell's beating of Denny (492).[16] He certainly prides himself on his moral conscience, but he is really just a moralistic version of the Captain, a sadist with standards. Like the Captain, the Doctor is uncomfortable in the presence of masses: "His agitation grew

---

[15] At the most extreme point of authoritarian caricature, the Captain is shown to be an advocate of interdiction because he was once severely punished by his father for ignoring a sign that read "Verboten" (428; see also 173–74).

[16] Brinkmeyer argues that Porter identified with Dr. Schumann and that his failings are the novel's failings. "Porter may have seen *Ship of Fools* as an attempt to correct twentieth-century chaos and madness, but what the novel finally became was something close in spirit to Dr. Schumann's calculated detachment and idealism—not a corrective for but an embodiment of the very problem it supposedly combated" (220).

as he felt the oppression of the increasing millions of subhuman beings, the mindless grave-stuff not even fit to be good servants, yet whose mere mass and weight of negative evil threatened to rule the world" (317). The Captain describes "subhuman beings" as rats; the Doctor calls them evil. The Captain fantasizes about extermination; the Doctor dreams of righteousness.[17] This comes to the fore in the Doctor's abortive romance with La Condesa, the exiled Cuban noblewoman who claims to have no conscience but honor (192). The Doctor tries to cure her of her drug addiction, but he falls in love with her in the course of the treatment. He believes he can diagnose the patient's vices from her symptoms, but his own weak heart—he nearly dies in the novel and does so in the film—suggests a lack of compassion, or perhaps a confusion of compassion with passion (197). To wean La Condesa from one drug he substitutes another, shifting her addiction and establishing himself as the dealer. A dream, triggered by his own use of what is perhaps the same soporific, suggests that his possession of La Condesa—he imagines she is a little ball—is his solace for having to treat the masses he despises (469). Dr. Schumann is not oblivious to these contradictions: he accuses himself of "criminal sentimental cruelty" and "moral collapse" (373). This does not, however, change the way he feels or acts toward the addict who responds with a desperation that is easy to mistake for passion: "don't stop giving it. Don't go away. I love your good advice" (121). The advice, of course, comes with the medicine, at least until the Doctor abandons La Condesa to her island exile on Santa Cruz de Tenerife. The depth of her affection might be gauged by the fact that she tears up his parting letter without reading it. The Captain hints at criminal negligence, but he is jealous of her affections and therefore unreliable as a judge; in any event the Doctor returns to the Captain's table at the end, where—as another passenger puts it—they are "all good Germans together" (474, 494).

This foreboding affirmation of German identity does not contradict the general tone of the novel, but it does qualify those passions that otherwise tend to put everyone in the same boat. Porter had trouble finishing her book, and the abrupt ending breaks with those aspects of the pornographic imagination that represent passion as the driving force of history, and character—whether personal or national—as an abstraction. Some contemporary German reviewers saw the novel as unfairly anti-German (one reviewer called the novel a "Dokument des Hasses" [Unrue 254]), but it is important to weigh the instantiated evil of the Captain's table against the

[17] Doctor Schumann is puritanical, a version of Cotton Mather whom Porter described in three essays she hoped to turn into a book; he spreads the infection because he believes himself to be morally immune (*Collected* 337).

indiscriminate sex and violence that bothered Solotaroff. Even those characters who never have a seat at the table—the Spanish dancers, Ric and Rac, Denny, Treadwell, Löwenthal—are implicated in the general reign of unreason. Returning the Doctor to the fold, however, does serve to differentiate the passengers and crew whose destination is Bremerhaven from those who decide to go elsewhere. The key defectors are the American artists Jenny Brown and David Scott, who true to the principle of doubling and twinning evident everywhere in the novel, jointly inherit Charles Upton's artistic legacy from "The Leaning Tower."

Jenny and David fight about their destination for the entire trip: "This would be such a nice voyage if only we knew where we were going!" (*Ship of Fools* 148, see also 396). Even at the end of the novel it is not clear where they are heading, only that they will stay together for the time being (496). "The quarrel between them" is unending, "a terrible treadmill they mounted together and tramped round and round until they were wearied out or in despair" (43). It drives them to behavior that resembles that of the other passengers: David gets drunk and Jenny dances provocatively with the Spaniards and flirts with Freytag. However, the desperate romanticism behind the quarrel also distinguishes them from their fellow passengers; it is because they "hoped to be the ideal image of the other" that they invariably expose one another's "evil natures" (44). That they manage to remain together at all is due in part to the psychological sobriety that descends on David in his drunken stupor: "There never was, there couldn't possibly be, any such living girl as he had dreamed Jenny was" (450).

Scholars agree that Jenny and David are the most autobiographical figures in the novel, standing for the young Porter and her third husband Eugene Dove Pressly, whom she met in Mexico (Givner 246–47, Unrue 255–56). Porter and Pressly voyaged together to Europe on the *Werra* (in the novel the ship is called the *Vera*) in 1931 when she received her second Guggenheim Fellowship; he left her in Berlin to travel on to Spain; they married in 1933 and lived together in Paris; Porter divorced him after she returned from Europe in 1938 (Stout 96–102). Later she seemed to grow nostalgic about the marriage, which she commemorated in a poem, "After a Long Journey (to Gene … Berlin, Fall, 1931)," published in *Mademoiselle* in 1957—but rejected by *Encounter*—and later included in her *Collected Essays* (Stout 111).[18] It begins "This was never our season" and provides snapshots of their journey that would later surface in the novel, including a stanza dedicated to

[18] Stout: "'After a Long Journey' also develops an important theme of the interrelation of personal and political life that would emerge both in 'The Leaning Tower' and in *Ship of Fools* and, by implication, in much of her work" (111).

the place of La Condesa's exile, Santa Cruz de Tenerife (492). The centerpiece is a cold meeting in the Tiergarten, when "Kisses freeze in our mouths" (*Collected* 491). The poem attempts to counter this winter of their marriage by freezing time in memory ("Oh, let us remember!"). The commemorative form it fixes on is montage:

> All, all such memories are rayed metal, a star with a cutting edge,
> That shears one moment from another. Must we lose them all
> Or shall we do a montage of them, and frame it? (492)

The poem materializes this framed montage as elegy and apostrophe: it resuscitates Gene Pressly as a participant in the ritual of remembrance even as it admits his absence. The object contemplated by the speaker and her partner in the park full of statues is their own relationship, rendered static through the cooling of passion, but monumental through poetic form.

Porter's montage-elegy for marriage is a version of what Joseph Frank famously calls "spatial form." Frank traces this form back to Pound's concept of imagism, summarizing the Poundian notion of the image as "a unification of disparate ideas and emotions into a complex presented spatially in an instant of time" (Frank 9). Frank argues that "modern poetry asks its readers to suspend the process of individual reference temporarily until the entire pattern of internal references can be apprehended as a unity" (13, 14). He also (and more controversially) applies the concept of spatial form to modernist narrative, which according to Frank tends to reduce the flow of historical time to circular patterns of myth and moments of psychological intensity. Porter's poem turns to imagism nostalgically, as a commemorative compensation for loss. Jenny and David's narrative is not classically modernist, but it can be understood as a novelistic variation on way spatial form functions in the poem. The marriage that the poem freezes as a monument manifests itself as an ongoing disagreement, and the static form of the montage is narrativized as the deferral of a destination indefinitely postponed.

The Jenny-David story is modernist and sentimental. Indeed it epitomizes the sentimental phase of modernism at midcentury, when art confronted the catastrophe of contemporary history and turned aside to prewar aesthetic debates. Jenny and David are discussing precisely the problem of modern art when they are confronted with the spectacle of the displaced persons being loaded into steerage. She is a primitivist, hoping to learn something authentic from the natives, and he, more cynical, believes that primitivism is simply a style, and a decadent one at that; the only valid aesthetic is a stringency of form and color that he does not think any woman can master (77). David keeps a close lid on his misogyny, but he is lecturing Jenny on racism—native racism towards the expatriate artists—when the sight of the masses silences them (56–59). This encounter stages modernism's confrontation with the problem of modernity: statelessness, de-individuation, mass violence. Porter turns to sex to represent this violence. What I have called her pornographic imagination explores the collective denial of individual personhood through characters whose passions push them to the limits of individuality. However, the novel retreats from pornography, and from the modern catastrophe, in its nostalgic rendering of Jenny and David. The subject of the novel is love and death, but in the end it holds up love as an antidote to death, turning the universal allegory of the ship into a quarantine vessel, and salvaging romance (of a sort) from the general wreckage of humanity.

The sentimentalism, which may have played a role in *Encounter*'s decision not to publish the poem, is as cultural as it is romantic. Porter wants to salvage the memory of a marriage, but she also wants to salvage art from the general shipwreck of the passions. As she put it in her essay "St. Augustine and the Bullfight," "Literary art, at least, is the business of setting human events to rights and giving them meanings the artist feels they should have—we do understand so little of what is really happening to us in any given moment" (*Collected* 94). This nostalgia for literary order might seem an unsatisfying solution to the emotional perversities everywhere apparent in the novel and signaled in the same essay: "Looking back nearly thirty-five years on my earliest days in Mexico, it strikes me that for a fairly serious young woman who was in the country for the express purpose of attending a Revolution, and studying Mayan people art, I fell in with a most lordly gang of fashionable international hoodlums" (94). However, even in her writing on Pound, Porter always wanted to protect art from the general reign of unreason it depicted. The artist who commits treason, she argues, should be hanged as a citizen, not as an artist (*Collected* 218). Art can represent passion as a political force, but in the end it is exempt from both passion and politics. It is a sculpture, a frozen monument.

The romance that is ultimately exempt from emotional perversities in *Ship of Fools* is the romance with art, or with high modernism. The irony is that this sentimental view of modernism was solidly middlebrow by midcentury. Fiedler made precisely this criticism of Porter in *Waiting for the End* (1964). One of her biographers describes Porter's reaction as follows:

> In *Waiting for the End* the critic Leslie A. Fiedler wrote of Katherine Anne Porter that she had "only in the past few years [...] clearly exposed herself as having gone over to ladies'-magazine fiction." She was so furious that when his picture appeared alongside a review of his book she scribbled around it, "This is what the Jews used to call a Kike—I don't know what that means but this nasty smug conceited smirk is the front for the most indecent mind and the pickiest envy of talent I know and it is pure Jewish as Seymour Kr__ says." (Givner 414; Fiedler 175)

Porter turns Fiedler into a Löwenthal through a twisted emotionalism analogous to Freytag's, blaming her own anti-Semitic outburst on the Jews. Her prejudices are most evident in her attempts to protect art—especially her own art—from the emotional perversions she knew to be widespread. Like Freytag she knows that "their abstractions and generalizations, their Rage for Justice or Hatred of Tyranny or whatever, too often disguised a bitter personal grudge," but like him she does not apply her observations to herself, or at least not to her own art (411). This is her most Poundian side, and it is hidden by the liberal individualism of her essays. Solotaroff is wrong, I think, to criticize her for her universalism. It is her anti-Semitism that probably bothered him, anti-Semitism put to the service of an aesthetic ideal. Brinkmeyer argues that the novel fails because Porter's anti-totalitarianism moved her to intolerance and authoritarianism, ultimately undermining the individual focus that characterized her best stories (220–21). However, I would argue that she remained true to liberal individualism, at least as a political ideal. Indeed, it was Porter's commitment to the liberal aesthetic that moved her to illiberalism. It was because she believed art to be fundamentally different from politics that she defended it with those emotions she held to be politically dangerous. Critics like Fiedler would move beyond liberalism in another direction, refusing to exempt art from the general ebb and flow of the passions, and turning to culture to find the kind of fulfilment that seemed to be repressed through liberalism's principle of toleration.

Love and Death at Midcentury

Sex was a common metaphor for violence at midcentury. A confluence of Freudian and Marxian theories led many thinkers to conclude that healthy affection was impossible in an industrial society, which perverted love into its opposite, i.e. mechanized death. Versions of this argument can be doubtless traced back to the Romantics, but a convenient midcentury benchmark is Horkheimer and Adorno's portrait of the Marquis de Sade as the counter-image of enlightenment rationalism in *The Dialectic of Enlightenment* (1944,

1947). Sade, they argue, can be considered the conceptual architect of the death camps. The geometrically organized spaces and torments in *The 120 Days of Sodom* are a blueprint for the kind of perverted rationalism—rational means for irrational ends—that would find its ultimate expression in totalitarianism (88–89, 118–19).

Horkheimer and Adorno do not turn Sade into a psychological case study; he personifies the abject side of enlightenment rationalism, which can be systematically cruel because it is impersonal or apathetic (96–97). Unreason, according to this formulation, is a manner of thinking or acting that achieves methodological consistency at the expense of thinkers and actors. The notion that systematic cruelty was a form of sadism did, however, lead many writers to conclude that perpetrators must be *eo ipso* sadists. The psychological analysis of the fascist as sadist played an important role in the writing of Herbert Marcuse and Klaus Theweleit, who argued that "acts of fascist terror spring from irreducible human desire," as Barbara Ehrenreich puts it in her foreword to *Male Fantasies* (xii). Wilhelm Reich and Norman O. Brown can also be grouped among those thinkers who considered fascism to be an affect-driven perversion, as can Bruno Bettelheim and the researchers (including Adorno) involved in defining the authoritarian personality.[19] Hannah Arendt would paint the famous counter-portrait of the Nazi as passionless bureaucrat ("The trouble with Eichmann was precisely that so many were like him, and that the many were neither perverted nor sadistic, that they were, and still are, terribly and terrifyingly normal" [276]), but the image of the perpetrator as someone who kills with a passion played a central role in the theories that came to be associated with the New Left and in a whole host of books and

---

[19] Marcuse argues that sexual repression is linked to political repression in *Eros and Civilization*. See Reich, *The Mass Psychology of Fascism*: "sexual repression strengthens political reaction and makes the individual in the masses passive and non-political; it [also] creates a secondary force in man's structure—an artificial interest, which actively supports the authoritarian order. When sexuality is prevented from attaining natural gratification, owing to the process of sexual repression, what happens is that it seeks various kinds of substitute gratifications. Thus, for instance, natural aggression is distorted into brutal sadism, which constitutes an essential part of the mass-psychological basis of those imperialistic wars that are instigated by a few" (31). See also Brown's *Love's Body*, which opposes what it calls "Conventional Anglo-Saxon political theory [which] dismiss[es] Nazism as an irrelevant aberration, a lunatic episode" (11), and focuses instead on the political significance of the fraternal organization, the band of brothers, the primal hoard, which unites behind a phallic symbol ("The penis is the head of the body" [134]). According to Brown, this phallic symbol is the driving force behind an apocalyptic politics: "In the Apocalypse, pomp, power and politics is discovered to be sex. Perverted sex; sado-masochistic sex" (75).

films ranging from *House of Dolls* and *Night Porter* to *Sophie's Choice* and *Schindler's List*.

Elsewhere Michael J. Hoffman and I have described these theories and films as examples of Holocaust pornography. The term is not meant to be derogatory: we argue that the eroticization of violence had an elegiac function after the war, transforming faceless victims into objects of desire and exhuming individuals—or at least individual bodies—from the statistical immensity of mass murder. (There is also a moral component to pornography: perpetrators cannot claim the excuse of "just following orders" if genocide is a crime of passion.) What Sontag calls the pornographic imagination has a long history, but the systematic dehumanization of modern warfare makes it humanism's genre of last resort. Pornography emerges at the limits of individualism, registering the impersonal nature of violence in its indiscriminate portrayal of bodies, pairings, and sexual activities, while at the same time reaffirming the subjective relevance of passion. The genre is *vain* in the etymological sense of empty: it does not discard the individual completely, but hollows him or her out as a container for the passion that is transmitted as directly as possible to the viewer or reader. This stimulus-response circuit, located at the limit of individualism, also marks one limit of representation, replacing symbolic reference with the direct transmission of feeling that Ruth Leys, in her study of trauma, calls "the pathos of the literal" (266–98). What trauma theory recuperates as compassion first emerged in the postwar years as passion; the early stirrings of mourning were easy to mistake for desire.

Passion was central to the philosophy of individualism that was at first more influential than critical theory and preceded it as an academic trend: existentialism. Sartre's "Portrait of the Antisemite," published in *Partisan Review* in 1946, argues that anti-Semitism is not an opinion but a passion (166). Sartre compares the Jew-hater to a man who goes to public pools because he is offended by the sight of women in bathing suits (170). He seeks out the object of his hatred, who is symbolically, when not actually, the victim of rape. Thus the term "Jewess," Sartre argues, "has a kind of flavor of rape and massacre," calling to mind not merely a Jewish woman but a woman dragged by her hair through a burning *shtetl* (175). Anti-Semitism is a form of sadism, and the sadist, as Sartre defines him in *Being and Nothingness*, seeks to relieve anxieties about his own freedom by denying the freedom of others (*Being and Nothingness* 522–23). This kind of domination plays a central role in virtually all forms of social interaction as Sartre conceives them. His paradigmatic social relationship is an eroticized version of the master-slave dialectic (320–22, 497). Thus all love, according to Sartre, vacillates between sadism and masochism: the sadist seeks to reduce the other to an object, and the masochist wants to see himself reduced to an object in the eyes of the sadist (320–21, 492–93).

The sadomasochistic struggle threatens to hollow out the individual, or make him a slave to his body, but the moral Sartre draws from it is freedom. Sartre's imagination is pornographic in reverse; he wants to liberate the individual from the seraglio of passion. He excerpts Faulkner's description of the castration-murder of Joe Christmas in *Light in August* to argue that the victim of lynching, when he looks at his tormenter, "causes the meaning and goal of sadism to collapse" (526). Joe Christmas's crucifixion establishes the etymological meaning of passion—passivity. However it is the lyncher—not his victim—who is passive; he chooses to hate in the same way the anti-Semite chooses to be "massive and impenetrable" like a "stone" ("Portrait of the Anti-Semite" 166). Passion offers perpetrators the false comfort of compulsion. It is related to the "clogged consciousness" Sartre associated with sexual desire, but also to the personal renunciation of freedom he called bad faith (*Being and Nothingness* 504, 110).

The reference to Faulkner also establishes the contradictory meaning passion has for the victim: transcendence. Lacan criticized "the philosophy of being and nothingness" for imagining "a freedom that is never more authentic than when it is within the walls of a prison [...] a voyeuristic-sadistic idealization of the sexual relation [...] a consciousness of the other than [*sic*] can be satisfied only by Hegelian murder" (6). Lacan is correct in one sense: imprisonment is indeed the archetype of existence in Sartre's ontology, hence the famous aphorism that we are "condemned to be free" (*Being and Nothingness* 623). Many found the politics that Sartre extrapolated from his metaphysics untenable, but his philosophy was political in its inception and was compatible with the liberal defense of lyricism which, as I have already argued, imagines the "free" poet to be alone in a cell.[20] Liberalism recovers freedom at the moment of its disappearance by making the "overheard" lyric the measure of free speech; Sartre recovers freedom by describing the perpetrator as the slave to passion, and appointing the victim as witness and judge.

Other postwar accounts of sex and violence dispensed with the problem of freedom altogether. Passion was not a choice but a fact of nature; the individual could not control it, but it might be regulated for the collective good.

[20] Even liberalism, Sartre argues, runs against its own "perilous reef" when it tries to force people to be free (*Being and Nothingness* 528–30). For a critique of Sartre's politics as untenably romantic, see Burkle in Mary Warnock's *Sartre*, 335. Arendt, in her ongoing footnote battle with Sartre, sees the existentialist's latter work especially as prone to glorify violence (*Crises of the Republic* 186).

This was the thesis of Gershon Legman's *Love and Death*, a "study in censorship" published the same year as the Bollingen controversy (1949). Legman claimed that the legal degradation of sex through obscenity laws turned a generation of readers into armchair "lynchers" who read mystery novels and comic books to kill symbolically, but with pleasure, because they were denied the healthy enjoyment of erotic literature (16–17, 19). The opening pages make it clear that Legman thought more to be at stake than personal pathology. The normalization of literary murder could have dire political consequences: "In the same way Germans were given to understand that Jews are not human and, as such, can properly be gassed, electrocuted, and incinerated wholesale. In precisely the same way we are thrilled by a newsreel of the burning to death of a Japanese before our eyes" (13). Legman does not leave any room for choice in his theory. Passion is an irresistible force that drives people to love or hate depending on how it is directed; the individual is little more than a channel for the emotions passing through him. Legman sought to open the channels by acting as a missionary for pornography. He wanted to acquaint his contemporaries with their own sexual drives in order to prevent another genocide or atomic bomb. Ironically, his endorsement of pornography was considered pornographic by the postmaster general, who ordered the confiscation of *Love and Death* for violation of obscenity laws. To escape prosecution Legman fled to France, where he worked as an independent scholar assembling anthologies of dirty jokes and limericks and served as editor for the short-lived Beat journal *Neurotica*.[21] (He was also an expert on origami.)

The simplicity of Legman's thesis made it suitable for sloganeering (he claimed to be the originator of "make love, not war"). The book that assumes the mantle of his legacy (along with his title) complicated the thesis by expanding the generalized notion of sexual repression into a model for national culture. Fiedler's *Love and Death in the American Novel* rejects Legman's homology between political and psychological repression but not their relation, which Fiedler argues is culturally mediated. Culture expresses the dreams but also disguises the failures of national politics; the problem is not censorship so much as collective disavowal (Fiedler xxi). Fiedler acknowledges Legman's influence in the section of the study borrowing another one of his titles: "Avatars of the Bitch" (Fiedler 318–19). Legman had argued that sexual repression turned women into harpies, who revenge themselves in literature and in reality (the relation is again homologous) by tormenting men (Legman 58–59). For Fiedler the "petticoat government" of women is not what the average American but the typical American protagonist flees.

[21] On Legman, see Susan Davis and Brottman.

Huck lights out for the territories with Jim because he knows civilization means Aunt Sally. In this he is like Ishmael fleeing to the *Pequod* and Queequeg, Leatherstocking fleeing to the wilderness and Chingachgook, and Rip van Winkle fleeing his shrewish wife to drink with the ghosts of Dutch explorers (xxi).

Critics like Richard Chase and Ralph Ellison were quick to point out the reductive, ahistorical tenor of Fiedler's argument—and indeed of myth criticism in general (Chase, "Leslie Fiedler" 13; Ellison 216). Fiedler's broad brushstrokes could transform almost any American novel into variations on a single theme. That theme is the traditional one of independence. It has psychological and political components, and both contribute to Fiedler's central insight that independence remains incomplete. American protagonists fleeing the sickness of civilization invariably spread the disease, as did the founding fathers (or genre founders) before them:

> To write, then, about the American novel is to write about the fate of certain European genres in a world of alien experience [...] a world which had left behind the terror of Europe not for the innocence it dreamed of, but for new and special guilts associated with the rape of nature and the exploitation of dark-skinned people; a world doomed to play out the imaginary childhood of Europe. (xxvi)

Few would dispute Fiedler's claims about the flawed origin and character of national politics, but his conclusions about culture are breathtakingly monolithic. Fiedler argues that all cultural narratives—all myths and symbols—are expressions of a collective cultural psyche. The American psyche believes itself to be innocent because it accepts a European myth; but this act of psychological repression leads to political repression as the collective psyche acts out its violent origins (xi, xviii, xxi, 332). The relation between nation and narration in Fiedler's theory is not ideological but symptomatic. He does not believe that culture mystifies economics or politics in any systematic way (e.g., ideology as the means of reproducing the means of production or the lived relation to the real). Rather, culture is the consciousness and in some ways the unconscious of the nation, erected over the abyss of political and psychological denial.

Fiedler's goal was to shock America into growing up. Beginning with his infamous essay on the Rosenbergs, he set out to put an "end to innocence" by exposing the violence implicit in modern mythologization. The Rosenbergs were guilty of internalizing a communist myth; even in their most private moments they "blasphemously deny their own humanity" by confusing themselves with communist banalities (21). They deluded themselves into thinking they were innocent because a political myth told them they were, and they repressed the authentic feelings—the passion—that could have made them adults (20). Fiedler willingly abandoned the Rosenbergs to their fate to eviscerate the mystifying power of communism. His other projects of demystification would not require such obvious victims. In his methodology, although not in his politics, Fiedler shows the influence of both Legman and Sartre. He is like Legman in his belief that culture can be understood psychologically as a collection of passions and repressions. He is like Sartre in his belief that some forms of passion—those grounded in resistance—are more authentic than others. The archetypical American protagonist is an exile who realizes that he can find no permanent home in the stories other people tell about him. "In his relationship to his lot," argues Fiedler, "his final resolve to accept what is called these days his 'terrible freedom,' Huck seems the first Existentialist hero" (589).

Existentialism is the philosophy of individual consciousness, but Fiedler is an existentialist of the collective. Fiedler's protagonist is an individual on a grand scale, so grand that it is not, properly speaking, an individual at all. It is identity[22]—the American identity that takes responsibility for its own "terrible freedom" in declaring its independence from alien myths. Once Fiedler had defined the project of American cultural identity, he would help redirect American studies as it turned its attention to smaller collectivities

---

[22] The spokesman and in many ways the founder of this postwar notion of identity was Erik Erikson. His 1968 book, *Identity: Youth and Crisis*, explains how the concept of identity developed in response to the limitations of the psychological version of individualism known as ego psychology (45). "The concept of the ego, then, was first delineated by the definitions of these counterplayers, the biological id and the sociological 'masses.' The ego, the individual center of organized experience and reasonable planning, stood endangered by both the anarchy of the primeval instincts and the lawlessness of the group spirit" (46). Ego psychology can be seen as an attempt to defend the embattled self from the primitive feelings originating below its control and from the social forces originating beyond. However, the atrocities of World War II showed that the forces most in need of being accounted for were those beyond individual control (Erikson began developing his theories by working with veterans). Identity is an attempt to explain not the isolated but the situated self. Erikson turns to two "bearded authorities" in an attempt to explain the concept that carries him beyond the limits of individualism: William James who describes identity as "a subjective sense of an invigorating sameness and continuity" (19), and Freud who spoke of his Jewishness as "a deep communality known only to those who shared in it, and only expressible in words more mythical than conceptual" (20–21). "The two statements and the lives behind them serve to establish a few dimensions of identity and, at the same time, help to explain why the problem is so all-pervasive and yet so hard to grasp: for we deal with a process "located" *in the core of the individual* and yet also *in the core of his communal culture*, a process which establishes, in fact, the identity of those two identities" (22).

engaged in similar struggles against America's dream of itself: "the psychically oppressed flounder in their attempts to come to terms with the burden imposed upon them: the obligation [...] to act out, in addition to their own authentic roles, secondary ones corresponding to the inner necessities of quite alien others" (*Waiting for the End* 119). Fiedler lit out for the new territories of Jewish American identity, Native American identity, African American identity, and the identities of the youth and drug subcultures, opening new frontiers of cultural authenticity (Winchell, *Too Good* 53). The one noteworthy exception among his causes was feminism. The sex-violence nexus at the center of Fiedler's theories required women to be objects of desire or fear, linked to the id or the superego but never aligned with consciousness (*Love and Death* 330). When women travel to the frontier they do not embody the possibility of freedom, according to Fiedler, but invite the threat of miscegenation (*Waiting for the End* 113).

Waiting for the End applies Fiedler's insights about the collective (androcentric) struggle to end American innocence at midcentury. Jewish identity—or what Fiedler calls the "Judaization of American culture"—turns out to be central in two ways (67). Fiedler draws attention to a Cold War "détente" "between Gentile and Jew in the United States" that reverses the mandatory anti-Semitism of the high modernists (Fiedler mentions Pound's "the yidd is a stimulant" here [80, 67]). Also, he suggests that American culture was actually Jewish all along: "These great figures out of our deepest imagination, whom we had thought essentially American, we now learn are—or at least can be made to seem—characteristically Jewish as well. It is not a matter of cultural kidnapping, but of the discovery of cultural resemblances" (85). Huckleberry Finn was an existentialist, and his heirs are the absurd and alienated heroes Augie March and Holden Caulfield (83–84, 85). In a sense, American heroes have always been Jewish existentialists because American culture has always struggled to declare its independence from alien myths (89). There is an elegiac component to this argument, an attempt to make Jewish experience central to American culture after the European genocide. However, there is a contemporary component as well. The American psyche, still laboring under the European myth of innocence, has to liberate itself from a new terror at midcentury. Fiedler's experiences as a Fulbright professor in Italy taught him that "*all* Americans [...] are the Jews of the second half of the twentieth century: refused (outside of their own country, at least) any identity except the general one contained in a name which is an abusive epithet. "*Americans go home*!" (102, 88).

Fiedler sets out to describe what is archetypically American about American culture, but his concerns turn out to be international and contemporary. After World War II and in the context of the Cold War, Americans and Jews have a common cross to bear. Fiedler detects similarities in the accusations "You killed our Julius and Ethel Rosenberg!" and "You killed our Christ!" (102–03). His fears about an anti-American pogrom proved misguided, but they were stimulated by his analysis of the passionate nature of racism—an analysis that resonated with those of other midcentury writers. Fiedler believed that racist stereotypes, driven by collective passion, could lead to genocide. He also believed that Jews and Americans were in key positions to help forge a new, post-racist identity because they had the means to counter dominant passions and myths: "The Jewish-American mind, conditioned by two thousand years of history, provides other Americans with ways of escaping the trap of vacillation between isolationism and expatriation, chauvinism and national self-hatred" (83). The cumulative experience of the Jewish-American psyche teaches the lesson of exile. It does so in a literary language—a genre— that exploits the comic potential of never being one thing or the other: vulgar humor. The typical midcentury narrative is abject and transcendent; it traces the inner migration or "inpatriation" of Jewish figures moving as far west as Montana (where Fiedler taught). "Within the past couple of years the first fictional treatment of this new migration, a comedy involving an urban Jew in a small university community in the West, has appeared" (83) Fiedler is referring to Malamud here, but he could be describing the plot of his own short story "Pull Down Vanity."

Fiedler's poet protagonist Milton Amsterdam evokes Delmore Schwartz —a Schwartz who got the teaching position he was looking for instead of dying alone in New York. Amsterdam teaches at a private school in Texas, but he is visiting a Midwestern university to lead a seminar on poetry. A critic from New York also lecturing at the seminar "outs" him as Jewish, and he immediately becomes the target of ethnic stereotyping. Judy, the beautiful department secretary, pursues him as a sexual partner, in part to convince him to read her husband's poetry. Hank, a graduate student who has lost his self-confidence, writes in the style of Sandburg. The Midwesterners are types, corn-fed giants with chests bursting from their sweaty t-shirts and low-cut summer dresses. Judy's body literally strains the seams of her clothing, and Amsterdam dwells on the fact that she wears no underwear (140). Among the cast of characters is a Jewish sociologist who is also a type; he is doubly inauthentic because in addition to embodying an anti-Semitic caricature, he also buys into the communist myth (138). These repertoire figures are the supporting cast for Amsterdam's self-liberation from the Jewish myth (he is already post-Communist). He resists Judy's seductions, described in the language of rape (140, 143, 155), and remains detached while she stimulates herself on his flaccid body ("I felt [...] a relaxed sense of triumph over all the women I had ever known" [158]). Shortly thereafter he parries the jealous attacks of her husband through what can only be described as Jewish jiu-jitsu (165). Hank is so drunk that he knocks himself down on Amsterdam's body in the same way Judy brings herself to orgasm. Amsterdam resists the sexuality and violence of these graduate school Gentiles by remaining impassive to their arousal. Leaving the party, he discovers his own passion—presumably for writing—in an erection that points him home: "It was then that my desire flowed back into me, idiotically, uncomfortably, to the crowing of the first cocks; and I hobbled down the street, pointing my own way home and feeling for the first time that summer almost cold" (167).

This erection is the authentic locus of identity for Fiedler. It leaves Amsterdam cold because he escapes from the anti- and philo-Semitic myths that are the products of other people's passion.[23] The end to innocence is the sexual awakening into the self. *Time* magazine criticized *Tear Down Vanity* (the collection of short stories) as academic kitsch. However, it is actually academic pornography, as Chase suggests, in which passion plays the lead role, and the bodies—while clearly incarnations of cultural types—channel a cultural narrative that speaks through them (Chase, "Leslie Fiedler" 8). Fiedler's protagonist is an individual on the verge of disappearing, a plaything for other people's passions who finally inhabits himself through the sexual experience of his own ethnicity. His body is authentic not because of its genes or chromosomes, but because it is already the seat of the collective psyche: it embodies the contours of Jewish experience.

Fiedler, as I have already pointed out, locates this collective psyche in the "special Jewish vulgarity" he finds in Roth, and also presumably in his own fiction, but also in the poetry of Karl Shapiro and especially Allen Ginsberg (*Waiting for the End*, 83, 233, 239). He insists on reading both poets in relation to Pound. Ginsberg, as I pointed out in chapter one, admired Pound; Fiedler recalls the "Ez for Pres" graffiti campaign he waged in bars throughout the 1950s (240). With Shapiro, of course, the case is more difficult, but Fiedler does draw a line of influence through Whitman and argues that the only place for poets at midcentury America is in the academy or the asylum (238, 185–86). Fiedler sees poets as victims of the myths mass culture imposes on them; he claims a jury would find any poet guilty of treason with

[23] "When either the cult of the primitive or a genteel tradition is in the ascendency, the Jew is likely to be regarded as the Adversary; for he is the anti-type of Negro and Indian, a projection of the feared intelligence rather than the distrusted impulse, and 'genteel' equals Gentile in the language of the psyche. Neither paleface nor redskin, neither gentleman nor genital man, to what can the Jew appeal in the American imagination, which seems to oscillate helplessly between these two poles? Is he doomed to remain merely the absolute un-American, everybody's outsider?" (Fiedler, *Waiting for the End* 82).

the exception of Frost (185–86, 189). Poets are witnesses of their own exclusion in the same way members of minority groups are: "I am talking about our sense of acting out our national destiny in the presence of *witnesses* involved in that destiny (through fear and hate, we know; through love as well, we hope) by virtue of their color, but by the same token detached from it" (114). The fictional Milton Amsterdam can affirm his affinity to Pound by vulgarly affirming his Jewishness because he insists on bearing witness to the powerful myths that would deny him his own identity (see *Waiting for the End* 123–124). By the 1960s Fiedler was arguing that the Baldwins, not Bellows would be the true heirs to this lyricism of identity; Jewishness and philo-Semitism had already become too mainstream to raise any eyebrows (66, 106).

The lyricism of identity scandalizes because it is embodied, but Fiedler knows that ethnicity can be performed. "'Do we have to become Gentile Jews before we can become White Negroes?' an impatient and reasonably hip youngster from a college audience I addressed recently asked me; and he was only half kidding" (88). Fiedler's half-humorous answer to the graduate student in this story, a biographical supplement to "Pull Down Vanity," is yes. The fictional poet Milton Amsterdam's erection points the way to an embodied lyricism. However, it also points to John Berryman's performative concept of the "imaginary Jew." Berryman's poetry of ethnic impersonation will be the subject of the next chapter.

Pound in his double incarnation—as propagandist for fascism and as prisoner in a cage—served as a persistent reminder of the role played by unreason in politics. To represent unreason writers like Porter and Fiedler turned to the themes of sex and violence, and to pornographic representations of passion. Their writing challenged the individual bias of midcentury libe¬ralism. Characters became abstract, passions the material agents of political and historical change. Porter ultimately tried to sequester passion away from politics by containing it in art. She was nostalgic for romance and for the formal coherence of high modernism. Fiedler, on the other hand, considered cultural patterns of perversion—understood as mythic archetypes—to be expressions of a collective psyche. His theories would help effect the transition from individualism to identity in Cold War literature by providing affective rationale for the collective architecture of selfhood. Identity, as he describes it, is a post-individualist concept of selfhood. It rejects cultural myths in order to embrace an experience at once personal and collective.

CHAPTER 6

Imaginary Jews and True Confessions: Ethnicity, Lyricism, and John Berryman's *The Dream Songs*

> . . . Jews, who have changed much in the course of history, are certainly no race, [but] the anti-Semites in a way are a race, because they always use the same slogans, display the same attitudes, indeed almost look alike.
>
> — Max Horkheimer, "Sociological Background" (6)

John Berryman's "The Imaginary Jew," published in the *Kenyon Review* of 1945, is in some ways a rather programmatic account of one man's conversion from parlor anti-Semitism to a feeling of solidarity with Jews. The climax occurs when a bigot accuses the narrator of being Jewish in order to discredit him in an argument over Roosevelt's foreign policy prior to the American entry into World War II. The accusation completely unnerves the narrator in ways he does not immediately understand, and he is shocked to see that it discredits him in the eyes of the crowd, which has assembled at Union Square to hear impromptu debates. Later, after leaving the scene of his embarrassment, he decides to lay claim to this mistaken, or *imaginary*, identity, and comes to the following conclusion about the nature of prejudice:

> My persecutors were right: I was a Jew.The imaginary Jew I was as real as the imaginary Jew hunted down, on other nights and days, in a real Jew. Every murderer strikes the mirror, the lash of the torturer falls on the mirror and cuts the real image, and the real and the imaginary blood flow down together. (Berryman, *Recovery* 252)

The story garnered some attention when it appeared in 1945. It was Berryman's first major publication and it won him the *Kenyon Review* award for the best contribution of the year, bringing him a badly needed prize of $500. It was reprinted in international journals and periodicals. Berryman himself was to return to the theme and even the phrase "the imaginary Jew" throughout his career, referencing it in his *Dream Songs* and in the autobiographical novel *Recovery* he did not complete before his suicide.

"Imaginary Jews" were quite common in the late 1940s, although given our current sensibilities about ethnicity the prevalence of such impersonations might strike us as strange. Arthur Miller's novel *Focus*, published the same year as Berryman's short story, tells the story of a man who begins to "look Jewish" when failing eyesight compels him to wear glasses.[1] By the end of the novel his family and neighbors have turned on him, and he resolves to join forces with the only Jew on his street to face down a violent anti-Semitic attack. In other words, he chooses to "look Jewish" not only as an *object* of other people's perception but as a *subject*. Laura Z. Hobson's novel *Gentleman's Agreement*, about a WASP reporter who impersonates a Jew to uncover anti-Semitism in New York and Connecticut, reached the top of the *New York Times* bestseller list in 1947. The film adaptation of the novel, directed by Elia Kazan and starring Gregory Peck, won three Oscars and was nominated for several more.

Identifying with Jews, and especially Jewish victims of the Holocaust, was also a common practice in midcentury American poetry. Sylvia Plath's "Daddy," "Lady Lazarus," and "Getting There," all from 1962, are the most obvious and widely cited examples. The list could be extended to include Robert Lowell (Mordecai Myers in *Life Studies*), Charles Olson (*The Distances*), Randall Jarrell ("In the Camp there Was One Alive," "A Camp in the Prussian Forest"), and Anne Sexton ("After Auschwitz"). (If we add Jewish American poets to the list of those identifying with Holocaust victims, it would grow to include Allen Ginsberg, Charles Reznikoff, Denise Levertov, Hilda Schiff, and Anthony Hecht, whose army unit helped liberate Buchenwald.)[2] The imaginary Jew was not a major postwar figure, but it was certainly a consistent one, and this consistency makes its subsequent disappearance—and its strangeness from a contemporary perspective—all the more striking.[3]

The imaginary Jewishness evident in postwar poetry and culture completely reversed the anti-Semitism typical of some prewar modernism, which tended to represent Jews through grotesque images rather than as figures of

---

1 The minor metaphorical difference between Miller's use of a distorting lens and Berryman's mirror disappears in the 1984 preface to *Focus*, which restates the moral of the novel in terms of "the mirror of reality" (5).

2 For this list, I am indebted to Schiff, Gubar, and Flanzbaum.

3 On the prevalence of the imaginary Jew in postwar fiction see Fiedler's *The Jew in the American Novel*: "What, after all, *is* a Jew in this world where men are identified as Jews only by mistake, where the very word becomes merely an epithet arbitrarily applied? It is difficult to make a novel about anti-Semitism when one is not sure exactly what, beside being the butt of anti-Semites, makes a man a Jew" (47–48). Much of the material from this small book would go into *Waiting for the End*.

identification. The passages I have already identified in Pound's *The Cantos* are representative of the trend, as are T. S. Eliot's "Burbank with a Baedeker: Bleistein with a Cigar" and "Sweeney among the Nightingales," Djuna Barnes's *Nightwood*, the novels of Nathanael West (sometimes pointed to as examples of "Jewish self-hatred") and even aspects of James Joyce's otherwise sympathetic representation of Leopold Bloom in *Ulysses*.[4] As Fiedler puts it in *Waiting for the End*, "Philo-Semitism is required—or perhaps, by now, only assumed—in the reigning literary and intellectual circles of America, just as anti-Semitism used to be required—and after a while only assumed—in the Twenties" (66).

Recent criticism has tended to judge the "imaginary Jew" almost as harshly as Eliot's line in "Gerontion," "the jew squats on the window-sill" (Eliot, *Collected Poems* 29), and Pound's disparaging remarks about "the intramural, the almost intravaginal warmth of / hebrew affections" (35/172) and the "big jews' vendetta on goyim" (52/257). Hilene Flanzbaum, for instance, accuses Berryman—and through him postwar American culture generally—of misappropriating the Jewish identity that contemporary Jewish poets such as Karl Shapiro ignored ("The Imaginary Jew," 25, 28–30). While this accusation registers our contemporary discomfort with ethnic impersonations, it fails to account for their pervasiveness. It also fails to recognize the explicitly *imaginary* nature of Berryman's Jewishness—an identity he never claimed to be his own.

Berryman is an important test case here because he comes under fire from two divergent critical discourses in ways that highlight their common assumptions about ethnic and lyric identity. The criticism directed against Berryman's supposedly inappropriate "ethnic" identification recapitulates the first wave of sustained anti-Berryman criticism to emerge in the 1970s, when he was accused of being too personal (wrapped-up in quotidian problems) or personal in the wrong way (expressing these problems through the indirection of *dramatis personae*). In a sense, Berryman gets lost in the transition from prewar anti-Semitism to contemporary multi-culturalism in the

4 For a general discussion of the "discourse of semitism" in English literature see Bryan Cheyette's *Constructions of 'the Jew' in English Literature and Society*, especially the introduction and conclusion, and the final chapter on "Modernism and Ambivalence: James Joyce and T. S. Eliot." Cheyette makes the important point that 'the Jew' is not a fixed or mythic character, but rather an indeterminate symbol—and a symbol of indeterminacy—which can serve as both grotesque image and object of desire and/or identification (3–4, 268). Also see Anthony Julius, *T. S. Eliot: Anti-Semitism and Literary Form*; Christopher Ricks, *T. S. Eliot and Prejudice*. On Pound see Robert Casillo, *The Genealogy of Demons*. For a discussion of West see Stacey Olster and Fiedler's remarks in *Waiting for the End*.

same way that he gets lost in the shift from high modernism to confessional poetry.

The determinate context here is indeed confessional poetry, widely understood by Berryman's contemporaries to be an authentically personal lyricism rebelling against Eliot's doctrine of "impersonality."[5] Berryman resisted applying the term "confessional" to his own poetry, and even those who actively cultivated the label rarely subscribed to a form of lyricism as naïve or spontaneous as their supporters (and detractors) claimed. However, confessional poetry did self-consciously cultivate *personality* in an agonal relation to the doctrine of *impersonality* propounded by Eliot and Pound, and in defiance of the individualism used to defend Pound's right to poetic free speech. The new poetry cultivated a lyricism of identity, focusing, in sometimes embarrassing detail, on the particular experiences of identifiable speakers in concrete emotional, professional, and even therapeutic situations. This "situatedness," in turn, became an important motif in the struggle waged by the feminist and ethnic literatures of the 1960s and 1970s against the abstract universals of both traditional (high modernist) culture and liberal individualism.[6] There is a sense in which poetry becomes personal before the personal becomes political.

Berryman, opposing both tradition and the younger talents, is neither impersonal nor personal but *impersonating*. He does not differ from Eliot and Pound in his reliance on personae, masks, or dramatic monologue and dialogue; nor does he diverge from the confessionals in the painful subject matter he called "the soul under stress" (Kostelanetz 345). Rather, it is his construction of identity that is discordant—and in a way that calls the assumptions of both his predecessors and peers into question. From the

---

5 Robert Shaw offers the following definition of confessional poetry in the introduction to his edited volume *American Poetry Since 1960*: "The basic challenge [...] was directed against the Eliotic cult of impersonality. The poet no longer hedged himself about with ironic literary allusions, but presented the reader with (we were asked to believe) unvarnished portraits of himself, the more warts the better" (11).

6 David Simpson defines situatedness as a compromise formation; we know we cannot offer an essentialist account of ourselves, but we suspect such an account would have something to do with background and location: "*Situatedness*, I have been suggesting, is one of the currently fashionable neologisms that claims to indicate if not a breakthrough then at least a temporary accommodation with the intractable demands placed on the self toward justifiable self-description. To announce one's situatedness appears to pre-empt the accusation that one is not being adequately self-aware, and at the same time to provide a limited authority to speak from a designated position" (195). For a complementary account of the way "identitarian" considerations begin, in the 1960s, to replace Cold War concerns with value and belief, see Walter Benn Michaels, *The Shape of the Signifier*.

perspective of Berryman's poetic practice, Eliot's impersonality comes to resemble the invisibility of white male privilege; and confessional personality appears to invert the values without challenging the basic structure of modernist prejudice. Berryman's dramatic impersonations, in no way atypical of literary and filmic narratives of the 1940s and 1950s, deliberately oppose some of the basic principles of twentieth-century verse, and in doing so reveal the ethnic assumptions behind modernist theories of lyricism as well as the hidden lyricism of contemporary ethnicity.

The ethnic lyricism typical of high modernism and confessional poetry is fundamentally melancholic, preoccupied with an Other it can neither ignore nor assimilate. The Other is an excluded or missing object whose "absent presence" effectively restricts the modes of poetic expression to the philippic and the elegiac, and the means to parody, apostrophe, and prosopopoeia. Just as Eliot's grotesque anti-Semitic imagery cannot be separated from his call, in *After Strange Gods*, to limit the number of Jews in communities in order to "protect" cultural tradition (20), Plath's fascination with Jews and Nazis is not to be separated from the recent memory of mass deportation and murder. The political impulses here are fundamentally opposed, but both poetic practices depend, in the proleptic or the commemorative modes, on the representation of Jewish identity as *absence*. Berryman, in contrast to Pound and Plath, neither excludes nor elegizes Jews; he impersonates them, as well as African Americans and women, in a deliberately theatrical way. His impersonations are part of a twofold strategy to dramatize the dangerous links between imagination and violence in modernist poetry, and to reveal the modernist poetic persona's deep investment in racial or ethnic identity.

The theory supporting Berryman's poetic project involves the mirror of anti-Semitism alluded to at the end of his short story. It was widely assumed in midcentury psychology that prejudice turns its object into an inverted mirror, simultaneously reflecting and alienating those aspects of personality the bigot is incapable of facing in himself. Berryman's poetry attempts to transform this violent mirroring into recognized interdependency. To borrow Berryman's own terminology, his "imaginary Jew," far from appropriating or rejecting a "foreign" identity, shows how "selving" is linked to "othering," whether we like it or not (*Dream Songs* 44 and 66; 48, 73).

"The Imaginary Jew" and the Mirror of Anti-Semitism

"The Imaginary Jew" evidently had a strong personal significance for Berryman, who is described by one of his biographers as having briefly flirted with anti-Semitism during his student days (Mariani 31). The short story is based on an actual incident in 1941 that alerted him to the dangers of prejudice and racist stereotyping. He tried to write about the incident for four years—in verse and prose—before finally deciding on the short story format. This casting about for a form is significant. The short story allowed Berryman to work out at the level of plot, setting, and characterization certain relations between image and identity that would later prove crucial in his poetry. I will pursue this point in the next section. First, I want to examine the relations between image, identity, and prejudice as they appear in the short story, along with the similarities between the short story's account of prejudice and those put forth by theories of anti-Semitism that were current at the time of its composition.

A close reading of the story does not support the claim that Berryman is trying to "appropriate" Jewish identity. There are some hints, for instance, that the man who mistakenly—and threateningly—accuses the narrator of being Jewish is also the narrator's double. This doubling is suggested by the fact that the bellicose aggressor in the story is Irish (as was Berryman), and even more strongly by the image of the mirror at the end of the story and the repetitive and ambiguous syntax. There is also a telling repetition of the key word "cut" to evoke both anti-Semitic violence and circumcision, when the bigot ultimately challenges the narrator to show his penis to prove his identity (*Recovery* 252).

While the story plays up the connections between the non-Jewish narrator and his anti-Semitic antagonist in their violent but also strangely intimate encounter, it repeatedly warns against the narrator's reactive tendency to over-identify with Jews. In fact, there are several warnings against the dangers of joining image and reality through either over-identification *or* prejudice, which are presented as mirror-images of one another. The narrator informs us, apropos of nothing, that in a moment of excitement he inadvertently scratched a record of Haydn's *London Symphony* where "oboe joins the strings" in the final movement. Other significant details call seemingly arbitrary moments of "joining"—either of aggressor and victim or victim and Jew—into question. There is a seemingly gratuitous reference, for instance, to a female badger who keeps turning summersaults, "quitting the wall, by the way, always at an angle in fixed relation to the angle at which she arrived at it" (244). This observation, seemingly irrelevant to the central conflict of the story, is picked up in an apparently random description of the mind's "weak [...] talent" to conceptualize pure relation, described as the "immaculate relation of K alone," the alphabetic character here describing, when considered as an ideogram, the badger's approach and retreat from the wall at an oblique angel (244).[7] These details, existing in a relation of supplementarity to the main plot events, throw those events into a new light, warning against the dangers of confusing image and identity through either prejudice or over-identification. In other words, the short story endorses neither the anti-Semitic identification of the Jew with Jewish stereotypes, nor the philo-Semitic identification of the non-Jew with the Jew. Identification necessarily involves imagination, or the projection of images of the self onto the other, but the moral of the story is that imagination can also lead to acts of violence. Accusations of identity theft seem to miss the mark.

The point of the story is not identifying with Jews but imagining "the Jew" as a "real image," to use Berryman's term, i.e. as a symbol that can actually designate victims of real violence. Berryman was concerned with the way symbols produce reality, and with how reality is materialized through the bodies of victims forced to stand for the social groups to which they allegedly "belong."[8] These concerns had a pressing political significance in 1945. Thus Berryman goes to some lengths to contextualize his story in relation to German violence against Jews (the narrator mentions 1933, the year of Hitler's rise to power, as the date he became aware of anti-Semitism in his American college) and in relation to other examples of American prejudice (the narrator describes himself as a "nigger-lover," despising the term and lacking a cognate to explain his affection towards Jews [246]).

Berryman's triangulation of American anti-Semitism between Nazi genocide and homegrown racism places the story firmly in the context of mid-century American responses to the Holocaust. Most early theorists were concerned with the practical problem of putting a stop to anti-Semitism—and indeed all forms of prejudice—once and for all. Their motivation was not elegiac or commemorative but preventative. It was assumed that the war could actually lead to an increase of anti-Semitism in the United States, especially among returning veterans who, traumatized by combat and frustrated with civilian life, would look to vent their frustrations on scapegoats. This is what was understood as having happened in Germany after World War I. Max Horkheimer made the dire observation in Ernst Simmel's landmark volume *Anti-Semitism* (1946) that anti-Jewish prejudice was a stronger social factor in the United States in 1945 than it was in Germany before

[7] The letter K seemed to have a special significance for Berryman whose precise nature I have not been able to determine, although it may have been connected to the postwar rage for Kafka. See Dream Song 105 for another example of its use.

[8] See Scarry for a more recent articulation of the way organized violence transforms the bodies of victims into emblems of coercive power.

Hitler's rise to power ("Sociological Background" 5), and Douglass Orr predicted that veterans would be extremely susceptible to prejudice ("Anti-Semitism" 95). This is, in fact, the premise of one of the most important studies of its day, the famous *Dynamics of Prejudice* (1950) by Bruno Bettelheim and Morris Janowitz, which bases its analysis of social attitudes towards Jews and African Americans on a survey of returning veterans.

This is not the place to evaluate Bettelheim and Janowitz's ego-psychological model, which theorizes the anti-Semitic portrait of the "Jew" in terms of character traits associated with the superego (e.g. greed, control) and the "Negro" in terms of those traits associated with the id (e.g. irrational drives).[9] Such studies tend to be overlooked today not merely because of their theoretical apparatus but because the very situation they set out to describe seemed like ancient history after a decade. Bettelheim and Janowitz's follow-up study of 14 years later, *Social Change and Prejudice*, expresses the authors' surprise that anti-Semitism seemed to have almost disappeared in the United States, at least according to available indicators, while prejudice against African Americans remained disturbingly strong. The Bettelheim-Janowitz studies allow us to date with some precision the remarkable transformation that is now commonly called the "whitening" of American Jews.[10] It was during this period of "whitening"—the late 1950s and early 1960s—that the figure of the "imaginary Jew" became embarrassing; in popular culture it was replaced by what might be termed the progressive blackface of books such as John Howard Griffin's *Black Like Me* (1961) and by more provocative impersonations like Norman Mailer's "white negro" (1957). Berryman also puts on blackface in the 1960s, but without abandoning his early experiments in imaginary Jewishness. Those who point to Berryman's imaginary Jew as an example of identity theft ignore both its multiple resonances with contemporary theories of anti-Semitism and the historical significance of Jewish social integration.

What is significant about the Bettelheim-Janowitz model for our purposes is the assumption that prejudice has more to do with the character of the bigot than the supposed characteristics of his victim. This claim, novel for its time, defined prejudice as a form of mis-identification or morbid projection. Berryman's metaphor for this is the "mirror" struck by the murderer at the

---

9 Here is Fiedler's version of the theory in *Waiting for the End*: "When either the cult of the primitive or a genteel tradition is in the ascendency, the Jew is likely to be regarded as the Adversary; for he is the anti-type of Negro and Indian, a projection of the feared intelligence rather than the distrusted impulse, and 'genteel' equals Gentile in the language of the psyche" (82).

10 See Brodkin.

end of his story (*Recovery* 252). Variations on the theme of mirroring are evident in many of the influential theories of the day, including the Simmel volume (51), and in Jean-Paul Sartre's *Anti-Semite and Jew*, the first chapter of which appeared in *Partisan Review* in 1946 (13). The mirroring argument is also evident in Hannah Arendt, who was critical of psychoanalysis and of Sartre.[11] Mirroring also plays a prominent role in the chapter on anti-Semitism in Horkheimer and Adorno's *Dialectic of Enlightenment* (187). Anti-Semitism was widely understood to be a neurotic projection, a pathology having more to do with the character of the anti-Semite than the supposed characteristics of the Jew. At the group level projection was understood to take on the dangerously delusional character of psychosis, which could easily lead to a massive negation of reality through acts of mass violence (Simmel, "Anti-Semitism and Mass Psychology" 44). While such theories run the risk of denying a positive content to Jewish identity and thereby reducing Jews to mere projection screens of anti-Semites, they do point out the role played by "imaginary Jewishness" in the persecution of real Jews. Anti-Semites strike at their own dark imaginings in their victims, regardless of who those victims really are.

Genocide, Poetry, and the Doctrine of Impersonality

Berryman's ethnic impersonations were typical for the 1940s and 1950s and resonated with those theories of anti-Semitism stressing the way prejudice imagines its objects. Impersonation is not primarily self-invention for Berryman; it is an attempt to embody the images—and caricatures—produced by ethnic mirroring and projection. Arguments about ethnic "appropriation" miss the significance of Berryman's project because they depend on the

11 Sartre's formulated the concept of mirroring in a now-famous epigraph in *Anti-Semite and Jew*: "If the Jew did not exist, the antisemite would invent him" (13). In her preface to the 1967 edition of *The Origins of Totalitarianism*, Hannah Arendt remarks on the popularity of Sartre's definition, at the same time commenting on its unfortunate propagation of the "myth" that "Jewish self-consciousness was ever a mere creation of anti-Semitism" (xv). However, her discussion of the way the "tribal nationalism" of the early national socialists merely inverts a misconception of Jewish "chosenness" seems indebted to the same model of inversion she criticizes in Sartre (242–43). A thought experiment posed by Sidney Hook in his 1949 review of Sartre could be taken as the plot outline for Berryman's story and its literary and filmic relatives: "Let any Catholic Irishman or Boston Brahmin or Southern aristocrat move into a community in which he is unknown and pretend he is Jewish only to the extent of *saying* he is Jewish, and he will be treated like all other Jews including those who do not *say* they are Jewish but whom the Gentile community regards as Jews" (475).

assumption, which Amy Hungerford has shown to be typical of much writing about ethnicity after the Holocaust, that the text is a personified substitute for the author and bears the ethnic and cultural markers of the author's identity.[12] Berryman is not interested in claiming Jewish identity; his aim is to create "a compelling counter-image of the Jew, still somehow authentically American" to oppose the "Jewish character [...] invented, and [...] frozen into the anti-Jewish stereotype" (Fiedler, *The Jew* 8, see also 48). This is Leslie Fiedler's statement on the task of the Jewish American novelist in the 1960s. He was not referring to Berryman because Berryman was not Jewish, and his poetic strategy calls into question the "personalist" or "identitarian" assumption that only Jews could be interested in combating anti-Semitic stereotypes. Berryman's project is closer to what Kenneth Gross, in analyzing Shylock, calls "the inner life of a slander": "Shakespeare's startling achievement is that whatever we call Shylock's humanity emerges exactly through rather than simply in spite of the shapes of anti-Semitic abuse that frame his character onstage" (10).[13] (It should be remembered that Berryman was a Shakespeare scholar.) Berryman is not operating in the personal register at all, or even through the trope of personification. Instead he dramatizes his literary persona by impersonating those images that define the literary and political identity of "the Jew."

Berryman persisted in his impersonations until the end of his life in 1972, long after it became fashionable to do so, because they allowed him to work out certain formal problems of voice and persona. His writing consistently opposed both the doctrine of impersonality, as it was advocated by Eliot and Pound, and what in contemporary parlance is called ethnic essentialism.[14] The model of identity emerging from his writing is highly performative, and it relies on the structures of mirroring and projection he explored in "The Imaginary Jew." Poetry is like prejudice, for Berryman, in the way it projects and mirrors multiple identities. While Berryman would never confuse real

---

[12] Hungerford persuasively argues that the denial of individuality implicit in genocide encourages a strong identificatory response in writing after the Holocaust, and a tendency towards personification as a literary device. Personification, in her account, is the literary response to mass murder, and it depends on a theory of personality or personhood that views the individual as an embodiment of his or her culture (3–13).

[13] Also see Gross's account of how anti-Semitism provides the language and imagery for a character that embodies stereotypes while fundamentally contradicting them (17) and his description of the way "the Jew hold[s] up to the Christians a mirror of their own hatred" (73–74).

[14] See Berryman's account of the personality of the poem in Haffenden's *The Life of John Berryman* (351–52).

victims of violence with the characters in a short story or the *dramatis personae* in his verse, he does understand that imagining the Other, even in poetry, can have very real political implications. His later poetry in particular attempts to assign the lyric voice to the "Other," using this "external" vocalization point to describe "self." Traditionally his *Homage to Mistress Bradstreet* (1956) is pointed to as the breakthrough poem in this regard.[15] However, it is arguably Berryman's earlier preoccupation with anti-Semitism and genocide that led to his poetry of impersonation.

Berryman's preoccupation with the connections between poetry and prejudice are already evident in his 1948 "New Year's Eve," a poem showing the influences of the Auden school in its attempt to impose strict form (a variation of *ottava rima*) on a painful subject matter, resulting in pairings that perhaps sound forced or even disrespectful to contemporary ears, e.g.: "Ages we have sighed, / And cleave more sternly to a music of / Even this sore word 'genocide'" (456). We are likely to cringe at the jarring rhyme between "sighed" and "genocide," but the mere mention of the word (in quotation marks) is significant, as the UN Convention on the Prevention and Punishment of the Crime of Genocide that would offer the first legal definition of the neologism was not passed until *after* the publication of the poem (9 December 1948). Berryman's metaphor flies in the face of contemporary concerns over the possibility of writing poetry after Auschwitz, concerns usually linked to Adorno's dictum that "to write poetry after Auschwitz is barbaric."[16] The poem is not insecure about the ability of language to represent atrocity; on the contrary, it assumes that rhyme and meter can contain or make sense of genocide, and in doing so turns genocide into a metaphor of the universal human condition, so that Nazi cruelties become a symbol of what time does to everyone: "brownshirt Time chiefly our works will burn" (457).

---

15 See in particular Haffenden's discussion of the way Berryman materializes Bradstreet in order to present himself—or his poetic persona—as a figment of *her* imagination: "The true perspective on this state of affairs is illusorily reversed within the poem, since the figure of Anne Bradstreet is highly realized, while the poet himself is attenuated—no more than a voice. She is substantiated in order that Berryman may introduce himself almost as a projection of her fantasy" (*Commentary* 11).

16 Recent scholarship convincingly argues that the object of Adorno's critique is not so much the aesthetic discontinuity between representation and its object as the historical continuity between totalitarianism and the "total society" of consumer culture, which Adorno describes as an "open-air prison" in *Prisms* (34). See in particular Fredric Jameson's *Late Marxism: Adorno, or The Persistence of the Dialectic* (106) and Michael Rothberg's *Traumatic Realism: The Demands of Holocaust Representation* (35–36).

Berryman seems to have become dissatisfied with this universalizing approach to oppression—which *does* misappropriate Jewish victimization for the sake of poetic production—when he began to work on Ezra Pound. Although Pound would have a major influence on Berryman (*The Cantos* are in many ways a model for *The Dream Songs*), Berryman was uncomfortable with what he began to see as the linked Poundian problems of anti-Semitism and impersonality. Shortly after publishing "New Year's Eve" he began but never completed an essay entitled "Antisemitism Here," which was intended to support Pound as winner of the first Bollingen Prize. The unfinished piece apparently mentions the short story and admits that Berryman himself had gone through anti-Semitic phases. It represents this prejudice as typical for the American cultural establishment, citing as evidence Mark Van Doren's 1932 *Anthology of American Poetry*, which included only one Jewish voice. (Van Doren was Berryman's mentor and friend.) Rather than defending Pound's beliefs or actions during the war, Berryman seems to be making a "cast the first stone" argument: he and his readers should not sacrifice Pound for prejudices they share (Mariani 225).[17] The essay Berryman did eventually publish on Pound was originally intended to serve as the introduction to the 1949 New Directions edition of his *Selected Poems*. Berryman had been commissioned to come up with an alternative to the 1948 reissue of Eliot's 1928 edition for the London publisher Faber & Faber, and although Pound largely accepted Berryman's selections, he rejected the introduction, putatively on the grounds that it was too academic, but more likely because it does not refrain from mentioning anti-Semitism and fascism. After another failed attempt at an introduction by Rolfe Humphries—rejected by Pound for mentioning fascism and anti-Semitism—the volume eventually appeared without one.[18] Not until the 2010 appearance of Pound's *New Selected Poems and Translations*, edited by Richard Sieburth, was this omission in some sense corrected.

Since the 1960s scholars have been exploring the ways in which anti-Semitism not only embellishes (or blemishes) but actively informs Pound's and Eliot's poetry.[19] Maud Ellmann, for instance, has pointed to the political

---

[17] Haffenden points out in his *Life of Berryman* that in 1950 Berryman also published a poem on Pound which, while not unsympathetic to his plight, points an accusing finger at his anti-Semitism (214).

[18] See Hugh Witemeyer and Rolfe Humphries, "The Making of Pound's 'Selected Poems' (1949) and Rolfe Humphries's Unpublished Introduction."

[19] See Ricks, Julius, and Cheyette. In a review of Julius, Louis Menand argues that anti-Semitism was "a relatively minor aspect" of Eliot's thought: "part of the reason it was so half-baked even as anti-Semitism was that Eliot didn't give much attention to it,

significance of Eliot's and Pound's doctrine of impersonality, which she links to their efforts to instigate a cultural "revolution" against liberalism, usury, and supposed Jewish influence (14). It is true that Eliot's most famous essay on the topic, the influential "Tradition and the Individual Talent," remains scrupulously non-political on the surface, defining the "impersonal" emotion of art as a formal relation between the poem, the historical present, and literary tradition ("Tradition" 13–22). According to Eliot a poem is "depersonalized" when tradition speaks through it; it embodies a collectivity, which he defines as a sort of select club of the world's greatest poems. In the years leading up to World War II, however, Eliot was quite willing to be more specific about the kind of tradition he understood to be speaking impersonally. His *After Strange Gods* (1934) is framed as an elaboration of the concepts first presented in "Tradition and the Individual Talent" (15), and, as I pointed out in a previous chapter, it argues that "reasons of race and religion combine to make any number of free-thinking Jews undesirable" (20).

Berryman owned *After Strange Gods*, along with many of Eliot's books.[20] He was clearly aware of the motive behind the doctrine of literary impersonality and the kinds of personalities ("free-thinking Jews") excluded by it. In his rejected introduction to Pound, which appeared in the issue of *Partisan Review* containing William Barrett's editorial "A Prize for Ezra Pound" and the symposium it kicked off, Berryman argues that "the notion of the 'impersonality' of the poet," which he links to Eliot and describes as "perverse and valuable," actually works to conceal the "motive" he takes to be one of the most important sources of poetic inspiration (389). Berryman argues against Eliot and Eliot's Pound by claiming that we should consider Pound's motives *and* continue reading his poetry with those motives in mind. In other words, part of what we can learn from Pound as a poet has to do with his antagonism towards Jews. Most of Pound's defenders in the Bollingen controversy took the opposite tack and endorsed separating poetic considerations from political ones. This separation of the poetic from the political is what I have been calling the liberal aesthetic. Berryman's opposing claim is that the "subject" of Pound's poetry is the "life of the modern poet," that "Pound is his own subject *qua* modern poet," and that "the persona increasingly adopted, as the Poet's fate clarifies, is Pound himself" (385–86, 388, 393). He rejects *both*

---

and in most of the poetry and almost all of the literary criticism it fades into insignificance" (58). See Sharon Cameron's reading of the *Four Quartets* for an account of the way Eliot's own (late) practice of poetic impersonality strays from the orthodoxy and tradition he advocated in *After Strange Gods* (176).

20 Richard J. Kelly, *John Berryman's Personal Library: A Catalogue* (107).

the impersonality of Pound's art and any presumed autonomy of the aesthetic realm. Berryman does not offer a systematic account of how the motive of anti-Semitism informs Pound's poetry. In fact, at this early stage in his career Berryman's functional hemming-in of the role played by personality in verse (Pound represents himself as poet, not as himself) serves to minimize Pound's guilt (an odd and almost unintelligible footnote attempts to define treason as a private as opposed to a political affair) and to blame his reactionary politics on the widespread disregard of his poetry (387). However, Berryman's rejection of the doctrine of impersonality is also an attempt to make poetry political rather than simply "traditional." Ideology informs imagery, in other words, and imagery matters politically.

The Dream Songs, Impersonation, and Palatable Monstrosity

While working on the Pound essays Berryman also began a series of poems based on the *Black Book of Poland*, a documentary account Nazi atrocities in occupied territory, including the systematic murder of Polish professors. One of Berryman's biographers reports that reading about the murder of the intelligentsia moved him to tears (Haffenden, *Life* 206). Only three short poems from the project were published, and these vary in form and quality. One, like "New Year's Eve," is a variation on *ottava rima* ending in rhyming couplets. It describes life in the ghetto with a rhyme whose inappropriateness underscores the inadequacy of the elegiac landscape convention being applied: "Hands hold each other limper / while the moon lengthens on the sliding river." The third poem comments directly on the inadequacy of the elegiac tradition (Berryman, *Short Poems* 106–09).

Berryman subsequently gave up this "Mass for the Dead […] about the Nazi murderers of the Jews," as he later described the project: "I wasn't able at this time […] to find any way of making palatable the monstrosity of the thing which obsessed me" (Haffenden, *Life* 206). *The Dream Songs*, which obsessed Berryman for most of the remainder of his life, were originally intended to provide an "interlude" from the *Black Book* project, which he always meant to resume (Haffenden, *Commentary* 37). Their innovation is the figure of the imaginary Jew, and it is with the help of this figure that Berryman is able to make the monstrous "palatable." This term is misleading as it suggests Berryman was attempting to aestheticize catastrophe—something a closer look at the poetry shows he was not trying to do. What Berryman probably found unpalatable was the poetic form he had, until then, developed to represent prejudice, violence, and mass murder.

The Dream Songs employ a more flexible, dialogic structure, emphasizing multiple personae and points of view. The 385 songs are composed in six-line stanzas in groups of three, with irregular rhyme schemes and often inverted syntax. Their diction fluctuates between the formal and the colloquial; they juxtapose high and vulgar references, erudition and slang. Their themes are as varied as their diction and tone, ranging from banal everyday experiences to lust, envy, depression, melancholia, and existential angst. The unifying element of the sequence is a central figure named Henry, who impersonates African Americans—in a self-consciously minstrel style—as well as Jews.[21] The following is Berryman's widely-cited introductory note to the 1969 edition:

> The poem then, whatever its wide cast of characters, is essentially about an imaginary character (not the poet, not me) named Henry, a white American in early middle age sometimes in blackface, who has suffered an irreversible loss and talks about himself sometimes in the first person, sometimes in the third, sometimes even in the second; he has a friend, never named, who addresses him as Mr Bones and variants thereof. (vi)

While Berryman ironically denies his identity with his main character Henry, the poems present private details from his life as if they were Henry's experiences. Using a figure such as Henry as a mask is well within modernist tradition; but the changing points of view, the flirtation with minstrel conventions, the multiple identities all bound up in a single persona or ego structure—these techniques recall the projections and mirrorings elaborated in the ego-psychological analysis of prejudice. Henry does not try to become a Jew—the performance is too much like an exercise in method acting—but his imaginings do tell us something about poetic voice and its relation to tradition or "whiteness." Kevin Young has made a similar argument about Berryman's minstrelsy in his introduction to the new American Poets Project edition of Berryman's *Selected Poems*:

> Much of the force of *The Dream Songs* comes from its use of race and blackface to express a (white) self unraveling. Berryman explores the "blackness" of whiteness [...] even if, from another angle, he might be said to replicate in all too familiar a fashion the constant use of blackness by whites to say the unsayable. (xxiv–xxv)

---

[21] Berryman apparently read his dialect passages over the phone to Ralph Ellison, who joked about being a Mister Interlocutor—or Mister Tambo—to Berryman's Mister Bones, but ultimately found the poetry "fascinating" (Mariani 387).

One aspect of the "unsayable" articulated through Berryman's ethnic impersonations is the Holocaust. In the interest of showing the links between poems, I will start by analyzing Dream Song 41, which deploys imaginary Jewishness as personification or prosopopoeia, then move to 48, which mentions the figure by name.

The explicit mention of Warsaw ("phantoms of Varshava") in Dream Song 41 makes it likely that the poem emerged from Berryman's work on the *Black Book* project. It is the kind of poem that would presumably be objectionable to those accusing Berryman of identity theft. Not only does the poem impersonate a Jewish survivor, it repeats in each of the three stanzas variations on the refrain "Death is a German expert," "Death was a German / home-country," which is adapted from the English translation of perhaps the most famous Holocaust poem ever written: Paul Celan's "Death Fugue." The reduction of the protesting and poetic voice to an animalistic scream suggests the end of culture, humanity, and individuality.

> …it's not we would assert
> particulars, but animal; cats mew,
> horses scream, man sing.
>
> Or: men psalm. Man palms his ears and moans. (45)

The parallel transformation of "sing" to "psalm" to "palm" to blocking the ears and moaning in the second stanza effects the degeneration of poetry, and religious belief, to an animal level of existence or "bare life." The second part of that stanza ("odd and trivial") offers a double commentary on both the randomness of death and survival during the Holocaust, and the oddness and arbitrariness of the trope of remembrance for someone who did not actually witness the events. The wound on the instep at the end of that stanza ("a bullet splitting / my trod-on instep, fiery") puts the speaker in the position of Eve from Genesis 3:15, which metonymically also suggests the old anti-Jewish linking of Judaism to Satan. The wound in the foot may also allude to the death of Achilles. The injured foot explains the metaphor of lurching and stumbling in the final stanza, which itself stumbles through the broken rhyme-scheme and metrical feet, disrupting the a-b-c-a-b-c of the preceding two stanzas to emphasize the forced rhyme between "burned" and "German." Stumbling is significantly the opposite of the marching of the oppressors. By transforming "German expert" to "German home-country" in the poem's final line, Berryman changes the emphasis of Celan's original "Meister aus Deutschland," suggesting that the status of being nation-less is ultimately as material to death as a bullet or blow. This reflects his hard-won insight that imagination—whether mobilized to generate anti-Semitic stereotypes or, in this case, racist legal classifications—can be fatal. The vulnerability to denaturalization was the Achilles heel of the European Jewish population.

Dream Song 48 comments not only on the "imaginary" perspective of this Holocaust poem—"imaginary Jews, / like bitter Henry"—but on a loss of faith that may itself be traced back to the experience or memory of atrocity (Neiman 238–66). The diction suggests an argument on the street, but this is actually a moment of divine address or interpellation:

> He yelled at me in Greek,
> my God!—It's not his language
> and I'm no good at—his Aramaic,
> was—I am a monoglot of English
> (American version) and, say pieces from
> a baker's dozen others: where's the bread? (52)

The "my God!" in the second line is not (only) an expletive but the name of the implied divine addressor, Jesus, who instead of using his native Aramaic speaks through the language of the New Testament, Greek. This is recounted from the perspective of the irreligious speaker, whose comment on his own difficulty in mastering foreign languages ("a baker's dozen") leads, through metalepsis, to a series of ironic and irreverent reflections on the Second Coming and the Eucharist, as Henry answers his own rhetorical question about bread with the line, "but rising in the Second Gospel, pal." It is in part this irreverence that leads Henry to identify himself as an "imaginary Jew" (as the reference in the poem is plural, Jesus may be the other). Berryman's appropriation of his own figure—an appropriation that shifts the tenor of the metaphor from anti-Semitism to Christian theology—is striking. What does the loss of Christian faith or the historical criticism of the New Testament have to do with Jews and Judaism? Precious little. It is this kind of imaginative leap—blaming the loss of Christian faith on Judaism—that galvanizes the violent projection and mirroring explored by Berryman in his early short story. The Warsaw poem evokes the imaginary Jew as a victim; this one explores the kind of ethnic mirrorings and projections that can lead to violence and victimization.

The poem provides a different version of mirroring, with the speaker in the role of aggressor rather than victim.[22] Hence the reflections in the final

---

[22] Henry often refers to his capacity for violence and murder in *The Dream Songs*. The widely anthologized Dream Song 29 concludes with the following homicidal stanza: "But never did Henry, as he thought he did, / end anyone and hacks her body up / and

stanza on Henry's own uncomfortable, Macbeth-like ambitions ("Cawdor-uneasy"). References to "the death of love" and "the death of the death of love" suggest negative and positive states of grace, but also potentially murder—death in its transitive form—and the way violence begets violence through a dynamic René Girard termed mimetic. Henry is the potential murderer here, and there is at least a suggestion that a possible target is the "real" Jew behind the imaginary projection, since "the death of love," which could be read as the murder of Christ, is a standard anti-Jewish libel. When the Christ figure "sybills" "the death of death"—and it is difficult to read the word "sibyl" without thinking of Eliot—this again suggests Christian links to the ancient Greek language and mythology and hence to paganism. The Christianity alluded to in this poem is just as "heathen" as Judaism, but the accusation of heathenism has historically been used to justify Christian violence against Jews. Henry flees the anti-Semitism of this dynamic in the final line, but even this means conforming to a certain "image" of the Jew: namely the rootless, wandering cosmopolitan.

Juxtaposing Dream Songs 41 and 48 reveals a connection between the alienation of imaginary Jews and the factual exclusion of historical Jews from the "imagined community" of the nation. Exclusion is the deadly fact of a set of widely accepted fictions: ethnic, religious, and national. Exposing these fictions *as* fictions, as Berryman does, leads to another form of poetic exclusion—one not at all incompatible with the persona of the alienated poet. However, the speaker does not fully identify with the wandering Jew because he is also the expelling anti-Semite. Berryman at his best is not open to the accusations of identity theft because he does not claim a stable relation to Jewishness. His dramatic verse deploys impersonation in a way that allows him to avoid turning Nazi cruelty into a symbol of the human condition or Jews into figures of alienated poets. Or rather, his poetry does turn to such universalizing metaphors but immediately evacuates them of their pathos, either in the same poem or in linked poems in the series. Berryman represents himself as a white man, in blackface, who is a Jew but also an anti-Semite. The serial nature of these impersonations, and the relations established between them, are of central importance. The Warsaw poem impersonates Jewish identity, and the "imaginary Jew" poem comments on that impersonation as an exercise in masking and projection.

A more thorough analysis of the figure of the imaginary Jew in Berryman's work would look at Dream Song 53, where the speaker discusses "identifying" with everyone in the newspaper, including corpses; 82 which

---

hide the pieces, where they may be found. / He knows: he went over everyone, & nobody's missing. / Often he reckons, in the dawn, them up. / Nobody is ever missing."

explores the differences between Jehova and Yahweh; the series of elegies for Delmore Schwartz, especially 149 and 151, which states "let's all be Jews bereft"; and 220 which begins "—If we're not Jews, how can messiah come?" The complicated relations between imaginary Jewishness and minstrelsy also remain to be explored, for instance by looking at the discussion of passing in 119 and the commentary on burnt cork and blackface in 143. The mere mentioning of these themes will have to suffice as I now turn to the critical reception of Berryman's work.

Imaginary Jews, True Confessions, and Ethnicity

Throughout this chapter, I have referred to Hilene Flanzbaum as representative of those critics accusing Berryman of appropriating Jewish identity. Flanzbaum does not examine Berryman's poetry or offer an extended analysis of the way the figure of the imaginary Jew works in his short story. She is more concerned with what the story has to say about wider cultural trends, namely "the meaning of ethnicity, and especially the condition of Jewish ethnicity, in America in 1945" ("The Imaginary Jew" 28). Basing her argument on a comparison between Karl Shapiro and Berryman, she draws the following conclusions about the story's implications for ethnicity in postwar America:

> That Berryman is able to claim the category of Jewishness for himself spotlights the void in the cultural American landscape that the assimilated Jew has left. In other words, it is precisely Shapiro's claims to being American that have made becoming Jewish an option for gentile poets. Shapiro's assertion that he is not marginal and no one's victim corresponds to his lack of Jewish ethnicity; at the same time, his position thrusts Jewishness into the world of metaphor. (30)

Considering Shapiro's dissenting vote on the first Bollingen committee, I think it is inaccurate to claim that he somehow "lack[s] Jewish ethnicity." His changing attitude towards identity in general and Jewishness in particular is the subject of chapter two. However, it is clear that Shapiro's late rejection of identity—or what I have called his "elegy for identity"—is opposed to Flanzbaum's notion of ethnic memory. Flanzbaum's essay is the first piece in her influential edited volume *The Americanization of the Holocaust*, and the assertion that "Berryman is able to claim the category of Jewishness for himself" informs her general argument about how the Holocaust has become an American (as opposed to Jewish) symbol. Like the confessional poets he is made to stand for, Berryman is a "representative victim," i.e. one who feels victimized by "mainstream culture," so "in the post-Holocaust world, where the most recognizable feature of Jewish identity became victimhood, John Berryman has no problem slipping into the role" (30, 32). The appropriation of Jewish victim status, which "thrusts Jewishness into the world of metaphor," is the literary and historical prelude to the more contemporary problem Flanzbaum mentions in her introduction, namely that "Most Americans seem so well acquainted with at least some version of the Holocaust that they freely invoke it in metaphor, and often with an inflammatory casualness" (7). The appropriation of victim status and the universalization of the Holocaust as metaphor are countered, at least in part, by a third aspect of Americanization: the reclaiming of the Holocaust by American Jews as part of their own cultural memory after an initial decade or so of silence (32). In this struggle over who owns the Holocaust, Shapiro and Berryman play crucial roles in establishing the provenance of memory and distinguishing it from "mere" metaphor. Berryman is identified with the latter insofar as he appropriates somebody else's memories, and Shapiro with the former (albeit negatively) insofar as he represses his Jewish identity. These extremes define the range of what I call ethnic lyricism, the notion that the individual (poetic) utterance expresses the speaker's relation to a group.

What about Jewish American poets who did not experience the Holocaust directly? Flanzbaum deliberately contrasts Berryman with Shapiro, who is not a victim but a veteran and in a sense as close as a Jewish American poet could get to the Holocaust (although he served in the Pacific). A better comparison would have been Berryman's close friend Delmore Schwartz, who did not serve in the military and who actually wrote an essay, "The Vocation of the Poet," depicting modern poets as symbolic Jews (23). Flanzbaum needs to get as close as she can to first-hand experience because her distinction between memory and metaphor works best when applied to the poetry of actual survivors. It is difficult to maintain that Berryman is somehow more distant from the Holocaust than Schwartz or other Jewish American poets, although Flanzbaum's model of ethnicity is meant to suggest precisely that.

Ethnicity is a lyrical model of group identity in Flanzbaum, functioning analogously to individual identity in the way it links memory to event. Modern sociology from Maurice Halbwachs to Paul Connerton is more or less unanimous in the opinion that memories are collect*ed* rather than collect*ive*, that all social groups, whether ethnicities or nations, are to some extent produced by the metaphors they circulate and the stories they tell about themselves. Flanzbaum, however, reverses this analysis, assuming that ethnicity precedes memory and distinguishes it from metaphor, determining who has access to those stories that are understood as part of an ethnic heritage. Pushed to its extreme, such a theory verges on a model of causality as deterministic as any biological account of race: only those with some direct relation to an event can actually remember it, ethnicity somehow providing the connection when actual proximity fails.[23]

This story of Jewish cultural heritage and its usurpation as imaginary Jewishness is underwritten by what Flanzbaum states as her deliberately provocative "assumption" on the first page of the book, that Americans and American Jews said little about the Holocaust in the decade following World War II (1). She does not mean that the Nazi genocide was not discussed at all—such an assertion would be preposterous—but that it was discussed in universal terms, as a human rather than a particularly Jewish catastrophe.[24] A number of influential historians concerned with the "Americanization" of the Holocaust have postulated that the shock caused by the enormity of the Nazi atrocity, coupled with the postwar emphasis on assimilation, led to a general moratorium among Jews on the topic of the Holocaust until the 1960s, when the widely publicized Eichmann trial (1961) and the Six-Day War (1967) illustrated both the ongoing plight of the Jewish people and the strength and self-confidence of Israel as a nation.[25] This account is widely accepted, in part because it corresponds to the predominant psychological model of remembering in a traumatized individual: shock, followed by repression, slowly giving way to the "return of the repressed." Whether this model can be transferred from the individual to level of "collective consciousness" is an open question, but it certainly reveals a longing to convert history into memory and make the past the property of individuals or groups conceived as lyrical subjects. This shift from history to memory in current debates over the Americanization of the Holocaust, and the corresponding valorization of memory over "mere" metaphor, is typical of what Walter Benn Michaels has defined as post-historical and post-ideological turn in cultural politics, replacing questions of *what we believe* with those involving *who we are* (*Signifier* 24). According to this logic, not speaking (like Shapiro) is understood as a form of repression, and impersonation is tantamount to identity theft.

---

[23] Walter Benn Michaels's contribution to Flanzbaum's collection, "You Who Was Never There," criticizes precisely this alignment of memory with collective identity (181–97).

[24] Lawrence Baron, drawing attention to the significant corpus of scholarly and popular work on the Nazi genocide produced between 1945 and 1960, argues that many of these texts have been forgotten because their focus is not narrowly ethnic but universal (62–88).

[25] The broad outlines of this argument were established by Lipstadt. Her argument influenced Novick and Cole.

In literary criticism it is possible to date with some accuracy the shift from universalist approaches to Nazi genocide to particularist interpretations of the Holocaust as a Jewish catastrophe.[26] The decisive study is Alvin Rosenfeld's *A Double Dying: Reflections on Holocaust Literature* (1980), a book that anticipates Flanzbaum's arguments about appropriation. Rosenfeld takes Plath and (less systematically) Berryman to task for appropriating Jewishness and the Holocaust as metaphors for their own personal anguish (18, 178, 181).[27] The "exploitation of atrocity" evident in the "universaliz[ation] of Auschwitz as a murderous thrust against 'mankind'" and in its treatment as a "metaphor" for individual experience finds its fullest expression in confessional poetry, "where the vocabulary of the ghettos and camps is often employed as a public reference not for the pain of history but for private pain" (159, 167, 181, 174–75).

Like most critics of the poetic "appropriation" of the Holocaust as a symbol of personal anguish, Rosenfeld is more concerned with Plath than with Berryman. Nevertheless, his argument is directed explicitly against the "imaginary Jew," a concept he runs across in an early analysis of Plath by A. Alvarez. Alvarez famously claimed that Plath "is not just talking about her own private suffering [...]. She assumes the suffering of all the modern victims. Above all, she becomes an imaginary Jew" (qtd. in Rosenfeld 178).[28] Rosenfeld holds that "what is so terribly wrong with such criticism, as with the poetry that it offers easy sanction [...] is [the] radical imbalance between anyone's personal horrors of divided identity and the horrors brought on by the Nazis, an imbalance as fundamental as that between Belsen and Brooklyn" (178).

Rosenfeld misunderstands Alvarez's point in the way exemplified by Flanzbaum and criticized by Michaels, i.e. by assuming that lyricism expresses personal suffering attributable to group identity.[29] Alvarez, however, is not interested in comparing personal or group victimization; rather he places the concentration camps on a continuum of the various assaults on humanity perpetrated by mass society:

---

[26] For a concise account of this paradigm shift in Holocaust representation, see Alan Mintz's *Popular Culture and the Shaping of Holocaust Memory in America*.

[27] Flanzbaum is also indebted to Rosenfeld's "The Americanization of the Holocaust" in *Commentary* (June 1995), as she acknowledges in her notes.

[28] The passage is originally from A. Alvarez's essay "Sylvia Plath" in Charles Newman, *The Art of Sylvia Plath: A Symposium* (65). See also Rosenfeld's use of the term (181).

[29] Alvarez does criticize "Daddy" and "Lady Lazarus" for what he calls their "details," giving as an example the rhyming of "knees" with "Japanese." (Alvarez asks, in parentheses, "Do you just need the rhyme? Or are you trying to hitch an easy lift by dragging in atomic victims?") ("Sylvia Plath," 64). See also his *Savage God* (17).

> Individual suffering can be heroic provided it leaves the person who suffers a sense of his own individuality—provided, that is, there is an illusion of choice remaining to him. But when suffering is mass-produced, men and women become as equal and identity-less as objects on an assembly line, and nothing remains—certainly no values, no humanity. This anonymity of pain, which makes all dignity impossible, was Sylvia Plath's subject. ("Sylvia Plath" 65)

Plath's suffering, according to Alvarez, is not *comparable* to the victims of Nazi oppression, but it is the *result* of the same violent process of de-individuation at work in totalitarianism and in some aspects of democratic society. The placing of Western democracies and totalitarian regimes along a continuum is what is shocking about this argument; not the comparison of the suffering of a midcentury American poet with that of a camp inmate. However, we should remember that this argument against mass society, and the totalitarian undercurrents of (nominal) democracies, was a typical one for the non-communist left during the Cold War. Betty Friedan's *The Feminine Mystique* (1963), for instance, includes a chapter on "Progressive Dehumanization: The Comfortable Concentration Camp," in which she describes housewives as having "adjusted" to their suburban homes in the same way that prisoners "'adjusted' to the conditions of the camps[,] surrendered their human identity and went almost indifferently to their deaths" (305–06). Bettelheim put forth a version of the argument linking capitalist democracies to totalitarianism in *The Informed Heart*.

Confession, in this Cold War context, has less to do with the particulars of ethnic identity than with the general structure of society; it is metonymic rather than metaphoric, testifying to a situation rather than an identity. M. L. Rosenthal's influential 1967 definition of the confessional poet—the "individual as a *victim*"—should be distinguished from the cultural hero paradigm of the high modernists, but also from the ethnic lyricism of contemporary identity politics (15). For Rosenthal and his contemporaries, the act of poetic confession forges the link between the individual "experience of reality" and "symbolic embodiment of national and cultural crisis" (*New Poetry* 13).[30] It does not primarily or even necessarily give expression to ethnic—or for that matter sexual or class—identity.

Berryman's poetry, a product of the Cold War context, is as much opposed to the "impersonal" tradition of epic modernism as it is to the very

---

[30] In *The Confessional Poets*, Robert Phillips takes the personal trauma of the victim-poet to be symptomatic of larger social dynamics. Society is sick, in other words, but only poets can admit it (xi–xiii). Robert von Hallberg has pointed out that the lyric was the privileged form of Cold War poetry because it was taken to demonstrate the individualism supposed to be at the heart of democratic freedom, even—or perhaps especially—in its criticism of the mass society of which it was a part (25–26).

personal one of ethnic lyricism. His oddity helps explain his disappearance from the critical scene. Contemporary critics accuse him of identity theft, when they discuss him at all. An earlier generation of critics accused him of being both too personal and too impersonal, or simply personal in the wrong way.[31] In the 1980s there was some scattered praise of Berryman's densely populated verse as predictive of the various post-lyrical trends of postmodern poetics.[32] The most concerted effort to rehabilitate his reputation, however, has been conducted under the sign of empathy.[33] Discussing the short story "The Imaginary Jew," James Young argues that "[t]he fine line between empathetic identification [with Jews] and actual conversion fascinated Berryman—and became in itself a kind of no-man's-land in which he lived and wrote" (112–13). Susan Gubar's *Poetry after Auschwitz*, building on Young but not focusing explicitly on Berryman, explores identification as an elegiac *and* empathetic figure, which functions through simultaneously invoking and distancing the perspective of the dead (202). These are important points, but they remain trapped in the logic of identity politics—or ethnic lyricism—and miss what is perhaps the most innovative aspect of

---

[31] Rosenthal, for instance, sees Berryman as one of the poets at "the end of the confessional movement in American poetry" because his poetry depicts "a divided self" on the one hand and assumes that "every nuance of suffering brought out on the couch or in reverie is a mighty flood of poetic insight" on the other. In pointing to what he sees as the related problem of "commandeer[ing] political themes too facilely or fashionably," Rosenthal draws particular attention to "the presumed identification with the Jews of the Warsaw ghetto in Poem 41" (112–13, 119, 122–23). Even Berryman's supporters admit that the vast cast of characters in the poem lead to both problems of coherence and self-indulgence. See Bruce Bawer's *The Middle Generation: The Lives and Poetry of Delmore Schwartz, Randall Jarrell, John Berryman, and Robert Lowell* (163). See also Edward Mendelson's "How to Read Berryman's *Dream Songs*" in Robert B. Shaw's *American Poetry Since 1960* (35). Mendelson is for the most part supportive of Berryman's efforts to diversify poetic personality, emphasizing the importance of "dramatic indirection" and "dissociated personality" (29, 32). For other appreciative accounts on this point, see Steven K. Hoffman's account of the role the dramatic in confessional poetry (694). Ernest J. Smith argues that Berryman was after a "*less* obvious-lyricism" or a "survival-epic" (430, 432).

[32] Donald K. Hedrick makes this point in terms of Berryman's editorial and textual metaphors, which become increasingly central to his poetry in later years: "Individual lives are texts, as they are in the structuralist notions that Berryman anticipates" (297). See also Gustavsson.

[33] See Kathe Davis (63). Even a recent collection edited by Eric Haralson, *Reading the Middle Generation Anew*, does not offer so much a "re-reading" of Berryman but an account of how contemporary poets have been influenced by him. The essay by Stephen Burt, "My Name is Henri: Contemporary Poets Discover John Berryman," points to a recent poem by Joanna Fuhrman that picks up the figure of the imaginary Jew: "Glimpsing John Berryman Reborn as a Hasid" (234).

Berryman's verse. Berryman is not primarily concerned with recovering his identity or appropriating (even at a distance, and even in mourning) anyone else's; he seeks instead to bring slanders and stereotypes to life through impersonation. In other words, his poetry does not authorize its voice in the first person, as in the ethnic lyricism that grounds the metaphor of cultural memory by eliding the difference between first-person singular and plural; rather, his voice emerges in the second person, both nominative and predicative, as is revealed by the dialogic quality of *The Dream Songs*.

In other words, Berryman's poetry does not originate in the "I" of recollection but in the "you" of interpellation. The political implications of this second-person lyricism become clear in the way Berryman picks up on the figure of the imaginary Jew in his final, unfinished book *Recovery*, which was to have ended in a chapter entitled "The Jewish Kick." According to Berryman's notes, the chapter would have linked "the drive to become a Jew" to the need to "expiate imaginary transgressions—cf. Guardini—join son and dead friend [Delmore Schwartz]" (*Recovery* 239).[34] Berryman's son was Jewish because his divorced second wife was Jewish. The Guardini he refers to was the Catholic priest and professor Romano Guardini, who in a speech in Munich in 1955 argued that while there is no such thing as German collective guilt, as one man could not be guilty for the crimes committed by another, there is such a thing as collective responsibility (*Recovery* 236). Berryman quoted from this speech at length in a letter protesting the Vietnam War he sent to the editor of the *New York Times* while he was working on *Recovery*. The letter was never printed but is included among the author's notes in *Recovery*. Perhaps because of Vietnam, and the responsibility he feels for it as an American, he links Jewishness to what he calls in his notes, in capitals, "THE PRESENT SICK WHITE WORLD" (230).[35] Imaginary Jewishness is not a figure for Berryman's personality or identity but for his responsibility; it was also his point of protest against those Cold War policies he understood to be implicated in another genocide.

"The Imaginary Jew" is absolutely central to Berryman's poetic project and to his self-fashioning as a poet. To read the story as an attempt to appropriate Jewish identity, as Flanzbaum does, is to miss the strong elements of self-accusation and self-limitation implicit in the metaphor of mirroring, and to miss the fact that mirroring is indeed a metaphor, performing not only psychological and political but also literary work. The imaginary Jew is an

---

[34] Schwartz's interpolated name in the original.

[35] The editors of *Recovery* thought this provisional ending to be so relevant to Berryman's early short story that they appended "The Imaginary Jew" to the novel in place of a concluding chapter.

enabling fiction allowing Berryman to articulate his dramatic voice. It is also his point of entry into politics. Berryman resists Eliot's and Pound's doctrine of impersonality in the same way he resists their anti-Semitism, and he resists contemporary identity politics in the same way he resists first-person lyricism. Berryman does not claim to be the "other" or try to tell us about the "other"; rather, he is interested in how the process of "othering" (Dream Song 66) is linked to the process of "selving" (Dream Song 44). His poetic voice is so schizophrenic as to be epic in scope, and this does confront us with an early version of the multiple-identities typical of postmodern literature. More significant than Berryman's postmodernism, however, is his portrayal of anti-Semitism as a creative force, like poetry only much more violent, maintaining its myth of pure, almost lyrical identity by *materializing* otherness in the Jew.[36] Jewishness is not an "identity" in Berryman; it is the figure of a form of mirroring—a projection—that is implicated in both poetry and prejudice. In writing about the imaginary Jew, Berryman confesses something even more personal than ethnicity; he confesses imagination, and its power to create and destroy.

[36] Young makes a similar point about the *function* of imagery in motivating persecution: "The Holocaust Jew was not yet a figure in its own right when Berryman wrote his story, but it might be said that with knowledge of the Holocaust in mind, this figure accrued added weight and gravity. For he understood that the figurative Jew—the victim—was necessary for the actual victimization of Jews" (116).

Epilogue

The period covered in this study begins with the first Bollingen Prize, awarded to Ezra Pound for *The Pisan Cantos*, and extends through the late 1960s when the arguments used to defend the award fell out of favor. Pound received the Bollingen while facing treason charges for the pro-Mussolini radio broadcasts he made during World War II. *The Pisan Cantos* contain passages mourning the Fascist dictator and the social and economic order Pound believed he stood for. Nevertheless, most members of the Bollingen committee argued that Pound's politics were secondary to the lyricism he achieved by reflecting on his confinement in the American military prison outside of Pisa. The lyrical passages seemed to signal remorse, but more than Pound's attitude was at stake. Lyricism *per se* was taken to be the opposite of propaganda: a form of free speech answerable only to the dictates of self-reflection and valued primarily in open societies where artists were at liberty to speak their minds. This free speech argument, which distinguished poetry from politics in the name of liberal individualism, is what I call the liberal aesthetic. It was prominent in the early years of the Cold War but had the ironic effects of turning a Fascist poet into a spokesman for democracy and prison-poetry into a symbol of free speech.

These ironies proved unpalatable to a younger generation of poets and scholars who, like Pound, advocated more activist or avant-garde notions of poetry. A convenient comparison point, discussed in the introduction, is the National Book Award in Poetry for 1968, awarded to Robert Bly for *The Light Around the Body*. Bly openly challenged the liberal distinction between poetry and politics by speaking out against the Vietnam War in his verse and at the award ceremony; he also signed over his award money—$1000 in his case as in Pound's—to the antiwar movement. This gesture challenged the tenets of the liberal aesthetic by insisting on the political significance of verse.

Bly's gesture did not, however, challenge Pound. Bly echoes some of Pound's economic theories, and especially his claim that American bellicosity originated in Alexander Hamilton's economic policies (Pound, *Jefferson* 14, 20, 117). In "The Teeth Mother Naked At Last," for instance, Bly concludes the description of a jet fighter attack on a Vietnamese village with the observation: "This is Hamilton's triumph./ This is the advantage of a centralized bank" (*Selected* 76). Bly does not attribute Hamilton's economic perfidy to his "Hebrew" and "Scotch" "blood," as does Pound in *Jefferson and/or Mussolini* (20). However, both poets tap into a strand of populism, one from the right and the other from the left, to blame war on what Pound calls the "black death of the capitalist monetary system" (128).

The Bollingen committee rehabilitated Pound as a lyricist and de facto liberal, but Pound's influence was always strongest among those who rejected one or the other side of the liberalism/lyricism equation. Activist poets like Bly challenged the distinction between poetry and politics, others the conflation of poetry and personal conviction. Charles Olson's manifesto for "Projective Verse," published the year after the Bollingen decision, draws on an anti-lyrical tradition that Olson traces back to Pound (and William Carlos Williams). Olson called this anti-lyricism "objectism":

> Objectism is the getting rid of the lyrical interference of the individual as ego, of the 'subject' and his soul, that peculiar presumption by which western man has interposed himself between what he is as a creature of nature (with certain instructions to carry out) and those other creations of nature which we may, with no derogation, call objects. (247)

Olson's attempt to place the human subject in nature as one object among many was consistent with Pound's efforts to let the landscape find its own poetic form through the topographical analogy he called "periplum" (see chapter one). This strand of Poundian poetics helped usher in an ecological poetry represented, for instance, by Gary Snyder, who in "Axe Handles" (1983) quotes Pound as the guardian of a long tradition of craftsmanship that has less to do with "making it new" than with adapting what has come before: "When making an axe handle/ the pattern is not far off" (5).

In the debates over lyricism spanning the last 70 years, Pound has served as both handle and axe: dividing personal forms of verse from more activist or avant-garde poetics and providing continuities between anti-lyrical traditions. In this study, I have focused not on poetic activism or anti-lyricism but on the alternate lyricisms developed by writers who were uncomfortable with Pound's rehabilitation as a liberal and a lyricist.

Chapter one begins with the exception, demonstrating how a widespread misreading of Pound, here exemplified by Allen Ginsberg, authorized a form of personal lyricism that had little to do with Pound's notion of the "periplum" or his conception of socially relevant poetry. Bishop's very different attempt to come to terms with Pound in "Visits to St. Elizabeths," which I argue provides a map of institutional spaces rather than a gauge of personal experience, suggests that some of Pound's contemporaries were uncomfortable not only with turning him into a lyricist, but with the institutionalization of lyricism at midcentury.

Chapter two illustrates a dominant cultural shift from the lyricism of individualism to the lyricism of identity by showing how Shapiro traverses this trajectory in reverse. Shapiro initially spoke out as a Jew to protest Pound's anti-Semitism. He turned identity into a mode of lyrical and political expression to challenge the tenets of liberal individualism, or at least the individualism supposedly represented by Pound. Later in the career that suffered, as Shapiro felt, because of his criticism of Pound, he returned to an individualistic notion of poetry and saw Jewishness not in terms of group identity but as a figure of personal alienation and anxiety.

Chapter three turns to Auden, Shapiro's poetic model, as the representative of a poetics less concerned with individual expression than with group dynamics. Auden sensed that the midcentury fascination with individualism would serve as the common ground for an emergent intellectual class. His verse drama on "anxiety," a keyword for both existentialists and cold warriors, named the age and dissected the conditions that made Pound's rehabilitation as a representative outsider possible. In the postwar context when "alienated" intellectuals gained institutional footing as university professors, Pound's own institutionalization served as a haunting reminder of the administrative connections between regulation and freedom.

Chapter four sketches the career of an intellectual opposed to Pound's rehabilitation and to the institutional structures supporting it: Peter Viereck, the award-winning (but forgotten) poet and political thinker whose father was imprisoned during the war as a Nazi agent. Like Shapiro, Viereck felt that his opposition to Pound damaged his career, but another factor was certainly his opposition to both the establishment liberalism he believed to be prevalent in universities, and to the anti-establishment conservative movement that began to gain momentum in the 1950s. Increasingly at odds with liberals and conservatives alike, Viereck turned to a body-centered, in some ways pornographic style of verse to lay claim to biological truths that he felt were older and more relevant than political and cultural trends.

Chapter five, on Porter and Fiedler, demonstrates how pornographic conventions challenged liberal individualism by situating the abstract individual in a gendered and ethnically marked body. Both writers, in spite of their disagreements, thought that Pound represented a kind of unreason that would become more dangerous if culturally repressed. They both turned to the body, or more accurately to embodied representations of sex and violence, to show how unreason can infect society like an epidemic. Pound, in their writing, is less a representative individual than a personification of those forces that negate individualism in times of crisis.

The final chapter on Berryman argues that ethnicity, in its lyrical form, is not so much embodied as performed. Berryman forged his lyrical voice by identifying with minority figures such as the "imaginary Jew," both to counter the danger posed by Pound and to capitalize on material Pound had deemed un- or anti-poetic. The "imaginary Jew" also challenged the tendency in liberal individualism to reduce all differences to differences in opinion. The target of an anti-Semitic slur is denied individuality by being forced to serve as the representative of the insulted group. Berryman inhabits the slur to forge a new poetic voice, in effect creating lyrical identity out of an insult.

The "reaction" in my title *The Pound Reaction* is meant in a double sense. I have tried to show how a generation of poets and scholars reacted to Pound's reactionary politics by recuperating what they saw as the lyrical and individualistic aspects of his poetry. I have also shown how another group of writers reacted to this reaction by problematizing, in various ways, the free speech equation between lyricism and liberalism. My aim has been to provide a backstory to the recent academic preoccupation with identity. Identity, I argue, is an attempt to correct a deficit in liberal individualism, specifically its principled blindness to groups. It is, after all, groups that are targeted by the kind of illiberal thinking exemplified by Pound. Identity, insofar as it functions as a poetic trope, personalizes group membership as voice.

A further study would show how the poetic model of identity that emerges in reaction to the liberal aesthetic is related to a kind of ethnic impersonation that has itself fallen out of favor. Berryman shared the Bollingen Prize with Shapiro in 1969, but his reputation declined as readers became wary of his impersonations, especially those involving the blackface minstrelsy of his poetic persona Henry (discussed in the last chapter). Recently the poet Tyehimba Jess has exorcised Berryman's blackface by appropriating the voice of his Henry to tell the forgotten story of Henry "Box" Brown, who "escaped from slavery in 1849 by mailing himself from Virginia to Philadelphia in a 3 x 2 x 2.6 wooden crate" (Jess 78). If Berryman creates his distinctive lyrical voice by impersonating identity, Jess appropriates Berryman's impersonation to channel the voice of someone who cannot speak for himself, creating a hybridized verse "*in which the escaped slave and traveling mesmerist Mr. Henry "Box" Brown blackens the voice of poet Mr. John Berryman's "Henry" from Dream Songs and liberates him(self) from literary bondage!*" as Jess puts in his epigraph (78, italics in original). Jess's project criticizes Berryman but is also a tribute to his style—one intended to "free" the poet from his bondage to the minstrel tradition in a way that mimics Berryman's channeling of Anne Bradstreet in his *Homage to Mistress Bradstreet* (1953). If ethnic impersonation is part of the box that buried Brown's memory, it is also the sounding board of his resurrection.

Jess's rewriting of Berryman reveals an aspect of lyrical structure that has haunted poetry since Mill defined it as eloquence overheard, and certainly since Pound received the Bollingen Prize. Mill, as I point out in the introduction and chapter one, compared the lyric to the monologue of a prisoner in a cell. Pound plays the role of prisoner in the story the liberal aesthetic tells about the lyric, but the structure of incarceration or "boxing" repeats itself in the transition from lyrical individualism to the lyricism of identity. This is partly a structural issue: the pathos of lyricism depends on the revelation of something deep, hidden, or private. The liberal aesthetic, with its emphasis on the individual, argues that that which is hidden is relevant because it is personal. The lyricism of identity, on the other hand, tropes the hidden part of identity as that aspect of selfhood—namely group membership—ignored by liberalism as a matter of principle.

The tension between these two models of selfhood, and the kinds of incarceration or seclusion both seem to require, is evident, for instance, in Ralph Ellison's *Invisible Man*. It is significant that the crazy veteran who advises the young protagonist to take advantage of the fact that "You're hidden right out in the open—that is, you would be if you only realized it" is on his way to St. Elizabeths (153, 154). The name of Pound's mental hospital anticipates the narrator's self-incarceration at the conclusion of the novel, when he hides himself in a cellar in preparation for the coming out in the open that is his first-person narration. Ellison's protagonist is torn between lyrical individualism and the lyricism of identity; he struggles to make the conditions of his isolation visible as blackness while refusing to submit to the models of ethnic identity parodied through his picaresque misadventures.

The author perhaps most relevant for an extension of my analysis would be Melvin B. Tolson, the midcentury poet whose Poundian verse—Poundian in terms of length, epic scope, and multi-lingual breadth of erudition—was largely ignored by his contemporaries. Like Ellison's protagonist, he remained invisible in plain sight, at least as far as the "poetry establishment" was concerned, to use an epithet favored by Shapiro. His two major works, *The Libretto for the Republic of Liberia* commissioned by the government of Liberia and published in 1953, and *Harlem Gallery: Book I, The Curator*, published shortly before Tolson's death in 1965, appeared with introductions by Allen Tate and Shapiro respectively. Both poets had been members of the inaugural Bollingen committee. Tate, who Rita Dove reports had gone out of his way to avoid meeting African American poets in the 1930s (Dove xvii), praises Tolson for transcending African American themes and locating himself squarely in the "Anglo-American poetic tradition": "In the end I found that I was reading *Libretto for the Republic of Liberia* not because Mr. Tolson is a Negro but because he is a poet, not because the poem has a 'Negro subject' but because it is about the world of all men" (Tate n.p.). Shapiro's introduction criticizes Tate's notion of the tradition: "Poetry today is an established institution which has many of the characteristics of a closed corporation. (One of the rules of the poetic establishment is that Negroes are not admitted to the polite company of the anthology.)" (11). Shapiro also describes Tolson as a poet of identity: "He is, to use the term he prefers, an Afroamerican poet, not an American Negro poet accommodating himself to the Tradition" (12). As Dove points out, many African American poets disagreed with Shapiro's characterization and saw Tolson's verse as conformist (Dove xviii). While Shapiro was perhaps thinking of his own exclusion from anthologies when he praised Tolson, there are many similarities between *Harlem Gallery* and, for instance, *In the Mecca* by Gwendolyn Brooks (Tate claimed Tolson was closer to Hart Crane than to Brooks). Tolson certainly understood himself as an African American poet: "Black Boy,/ in this race, at this time, in this place,/ to be a Negro artist is to be/ a flower of the gods, whose growth/ is dwarfed at an early stage—" (Tolson 343). However, his style, as Tate rightly argues, draws on recognizably modernist themes and forms.

The tension in his work between tradition and identity has made Tolson difficult to classify. The former Bollingen committee members, in their divergent assessments, place him between the cracks in the shift from the liberal aesthetic that dominated criticism in the 1950s to the lyricism of identity. They were also sliding into oblivion as a result of this shift but, perhaps because of their proximity to the fault line, offered telling accounts of the way the poetry landscape changed after the Pound scandal. I have tried to excavate these and other partially forgotten writers who participated in the important debates over lyricism and liberalism at midcentury. These debates, under different banners and slogans, continue today.

Bibliography

Abrams, M. H. *The Mirror and the Lamp: Romantic Theory and the Critical Tradition.* London: Oxford UP, 1971.

Adorno, Theodor W. *Prisms*. Trans. Shierry Weber Nicholsen and Samuel Weber. Cambridge, MA: MIT Press, 1981.

Adorno, Theodor W., et al. *The Authoritarian Personality*. New York: Harper, 1950.

Albright, Daniel. "Early Cantos I-XLI." *The Cambridge Companion to Ezra Pound*. Ed. Ira B. Nadel. Cambridge: U of Cambridge Press, 1999. 59–91.

—. *Untwisting the Serpent: Modernism in Music, Literature, and Other Arts*. Chicago: U of Chicago Press, 2000.

Allen, Robert L. "The Cage." O'Connor and Stone 33–38.

Allitt, Patrick. *The Conservatives: Ideas and Personalities throughout American History*. New Haven: Yale UP, 2009.

Altieri, Charles. *The Art of Twentieth-Century American Poetry: Modernism and After*. Malden, MA: Blackwell, 2006.

Alvarez, A. *The Savage God: A Study of Suicide*. New York: Random, 1972.

—. "Sylvia Plath." *The Art of Sylvia Plath: A Symposium.* Ed. Charles Newman. Bloomington: Indiana UP, 1970. 56–68.

Arendt, Hannah. "The Concentration Camps." *Partisan Review* 15.7 (July 1948): 743–64.

—. *Crises of the Republic*. New York: Harvest/Harcourt, 1972.

—. *Eichmann in Jerusalem: A Report on the Banality of Evil*. New York: Penguin, 1994.

—. *The Human Condition*, 2nd ed. Chicago: U of Chicago Press, 1998.

—. *The Origins of Totalitarianism*. San Diego and New York: Harvest/Harcourt, 1994.

Arendt, Hannah, and Mary McCarthy. *Between Friends: The Correspondence of Hannah Arendt and Mary McCarthy, 1949–1975*. Ed. Carol Brightman. New York: Harcourt, 1995.

Auden, W. H. *Collected Poems*. Ed. Edward Mendelson. New York: Random/Vintage, 1991.

—. *The Dyer's Hand*. New York: Vintage/Random, 1989.

—. *The Enchafèd Flood: Or, The Romantic Iconography of the Sea*. Page-Barbour Lectures. New York: Random, 1950.

—. *Forwards and Afterwards*. New York: Vintage/Random, 1989.

—. "In Memory of W. B. Yeats." *Collected Poems*. Ed. Edward Mendelson. New York: Vintage, 1991. 247–49.

—, ed. *Kierkegaard*. London: Cassell, 1955.

—. *Nones*. New York: Random, 1951.

—. "Yeats as an Example." *The Kenyon Critics: Studies in Modern Literature from the Kenyon Review*. Ed. John Crowe Ransom. Cleveland: World Publishing, 1951. 107–14.

Auerbach, Morton M. *The Conservative Illusion*. New York: Columbia UP, 1959.

Babbitt, Irving. *Democracy and Leadership*. Boston: Houghton/Riverside, 1962.
—. *The New Laokoon: An Essay on the Confusion of the Arts*. Boston: Houghton/Riverside, 1910.
Bahlke, George W. *The Later Auden: From "New Year's Letter" to* About the House. New Brunswick, NJ: Rutgers UP, 1970.
Barnhisel, Gregory. *James Laughlin, New Directions, and the Remaking of Ezra Pound*. Amherst: U of Massachusetts Press, 2005.
Baron, Lawrence. "The Holocaust and American Public Memory, 1945–1960." *Holocaust and Genocide Studies* 17:1 (Spring 2003): 62–88.
Barrett, William. "Dialogue on Anxiety." *Partisan Review* 14.2 (Mar.–Apr. 1947): 151–59.
—. "Further Comment on the Question of the Pound Award." *Partisan Review* 16.5 (May 1949): 520–22.
—. "A Prize for Ezra Pound." *Partisan Review* 16.4 (Apr. 1949): 344–47.
—. *What is Existentialism?* New York: Grove, 1964.
Barzun, Jacques. "Workers in Monumental Brass." Rev. of *Age of Anxiety*, by W. H. Auden and other books. *Harper's* Sep. 1947: back matter.
Bawer, Bruce. *The Middle Generation: The Lives and Poetry of Delmore Schwartz, Randall Jarrell, John Berryman, and Robert Lowell*. Hamden, CT: Archon, 1986.
Bayley, John. "W. H. Auden." Spears, *Auden* 60–80.
Baym, Nina, ed. *The Norton Anthology of American Literature*. 6th ed. 5 vols. New York: Norton, 2003.
Beach, Christopher. *ABC of Influence: Ezra Pound and the Remaking of American Poetic Tradition*. Berkeley: U of California Press, 1992.
Beach, Joseph Warren. *The Making of the Auden Canon*. Minneapolis: U of Minnesota Press, 1957.
Bell, Daniel. "The End of Ideology in the West." *The End of Ideology Debate*. Ed. Chaim I. Waxman. New York: Funk, 1968. 87–105.
—. "Passion and Politics in America." *Encounter* 6.1 (Jan. 1956): 54–61.
—, ed. *The Radical Right*. New York: Anchor/Doubleday,1964.
Bennett, Eric. "How Iowa Flattened Literature." *The Chronicle of Higher Education*. 10 Feb. 2014. 10 July 2014. <http://chronicle.com/article/How-Iowa-Flattened-Literature/144531/>.
Bernstein, Charles. *A Poetics*. Cambridge, MA: Harvard UP, 1992.
Berryman, John. *The Dream Songs*. New York: Farrar, 1982.
—. "The Imaginary Jew." *Recovery*. New York: Farrar, 1973. 243–52.
—. "New Year's Eve." *Partisan Review* 15.4 (1948): 456–58.
—. "The Poetry of Ezra Pound." *Partisan Review* 16.4 (1949): 277–394.
—. *Short Poems*. New York: Farrar, 1967.
Bettelheim, Bruno. *The Informed Heart: Autonomy in a Mass Age*. New York: Avon/Discus, 1979.
Bettelheim, Bruno, and Morris Janowitz. *Social Change and Prejudice, Including Dynamics of Prejudice*. New York: Free Press, 1964.
Bishop, Elizabeth. *The Complete Poems: 1927–79*. New York: Noonday/Farrar, 1991.
Blair, John G. *The Poetic Art of W. H. Auden*. Princeton, NJ: Princeton U Press, 1965.
Bly, Robert. *The Light Around the Body*. New York: Harper/Colophon, 1985.
—. *Selected Poems*. New York: Harper Perennial, 1986.

—. "National Book Awards Acceptance Speech for *The Light Around the Body*." 1968. 23 July 2014. <http://www.nationalbook.org/nbaacceptspeech_rbly.html#.U8-vOhAfMmQ>.

Bogan, Louise. *Achievement in American Poetry: 1900–1950*. Chicago: Regnery, 1951.

—. "Modernism in American Literature." *American Quarterly* 2.2 (Summer 1950): 99–111.

Bornstein, George, ed. *Ezra Pound among the Poets*. Chicago: U of Chicago Press, 1985.

Brinkley, Alan. *Liberalism and Its Discontents*. Cambridge, MA: Harvard UP, 1998.

Breslin, Paul. *The Psycho-Political Muse: American Poetry since the Fifties*. Chicago: U of Chicago Press, 1987.

Brinkmeyer, Robert H., Jr. *Katherine Anne Porter's Artistic Development*. Baton Rouge: Louisiana State UP, 1993.

Brodkin, Karen. *How Jews Became White Folks*. New Brunswick, NJ: Rutgers UP, 2000.

Brooks, Cleanth. "Auden's Imagery." Spears, *Auden* 15–25.

—. *Modern Poetry and the Tradition*. Chapel Hill: U of North Carolina Press, 1939.

Brooks, Cleanth, and Robert Penn Warren. *Understanding Poetry*. 3rd ed. New York: Holt, 1960.

Brooks, Gwendolyn. "In the Mecca." *The World of Gwendolyn Brooks*. New York: Harper & Row, 1971. 374–403.

Brooks, Van Wyck. *The Ordeal of Mark Twain*. London: Heinemann, 1922.

Brottman, Mikita. *Funny Peculiar: Gershon Legman and the Psychopathology of Humor*. Hillsdale, NJ: Analytic, 2004.

Brown, Norman O. *Love's Body*. New York: Random, 1966.

Brunner, Edward. *Cold War Poetry: The Social Text in the Fifties Poem*. Urbana: U of Illinois Press, 2001.

Buell, Frederick. *W. H. Auden as a Social Poet*. Ithaca: Cornell UP, 1973.

Bürger, Peter. *Theory of the Avant-Garde*. Trans. Michael Shaw. Minneapolis: U of Minnesota Press, 2007.

Burke, Edmund. "On Taste"; "On the Sublime and Beautiful"; "Reflections on the French Revolution"; "A Letter to a Noble Lord." *The Harvard Classics*, vol. 24. Ed. Charles W. Eliot. New York: Collier, 1959.

Burke, Kenneth. *The Philosophy of Literary Form*. 3rd ed. Berekely: U of California Press, 1973.

Burkle, Howard R. "Sartre's 'Ideal' of Social Unity." *Sartre: A Colletion of Critical Essays*. Ed. Mary Warnock. New York: Doubleday/Anchor, 1971.

Burnham, James. *The Managerial Revolution: Or What Is Happening in the World Now?* New York: Penguin, 1945.

—. *The Web of Subversion: Underground Networks in the U.S. Government*. New York: Day, 1954.

Burt, Stephen. "My Name Is Henri: Contemporary Poets Discover John Berryman." *Reading the Middle Generation*. Ed. Eric Haralson. Iowa City: U of Iowa Press, 2006.

Bush, Ronald. "Art Versus the Descent of the Iconoclasts: Cultural Memory in Ezra Pound's *Pisan Cantos*." *Modernism/Modernity* 14.1 (Jan. 2007): 71–95.

—. "Late Cantos LXXII-CXVII." *The Cambridge Companion to Ezra Pound*. Ed. Ira B. Nadel. Cambridge: U of Cambridge Press, 1999. 109–38.

—. "Modernism, Fascism, and the Composition of Ezra Pound's *Pisan Cantos*." *Modernism/Modernity* 2.3 (1995): 69–87.

Byron, Mark. "A Defining Moment in Ezra Pound's Cantos: Musical Scores and Literary Texts." *Literature and Music*. Ed. Michael J. Meyer. Amsterdam: Rodopi, 2002. 157–82.

Cameron, Sharon. *Impersonality: Seven Essays.* Chicago: U of Chicago Press, 2007.

Carruth, Hayden. "The Poetry of Ezra Pound." *Perspectives USA* 16 (Fall 1956): 129–59.

Carton, Evan, and Gerald Graff. "Criticism Since 1940." *The Cambridge History of American Literature*. Vol. 8. Ed. Sacvan Bercovitch. Cambridge: Cambridge UP, 2005. 263–472.

The Case Against the "Saturday Review of Literature": The Attack of the "Saturday Review" on Modern Poets and Critics. Fellows in American Letters of the Library of Congress. Chicago: Poetry, 1949.

Casillo, Robert. *The Genealogy of Demons: Anti-Semitism, Fascism, and the Myths of Ezra Pound.* Evanston, IL: Northwestern UP, 1988.

Celan, Paul. *Selected Poems and Prose.* Trans. John Felstiner. New York: Norton, 2001.

Chace, William M. *The Political Identities of Ezra Pound and T. S. Eliot.* Stanford, CA: Stanford UP, 1973.

Chambers, Whittaker. *Witness*. New York: Random, 1952.

Chase, Richard. "Contribution to 'Our Country and Our Culture: A Symposium (III).'" *Partisan Review* 19.5 (Sep.–Oct. 1952): 565–69.

—. "The Fate of the Avant-Garde." *Partisan Review* 24.3 (Summer 1957): 363–75.

—. "Leslie Fiedler and American Culture." *Chicago Review* 14.3 (Autumn–Winter 1960): 8–18.

Cheyette, Bryan. *Constructions of 'the Jew' in English Literature and Society.* Cambridge: Cambridge UP, 1993.

Cole, Tim. *Selling the Holocaust*. New York: Routledge, 2000.

Connerton, Paul. *How Societies Remember*. Cambridge: Cambridge UP, 1989.

Corn, Alfred. "History's Autobiography: Robert Lowell." *American Poetry, 1946–1965.* Ed. Harold Bloom. New York: Chelsea, 1987. 313–26.

Cornell, Julien. *The Trial of Ezra Pound.* New York: Day, 1966.

Cotkin, George. *Existential America*. Baltimore: Johns Hopkins UP, 2003.

Cousins, Norman, and Harrison Smith. "Follow-up editorial to Hillyer's 'Treason's Strange Fruit.'" *The Saturday Review of Literature* 11 June 1949: 20–21.

Cowley, Malcolm. *Exile's Return*. New York: Norton, 1934.

—. "Exploring a World of Nightmares: A Critic Looks at American Fiction in the Light of Freud's Teachings." Rev. of *Love and Death in the American Novel* by Leslie Fiedler. *New York Times Book Review* 27 Mar. 1960: 1, 40.

Davidson, Donald. "A Mirror for Artists." *I'll Take My Stand.* Baton Rouge: Louisiana State UP, 2006. 28–60.

Davie, Donald. "*The Cantos*: Toward a Pedestrian Reading." *Paideuma* 1.1 (Spring 1972): 55–62.

Davis, Kathe. "The Li(v)es of the Poet." *Twentieth Century Literature* 30.1 (1984): 46–68.

Davis, Robert Gorham. "Culture, Religion, and Mr. Eliot." *Partisan Review* 16.7 (July 1949): 750–53.

—. "The Question of the Pound Award" (contribution to a symposium). *Partisan Review* 16.5 (May 1949): 513–15.

—. "The New Criticism and the Democratic Tradition." *The American Scholar* 19.1 (Winter 1949–1950): 9–19.

Davis, Susan. "Eros Meets Civilization: Gershon Legman Confronts the Post Office." *Stop Me If You've Heard This: A History and Philosophy of Jokes*. Ed. Jim Holt. New York: Norton, 2008.

Dewey, John. "The Crisis of Human History: The Danger of the Retreat to Individualism." *Commentary* 1.5 (Mar. 1946): 1–9.

—. *Liberalism and Social Action*. The Page-Barbour Lectures. New York: Putnam, 1935.

Donaldson, Scott. *Archibald MacLeish: An American Life*. Boston: Houghton, 1992.

Donner, Wendy. "Morality, Virtue, and Aesthetics in Mill's *Art of Life*." *John Stuart Mill and the Art of Life*. Ed. Ben Eggleston, Dale E. Miller, and David Weinstein. Oxford: Oxford UP, 2011. 146–68.

Doob, Leonard W., ed. *"Ezra Pound Speaking": Radio Speeches of World War II*. Westport, CT: Greenwood, 1978.

Dove, Rita. Introduction. *"Harlem Gallery" and Other Poems of Melvin B. Tolson*. Melvin B. Tolson. Ed. Raymond Nelson. Charlottesville: UP of Virginia, 1999. xi–xxvi.

Du Bois, W.E.B. *Dusk of Dawn*. New York: Schocken, 1968.

—. *The Souls of Black Folk*. New York: Modern Library, 2003.

Eliot, T. S. *After Strange Gods: A Primer of Modern Heresy*. New York: Harcourt, 1934.

—. *The Cocktail Party*. London: Faber, 1958.

—. *Collected Poems: 1909–1962*. New York: Harcourt, 1991.

—. "Notes Towards a Definition of Culture." *Partisan Review* 11.2. (Spring 1944): 145–56.

—. *Notes Towards the Definition of Culture*. London: Faber, 1948.

—. "Religion and Literature." *Selected Essays*. By Eliot. London: Faber, 1958. 388–401.

—. "Tradition and the Individual Talent." *Selected Essays*. London: Faber, 1958. 13–22.

Ellison, Ralph. "Change the Joke and Slip the Yoke." *Partisan Review* 25.2 (Spring 1958): 212–22.

—. *Invisible Man*. New York: Vintage International, 1980.

Ellmann, Maud. *The Poetics of Impersonality: T. S. Eliot and Ezra Pound*. Brighton, Sussex: Harvester, 1987.

Ellmann, Richard, ed. *The New Oxford Book of American Verse*. New York: Oxford UP, 1976.

Elton, William. "A Glossary of the New Criticism." *Poetry* 73.3 (Dec. 1948): 151–61.

—. "A Glossary of the New Criticism." *Poetry* 73.4 (Jan. 1949): 232–45.

—. "A Glossary of the New Criticism." *Poetry* 73.5 (Feb. 1949): 296–307.

Erikson, Erik H. *Identity: Youth and Crisis*. New York: Norton, 1968.

Fiedler, Leslie A. "Come Back to the Raft Ag'in, Huck Honey!" *Partisan Review* 15.6 (June 1948): 664–71.

—. *An End to Innocence: Essays on Culture and Politics*. Boston: Beacon, 1955.

—. *The Jew in the American Novel*. New York: Herzl, 1966.

—. *Love and Death in the American Novel*. Cleveland: Meridian/World, 1962.

—. *Tear Down Vanity and Other Stories*. London: Secker, 1963.

—. "Traitor or Laureate: The Two Trials of the Poet." *New Approaches to Ezra Pound*. Ed. Eva Hesse. London: Faber, 1969. 365–77.

—. *Waiting for the End: The American Literary Scene from Hemingway to Baldwin.* London: Cape, 1965.
Filreis, Alan. *Counter-Revolution of the Word: The Conservative Attack on Modern Poetry, 1945–1960.* Chapel Hill: University of North Carolina Press, 2008.
Fitzgerald, Robert. "The Present State of Poetry." *New Republic* 118 (5 Jan. 1948): 25–26.
—. "Gloom and Gold in Ezra Pound." *Encounter* 7.1 (July 1956): 16–22.
—. "'What thou Lovest Well Remains.'" *Ezra Pound: The Critical Heritage*. Ed. Eric Homberger. London: Routledge, 1972. 359–63.
Flanzbaum, Hilene. "The Imaginary Jew and the American Poet." Flanzbaum, *Americanization* 18–32.
—, ed. *The Americanization of the Holocaust*. Baltimore: Johns Hopkins UP, 1999.
Fletcher, Angus. *Allegory: The Theory of a Symbolic Mode*. Ithaca: Cornell UP, 1964.
Fluck, Winfried. "The Humanities in the Age of Expressive Individualism and Cultural Radicalism." *Romance with America?* Ed. Laura Bieger and Johannes Voelz. Heidelberg: Universitätsverlag Winter, 2009. 49–68.
Foster, Hal. *The Return of the Real.* Cambridge, MA: MIT Press, 1996.
Frank, Joseph. *The Widening Gyre: Crisis and Mastery in Modern Literature*. Bloomington: Indiana UP, 1963.
Freud, Sigmund. "Trauer und Melancholie." *Sigmund Freud-Studienausgabe*, vol. 3. *Psychologie des Unbewussten*. Frankfurt am Main: Fischer, 1981. 193–212.
Friedan, Betty. *The Feminine Mystique*. New York: Norton, 1963.
Frye, Northrop. *Anatomy of Criticism*. Princeton, NJ: Princeton UP, 1990.
—. *Fables of Identity: Studies in Poetic Mythology*. New York: Harcourt, 1963.
Fuller, John. *A Reader's Guide to W. H. Auden*. London: Thames, 1970.

Gaddis, John Lewis. *George F. Kennan*. New York: Penguin, 2011.
Galbraith, J. K. "Eisenhower and the Conservative Revolution." *Commentary* 16.2 (Aug. 1953): 99–104.
Gelpi, Albert. "Adrienne Rich: The Poetics of Change." *American Poetry Since 1960*. Ed. Robert B. Shaw. Cheadle: Carcanet, 1973. 123–43.
Gilbert, Roger. *Walks in the World: Representation and Experience in Modern American Poetry*. Princeton, NJ: Princeton UP, 1991.
Ginsberg, Allen. *Collected Poems: 1947–1980*. New York: Harper, 1984.
Girard, René. *Violence and the Sacred.* Trans. Patrick Gregory. Baltimore: Johns Hopkins UP, 1979.
Givner, Joan. *Katherine Anne Porter*. New York: Simon, 1982.
Goodman, Paul. "Tall Ideas Dancing." Rev. of *Terror and Decorum* by Peter Viereck. *Poetry* 73.5 (Feb. 1949): 289–91.
Goodwin, Ken. *The Influence of Ezra Pound.* London: Oxford UP, 1966.
Gopnik, Adam. Foreword. *Randall Jarrell on W. H. Auden*. Ed. Stephen Burt and Hannah Brooks-Motl. New York: Columbia UP, 2005. vii–xiv.
Gottlieb, Susannah Young-ah. *Regions of Sorrow: Anxiety and Messianism in Hannah Arendt and W. H. Auden.* Stanford, CA: Stanford UP, 2003.
Greenberg, Clement. "Venusberg to Nuremberg." Rev. of *Metapolitics* by Peter Viereck. *Partisan Review* 8.6 (Nov.–Dec. 1941): 508–12.
Greenberg, Herbert. *Quest for the Necessary: W. H. Auden and the Dilemma of Divided Consciousness.* Cambridge, MA: Harvard UP, 1968.

Griffin, Howard. "A Dialogue with W. H. Auden." *Hudson Review* 3.4 (Winter 1951): 575–91.

Griffin, John Howard. *Black Like Me*. Boston: Houghton, 1961.

Gross, Andrew S. and Michael J. Hoffman. "Holocaust Obscenity: Representing Genocide as a Crime of Passion." *Projecting Words, Writing Images: Intersections of the Textual and the Visual in American Cultural Practices*. Ed. John R. Leo and Marek Paryz. Newcastle upon Tyne: Cambridge Scholars, 2011. 209–34.

Gross, Kenneth. *Shylock Is Shakespeare*. Chicago: U of Chicago Press, 2006.

Gubar, Susan. *Poetry after Auschwitz: Remembering What One Never Knew*. Bloomington: Indiana UP, 2003.

Guillory, John. *Cultural Capital: The Problem of Literary Canon Formation*. Chicago: U of Chicago Press, 1993.

Gustavsson, Bo. *The Soul under Stress: A Study of the Poetics of John Berryman's "Dream Songs."* Diss. Uppsala University, 1984. Uppsala: Academiae Ubsaliensis, 1984.

Guttmann, Allen. *The Conservative Tradition in America*. New York: Oxford UP, 1967.

Habermas, Jürgen. *Strukturwandel der Öffentlichkeit: Untersuchungen zu einer Kategorie der bürgerlichen Gesellschaft*. Neuwied: Luchterhand, 1962.

Haffenden, John. *John Berryman: A Critical Commentary*. New York: New York UP, 1980.

—. *The Life of John Berryman*. Boston: Routledge/Paul, 1982.

Halberstam, David. *The Fifties*. New York: Villard, 1993.

Halbwachs, Maurice. *On Collective Memory*. Ed. and trans. Lewis A. Coser. Chicago: U of Chicago Press, 1992.

Hayek, Friedrich A. *The Road to Serfdom: The Collected Works*. vol. 2. Ed. Bruce Caldwell. Chicago: U of Chicago Press, 2007.

Hamilton, Ian. *Robert Lowell: A Biography*. New York: Vintage, 1983.

Hansen, Miriam. *Ezra Pounds frühe Poetik und Kulturkritik zwischen Aufklärung und Avantgarde*. Stuttgart: Metzler, 1979.

Harrison, John Raymond. *The Reactionaries*. London: Gollancz, 1966.

Harvey, David. *The Condition of Postmodernity*. Cambridge, MA: Blackwell, 1993.

Hedrick, Donald K. "Berryman Text Dreams." *New Literary History* 12 (1980): 289–302.

Hesse, Eva. *Ezra Pound: Von Sinn und Wahnsinn*. München: Kindler, 1978.

—. *"Ich liebe, also bin ich": Der unbekannte Ezra Pound*. Berlin: Osburg, 2008.

Heydt, Colin. "Mill, Life as Art, and Problems of Self-Description in an Industrial Age." *John Stuart Mill and the Art of Life*. Ed. Ben Eggleston, Dale E. Miller, David Weinstein. Oxford: Oxford UP, 2011. 264–90.

Heymann, C. David. *Ezra Pound: The Last Rower*. New York: Seaver, 1976.

Higham, John. "Changing Paradigms: The Collapse of Consensus History." *Journal of American History* 76.2 (Sep. 1989): 460–66.

Hillyer, Robert. "Poetry's New Priesthood." *Saturday Review of Literature* (18 June 1949): 7–9; 38.

—. "Treason's Strange Fruit." *Saturday Review of Literature* (11 June 1949): 9–11.

Himmelfarb, Gertrude. *On Liberty and Liberalism*. New York: Knopf, 1974.

Hobson, Laura. *Gentleman's Agreement*. New York: Simon, 1947.

Hobswam, Eric. "Identity Politics and the Left." *New Left Review* 217 (May–June 1996): 38–47.

Hoffman, Michael J. "From Cohn to Herzog." *Yale Review* 58 (1969): 342–58.
—, and Andrew S. Gross. "Holocaust Pornography: Obscene Films and Other Narratives." *Polish Journal for American Studies* 4 (2010): 75–94.
Hoffman, Steven K. "Impersonal Personalism: The Making of a Confessional Poetic." *ELH* 45.4 (Winter 1978): 687–709.
Hook, Sidney. "Reflections on the Jewish Question." *Partisan Review* 16.5 (May 1949): 463–82.
Horkheimer, Max. "Sociological Background of the Psychoanalytic Approach." Simmel, *Anti-Semitism* 1–10.
Horkheimer, Max, and Theodor W. Adorno. *Dialectic of Enlightenment*. Trans. John Cumming. New York: Continuum, 1993.
Howe, Irving. "Mass Society and Post-Modern Fiction." *Partisan Review* 26.3 (Summer 1959): 420–36.
—. "The New York Intellectuals." *The Decline of the New*. New York: Harcourt, 1970. 211–68.
—. "This Age of Conformity." Phillips and Rahv 145–64.
Hungerford, Amy. *The Holocaust of Texts: Genocide, Literature, and Personification*. Chicago: U of Chicago Press, 2003.

Ickstadt, Heinz. "William Carlos Williams and German Post-war Poetry." *Europe and America: Cultures in Transition*. Ed. Britta Waldschmidt-Nelson, Markus Hünemörder, Meike Zwingenberger. Heidelberg: Universitätsverlag Winter, 2006. 131–46.
Irons, Peter. "On Repressive Institutions and the American Empire." *The New Left: A Collection of Essays*. Ed. Priscilla Long. Boston: Extending Horizons, 1969. 87–113.

Jackson, Virginia. *Dickinson's Misery: A Theory of Lyric Reading*. Princeton, NJ: Princeton UP, 2005.
Jameson, Fredric. *Late Marxism: Adorno, or, The Persistence of the Dialectic*. London: Verso, 2000.
—. *The Political Unconscious: Narrative as a Socially Symbolic Act*. Ithaca: Cornell UP, 1981.
—. "Postmodernism and Consumer Society." *The Norton Anthology of Theory and Criticism*. Ed. Vincent B. Leitch, et al. New York: Norton, 2001. 1960–74.
Jarrell, Randal. "*Freud to Paul:* The Stages of Auden's Ideology." *Partisan Review* 12 (Fall 1945): 437–57.
—. *Little Friend, Little Friend.* New York: Dial, 1945.
Jess, Tyehimba. "Mirror of Slavery/Mirror Chicanery: The Freed Songs of Berryman/Brown." *jubilat* 24 (Nov. 2013): 78–94.
Johnson, Niel M. *George Sylvester Viereck: German-American Propagandist*. Urbana: U of Illinois Press, 1972.
Joyce, Frank. "Racism in the United States." *The New Left: A Collection of Essays*. Ed. Priscilla Long. Boston: Extending Horizons, 1969. 128–50.
Julius, Anthony. *T. S. Eliot: Anti-Semitism and Literary Form*. Cambridge: Cambridge UP, 1995.

Kampf, Louis, and Paul Lauter, eds. *The Politics of Literature: Dissenting Essays on the Teaching of English*. New York: Vintage, 1973.

Kantorowicz, Ernst. *The King's Two Bodies: A Study in Mediaeval Political Theology*. Princeton, NJ: Princeton UP, 1957.

Kazin, Alfred. *New York Jew*. New York: Syracuse UP, 1996.

—. *Starting Out in the Thirties*. London: Seeker, 1966.

Kelly, Richard J. *John Berryman's Personal Library: A Catalogue*. New York: Lang, 1999.

Kennan, George F. *American Diplomacy, 1900–1950*. Chicago: U of Chicago Press, 1951.

—. *Democracy and the Student Left*. Boston: Little, 1968.

—. "International Exchange in the Arts." *Perspectives USA* 16 (Fall 1956). 6–14.

— [X]. "The Sources of Soviet Conduct." *Foreign Affairs* 65.4 (Spring 1987): 852–68.

Kenner, Hugh. *The Poetry of Ezra Pound*. London: Faber and Faber, 1951.

—. *The Pound Era*. Berkeley: U of California Press, 1973.

—. "The Rose in the Steel Dust." *Hudson Review* 3.1 (Spring 1950): 66–123.

Kimmage, Michael. *The Conservative Turn*. Cambridge, MA: Harvard UP, 2009.

—. "The Plight of Conservative Literature." *A New Literary History of America*. Ed. Greil Marcus and Werner Sollors. Cambridge, MA: Belknap/Harvard UP, 2009. 948–53.

Kimpel, Ben, and T. C. Duncan Eaves. "Two Notes on Ezra Pound's 'Cantos.'" *Modern Philology* 78.3 (Feb. 1981): 285–88.

Kirk, Russell. *The Conservative Mind: From Burke to Eliot*. New York: Equinox/Avon, 1973.

—. *Eliot and His Age: T. S. Eliot's Moral Imagination in the Twentieth Century*. New York: Random, 1971.

Kostelanetz, Richard. "Conversations with Berryman." *Massachusetts Review* 11 (1970): 340–47.

Kracauer, Siegfried. *From Caligari to Hitler: A Psychological History of the German Film*. Princeton, NJ: Princeton UP, 1971.

Kristol, Irving. "How Basic is 'Basic Judaism'?" *Commentary* 5.1 (Jan. 1948): 27–34.

Lacan, Jacques. *Écrits: A Selection*. Trans. Alan Sheridan. New York: Norton, 1977.

Lan, Feng. *Ezra Pound and Confucianism: Remaking Humanism in the Face of Modernity*. Toronto: U of Toronto Press, 2005.

Lander, Jeannette. *Ezra Pound*. Köpfe des XX Jahrunderts (no. 51). Berlin: Colloquium, 1968.

Laughlin, James. *Pound As Wuz*: *Essays and Lectures on Ezra Pound*. Saint Paul: Graywolf, 1987.

Lauter, Paul. "The Jewish Hero: Two Views." *New Republic* 24 Nov.. 1958: 18–19.

Lears, Jackson T. *The Culture of Consumption*. New York: Pantheon, 1983.

Legman, Gershon. *Love and Death: A Study in Censorship*. New York: Breaking Point, 1949.

Leick, Karen. "Ezra Pound v. *The Saturday Review of Literature*." *Journal of Modern Literature* 25.2 (Winter 2001–2002): 19–37.

Leitch, Vincent B. *American Literary Criticism from the Thirties to the Eighties*. New York: Columbia UP, 1988.

Lentricchia, Frank. *After the New Criticism*. Chicago: U of Chicago Press, 1980.

Levenson, Michael. A Genealogy of Modernism: A Study of English Literary Doctrine, 1908–1922. Cambridge, MA: Cambridge UP, 1984.

Leys, Ruth. *Trauma: A Genealogy*. Chicago: U of Chicago Press, 2000.

Lind, Michael. *Up from Conservatism: Why the Right is Wrong for America*. New York: Free Press, 1996.
Lindbergh, Charles A. "What Substitute for War?" *Atlantic* 165.3 (Mar. 1940): 304–08.
Lipstadt, Deborah. "America and the Memory of the Holocaust, 1950–1965." *Modern Judaism* 16.3 (1996): 195–214.
Lowell, Robert. *Collected Poems*. Ed. Frank Bidart and David Gewanter. New York: Farrar, 2003.
Lyotard, Jean-François. "Defining the Postmodern." *The Norton Anthology of Theory and Criticism.* Ed. Vincent B. Leitch, et al. New York: Norton, 2001. 1612–14.

Macdonald, Dwight. *Discriminations: Essays and Afterthoughts, 1938–1974*. New York: Viking/Grossman, 1974.
—. "Homage to Twelve Judges (an editorial)." O'Connor and Stone 46–48.
MacLeish, Archibald. *Actfive and Other Poems*. New York: Random House, 1948.
—.*Collected Poems*. Boston: Sentry/Houghton, 1962.
—. *Freedom Is the Right to Choose*. Boston: Beacon, 1951.
—. *Poetry and Opinion: A Dialog on the Role of Poetry*. Urbana: U of Illinois Press, 1950.
—. *A Time to Speak: The Selected Prose*. Boston: Houghton, 1946.
Mailer, Norman. *Armies of the Night*. New York: Signet, 1968.
—. "The White Negro: Superficial Reflections on the Hipster." *Advertisements for Myself.* London: Panther/Granada, 1972. 269–89.
Malin, Irving. *Jews and Americans*. Carbondale: Southern Illinois UP, 1965.
Marcuse, Herbert. *Eros and Civilization*. London: Routledge/Paul, 1956.
Mariani, Paul. *Dream Song: The Life of John Berryman*. New York: Morrow, 1990.
Matthiessen, F. O. *American Renaissance: Art and Expression in the Age of Emerson and Whitman*. London: Oxford UP, 1949.
—, ed. *The Oxford Book of American Verse*. New York: Oxford UP, 1950.
—. "Statement on Ezra Pound." *The Case of Ezra Pound.* Ed. Charles Norman. New York: Bodley, 1948. 57–60.
Maxwell, Glyn. "W. H. Auden's 'The Age of Anxiety.'" *The Guardian* 10 Apr. 2010. 13 Mar. 2015 <http://www.theguardian.com/books/2010/apr/10/auden-age-anxiety-leonard-bernstein>.
May, Larry, ed. *Recasting America: Culture and Politics in the Age of Cold War.* Chicago: U of Chicago Press, 1989.
McCarthy, Mary. "The Arthur Miller Case." *Encounter* 8.5 (May 1957): 23–25.
McGurl, Mark. *The Program Era: Postwar Fiction and the Rise of Creative Writing.* Cambridge, MA: Harvard UP, 2009.
Menand, Louis. *American Studies*. New York: Farrar, 2002.
—. "T. S. Eliot and the Jews." *American Studies*. New York: Farrar, 2002. 54–75.
Mendelson, Edward. *Early Auden*. London: Faber, 1981.
—. "How to Read Berryman's *Dream Songs*." *American Poetry Since 1960*. Ed. Robert B. Shaw. 29–44.
—. *Later Auden*. New York: Farrar, 1999.
Meyer, Frank S. *The Conservative Mainstream*. New Rochelle: Arlington, 1969.
Michaels, Walter Benn. *The Shape of the Signifier: 1967 to the End of History*. Princeton, NJ: Princeton UP, 2004.
—. "You Who Never Was There." Flanzbaum, *Americanization* 181–97.

Middlebrook, Diane Wood. "What Was Confessional Poetry?" *The Columbia History of American Poetry*. Ed. Jay Parini. New York: Columbia UP, 1993. 632–49.

Mill, John Stuart. *Essays on Poetry*. Ed. F. Parvin Sharpless. Columbia: U of South Carolina Press, 1976.

—. *On Liberty*. London: Routledge, 1907.

Miller, Arthur. *Focus*. Middlesex: Penguin, 1986.

Miller, John J. "Veering Off Course: The *New Yorker* Tries to Revive Peter Viereck." *National Review* 26 Oct. 2005. 13 Mar. 2015. <http://www.nationalreview.com/article/215772/veering-course-john-j-miller>.

Millier, Brett C. *Elizabeth Bishop: Life and the Memory of It*. Berkeley: U of California Press, 1993.

Mills, C. Wright. "Letter to the New Left." *Power, Politics and People*. New York: Oxford UP, 1963. 247–59.

—. *Power, Politics and People*. New York: Oxford UP, 1963.

Mintz, Alan. *Popular Culture and the Shaping of Holocaust Memory in America*. Seattle: U of Washington Press, 2001.

Molesworth, Charles. *The Fierce Embrace*. New York: Columbia, UP, 1979.

Moody, A. David. *Ezra Pound: Poet*. Vol. 1: *The Young Genius, 1885–1920*. Oxford: Oxford UP, 2007.

Nash, George H. *The Conservative Intellectual Movement in America Since 1945*. New York: Basic, 1976.

Neiman, Susan. *Evil in Modern Thought: An Alternative History of Philosophy*. Princeton, NJ: Princeton UP, 2002.

Nicholls, Peter. "Beyond *The Cantos*: Pound and American poetry." *The Cambridge Companion to Ezra Pound*. Ed. Ira B. Nadel. Cambridge: U of Cambridge Press, 1999. 139–160.

Norman, Charles. *The Case of Ezra Pound*. New York: Bodley, 1948.

Novick, Peter. *The Holocaust in American Life*. Boston: Houghton, 1999.

O'Connor, William Van. *Sense and Sensibility in Modern Poetry*. Chicago: U of Chicago Press, 1948.

O'Connor, William Van, and Edward Stone, eds. *A Casebook on Ezra Pound*. New York: Crowell, 1959.

Olson, Charles. "Projective Verse." *Collected Prose*. Eds. Donald Allen and Benjamin Friedlander. Berkeley: U of California Press, 1997.

Olster, Stacey. "The 'Other' in Nathanael West's Fiction: Jewish Rejection or Jewish Projection." *MELUS* 15.4 (1988): 51–65.

Ong, Walter J. "J. S. Mill's Pariah Poet." *Philological Quarterly* 29.3 (July 1950): 333–44.

Orr, Douglass W. "Anti-Semitism and the Psychopathology of Everyday Life." Simmel, *Anti-Semitism* 85–96.

"Our Country and Our Culture (I)." *Partisan Review* 19.3 (May–June 1952): 282–326.

"Our Country and Our Culture (II)." *Partisan Review* 19.4 (Jul.–Aug. 1952): 420–50.

"Our Country and Our Culture (III)." *Partisan Review* 19.5 (Sep.–Oct. 1952): 562–97.

Overmyer, Grace. *Government and the Arts*. New York: Norton, 1939.

Parker, Robert Dale. *The Unbeliever: The Poetry of Elizabeth Bishop*. Urbana: U of Illinois Press, 1988.

Perelman, Bob. *The Trouble with Genius: Reading Pound, Joyce, Stein, and Zukofsky*. Berkeley: U of California Press, 1994.

Perloff, Marjorie. *The Dance of the Intellect: Studies in the Poetry of the Pound Tradition*. Chicago: Northwestern UP, 1996.

—. *Differentials: Poetry, Poetics, Pedagogy*. Tuscaloosa: U of Alabama Press, 2004.

—. "Fascism, Anti-Semitism, Isolationism: Contextualizing the 'Case of EP.'" *Paideuma* 16.3 (Winter 1987): 7–22.

Phelps, Wallace. "Eliot Takes His Stand." *Partisan Review* 1.2 (Apr.–May 1934): 52–54.

Phillips, Robert. Afterword. *Essay on Rime with Trial of a Poet*. By Karl Shapiro. Ed. Phillips. Ann Arbor: U of Michigan Press, 2003. 105–15.

—. *The Confessional Poets*. Carbondale: Southern Illinois UP, 1973.

Phillips, Siobhan. *The Poetics of the Everyday: Creative Repetition in Modern American Verse*. New York: Columbia UP, 2010.

Phillips, William, and Philip Rahv, eds. *The Partisan Review Anthology*. New York: Holt, 1962.

Pilandri, Angela Jung. "Ezra Pound and His Italian Critics." *Tamkang Review* III.2 (1972): n. pag. Rpt. in University of Oregon Libraries. n.d. 13 Mar. 2015. <http://library.uoregon.edu/ec/e-asia/read/angela.pdf>.

Plath, Sylvia. *The Collected Poems*. Ed. Ted Hughes. New York: Harper, 1981.

Podhoretz, Norman. "Hannah Arendt on Eichmann: A Study in the Perversity of Brilliance." *Commentary* 36.3 (Sep. 1963): 201–08.

Porter, Katherine Anne. *The Collected Essays and Occasional Writings of Katherine Anne Porter*. New York: Lawrence/Delacorte, 1970.

—. *The Days Before*. New York: Harcourt, 1952.

—. *Flowering Judas and Other Stories*. New York: Signet, 1970.

—. *The Leaning Tower and Other Stories*. New York: Harcourt, 1944.

—. *The Never-Ending Wrong*. Boston: Little/Atlantic Monthly, 1977.

—. *Ship of Fools*. New York: Back Bay/Little, 2000.

Pound, Ezra. *ABC of Reading*. New York: New Directions, 1987.

—. *The Cantos of Ezra Pound*. New York: New Directions, 1996.

—. "Gedichte." Trans. Eva Hesse. *Perspektiven* 16 (Fall 1956): 60–77.

—. *Guide to Kulchur*. New York: New Directions, 1970.

—. *Jefferson and/or Mussolini*. New York: Liveright, 1936.

—. *New Selected Poems and Translations*. Ed. Richard Sieburth. New York: New Directions, 2010.

—. *Personae*. New York: New Directions, 1926.

—. *The Pisan Cantos*. Ed. Richard Sieburth. New York: New Directions, 2003.

—. "A Retrospect." *The Literary Essays of Ezra Pound*. Ed. T. S. Eliot. London: Faber, 1954. 3–14.

—. *Selected Letters 1907–1941*. Ed. D. D. Paige. London: Faber, 1971.

—. *Selected Poems of Ezra Pound*. New York: New Directions, 1957.

—. *Selected Prose: 1909–1965*. Ed. William Cookson. London: Faber, 1973.

—. *A Walking Tour in Southern* France. Ed. Richard Sieburth. New York: New Directions, 1992.

"The Question of the Pound Award." *Partisan Review* 16.5 (May 1949): 512–22.

Rahv, Philip. "Disillusionment and Socialism." *Partisan Review* 15.5 (May 1948): 519–29.

—. *The Myth and the Powerhouse*. New York: Farrar, 1965.

Ransom, John Crowe. *God without Thunder: An Unorthodox Defense of Orthodoxy*. Hamden, CT: Archon, 1965.

—. *The New Criticism*. Norfolk, CT: New Directions, 1941.

—. *The World's Body*. New York: Scribner, 1938.

Ransom, John Crowe, Delmore Schwartz, and John Hall Wheelock. *American Poetry at Mid-Century: Lectures Presented Under the Auspices of the Gertrude Clarke Whittall Poetry and Literature Fund*. Washington D.C.: Library of Congress, 1958.

Rasula, Jed. *The American Poetry Wax Museum: Reality Effects, 1940–1990*. Urbana, IL: National Council of Teachers of English, 1996.

Rawls, John. *Political Liberalism*. New York: Columbia UP, 1996.

Read, Herbert. *Poetry and Anarchism*. London: Faber, 1941. Rpt. with Folcroft Library, 1970.

Reck, Michael. "A Conversation between Ezra Pound and Allen Ginsberg." *Evergreen Review* 55 (June 1968): 27–29; 84.

Reich, Wilhelm. *The Mass Psychology of Fascism*. Trans. Vincent R. Carfagno. New York: Farrar, 1970.

Reiss, Tom. "The First Conservative: How Peter Viereck Inspired—and Lost—a Movement." *New Yorker* 24 Oct 2005. 13 Mar. 2015 <http://www.newyorker.com/magazine/2005/10/24/the-first-conservative>.

Rice, Philip Blaire. "Existentialism and the Self." *The Kenyon Critics: Studies in Modern Literature from the Kenyon Review*. Ed. John Crowe Ransom. Cleveland: World Publishing, 1951. 200–24.

Ricks, Christopher. *T. S. Eliot and Prejudice*. London: Faber, 1988.

Riesman, David. *Individualism Reconsidered*. London: Collier-Macmillan/Free Press, 1964.

—. "Psychological Types and National Character." *American Quarterly* 5.4 (Winter 1953): 325–43.

Rosen, Frederick. *Mill*. Oxford: Oxford UP, 2013.

Rosenberg, Harold. "The Herd of Independent Minds." *Commentary* 6.3 (Sep. 1948): 244–52.

—. "Jewish Identity in a Free Society." *Commentary* (June 1950): 508–14.

—. *The Tradition of the New*. New York: Horizon, 1959.

Rosenfeld, Alvin H. "The Americanization of the Holocaust." *Commentary* 99.6 (1995): 35–40.

—. *A Double Dying: Reflections on Holocaust Literature*. Bloomington: Indiana UP, 1980.

Rosenstock-Huessy, Eugen. *Die europäischen Revolutionen und der Charakter der Nationen*. Stuttgart: Kohlhammer, 1961.

Rosenthal, M. L. *The Modern Poets: A Critical Introduction*. New York: Oxford UP, 1960.

—. *The New Poets: American and British Poetry Since World War II*. New York: Oxford UP, 1967.

Rothberg, Michael. *Traumatic Realism: The Demands of Holocaust Representation*. Minneapolis: U of Minnesota Press, 2000.

Ryan, Claes G. "The Legacy of Peter Viereck: His Prose Writings." *Humanitas* 19.1–2 (Spring/Fall 2006): 38–49. 13 Mar. 2015 <http://www.nhinet.org/ryn19-1.pdf>.

Sartre, Jean-Paul. *Anti-Semite and Jew*. Trans. George J. Becker. New York: Schocken, 1976.
—. *Being and Nothingness: A Phenomenological Essay on Ontology*. Trans. Hazel E. Barnes. New York: Washington Square/Pocket, 1966.
—. "Gentile and Jew." Trans. George J. Becker. *Commentary* 5.6 (June 1948): 522–32.
—. "Portrait of the Antisemite." Trans. Mary Guggenheim. *Partisan Review* 13.2 (Spring 1946): 163–78.
—. "Portrait of the Inauthentic Jew." Trans. George J. Becker. *Commentary* 5.5 (May 1948): 389–98.
—. *Search for a Method*. Trans. Hazel E. Barnes. New York: Knopf/Vintage, 1963.
—. "The Situation of the Jew." Trans. George J. Becker. *Commentary* 5.4 (Apr. 1948): 306–17.
Saunders, Frances Stonor. *The Cultural Cold War: The CIA and the World of Arts and Letters*. New York: New Press, 2000.
Scarry, Elaine. *The Body in Pain*. New York: Oxford UP, 1985.
Schiff, Hilda. *Holocaust Poetry*. London: Harper, 1995.
Schlesinger, Arthur M., Jr. *The Vital Center: The Politics of Freedom*. Cambridge, MA: Riverside/Houghton, 1949.
Schneider, Gregory L. *The Conservative Century: From Reaction to Revolution*. Lanham, MA: Rowman, 2009.
Scholes, Robert. "The Illiberal Imagination." *New Literary History* 4.3 (Spring 1973): 521–40.
Schryer, Stephen. "Fantasies of the New Class: The New Criticism, Harvard Sociology, and the Idea of the University." *PMLA* 122.3 (May 2007): 663–78.
Schwartz, Delmore. "Karl Shapiro's Poetics." *Nation* 161.19 (10 Nov. 1945): 498.
—. Contribution to "Our Country and Our Culture: A Symposium (III)." *Partisan Review* 19.5 (Sep.–Oct. 1952): 593–97.
—. "The Vocation of the Poet." *Selected Essays of Delmore Schwartz*. Ed. Donald Dike and David Zucker. Chicago: U of Chicago Press, 1970. 14–23.
Shapiro, Karl. "American Poet?" Shapiro, *Creative Glut* 231–52.
—. *Collected Poems: 1940–1978*. New York: Random, 1978.
—. *Creative Glut: Selected Essays of Karl Shapiro*. Ed. Robert Phillips. Chicago: Dee, 2004.
—. "The Critic in Spite of Himself." Shapiro, *Creative Glut* 306–29.
—. *Edsel*. New York: Geis Assoc., 1971.
—. English Prosody and Modern Poetry: Annual Tudor and Stuart Club Lecture Delivered on April 18, 1947. Baltimore: Johns Hopkins UP, 1947.
—. *Essay on Rime*. New York: Reynal, 1945.
—. "Ezra Pound: The Scapegoat of Modern Poetry." *In Defense of Ignorance*. By Shapiro. New York: Random, 1960. 61–86.
—. Introduction. *Harlem Gallery: Book I, the Curator*. M. B. Tolson. New York: Twayne Publishers, 1965. 11–15.
—. "The Jewish Writer in America." Shapiro, *Creative Glut* 296–305.
—. *Karl Shapiro: Selected Poems*. Ed. John Updike. Library of America/American Poets Project: 2003.

—. "The Poetry Wreck." Shapiro, *Creative Glut* 253–62.
—. "Poets and Psychologists." *Poetry* 80.3 (1952): 166–84.
—, ed. *Prose Keys to Modern Poetry*. New York: Harper, 1962.
—. "The Question of the Pound Award" (contribution to a symposium). *Partisan Review* 16.5 (May 1949): 518–19.
—. *Reports of My Death*. Chapel Hill, NC: Algonquin, 1990.
—. "The Retreat of W. H. Auden." Shapiro, *Creative Glut* 65–85.
—. "To Abolish Children." Shapiro, *Creative Glut* 330–39.
—. *Trial of a Poet*. New York: Reynal, 1947.
—. *V-Letter*. New York: Reynal, 1944.
—. *The Younger Son*. Chapel Hill, NC: Algonquin, 1988.
—, and Robert Beum. *A Prosody Handbook*. New York: Harper, 1965.
Shaw, Robert, ed. *American Poetry Since 1960*. Chatham: Mackay, 1973.
Shorer, Mark. "We're All on the Passenger List." Rev. of *Ship of Fools* by Katherine Anne Porter. *New York Times Book Review*. 1 Apr. 1962: 1; 5.
Sieburth, Richard. "In Pound We Trust: The Economy of Poetry/The Poetry of Economics. *Critical Inquiry* 14.1 (Autumn 1987): 142–72.
—. Introduction. *The Pisan Cantos*. By Ezra Pound. Ed. Sieburth. New York: New Directions, 2003. ix–xliii.
—, ed. *A Walking Tour in Southern France: Ezra Pound among the Troubadours*. New York: New Directions, 1992.
Simmel, Ernst, ed. *Anti-Semitism: A Social Disease*. New York: International Universities Press, 1946.
—. "Anti-Semitism and Mass Psychology." Simmel, *Anti-Semitism* 33–78.
Simpson, David. *Situatedness, or, Why We Keep Saying Where We're Coming From*. Durham, NC: Duke UP, 2002.
Smith, Adam. *The Wealth of Nations*. New York: Modern Library, 1937.
Smith, Ernest J. "John Berryman's 'Programmatic' for 'The Dream Songs' and an Instance of Revision." *Journal of Modern Literature* 23.3/4 (Summer 2000): 429–39.
Snodgrass, W. D. *The Fuehrer Bunker: The Complete Cycle*. Brockport, NY: BOA, 1995.
Snyder, Gary. *Axe Handles*. Berkeley: Avalon/ Shoemaker/Hoard, 2005.
Solotaroff, Theodore. "'Ship of Fools' and the Critics." *Commentary* 4.34 (Oct. 1962): 277–86.
Sontag, Susan. "The Pornographic Imagination." *Styles of Radical Will*. New York: Picador/Farrar, 1969. 35–73.
Spears, Monroe K., ed. *Auden: A Collection of Critical Essays*. New Jersey: Prentice Hall, 1964.
—. *The Poetry of W. H. Auden: The Disenchanted Island*. New York: Oxford UP, 1963.
Stanford, Donald E. *Revolution and Convention in Modern Poetry: Studies in Ezra Pound, T. S. Eliot, Wallace Stevens, Edwin Arlington Robinson, and Yvor Winters*. Newark: U of Delaware Press, 1983.
Stark, Robert. *Ezra Pound's Early Verse and the Lyric Tradition: A Jargoner's Apprenticeship*. Edinburgh: Edinburgh UP, 2012.
Steiner, George. *In Bluebeard's Castle: Some Notes Towards the Re-definition of Culture*. London: Faber, 1971.
Stout, Janis P. *Katherine Anne Porter: A Sense of the Times*. Charlottesville: U of Virginia Press, 1995.

Sultan, Stanley. "Was Modernism Reactionary?" *Journal of Modern Literature* 17.4 (Spring 1991): 447–64.

Tate, Allen. "Ezra Pound and the Bollingen Prize." *Essays of Four Decades* by Tate. Chicago: Swallow, 1968. 509–16.
—. "Further Remarks on the Pound Award." *Partisan Review* 16.5 (May 1949): 666–68.
—. Preface. *Libretto for the Republic of Liberia.* M. B. Tolson. New York: Twayne Publishers, 1953. [ii–iv].
—. "Preface to *Reactionary Essays on Poetry and Ideas*." *Essays of Four Decades* by Tate. Chicago: Swallow, 1968. 611–14.
—. "The Question of the Pound Award" (contribution to a symposium). *Partisan Review* 16.5 (May 1949): 520.
Taylor, Charles. *The Ethics of Authenticity*. Cambridge, MA: Harvard UP, 2003.
Terrell, Carroll F. *A Companion to the Cantos of Ezra Pound*, vols. 1 and 2. Berkeley: University of California Press, 1984.
Theweleit, Klaus. *Male* Fantasies, vol. 1: *Women, Floods, Bodies, History*. Trans. Stephen Conway, et al. Foreword by Barbara Ehrenreich. Minneapolis: U of Minnesota Press, 1987.
Tocqueville, Alexis de. *Democracy in America*. Trans. George Lawrence. Ed. J. P. Mayer. New York: Harper/Perennial, 1988.
Tolson, Melvin B. *"Harlem Gallery" and Other Poems of Melvin B. Tolson*. Ed. Raymond Nelson. Charlottesville: UP of Virginia, 1999.
Torrey, E. Fuller. *The Roots of Treason: Ezra Pound and the Secrets of St. Elizabeths*. London: Sidgwick, 1984.
Travisano, Thomas J. *Elizabeth Bishop: Her Artistic Development*. Charlottesville: UP of Virginia, 1988.
Travisano, Thomas with Saskia Hamilton, eds. *Words in Air: The Complete Correspondence between Elizabeth Bishop and Robert Lowell*. New York: Farrar, 2008.
Trilling, Lionel. *The Liberal Imagination*. New York: Doubleday Anchor, 1953.
—. "On the Modern Element in Modern Literature." Phillips and Rahv 263–79.

Unrue, Darlene Harbour. *Katherine Anne Porter: The Life of an Artist*. Jackson: UP of Mississippi, 2005.

Vendler, Helen. *Last Looks, Last Books: Stevens, Plath, Lowell, Bishop, Merrill*. Princeton, NJ: Princeton UP, 2010.
Viereck, Peter. "Beyond Revolt: The Education of a Poet." *The Arts in Renewal*. Ed. Lewis Mumford. Philadelphia: Philadelphia UP. Rpt. Freeport, NY: Books for Libraries Press, 1969. 32–66.
—. "But—I'm a Conservative!" *Atlantic* 165.4 (Apr. 1940): 538–43.
—. *Conservatism Revisited and The New Conservatism—What Went Wrong?* New York: Macmillan/Free Press, 1962.
—. *The First Morning*. New York: Scribner, 1952.
—. *Metapolitics: The Roots of the Nazi Mind.* New York: Capricorn, 1965.
—. "My Kind of Poetry." *The Saturday Review of Literature* 32 (27 August 1949): 7–8; 35–36.
—. "Parnassus Divided." *Atlantic* 184 (Oct. 1949): 67–70.

—. "Pound at 100: Weighing the Art and the Evil." *New York Times Book Review* 29 December 1985: section 7, p. 3. Also in Viereck, *Strict Wildness*. New Brunswick: Transaction Publishers, 2008. 49–52.

—. "Pure Poetry, Impure Politics, and Ezra Pound (The Bollingen Prize Controversy Revisited)." *Commentary* 11.4 (Apr. 1951): 340–46.

—. "Pure Poetry, Impure Politics: The Implications of Ezra Pound and the Bollingen Controversy." *Dream and Responsibility: Four Test Cases of the Tension between Poetry and Society*. Washington, DC: UP of Washington, DC, 1953. 1–22.

—. *Shame and Glory of the Intellectuals: Babbitt Jr. vs. the Rediscovery of Values*. Boston: Beacon, 1953.

—. *Strict Wildness: Discoveries in Poetry and History*. Piscataway, NJ: Transaction, 2008.

—. *Strike through the Mask! New Lyrical Poems*. New York: Scribner, 1950.

—. *The Unadjusted Man: A New Hero for Americans*. Boston: Beacon, 1956.

—. "Vaginolatry." *Massachusetts Review* 43.4 (Winter 2002): 670–75.

Viereck, Peter, and Robert Edwin. *Terror and Decorum: Poems 1940–48*. New York: Scribner, 1950.

Voelz, Johannes. *Transcendental Resistance: The New Americanists and Emerson's Challenge*. Hanover, NH: UP of New England, 2010.

Von Hallberg, Robert. "Poetry, Politics, and Intellectuals." *The Cambridge History of American Literature*, vol. 8. Ed. Sacvan Bercovitch. New York: Cambridge UP: 2005. 9–260.

Weil, Simone. "Reflections on War." *Politics* (Feb. 1945): 51–56.

Wilhelm, J. J. *Ezra Pound: The Tragic Years, 1925–1972*. University Park: Pennsylvania State UP, 1994.

Williams, Linda. *Hard Core: Power, Pleasure, and the Frenzy of the Visible*. Berkeley: U of California Press, 1989.

Williamson, Alan. *Pity the Monsters: The Political Vision of Robert Lowell*. New Haven, CT: Yale UP, 1974.

Winchell, Mark Royden. *Leslie Fiedler*. Boston: Twayne, 1985.

—. *Too Good to Be True: The Life and Work of Leslie Fiedler*. Columbia: U of Missouri Press, 2002.

Winnick, R. H., ed. *Letters of Archibald MacLeish, 1907–1982*. Boston: Houghton, 1983.

Winters, Yvor. "T. S. Eliot, or the Illusion of Reaction." *In Defense of Reason*. Denver: U of Denver Press, 1947. 460–500.

Wise, Gene. "'Paradigm Dramas' in American Studies: A Cultural and Institutional History of the Movement." *Locating American Studies: The Evolution of a Discipline*. Ed. Lucy Maddox. Baltimore: Johns Hopkins UP, 1999. 166–214.

Witemeyer, Hugh. "Early Poetry 1908–1920." *The Cambridge Companion to Ezra Pound*. Ed. Ira B. Nadel. Cambridge: U of Cambridge Press, 1999. 43–58.

Witemeyer, Hugh, and Rolfe Humphries. "The Making of Pound's 'Selected Poems' (1949) and Rolfe Humphries' Unpublished Introduction." *Journal of Modern Literature* 15.1 (1988): 73–91.

Young, James. *Writing and Rewriting the Holocaust*. Bloomington: Indiana UP, 1990.

Young, Kevin. Introduction. *Selected Poems*. By John Berryman. Ed. Young. New York: Library of America, 2004. xvii–xxv.

Index